HEMISPHERIC
PERSPECTIVES
ON THE
UNITED STATES

HEMISPHERIC PERSPECTIVES ON THE UNITED STATES

Papers from the New World Conference

Edited by Joseph S. Tulchin
With the Assistance of María A. Leal

Contributions in American
Studies, Number 36

GREENWOOD PRESS
WESTPORT, CONNECTICUT • LONDON, ENGLAND

Library of Congress Cataloging in Publication Data

New World Conference, San Antonio, Tex., 1975.
 Hemispheric perspectives on the United States.
 (Contributions in American studies ; no. 36 ISSN
0084-9227)
 Includes index.
 1. United States—History—Congresses. 2. America—
Civilization—Congresses. 3. Latin America—Relations
(general) with the United States—Congresses.
4. United States—Relations (general) with Latin
America—Congresses. I. Tulchin, Joseph S., 1939-
II. Leal, María A. III. Title.
E172.9.N48   1975   973   77-87973
ISBN 0-313-20053-X

Library of Congress Catalog Card Number: 77-87973
ISBN: 0-313-20053-X
ISSN: 0084-9227

First published in 1978

Greenwood Press, Inc.
51 Riverside Avenue, Westport, Connecticut 06880

Printed in the United States of America

10 9 8 7 6 5 4 3 2 1

1-12-79

TO MY MOTHER
AND THE
MEMORY OF MY FATHER

Contents

II. ARTS AND CULTURE IN THE AMERICAS

III. THE UNITED STATES AND THE HEMISPHERE: SPECIAL PROBLEMS

Series Foreword

In introducing this volume, Joseph S. Tulchin has recounted the process by which the Bicentennial Committee on International Conferences of Americanists (BCICA) planned and produced five global meetings. Before the first of these conferences had taken place, the Greenwood Press, through its Contributions in American Studies Series, had contracted for the world rights to the publication of all five conferences. This was done with a commitment to the idea that, regardless of their abstract merit, the proceedings of these meetings would comprise an extensive and memorable landmark in the history of the study of the United States around the world.

An understanding of the United States does not increase evenly around the world any more than it does within the nation's borders. Yet the level, as well as the nature, of this understanding is of no mean importance. Foreign insights reveal aspects of the national experience that will have escaped native eyes. Apprehensions from abroad reveal ways in which Americans have failed to present themselves fully, clearly, or favorably. Foreign attitudes help determine America's future role among nations.

These insights, apprehensions, and attitudes are by no means static. Changes in them are as interesting and important as their state at a given moment. Comparisons demand benchmarks. Rarely does there come into view so elaborate and useful a benchmark as that provided by these five meetings of students of the United States.

Robin W. Winks, who chaired BCICA, has brought together a group of essays selected from all five global meetings. Titled *Other Voices, Other Views*, it has recently been published.

But the volume now in hand is the first broadly representative collection of the proceedings of a single conference to be made available in English for general distribution. We hope to see others and continue to encourage their production. Meanwhile we offer our sincere congratulations to Joseph S. Tulchin and his colleagues who have persisted in their labors to bring into print this landmark in which the future will take an interest perhaps unsuspected by the present.

ROBERT H. WALKER
Series Editor

Introduction

The Bicentennial Committee on International Conferences of Americanists (BCICA) planned five regional conferences on American Studies for 1975-76 in the Americas, Europe, Africa, the Middle East and Southeast Asia, and the Far East. The formal occasion for the conferences was the approaching Bicentennial of the United States. More specifically the conferences were viewed as opportunities to take stock of and, where possible, to stimulate the study of this nation abroad.

Although no attempt was made to promote unanimity on the question of what American Studies were or should be, it was agreed that the comparative approach was especially relevant in the international context in which the conferences would take place. Just as the United States had entered into a new stage in its relationships with other countries of the world, reflecting the political and economic complexities of the new era, so perhaps the study of this country should adapt itself more readily to the cross-cultural influences and interests that were reshaping the world community. If U.S. citizens ever assumed their civilization was unique or that their way of doing things was best for everybody else, they certainly did not do so now. The keynote to the new era was cooperation and interdependency, so there was no place in the study of the United States for nationalism or parochialism. The conferences derived a good deal of their underlying philosophy from those many Americanists abroad who believed the comparative approach best served their needs and interests.

The dates and sites of the 1975-76 conferences were as follows: April 19-23, the European conference in Salzburg; September 4-7, the Asia and Pacific regional conference in Fujinomiya, Japan; September 13-16, the North Africa, Middle East, and South Asian conference in Shiraz, Iran; November 4-8, the New World conference in San Antonio, Texas; and, finally, the African conference in Lagos, Nigeria, March 31-April 4, 1976.

The New World conference (NWC) stood out from the other regional conferences by extending to the participants and observers the opportunity to attend the Biennial Convention of the American Studies Association (ASA). A cosponsor of the NWC with BCICA, the ASA took pains to integrate the two meetings. There is no doubt that those who attended the New World conference benefited from the opportunities and intellectual stimulation afforded by the ASA convention. There was something in the rich and variegated ASA program to interest everyone; foreign students of the United States met with their U.S. counterparts whose books they had read and whose teaching materials they had used in their classrooms; fourteen of the conferees even served as full-fledged participants on eight ASA panels, demonstrating to all the high quality of American Studies outside the United States. To secure these advantages, unique among the regional conferences, the NWC had to accept two disadvantages. First, because participants mingled freely with the ASA convention-goers, the sense of a close-knit group brought together from distant countries for a specific purpose was dissipated. Second, holding the NWC on United States soil meant that BCICA had to take on the responsibility, together with the ASA, of organizing the conference. A special program committee was appointed with Canadian and Latin American representation to solicit applications and to select the participants.

The NWC brought together fifty-nine scholars from fifteen different countries in the hemisphere. Eleven sessions were organized, following the general outline proposed by BCICA for the five regional Bicentennial conferences, in addition to the ASA panels. The NWC was the first hemispheric academic gathering of students of the United States. Its significance was enhanced by the broad disciplinary representation of the participants and by its deliberate emphasis on comparative study. This is what held the conference together and provided much of its intellectual excitement. The study of the United States in this hemisphere varies from formal academic American Studies programs modeled on counterparts in the United States, most typically in Canada, to the work of individuals who never refer to themselves as American Studies specialists, but who study the United States in order to know more about it or to understand their own country through the prism of comparative study. Representatives of this mode of analysis—who might include businessmen, lawyers, or architects studying the way things are done in the United States or social scientists following the hortatory dictum of the dependency theorists to learn more about the imperialist center of the capitalist system—were included in the NWC along with practitioners of more traditional modes of American Studies.

The papers from the NWC have been collected and edited for publication for two reasons. Most obviously, they constitute the record of a unique historical event and demonstrate the extraordinary diversity of activity that was called forth by the Bicentennial of the United States. More important, coming from a broad spectrum of academic disciplines and a wide variety of viewpoints, these papers offer us a new perspective on our own society and culture. We have a great deal to learn about ourselves from the way others see us; we have a great deal to learn about the world outside our boundaries from the reactions to us from overseas. The papers in this volume will make a significant contribution to our self-awareness even though most of them were not written with a didactic purpose in mind. They have been organized here according to the themes of the conference. They do not constitute an organic whole, and no effort has been made to relate them or to tie them together to suit heuristic purposes conceived after the conferences.

I want to thank Karla A. Robinson, who served as program assistant in the early stages of organization, and María A. Leal, who ran the planning committee office, orchestrated the complex affairs of the conference secretariat, and worked with me to prepare these papers for publication.

JOSEPH S. TULCHIN

I. THE AMERICAN REVOLUTION IN CROSS-CULTURAL PERSPECTIVE

The United States: Revolution, Independence and Interdependence

William H. Goetzmann

I should like to begin by stating the obvious.
Revolution and independence are not the same thing.
This fact seems to have been obscured during our national birthday celebration, and much more stress has
been put upon revolution, admittedly a fashionable word
these days, than upon independence. This is true for a
number of reasons. Revolution is dramatic. It is epic.
It is dynamic. Independence is a condition. Revolution connotes images and visions of struggle and heroism, of pamphleteers and ragged soldiers, of "times
that try men's souls," of Tom Paine, George Washington,
Simón Bolívar, and Louis Riel. Independence for the
successful revolutionary is an anticlimax. It is abstract, implying termination and stasis, like the happy
ending of a fairy tale or a motion picture, whereas
revolution may be a permanent dynamic condition--an
ongoing focus for the hopes and dreams of a people.
Revolution is, above all, myth--the most powerful myth
of modern times and certainly the most powerful myth,
along with that of the frontier described by Frederick
Jackson Turner, in American civilization. It behooves
us, then, to be fully aware of the humanistic and
spiritual quality of revolution as myth in the growth
of U.S. civilization. The tradition of revolution
explains America's tumultuous political past, its
succession of political slogans suggesting an endless
progression of "new deals," reconstructions, and new
frontiers. The tradition or myth of revolution also
explains the North American's passion for novelty.
Steamboats, railroads, bridges, superhighways, automobiles, motorcycles, strip culture, and the easy rider--
all have something to do with the North American myth of
continuing revolution, with its passion for the new.
The United States in a bountiful continent has been

celebrating the "endless birthday party" for 200 years.
The myth of revolution has supplied the dynamic. It
has instilled the spirit into the revelers.

And yet most of our current scholars do not see
the American Revolution as being very revolutionary at
all. It is most frequently contrasted with the French
Revolution and the Russian Revolution and found wanting
in revolutionary quality. The French Revolution, carried forward on the rising tide of romantic folk spirit,
seemed once and for all to have overturned the established orders in favor of the people--the masses. It
has appeared to be a true social and class revolution.
It produced an ideology of revolution--or at least a
stirring rhetoric of revolution--that seemed to be addressed to the masses and promised, if not to abolish
the peasantry, at least to ameliorate its condition.
Since the United States had no explicitly acknowledged
peasant class, its revolutionary leaders, alas, produced no such rhetoric. People like Jefferson and
Franklin believed America to be a classless society,
while leaders like Adams and Hamilton, if they believed
otherwise, dared not admit it. American revolutionary
leaders wished only to throw off the impediments of
the British Empire so as to allow "the new man, the
American" to realize the opportunities that nature's
abundance offered to him. But this meant that American
revolutionary leaders, aside from Tom Paine, produced
no rhetoric or ideology of cataclysmic class revolution.

Likewise in this respect, they do not compare in
their apocalyptic visions with the leaders of the
Russian Revolution. There was no Marxist teleology,
nor myth of the working class to aid them in a country
where everyone was of the working class and believed
himself the better for it. And there was no brutal
Czarist repression, no downtrodden peasantry (except
the Negro slave), no secret police, no Siberia.

By all current standards the American Revolution
seems "prerevolutionary"--no peasants to liberate, no
masses to unchain, no classes to overthrow. From time
to time, however, historians with a perverse, pragmatic
bent have looked to the consequences of the two "modern"
revolutions and have been mildly dismayed to find that
as revolutions they had not accomplished so much after
all.

Nonetheless, the main scholarly battleground as it
concerns the American Revolution today seems inevitably
to have reference to the two "real" revolutions in France
and Russia. One group of scholars believed that the
American Revolution was fought less over "home rule"
than over "who should rule at home" and has searched

diligently for evidence indicating that a class struggle
was somehow involved in our revolution, too. "New"
historians have found startling evidence of such events
as sailors' riots against their masters--certain evidence of a colony-wide class struggle. Students of the
Great Awakening often see that strange event less in
religious terms than in socioeconomic terms. The
Awakeners, all the way from Charleston to Boston, were
the true peasant masses pitted against the tie-wig
elites and their pulpit puppets like Charles Chauncey
and Jonathan Mayhew. It was these awakened peasant
masses, inspired by Jonathan Edwards's millennial rhetoric of communitarianism, who led the vanguard of revolution. Still other interpreters point with pride to
the period after the Revolution--to the democratizing
provisions of the Northwest Ordinances, to the new
state constitutions that carried republicanism to the
extreme and enthroned the country legislator, to Shays's
and other incipient rebellions, to the constitutional
convention device, to the relative increase in the
franchise--and declare that the Revolution was after all
class-motivated and class-propelled, judging from its
short-term results. Another school points tellingly to
the fact that the Federalists, in order to promote the
Constitution and then to stay in power, had to adopt
the "leveling" rhetoric of republicanism, implying that
no Federalist believed a word of it. One of the abid-
ing problems with this interpretation is, of course,
the question as to whether or not republican yeomen in
town or country considered themselves masses and classes either in the revolutionary period or even later in
the Jacksonian period. This question should provide a
field day for an emerging generation of quantitative
historians.

    Certain interpreters of the Revolution remain old-
fashioned. They still search for an ideological tradition among American leaders that not only provided
the "cement" for revolutionary solidarity, but also
bears comparison with the better-known rhetoric and
ideology of France and Russia. The most notable work
of this genre, Bernard Bailyn's prizewinning Ideological
Origins of the American Revolution, sees the colonists
being persuaded to revolt by appeals to classical models of Roman republican virtue, Puritan values, the
English legal tradition, the works of British and Continental philosophers, and, most viscerally, the English
Whig tradition of "coffee house radicalism" best exemplified in Cato's Letters by Trenchard and Gordon.
Because the American colonies had a high degree of literacy, because the printing of pamphlets and penny
papers was becoming the rage in America, because news
traveled surprisingly fast in what was in the 1770s a
seaboard nation, Bailyn's thesis must be considered as

something more than an old-fashioned elitist interpretation. But the ideological interpretation seems forced
to concede that the Revolution itself was incidental,
after the fact, and that the real change had taken place
some years before in "the minds and hearts of the people." If so, why the necessity for independence?

Perhaps this can be explained; and in so explaining
it, I can possibly suggest still another characteriza-
tion of the American Revolution.

The one concept that seems to have taken hold in
prerevolutionary North America was the belief in the
natural right to liberty. First the pilgrims, then the
Puritans came, seeking religious liberty in their own
peculiar fashion. To the south, on the Chesapeake, the
one thing the proprietors of the Virginia Company
learned was the folly of attempting to attract plantation workers without giving them some chance to own
their own land in the vastness of America. As the
Middle Colonies developed, Pennsylvania prospered on its
climate of tolerance--religious, economic, and even
ethnic--which attracted thousands of settlers and not
only made Philadelphia the most prosperous and the most
tolerant city in the colonies, but also opened up the
back country to rich and prosperous settlement. And in
New York, not only had the Hudson River patroon system
failed and had Manhattan become a polyglot city of all
sorts of people, religions, and occupations, but it was
so recognized by British authorities who, when they
conquered it from the Dutch, allowed most indigenous
institutions to stand. Religion at times became an
issue, because British rulers lived in an age when the
spirit of the Reformation reinforced a natural imperial
competition with Catholic France and Spain; consequently
they endorsed, at times even enthusiastically, the holy
aspects of the English mission to North America. But
when intense religious conflicts arose in the mid-
seventeenth century, the reaction of Britain's rulers
was always toward broadened toleration. In the meantime, throughout the colonies locally dominated political institutions began to develop little by little:
from the famous Virginia House of Burgesses to the New
England town meetings built upon the base of religious
congregationalism. This whole broad imperial outlook
on the part of Britain has been termed a policy of
"salutary neglect," but, on the contrary, it would be
more accurate to say that it was a policy of headlong,
opportunistic imperial development in which large numbers of grateful, loyal, functioning citizens were seen
to be England's best resource in the competition with
Spain, France, and Holland. To achieve this strength
in the shortest possible time, within the broad outlines

of a traditional mercantilist design, there prevailed
a middle-class laissez-faire policy that even counte-
nanced indentured servitude and slavery. This laissez-
faire policy Americans came to equate with liberty,
which they believed to be traditional not only in their
own long colonial experience, but also in the rights of
Englishmen under the British Constitution. Eventually
American philosophers, following John Locke, traced the
natural right to liberty--or laissez faire--back
through the best times in ancient history to the mythical origins of man in a state of nature. Through a
process of historicism they made such rights fundamental
to the nature of man himself and thus perceived the
never-ending quest for these rights as something holy.

The striking fact about all this is that for such
a very long time, with minor exceptions, the interests
of Britain and its North American colonies seemed to
coincide. The most bitter struggles seemed to take
place within the colonies themselves--partially due to
growing pains that continually jostled, threatened, or
at times replaced the status positions of colonial
leadership groups. By the Peace of Paris in 1763,
which ended the French and Indian War, in North America
itself a new status revolution had taken place, one
fully as profound as the ousting of the French from the
backwoods heartlands of America. Religion per se had
lost its monopoly on the definition of the good life in
America. The Great Awakening had subsided for a time,
like a sudden storm blown out to sea, and with it had
gone the minister's authority in the vanguard of continental leadership. Instead, new men ruled--merchants
made rich on war profits, lawyers made rich on merchants' profits and squabbles, and, most important of
all, a new intellectual class who gained great sway
over the minds of Americans through the media of newspapers, almanacs, circulated letters, politically
oriented sermons, manifestos, and pamphlets. Such figures as Samuel Adams, Benjamin Franklin, James Otis,
Patrick Henry, John Dickinson, Thomas Jefferson, and
Tom Paine spring immediately to mind. Replacing the
minister, who had struggled over freedom of conscience
and the merits or demerits of private revelation, these
new men--the American philosophers--directed their
energies, using every basic strand of traditional
Western thought, to defining and arguing the nature of
human liberty in this world, rather than the next.

But why had they arisen as contenders and leaders
at all? Why did they feel compelled to precipitate a
crisis within what seemed to be a harmonious British
Empire governed, by their own admission, under the most
enlightened constitution and set of laws that Western
man had ever devised? Clearly, purely economic motives

were not the most important. The Navigation Acts, with
the exception of controls over sugar and molasses, were
largely beneficial to the colonists. And as Oliver
Dickinson has shown, these acts were so loosely enforced
as to make smuggling take on the character of legitimate
business enterprise. The King seemed to wish nothing
but goodwill for his colonies and even made an American,
Benjamin West, his court painter. Both King and Parliament were proud of their newly won North American empire.
Parliament, as Namier and his followers have shown, was
hardly a united body, but rather a collection of local
representatives bound up with a limited set of consti-
tuents, parochial concerns, and the game or sport of
jockeying for status and glory within the confines of
the houses themselves. Despite the great names of
Parliament handed down to us by British historians,
despite the striking personalities of Walpole, Pitt,
Fox, Burke, Townshend, North, Grenville, and the like,
the British Parliament seems really to have differed
little in its instincts from a Virginia House of Burgesses or a Massachusetts assembly. It was excessively
local in character. At a time when worldwide intellectual currents were sweeping through Western civilization and when Britain itself had acquired a global
empire, Parliament seemed almost testy at the inconven-
ience of interrupting its sport and attending to the
responsibilities of its new empire.

The best way out was to delegate authority; and by
1763, with regard to foreign policy, Britain had the
largest, most cumbersome bureaucracy of its time--a
major triumph of spoilsmanship and shrewd obfuscation
in the eyes of some. As Esmond Wright describes it,
the following all had some control over the colonies:
the secretary of state for the Southern Department, the
Board of Trade and Plantations (made up of merchants),
the Treasury, the surveyor and auditor-general of the
colonies, the commissioner of customs, the secretary-
at-war, the Admiralty, the Admiralty Courts, the sur-
veyor-general of the King's Woods, the postmaster
general, and the bishop of London.

Beyond this, the experience of the French and
Indian War fastened a permanent, hostile bureaucracy on
America. To a man, the British commanders who partici-
pated in that campaign--Loudon, Amherst, Bouquet, Sir
William Johnson, and others--had nothing but contempt
for the continentals. Most colonies had furnished supplies and men only with greatest reluctance. And all
of the successful campaigns in the vast war of forest
and lakes were mounted by common British redcoats.
Accordingly, General Thomas Gage was appointed commander
in chief for North America to watch over the immense
hinterland and to guard against the unruly Americans.

In 1763 there was launched a new strategy, which Gage
enthusiastically carried out until 1774, when, too late,
he was relieved. American settlers were to be kept out
of the interior--the back country of Pennsylvania, Ohio,
Kentucky, and Illinois. So, too, were British regulars
to avoid becoming enmeshed in another vast land war in
the wilderness. Troops were to be stationed around the
fringes of the frontier to keep the settlers out and to
protect the Indians so that they might continue to furnish furs to British manufacturers. New York, because
of its strategic location vis-à-vis the Hudson River
Valley, was selected as the main headquarters of the
British army, and great numbers of troops were to be
quartered there and sent out as reinforcements to frontier garrisons. In addition, Britain sent among the
Indians its own agents, seeking trade and pacification
so as to avoid another war. And finally in 1763 a
royal proclamation was issued, forbidding Americans to
cross over and settle beyond the Alleghenies. This
offended thousands of would-be American settlers and
also groups of land speculators in the seaboard towns
who hoped to profit by dealing in the greatly extended
territories won by the British soldiers.

   Parliament suddenly became aware--doubtless prompted
by tax-paying clients from the landholding sections of
the realm--that the war and the keeping of the peace
had become very expensive. Revenue acts taxing the
colonies for what could be construed as a war in their
interests seemed essential. Unfortunately, the primary
act passed for securing revenue was the Stamp Act of
1765. This act fell most heavily on exactly the wrong
group in America--the new elite of merchants, lawyers,
publicists, and philosophes, whose every document from
newspapers and pamphlets to wills, cargo manifests, and
land deeds had to bear the King's stamp. Such a regulation directly threatened the most intelligent,
aggressive, and recently triumphant elite in the colonies. Further, this group had increasingly felt
threatened not only by the rising military establishment and its pretentious (if not contemptuous) officer
class, but also by still another British bureaucracy
fastened upon America. To the ever growing numbers of
customs agents, revenue collectors, English factors,
insurance agents, bondsmen, inspectors, Vice-Admiralty
Court officers, royal governors, and their growing
staffs of agents and spies now were to be added a
legion of stamp sellers and an armada of revenue cut-
ters and patrol boats. Colonial businessmen, farmers,
shippers, and publicists bitterly resented both the
artificial status enjoyed by these new parliamentary
favorites and the habitual extortion, overzealousness,
and racketeering that was common practice among those
who swelled the King's bureaucracy in North America in

pursuit of "the main chance." What today might be
called "big government" and its real or imagined in-
fringement on their liberties seems most to have an-
gered the colonists. Not money alone nor legalistic
arguments over internal versus external taxation aroused
the colonists; rather, it was the psychological threat
to their liberties and to the newly won leadership
status of the vocal colonial elite class. Moreover, the
obvious venality, racketeering, and profligate behavior
of the King's military officers and his civilian agents
helped build up an image of rampant dissolution and
immorality emanating from Britain itself, particularly
in the minds of sober New Englanders and staid planters
like George Washington. The bad example of the low-
principled, high-living King's agents in America began
to change the colonials' image of Britain itself.

Out of all these circumstances came the first
crisis, the Stamp Act Crisis of 1765, which united the
colonies for the first time in opposition to the Crown.
The mobs; the haranguing; the harassment of officials,
which included hanging them in effigy; the sermons
praying against episcopacy, which somehow was linked
with stamps; the writings of James Otis; the formation
of the Stamp Act Congresses; and the nonimportation
agreements--all caused the cancellation of the Stamp
Act in 1766, but an obiter dicta, the Declaratory Act
of the same year, asserted Parliament's power to tax
the colonies. In the following decade came the series
of British acts that seemed to lead inevitably to revolution. The creation of Vice-Admiralty Courts suspend-
ing trial by jury in one's own country; the Townshend
Acts taxing the colonies on articles in such a way as
to ensure, as the London Magazine of 1766 put it, that
"the American is apparelled from head to foot in our
manufactures . . . he scarcely drinks, sits, moves,
labours or recreates himself without contributing to
the emolument of the mother country"; the forcible
quartering of troops in private homes; the hiring of
Hessian mercenaries to hold down "freeborn Englishmen";
the awful atrocity of the Boston Massacre in 1770, in
which five people were shot by soldiers; the granting
of a tea monopoly to the East India Company; and,
finally, the Coercive or Intolerable Acts--such actions
caused the colonists to take a more than casual interest
in their liberties. Indeed, in the critical decade
between 1764 and 1774, liberty became an American obses-
sion, a violent passion that led to revolution.

Behind all British imperial policy--indeed, one of
the chief causes for assuming the "hard line" that
eventually lost America--was the continued advice of
General Gage and the military-bureaucratic establishment in the colonies. In nearly every dispatch for a

decade, Gage sounded the alarm, urged a "get tough" policy, and called for an ever larger army and naval establishment. Gage's dispatches and reports were echoed by other officers and by civil officials such as Governor Bernard of Massachusetts and a resident of the same state, Hutchinson, whose lavish house had been sacked by a mob. As the crucial decade moved along, and as nearly every Crown officer became a target of abuse, the advice flowing into Parliament and the King from those who were assumed to be the most expert--the men on the spot--counseled tighter restrictions, a greater bureaucracy in America, a larger show of military strength, and a policy of bringing America to heel. The Crown's men on the spot not only glossed over their own countless peccadilloes and examples of bad judgment, but they also failed to face up to the obvious; that is, such a policy meant civil war, an expensive conflict that Britain just might lose along with its North American empire, should France be drawn into it. More than any other factor, this proconsul strategy of offending the civil leaders and needlessly showing military, economic, and bureaucratic coercion seems to have led to the American Revolution.

In any case, British strategy failed. Besides organizing the colonists as never before, it brought to the front the natural leaders in America. Further, it so mobilized the intellectual talents of these leaders as to generate a new kind of revolution--an ideological revolution. By 1776 the war, which had already begun in April 1775 at Lexington and Concord, had turned into something quite different from a legal struggle. It had become the philosophe's war, an ideological struggle that was made to represent the culmination of the Enlightenment struggle for the rights of man in a better environment shorn of the last vestiges of decadent feudalism. What better place than America--"Nature's Nation"--for the opening struggle in the great cause of liberty that Tom Paine so optimistically declared "the birthday of a new world." Thus, the American Revolution came to have its ideological dimension born out of the exigencies of a historical situation involving "big government" and callous proconsulship in the service of imperialism. Liberty was nature's basic law, and liberty was now not possible without independence.

Whatever interpretation one chooses to put upon it, the American Revolution had one outcome which the French and Russian revolutions did not, but which is of vital importance as a model to countries in this hemisphere-- independence for a new nation. This all-important concept is largely taken for granted by North American cultural analysts, who are mainly intent upon keeping

alive the revolutionary myth. To others in the hemisphere and around the world, even those who have been
born of revolution, independence cannot be taken for
granted. Thus it would seem important on this occasion
to examine more closely just what independence meant or
consisted of for the North American.

I have already suggested that it meant liberty and,
to a very large extent, laissez faire. But this is too
simple. Liberty meant a natural right to individual
self-determination by man as a member of human society
that existed before government. The American's emotional belief in liberty as a given attests to the profound
impact of ideas on society at all levels. Without this
emotional belief in the right to liberty the American
would have found no cause for grievance against the
King and his ministers. But liberty and independence
were largely perceived in Lockean terms, which meant
that each individual had personal inviolable rights,
that he also existed in society, that rights thus depended upon a certain mutuality between individuals,
and that, recognizing this, men formed governments and
delegated authority to secure these rights both among
themselves and with regard to outside social entities.
Independence thus meant that condition, both personal
and societal, that denoted the ability to secure true
liberty.

Thus far the North American independence existed
in theory on all levels of life. It was personal,
societal, and governmental, always recognizing that
personal and societal independence took precedence over
that of the state. In the United States from the beginning, due to the unfortunate experience with the Crown
and its agents and due to the philosophy of John Locke,
the individual and society were always more important
than the state. That was true independence. The state
existed to maintain this condition both internally and
externally. But, it was soon recognized, the State--
that is, the new United States of America--could not
automatically guarantee either itself or its citizens
true independence in the family of nations. Certain
internal problems of liberty or independence were
ignored or postponed by the founding fathers. The whole
range of states' versus national rights, the interpretation of the Bill of Rights and other clauses in the
Constitution relating to liberties on every level, the
question of slavery, and the status of the Indian were
all left either to the courts or to battlefields to
decide.

Likewise on the international level, independence--
liberty and freedom of action as a nation--was not guaranteed for all times by the Revolution. Hamilton,

perhaps more than any other founding father, worked
assiduously to make independence a permanent condition.
His financial plans for funding the war debt and creating a stable national bank were aimed at securing national credit abroad; his plan to encourage home manufactures looked toward continental economic self-
sufficiency; and his support for Jay's treaty with
Britain was aimed at securing not only lasting peace
with the mightiest power on earth through mutuality of
interest, but also genuine recognition of America's
existence by that power--a situation somewhat akin to
Israel's in the Middle East today. None of these measures was final, however. Throughout the early years of
its existence, the United States struggled for independence, on into the War of 1812, and, I would maintain,
throughout the first half of the nineteenth century,
when the Balkanization of the country was an ever possible threat and when economic growth was largely dependent upon foreign loans and the equivalent of multinational corporations, such as world cotton brokers,
Baring Brothers Bank, and foreign owners of our railroads and canals, mines and cattle ranches. Americans
soon learned that independence, once achieved, was and
still remains not easy to maintain, that independence
as much as revolution implies an ongoing, dramatic
struggle.

Because of this, one is tempted to conclude that
just as there was a myth of revolution that stirred
America, there was also a myth of independence. The
myth began with John Locke's fable of man in a state of
nature endowed with his natural rights. Its story
line--necessary for all myths or tales of the tribe--
carries the weight of the American republican experiment,
laissez faire, avoidance of extreme ideologies, faith
in democratic self-government, notions of world security, and belief in a fundamental order that takes precedence over nations and states.

But it also seems clear that from the beginning,
for the North American, independence was a relative
thing. It was so in Locke's fable, which implied
mutuality, and it worked out thus in the history of our
people on all levels. Independence evolved in response
to situations, and it was never perfect. Rather, independence involved a great contradiction. It was not
possible without at the same time assuming a position
of dependence. Independence depended upon mutuality
among individuals, societies, and nations. It is
variously a concept, a myth, a situation, and a position
in the world and in time, one that perhaps deserves
study by North American scholars during these Bicentennial years fully as much as does the idea of revolution.

The Impact of the American Revolution on the Independence of Guatemala

Reyes Antonio Pérez Rojas

The following remarks are meant to point out ways
in which the American Revolution and the independence
of Central America are interrelated. At the time of
independence, Guatemala comprised all of what today
is called Central America. Independence came on
September 15, 1821, a little less than fifty years after
the American Revolution.

THE MEANING OF AMERICAN INDEPENDENCE IN THE NEW WORLD

Diverse causes created the conditions that led the
nations of the New World to seek their independence.
One important factor was a consciousness of difference
among the Europeans who had come to America, a new consciousness without which the desire for self-government
and the search for sovereignty would never have arisen.

Nearly every region of America achieved its independence in a different way. But the fight for liberty
was the same and united patriots everywhere. This environment of unrest, which accentuated the feeling of
European oppression, prevailed at the time of U.S. independence. The significance of this historical fact
was great for those engaged in their own independence
struggles. Individuals fighting for independence were
able to obtain popular support for their goals. The
University of San Carlos of Guatemala, already more
than a century old, had fostered a well-informed intellectual class with progressive ideas recently inspired
by French and English philosophers.

In Guatemala more than ten persons worked to clarify and promote the desire for independence. Among
them two merit special mention: José Cecilio del Valle

and Pedro Molina. Both were brilliant writers whose
public discussions--del Valle in his newspaper, The
Friend of the Motherland; Molina in his newspaper,
The Constitutional Editor, later called The Genius of
Liberty--contributed significantly to shaping the
Guatemalan spirit that was to achieve independence from
Spain. Del Valle and Molina greeted American indepen-
dence with enthusiasm. Thus, for example, del Valle
wrote: "The North of America got itself in motion in
1774, and by declaring its independence from the
British government set an example for Mexico and Guate-
mala, Chile and Argentina."[1]

The local relevance that del Valle attributes to
the independence of "the North of America" is explained
by intangible bonds of solidarity among the peoples of
the new continent who were trying to liberate themselves from European rule. The American Revolution had
important repercussions among the peoples of the New
World. Charles C. Griffin, among others, perceived the
profound significance of the great American achievement:

> The American revolution was the most important
> happening in the New World at the time. It
> created a precedent for future colonial rebel-
> lions and introduced a new element into inter-
> national relations in the continent. Moreover,
> at this time the United States organized an
> effective system of federal government, strong
> enough to face external threats and internal
> discord.[2]

Thus, the image that the other Americans of the continent had before their eyes was complete and constituted
a reliable example to follow.

AMERICAN IDEOLOGICAL UNITY

The North American case appeared to have profound
significance in the eyes of anticolonialists. There
was agreement not only with respect to the ideals of
freedom, but also with respect to the ideas on which
they rested. The ideas of the Encyclopedia, the Enlightenment, and the doctrine of natural rights prevailed throughout the New World. Locke's Essay on
Civil Government, together with the Declaration of the
Rights of Man of the French Revolution and other
"modern" ideas, inspired the fight against colonialism.
The Declaration of Independence of the United States
was a concrete application of the ideas behind independence struggles of our nations. But the ideology of
freedom was not limited to the intellectual elite.

Besides the newspaper efforts of del Valle and Molina, in Guatemala other methods were used to spread those ideas among larger segments of the population. In 1829, soon after independence, for example, a pamphlet entitled <u>Project of political catechism for those who will vote in the elections of authorities of popular appointment in Central America</u> was printed and circulated in Guatemala. Needless to say, it was liberal, emphasizing ideas of independence. Thus, ideological unity was not limited to intellectuals.

CAUSES OF GUATEMALAN AND CENTRAL AMERICAN INDEPENDENCE

We can affirm, in agreement with our forefathers, that the thirst for justice was common to all independence movements in America. José Cecilio del Valle, writing about the role of reason in government, stated:

> Let us question this divinity: let us listen to its oracles. Let us note the causes of the revolutions of Greece and Rome, of Sweden and France, of the United States and of South America, and after realizing that injustice is the first origin of all of them, let us at last learn to be just if we want to be independent.[3]

But the thirst for independence was caused by concrete and specific wants. The distinguished Guatemalan historian, José Mata Gavidia, outlined the causes of the independence movement in Guatemala.[4]

> If America had been well treated by Spain it probably would have changed the destiny of the world, and it is possible that the independence movement would not have taken place in the nineteenth century. But human exploitation opened the gate to discontent. This discontent was nurtured by:
> 1. The systematic violation of justice against Indians, Creoles, and Spaniards who had settled here for life;
> 2. The awarding of government jobs to persons from Spain, thus affronting the Creoles;
> 3. Restrictions on commerce and the monopoly of sales, which caused indignation to Creoles and resident Spaniards alike; and
> 4. Restrictions on the expression of thought and university culture, which exasperated the elite of American thought: clergymen and university graduates.

According to the preceding text, the fight for independence was fundamentally one between the exploiters and
the exploited. According to the same author, "the
circumstances of the independence of the United States
and the fact of the French Revolution were merely its
historical antecedents but not its . . . origin." The
same opinion--that is, what was sought was the organization of a nonoppressive government--is expressed by
José Cecilio del Valle: "To be against the freedom of
America would have amounted to fighting against the
spirit of the century, to resist public opinion, to be
unjust and to become an object of contempt. . . . In
the future the New World will not be, as it has been in
the past, an unhappy appendage of the old."[5]

This brief causal account of the independence of
Guatemala has shown more than one point of comparison
with U.S independence. Both were movements against
the exploitation in which, in different ways, their
respective colonial masters were engaged.

THE IMPACT OF THE AMERICAN REVOLUTION IN GUATEMALA

I share Mata Gavidia's opinion that the independence of the United States cannot be considered,
strictly speaking, a cause of the independence of Central America. But the American Revolution was much
more than a mere historical antecedent, for it fulfilled at least three functions favoring the independence of our nations. It was an example, a living
experiment, and a fundamental premise of discussions in
favor of independence.

Example and Motive for Revolutionary Thought

U.S. independence and its effects exerted a powerful influence on the concept of independence held
throughout the rest of America. Pedro Molina wrote:
"Our century will be famous in history for its enlightenment. Thanks to it despotism is fought everywhere
and superstition dethroned. In the midst of the catas-
trophies that accompany revolutions we cannot help but
admire the heroism of the men that sustain them. . . ."[6]

The fight for independence in the United States
became a shining example to be imitated and provided
material for revolutionary enthusiasm. The cause and
the men were often referred to as prototypes of what
ought to be done. In Guatemala, the exploits of George
Washington, the Constitution of the United States, and
the writings of Benjamin Franklin were all well known
and were referred to in the writings of our political
thinkers of the time.

A Possibility Becomes a Reality

Ideas about constitutionalism, republicanism, and
so on were entertained, but there was no reference to
the possibility of their being applied in Guatemala.
The independence of the United States, the attempts to
consolidate it, and the efforts to derive beneficial
results from it provided an empirical referent to the
ideas entertained by our political philosophers.
Griffin points this out: "As governments sought or
achieved their independence, general ideas such as those
contained in the Declaration of Independence of the
United States were given a more definite practical
significance."[7]

Ideas of independence in the rest of America were
greatly aided by the fact that it was possible to point
out a case that embodied in practice what was proclaimed
in theory. The contemporary Cuban situation is similar
to this. For Latin American socialists, Cuba is the
living experiment of a new form of government, and that
is why there is so much interest in its future. Thus,
the socialist world does everything to make the experiment a success. The American revolution fulfilled a
similar function and, in my opinion, did it very well.

Spanish Support for American Independence

An oft-neglected fact is the role played by King
Charles III, whose backing of the independence of the
United States also favored Spanish American independence.
As a matter of fact, both France and Spain contributed
to the independence of North America, but it is hard to
determine if and to what extent the Spanish government
was conscious of the significance of its support of the
North Americans' fight against England. What is clear
is that this support was interpreted by Spanish American freedom fighters as favorable to their cause. Thus,
Pedro Molina wrote:

> Tired of suffering the yoke of English domi-
> nation the North American colonies decided to
> separate themselves from their metropolis.
> Thirteen colonies raised the flag of freedom
> and organized a government by themselves.
> Great Britain, insulted by this behavior,
> considered the colonies rebellious, sent
> troops to put the rebellion down, and tried
> everything that might contribute to preserve
> such valuable possessions. . . . War broke
> out; both of the nations in conflict appealed
> to other nations: the one claimed the rights
> of a mother, the other complained about the
> abuses it suffered. Whoever showed approval

of one of the parties thereby justified its
conduct.
          What did Spain do . . . ? She helped the
Americans, recognized their independence, protected them in their strivings, took sides
against England and, in a word, considered
the insurrection of the United States to be
just.--In so doing Spain . . . indirectly
invited her own [colonies] to imitate those
of England. . . . Therefore, Spain cannot
fairly label criminals those who follow
Washington's example, whom she helped and
protected.[8]

The conclusion of Molina's argument, which rested
on the help given by Spain to North America, was evident: "Spain has no more right over her colonies than
England had over hers. She publicly recognized that
the separation of the latter was just. Therefore, she
could not deny the right of the former to their separation without showing gross inconsequence and incurring
a contradiction of principles."[9]

Thus, consciously or not, in helping the North
American cause, Spain was not merely giving aid and
comfort; it was also acquiring a logico-practical commitment to accept the claim of its own colonies to the
right to independence.

THE RESPONSIBILITIES OF A POWERFUL NATION

I have pointed out at least three important functions that the American Revolution had. The nations of
the rest of America were able to judge the merits of
the process, and the United States fulfilled its historical mission. As the Count of Aranda wrote, several
years before the independence of Spanish America,

This federal republic [the United States] was
born a pygmy, so to speak, and it needed the
support and the strength of such powerful
nations as France and Spain to attain its independence. The day will come when she will
grow and become a giant and even a colossus
in those parts. Then she will forget the
benefits she derived from those nations and
will only think of becoming greater. . . .
The first action will be to get hold of
Florida in order to dominate the gulf of
Mexico. After thus causing us trouble in
our relations with the New Spain it will
aspire to conquer this vast empire, which
we cannot defend against a formidable

opponent, established in the same Continent, and which is its neighbor."[10]

Whether or not the Count of Aranda's forecast was right is a question that only the North Americans can answer. We Latin Americans have our own answer, which runs through the social movements of our time. In its own time the United States provided a living and stimulating example. It represented a desirable society and a tolerant, respectful, and enterprising national spirit. It seemed to be a model after which we could pattern our striving. But North Americans today ought to ask themselves two questions: Are we still an example for the enslaved world? Do we still represent the movement toward a satisfactory society for man? In turn, we Latin Americans should ask ourselves, Can we still be sure that the United States constitutes the vanguard of the fight for freedom? Can it still show us heroes of liberation?

These questions, among others that could be asked, urgently require answers of the North American people if they still want to be the world's leaders, as the American Revolution enters into its third century.

NOTES

1. Editorial José de Pineda Ibarra, Colección Documentos, vol. 2, El Amigo de la Patria (Guatemala: Editorial José de Pineda Ibarra, 1969), p. 180.

2. El Período Nacional en la Historia del Nuevo Mundo, trans. Emilia Romero Del Valle, Instituto Panamericano de Geografía e Historia (Mexico), pub. no. 261, 1962, p. 8.

3. Del Valle, El Amigo de la Patria, p. 209.

4. "Pronósticos Hispánicos de Emancipación Americana" (Paper delivered to the Guatemalan Society of Geography and History, September 12, 1962).

5. Del Valle, El Amigo de la Patria, p. 183.

6. Editorial José de Pineda Ibarra, Colección Documentos, vol. 3, El Editor Constitucional (Guatemala: Editorial José de Pineda Ibarra, 1969), p. 603.

7. Griffin, El Período Nacional, p. 15.

8. Molina, El Editor Constitucional, p. 675.

9. Ibid.

10. Quoted by José Mata Gavidia, *Anotaciones de Historia Patria Centroamericana*, 2d ed. (Guatemala: Editorial Universitaria, 1969), pp. 257-58.

The United States and the River Plate: Interrelations and Influences Between Two Revolutions

Hernán Asdrúbal Silva

There were many internal and external factors that affected the revolutionary process of the River Plate. A discussion of its features and influences is thus rather complex, and, hence, there exist differences among the many theses that attempt to explain it. Nevertheless, one can point out some basic elements that recur to explain not only the revolutionary phenomenon, but also the conditions under which it was able to develop.

One cannot speak directly of an official or semi-official North American policy facilitating the separation of the River Plate from the Spanish Crown, as one can observe of the English. However, the interrelations that were encouraged, especially at the end of the eighteenth century, are undoubtedly significant for a better understanding of this process. For this reason I will not only consider the formal relationship between the two regions, but also will try to demonstrate, starting from the last quarter of the eighteenth century, to what extent the informal interrelations with North America influenced South American history.

A short time after the independence of the United States was declared, the English ambassador suggested to the Madrid government that "it would be very pleasing to his Highness" if the ports of Spain were closed to North American ships, as Portugal had already done. Nevertheless, on 20 September 1776, after the international situation had been studied, José de Galvez sent a communiqué to the governor of Buenos Aires:

> These antecedents have caused the King to
> consider this matter, and, having thought
> that blocking up his ports to the Americans

would cause their turning into enemies of
Spain and indiscriminately capturing our
ships overseas, without our being left any
possibility for an indemnity, not even to
punish this violation, his Highness has
decided that the same Americans be cor-
dially admitted at the Spanish ports even
with their own flag instead of the British.[1]

The effects of this determination were not limited to
the United States and its struggle for independence. By
allowing a series of contacts that--although fundamentally related to the economy--had social, political, and
ideological consequences, the decision had a definite
influence on the Spanish American colonies.

Concurrent with the North American independence, a
significant event had modified and further stimulated
the already active economy of the River Plate, making
the legal and illegal trade with its ports even more
desirable. The new regulations issued after the creation of the viceroyship in 1776 established that the
silver obtained from the Peruvian mines should be channeled through Buenos Aires and Montevideo. This undoubtedly increased the interchange of raw materials
and coins, mainly for European or North American products, but also for other products from far-off regions,
like spices and silk fabrics from the East, to which
the traffic of slaves was added. Further, interest had
arisen in whales, seals, and walruses, which probably
complemented legal trading and constituted important
items of contraband.

Furthermore, in 1778, when the Crown ordered the
founding of settlements on the Patagonic coasts, it
warned that the danger of an occupation of those territories could come not only from the English, but also
from the North Americans. Hence the Royal Ordinance
of March 7, 1778, pointed out,

In order to discourage the English or their
insurgent colonists from thinking of settling down in the San Julian Bay or on the
same coast in order to catch whales in those
seas to which they have so earnestly devoted their efforts, His Majesty hereby
resolves that the Viceroy of Buenos Aires
and the treasurer of the Public Funds be
given precise and confidential instructions warning them that, by mutual agreement and as soon as possible, they must
arrange the formal founding and settlement
of the San Julian Bay.[2]

Spain's commitment to U.S. independence, which led them
to have an armed conflict with England, did not prevent
them from paying attention to their own territorial and
economic aims. And this was a well-founded preoccupation.

On the other hand, it is not at all accurate to
blame the San Ildefonso treaty of 1796 between Spain and
France, and the resulting new war with England, on the
onset of marauding by North American ships in the River
Plate. Long before this--and in confirmation of the
Crown's suspicions, which encouraged the creation of
Patagonic settlements--the danger represented by the
English and their North American ex-colonists was repeatedly stressed. For instance, in 1785 "the Viceroy
of Buenos Aires took notice of the considerable number
of English and Bostonian ships that frequented those
seas with the excuse of catching whales, possibly with
hidden intentions."[3] This call to attention was confirmed in April 1786, when D. Diego Gardoqui, sent by
the court to New York, wrote that since 1784 there were
"several North American commercial ships dealing with
the capture of whales on the coasts of the Falkland
Islands,"[4] on which they could have possibly settled
barracks to facilitate their activities. What in fact
caused the new war with Great Britain was that in 1797
the Cadiz merchants asked the king for permission to
use ships with a neutral flag, in order to resist the
serious difficulties inflicted on overseas commerce by
the English pirates.

The merchants' reaction merely reflected a general
crisis that seriously affected the economy of the whole
empire and Buenos Aires as well:

> Therefore, beginning in 1797 the colony suf-
> fered a painful social, political and economic
> evolution, in which the historian can find the
> elements leading directly to the Revolution.
> Once the commerce with Spain was interrupted,
> as well as any commercial relationship with
> other countries, an unbearable financial
> situation arose. In 1796 the export activity
> had exceeded 5,470,000 pesos; during 1797 it
> was less than 335,000 pesos.[5]

When Brackenridge referred to this situation in his report, he pointed out that "during the years that followed, while Spain was again at war with England, a
total stagnation affected the commerce with Buenos
Aires, except the contraband promoted by the United
States, which increased rapidly when the government
purposely overlooked this through unavoidable necessity."[6]

The authorization from Spain dated November 18, 1797, opened a great possibility to the North American ships. To the "products of legal trading," it not only added the smuggling of its goods, but also was the start of a great share of the worldwide interchange then rendered possible to the River Plate. As Chandler pointed out, from 1798 to 1810 at least 125 North American ships arrived in Buenos Aires and Montevideo. Thus, the commerce of the neutrals directly or indirectly favored the United States by allowing competition with Danish and Genoese vessels for the bulk of the intermediate commerce and by enabling the creation of new markets, not only in North America, but also in Europe and the East.

The frauds and contraband engendered by the commerce of the neutrals--especially the appearance of English ships flying North American flags in order to meet the requirements of the market--led the Cadiz Consulate to request the derogation of the Royal Ordinance of 1797. Their request was granted by the Crown in April 1799. The prohibition of dealing with foreign ships--set in force by the Marquis of Avilés, Viceroy of the River Plate, "not without having already been criticized by the Consulate's syndic"--caused an immediate reaction tending to circumvent it. Apart from the earnings obtained clandestinely or fraudulently, the most usual way of circumventing the royal disposition was for a ship transporting the merchandise to simulate another nationality. The ship entered the port bearing Spanish papers; once the merchandise was unloaded and the ship had departed from the roadstead, it assumed its real nationality. As a result, extreme precautions were taken to avoid this deception, such as requiring that ships be brought to port empty and their purchase be authentically demonstrated. In 1800, D. Francisco de Sar, who had obtained a license to buy two ships in the United States, was requested to carry the papers issued by the Spanish ambassador in North America, with documentation authenticated by the consul, in order to confirm the purchase in that country. Further, it was stipulated that in case of not being able to man the ships entirely with Spanish people, he should dismiss the foreigners as soon as he arrived in the River Plate; that he could not operate his ships before their being recognized as Spanish; and that he could not even sell them to foreigners.

However, since the war with England continued and it became mandatory to give a push to the Spanish economy, as well as to the colonial interchange and supply, the traffic of neutrals was permitted again in September 1801. The Germans took advantage of this opportunity to expand their markets. As soon as the system was

reestablished, a royal ordinance was issued, stating
that the Hamburg house of Bretano, Bovara and Urbieta
was allowed to send two neutral ships to Buenos Aires,
carrying 30,000 pesos' worth of merchandise of legal
commerce. These ships could return to Hamburg carrying products from the River Plate free from taxes, on
account of benefits rendered to the Crown.

North America also was favored by the expansion
of the German exporting activity. Of course, direct
traffic was an advantage. But in addition, this movement concerned German houses with affiliates in New
York, Philadelphia, Boston, and Baltimore.

The North Americans, who had taken over most
of this intermediate commerce, also carried
huge quantities of American products to the
neutral ports in northern Germany, taking from
these places what they needed from that part
of the world. In those times they had already
traded along all the coasts, many times by the
use of arms with insuperable force, and to do
this they needed many German products, which
were cheaper than the English. The splendor
of many great factories in Silesia, Saxony,
southern Hanover, Westphalia, and the like
started during that period.[7]

The dynamics of the international events were such
that in spite of the cessation of the English-Spanish
war of 1802, which should in theory have ended the commerce of neutrals, the traffic of these ships did not
disappear, although it decreased somewhat. Evidently,
it already had been incorporated into the system, and
when a new war broke out in 1805 as a consequence of
Spain's alliance with Napoleon, this activity was again
permitted.

Commerce with the United States must have been important at this time, since the North American nation
performed several functions: serving as intermediaries
in the export-import activities of other countries,
directly operating in the market for slaves, legally and
illegally introducing goods for consumption, and supplying ships and tools for the development of trades.
According to data provided by Chandler and Whitaker,
during 1801-02 at least forty-three American ships
operated in the River Plate, although their number declined over the two years that followed. In 1805,
twenty-two ships with North American flags arrived in
the port of Montevideo, half of which traded in slaves;
in 1806, thirty ships arrived in Montevideo, twenty
of them destined for the slave traffic. The usual cargo
also included articles such as rum, cognac, Baltimore

and Philadelphia flours, wine, furniture, fabrics, elements for navigation and drawing, saddles, horseshoes, and even some carriages. In exchange, these ships took with them mainly cattle products and coins.[8]

The closing of its sea routes as a consequence of the state of belligerency caused Spain serious financial problems. In January 1801, the viceroy of Buenos Aires was sent a "confidential circular," pointing out that "the urgent necessities of the Monarchy, in circumstances so unfortunate as those suffered by all Europe, and the essential necessity of supporting the obligations of the Crown impel it to take with utmost strength all imaginable steps to fulfill them." The loss by the Public Funds of the moneys coming from those domains with which all communication had been interrupted suggested the extraordinary practice of drafts: "The King has authorized the General Treasury to perform as many operations as it deems necessary, in order to obtain a prompt transfer of said funds to Spain, by starting relationships with trustworthy companies in the United States that will provide the exportation of silver or goods with the possibility of remitting the equivalent value."[9]

Direct contact with the River Plate was made not only through the ports of Buenos Aires and Montevideo, but also through the settlements on the Patagonic coasts, which received unscheduled ships and which, on more than one occasion, acted as improvised messengers and suppliers of food and equipment. This contact became even closer when the English invasions took place: it was a North American brigantine, commanded by Captain Carlos Boch, that was to carry back the settlers abandoning Puerto Deseado, having agreed to pay the captain a fee of $1,500.[10]

The economic interchange, which led to analyzing the necessity of permanent and fluid commercial possibilities, also permitted significant social relations, with a resulting exchange of knowledge and ideas. Important merchants from Buenos Aires, many of them connected with the consulate, established commercial contacts with and through North Americans. Moreover, several U.S. citizens--besides those constantly arriving and departing on cargo ships--settled in Buenos Aires, making personal contact with sectors of the population. This had a significant influence on the revolutionary process. Regarding commercial contacts, one need only point out the important relations established with the North Americans by the accommodating and expert financier, D. Tomas Antonio Romero. Devoted to the trading of the most diverse products--which did not exclude slaves--he was able to create an important

commercial network in which ships from New England
played an important role after 1798. The volume of his
business was very large; in October 1793 he had obtained royal authorization to ship products worth
250,000 pesos, excluding gold and silver; and in 1798,
when the trade of neutrals had already begun, he purchased from Whillam, Vernon and Associates of Newport
a slave ship valued at 44,180 pesos. J. M. Mariluz
Urquijo pointed out that in 1800 at least three ships
purchased in Boston and Providence arrived in Romero's
name.

Furthermore, the use of United States ships was
uninterrupted, even in those times when the trade of
neutrals was banned in theory. Thus, on April 22, 1801,
Captain Robert Gay from Boston arrived in the port of
Buenos Aires with a load consigned to Romero; and in
May 1804, the king approved the authorization requested
of him by the viceroy of Buenos Aires at the end of
1803 for Romero to use the Anglo-American frigate
Merrymack, which was destined for the slave trade.
This commercial relationship undoubtedly led to the
necessity of hiring Esteban Juicross, a North American
citizen from Boston, as purser for his company.

Besides Romero, other influential men in the River
Plate also devoted themselves to performing important
transaction with the United States. Referring earlier
to the purchase of ships, I mentioned Francisco de Sar,
who was a member of the consulate and the Municipal
Council; it is interesting to note that he was sanc-
tioned for bringing in North American products, among
which there were newspapers from Philadelphia. Agustín
de la Cuesta chartered ships to Providence; Manuel
Almagro bought ships in the United States; and Manuel
Duval constantly increased the number of his fleet with
ships also purchased in that country. This latter was
so economically powerful that on one occasion, being
faced with the danger of not being able to use the
frigate Angela Ana, which he had just bought in the
United States and which had arrived loaded with products instead of ballast, he ceded the total cargo--
valued at $23,301 (not including the steel cargo)--to
the High Court of Justice. Also, working on his own,
young Manuel de Sarratea, who would later be an outstanding figure of the Revolution, developed an important trade with North America. On several occasions he
sent Tomás O'Gorman to the U.S. in order to buy ships
and merchandise, and at the same time he established
firm relationships through permanent representatives in
Philadelphia.[11]

The trade was important, as well as the social
relations, both encouraging knowledge of the United

States. Buenos Aires also had a number of North Americans who in one way or another formed part of the population: American whale harpooners who came under contract to work along the Patagonic coasts; sailors who, for various reasons, had to remain longer and decided to settle permanently; different types of artisans; and, of course, merchants and adventurers who profited with the legal trading or smuggling, depending on circumstances. In 1804 the census of Buenos Aires showed the existence of 475 foreigners, including 250 Portuguese, 108 Italians, 57 French, 29 North Americans, 15 English, 8 Irish, and 2 Slavs. Although most of the North Americans were from Boston and Providence, the presence of a number from Connecticut and Philadelphia was recorded.

The war with England in 1805, the English invasions, and the situation of Spain after 1808--added to the problems inherent in international commercial relationships--modified this composition by about 1810: precautions had to be taken in regard to foreigners, many of whom were obliged to ally themselves with the viceroy or run the risk of being expatriated. "I have noticed a great number of English and American colonists spread in the towns of these domains and dwelling in them," D. Joaquín de Molina said in a letter dated May 1809 and addressed to the king to report "the latest happenings of his national mission with the viceroyship of Buenos Aires."[12]

Some of these merchants--adventurers who arrived from the United States in search of prosperity--formed important relationships not only socially, but also economically, with people who would later play a role in the process of independence; and some of them, such as W. White and D. Forest, even made close contact with the revolutionary governments. A good example was D. Forest, who took part in the smuggling trade with Spanish America beginning in 1801.

During his stay on the River Plate Forest became acquainted with Manuel Belgrano--on whom, we will see, he undoubtedly had an influence--and became commercially associated with Juan Larrea, then syndic of the consulate. He also established relations with his fellow citizen White, who cunningly handled Forest's finances at the capital of the viceroyship. His agency of overseas dispatches, which was closely connected with North American exporters, received merchandise consigned to local brokers, while the products from the River Plate were exported to other places in the world through him, especially when the attacks on the Spanish ships in 1804 and the war with England made it mandatory to use the North American flag.

The volume of the North American trade was large, which led Forest, based on his trading experience, to propose to President Jefferson in 1805 the creation of a consulate in the viceroyship. In 1798 the United States had already appointed a consul in Santiago, Cuba, and in 1800 it did the same in La Guaira, Venezuela. It is true that the Spanish Crown did not recognize these consuls, but the informal performance of their activity, as well as the colonial authorities' tolerance, obviated the need for formal recognition. Nevertheless, D. Forest's proposal, reiterated in 1807 to Secretary of State Madison (the previous one had not reached its destination) did not get an answer due mainly to the new government attitudes toward world trade, in spite of the data tending to demonstrate the importance of trading and the references to the English's trading activities.

After the English invasions, during which his fellow citizen William White held such a controversial commercial and political attitude,[13] Forest lodged at the house of Bernardino Rivadavia's father, whose acquaintance would prove valuable to him when he returned after the Revolution.

The invasions reactivated the old, well-rooted xenophobic position of the Buenos Aires inhabitants, which affected the North Americans as well as the English. Hence, on September 25, 1806, the following petition was read at the Municipal Council: "a petition signed by many neighbors and merchants in this city requesting that foreigners be expelled, that the colonial trade be no longer tolerated nor the North American expeditions be allowed to come--which have come with royal permit and are still coming; they based their request on the serious damages that would be inflicted on the government and the country, the same that this city has already experienced in its unfortunate loss."[14]

The people's suspicions led to repeated exonerations of foreigners, one of which pointed out that the well-known "David Forest, North American citizen, bugler of the Pueyrredón's Hussars Squadron, is lodging at D. Benito Rivadavia's home." Forest had evidently found a way to keep a certain balance by enlisting in the new corps commanded by Juan M. de Pueyrredon, in which D. Benito Rivadavia was Major Assistant.

This attitude evidently contradicted that of White, who had cooperated with the English during the two invasions and who was subject to trial for his "criminal, scandalous and intriguing" behavior. But beyond the judgment, one should consider the important local relationships that led to his conditional freedom, which drew a strong complaint from the Buenos Aires High Court of Justice against the Viceroy Santiago de Liniers. Among other harsh remarks the letter from the judges to the king pointed out:

> So deep were the suspicions that, from the beginning, were related to this Court of Justice--due to the nature of the cause and the previous actions preventing its knowledge-- that orders were expedited for a prompt conclusion of the process; and on considering the summary, this Court discovered White's criminal implications, the most serious transgressions, commercial relationships, and iniquities with neighbors of this city and of Montevideo, and a conspiracy of wickedness and intrigue that confirmed the previous suspicions, and it prepared for the delinquent an exemplary punishment.
>
> But when these events were known, his accomplices and protectors prepared themselves: the most criminal means were activated, the machinations increased, and the most cunning intrigues were carried out. The result was that the viceroy passed a report to this Court of Justice, ordering that the sentence be remitted and that White be released to his custody for reasons important to the royal service, which he did not express.[15]

Cisneros, who took over the River Plate government within an atmosphere of widespread conflict due to the division of parties and a complex international situation, had to expel those foreigners who could be considered as inspirers of revolutionary principles. Among them was D. Forest, whose evaluation, made years after his return to Buenos Aires, was as follows: "The last Viceroy Cisneros, obedient to Spain's principles of expelling foreigners, expatriated me from this country, almost ruining me with that oppressive and tyrannical attitude."[16]

It is practically impossible to establish to what extent these relationships, which originated during more than thirty years of direct exchange and mutual acquaintance, had an influence on the revolutionary process. But from the very moment that the separation of the Anglo-American colonies was known, a new factor began to erode the foundations of the Spanish Empire. As Ricardo Caillet Bois has pointed out, at least the most cultured inhabitants of the viceroyship learned

about the wars waged by the North American revolutionaries and about their aspirations, a viewpoint supported by the European gazettes reprinted in Buenos
Aires and the correspondence kept at that time.

The Count of Aranda expressed a real concern in his
famous political plan for a better government of the
Spanish provinces when he pointed out that "the independence of the English colonies is recognized, and
this means to me pain and fear. France has few possessions in America, but it should have considered that
Spain, its closest friend, has many, and that from now
on Spain will be exposed to the most terrible commo-
tion."[17]

In spite of the existing restrictions, direct interrelations occurred, and to them was added the knowledge of writings by some of the inspirers of the
North American revolutionary process. Just as the
traffic in commercial contraband could not be halted,
neither could the ideological traffic be limited, at a
period of time in which world events caused an accessi-
bility to outside ideas. I am not claiming that such
North American influences were the only ones, nor even
the most decisive, but I do wish to stress that they
contributed to enlarging the ideological structure,
together with the concepts already developed by the
Spanish tradition of the pure scholastics and the
learned reformers and by the ideologists of French and
British liberalism.

A clear example of this influence was given by
M. Belgrano in the introduction to his translation of
Washington's Farewell to the People of the United States
when, after expressing his admiration for the North
American hero, he pointed out that:

> His farewell reached my hands around 1805, and
> I must confess that notwithstanding my limited
> understanding, I saw in his principles the
> expression of wisdom based on the experience
> and constant observation of a man who had
> heartily devoted himself to procure the free-
> dom and happiness of his country.

> But as I saw mine in chains, I was filled
> with fury at the impossibility of destroying
> them and comforted myself by making some of
> my fellow citizens read them in order that
> someday they can take advantage of [these
> principles], if the Almighty should put them
> in the midst of such circumstances, or they
> can transmit those ideas to their children
> for their benefit if they should be fortunate

enough to work for the freedom of America."[18]

It is interesting that Franklin's articles were
published in the Weekly Report on Agriculture, Industry
and Commerce in 1803 and 1804; other such works appeared
in the records of some executors, for example, the will
of Apoliner Laynes made reference to the possession of
stamps picturing thirteen American generals. Furthermore, as soon as the Revolution took place, there
appeared publicly those writings that had previously
been kept on the most hidden shelves or passed silently
from hand to hand; now, their most fundamental aspects
were divulged openly in the press, while political
interest and discussions were intensified. Hence, when
the problem of the governmental structure was considered, La Gazette number 27, dated November 28, 1810,
issued an article including extensive remarks by Jefferson on Virginia. But another stage--the movement
from revolution to independence--had already begun;
it must also be considered in relation to North American interrelations and influences, disregarding the
strictly formal, diplomatic relationships and looking
instead at the economic, social, and ideological aspects
combining to shape it.

Just as the permanent relationship between the
United States and the River Plate took place mainly
through the commercial exchange, the unfortunate handling of that relationship at the beginning of the
Revolution was perhaps the cause of weakening this influence when the second level was reached. And simultaneously, the new English attitude, supported by a
favorable world situation, placed it in a privileged
position within South America.

Let us go back to the economic problem. Although
the North American ships continued coming rather frequently during 1807, their number was reduced as a consequence of the embargo declared by Jefferson and the
U.S. preoccupation to improve its trade with Spain,
even though this affected their trade with the colonies. While in 1806 the exports from the United States
to Spain were at least five times smaller than those to
the Spanish-American colonies, the dynamics of growth
were such that by 1811 the value of the merchandise
sent to Spain exceeded by three times that dispatched
to Latin America, including Brazil.[19]

The derogation of the embargo law in 1809 reacti-
vated the weakened North American commerce with Buenos
Aires, where at least thirty ships arrived in 1810.
But, evidently, English products had left little room
in the River Plate market for North American ones.
Nevertheless, the arrival of North American ships was

still rather frequent, due not only to the export goods
for the River Plate, but also to its serving as landfall
point for the commerce destined especially with the
Pacific via Cape Horn. Here the strong North American
interest in Chile had an influence, as did the traffic
that merchants like Girard, Astor, and Samuel Smith
made with Canton.

The aggressive British economic policy, then, as
well as the development of the revolutionary Spanish-
American movements, once again attracted U.S. attention
to these regions, although they always benefited from
the interests that linked them directly with Madrid.
But two and one-half months before the United States
appointed Joel Roberts Poinsett as "agent of the sailors and merchants in the . . . Port of Buenos Aires
and all those ports closer to it,"[20] on June 10, 1810,
Lord Strangford wrote to the Marquis of Wellesley
that "there seems to be a widespread belief that in
case the Spanish colonies declare their independence,
they must revert to the protection either of Great
Britain or of France and that there is no other government to which they will be inclined to look for help."
Nevertheless, there was another power unlikely to lose
this opportunity--which meant excluding England, by
any possible way, from all intervention in the Spanish
colonies' affairs. I am referring to the United States
of America.[21]

Spain's former preoccupation was now transferred
to the new master. Thus a new stage commenced.

NOTES

1. Facultad de Filosofía y Letras, Universidad Nacional
de Buenos Aires, Documentos para la Historia Argentina,
vol. 5, Comercio de Indias: Antecedentes Legales
(1778-1793) (Buenos Aires: Compañía Sudamericana de
Billetes de Banco, 1915), no. 83, pp. 381-82.

2. Archivo General de Indias, 5th sec., Audiencia de
Buenos Aires, leg. 326.

3. Archivo General de Indias, 5th sec., Audiencia de
Buenos Aires, leg. 70.

4. Facultad de Filosofía y Letras, Universidad Nacional
de Buenos Aires, Documentos para la Historia Argentina,
vol. 6, Comercio de Indias: Comercio Libre, 1778-1791
(Buenos Aires: Compañía Sudamericana de Billetes de
Banco, 1915), no. 138, pp. 324-25.

5. Ricardo Levene, "Introducción al Comercio de Indias," Documentos para la Historia Argentina, vol. 5, p. 107.

6. E. M. Brackenridge, La Independencia Argentina: Viaje a la América del Sur hecho por orden del Gobierno Americano en los años 1817 y 1818 en la fragata "Congress" [Spanish edition, trans. Carlos Aldao], vol. 2 (Buenos Aires: Talleres Gráficos Argentinos, 1927), p. 111. While the concept of total stagnation of commerce is somewhat exaggerated, his remarks on the development and encouragement of contraband are significant.

7. Karl Wilhelm Korner, "El Consul Zimmermann: Su actuación en Buenos Aires, 1815-1847," Boletín del Instituto de Historia Argentina, "Doctor Emilio Ravignani," 2d ser., vols. 7-8, nos. 11-13 (Buenos Aires, 1966), pp. 9-10.

8. Arthur P. Whitaker, Estados Unidos y la Independencia de América Latina, 1800-1830 (Buenos Aires: EUDEBA, 1964), passim.

9. Facultad de Filosofía y Letras, Universidad Nacional de Buenos Aires, Documentos para la Historia Argentina, vol. 7, Comercio de Indias: Consulado, Comercio de Negros y de Extranjeros (Buenos Aires: Compañía Sudamericana de Billetes de Banco, 1916), no. 118, p. 187.

10. Archivo General de la Nación, 9-16-5-7.

11. In December 1798, the king authorized the permit granted by the Marquis of Avilés "to D. Tomás A. Romero in order that a ship to be bought in the United States for the trade of slaves can carry arches and staves as ballast."

12. Facultad de Filosofía y Letras, Sección Historia, Universidad Nacional de Buenos Aires, Documentos Relativos a los Antecedentes de la Independencia de la República Argentina (Buenos Aires: Compañía Sudamericana de Billetes de Banco, 1912), no. 26, p. 271.

13. John Street says: "A good friend of the English during their occupation of Buenos Aires was the Yankee merchant W. White. White had traded with the Indian Ocean, and Popham had known him and had dealt with him there, resulting in Popham's owing the American a large sum of money. This could have impelled the commodore to attack Buenos Aires to ensure the payment of his debt. . . . Anyway, he was a useful ally when the English came. He was interpreter when the troops defending the city capitulated, and later Beresford

appointed him member of the commission in charge of
examining the English people living in Buenos Aires,
created to inform the British government. He also
carried out other official tasks." Artigas and the
Emancipation of Uruguay (Cambridge: Cambridge University Press, 1959).

14. Archivo de la Republica Argentina, Antecedentes
Políticos, Económicos y Administrativos de la Revolu-
ción de Mayo, República Argentina, Buenos Aires, vol. 1,
bk. 3 (La Plata: Talleres de Impresiones Oficiales,
1910), p. 9.

15. Documentos Relativos a la Independencia de la
República Argentina, pp. 12-13.

16. The National Archives, Microfilm Publications,
Dispatches from United States Consuls in Buenos Aires,
Argentina, 1811-1906 (Gabinete de Investigación de
Historia Americana y Argentina, Universidad Nacional
del Sur, M. 70, roll 2).

17. Vicente D. Sierra, Historia de la Argentina, vol.
3, Fin del Regimen de Gobernadores y Creación del
Virreynato del Río de la Plata, 1700-1800 (Buenos Aires:
Editorial Científica Argentina, 1967), p. 517.

18. Manuel Belgrano, Introducción a la Despedida de
Washington al Pueblo de los Estados Unidos (Buenos
Aires: Tipógrafo Dalmazia, 1902), p. 6.

19. Whitaker, Estados Unidos, p. 40.

20. Archivo General de la Nación, 10-1-4-14.

21. Facultad de Filosofía y Letras, Mayo Documental
(Buenos Aires: Universidad Nacional de Buenos Aires,
1965), pp. 287-95.

The American Revolution and Vietnam

David V. J. Bell

Comparison of events like Vietnam and the American Revolution can aim at different objectives. One might use comparative analysis to advance "scientific" theory or to test hypotheses through application to different "cases."[1]

Another objective of comparative analysis links the exercise more closely to policy formation and evaluation. Foreign policy especially seems to involve the application of various analogies drawn from previous (presumably similar) cases. The task of the historian, according to Ernest May, is to ensure that policy makers use historical analogies wisely. May sharply criticizes their failure to do so: "policy-makers ordinarily use history badly. When resorting to an analogy, they tend to seize upon the first that comes to mind. They do not search more widely. Nor do they pause to analyze the case, test its fitness, or even ask in what ways it might be misleading."[2] May is undoubtedly correct in his assessment, even if his conclusion that historians ought to be permanently appointed as policy advisers at various levels of government seems self-serving.

My paper has some implications for policy, but its primary thrust is in a different direction. I am comparing Vietnam and the American Revolution not to advance scientific theory, nor even to extract "lessons" for future policy makers. My concern is with perception and interpretation, or, less prosaically, ideology and propaganda.

In regard to historical comparison, it has been stated that "fools see similarities; wise men notice differences." In the two cases under consideration

here, this proverb needs modification. The differences
between Vietnam in the twentieth century and the thirteen colonies in the eighteenth are obvious and abundant. It is the similarities that are astounding and
remarkable.[3]

By pursuing and elaborating these similarities, I
may move closer to accomplishing an important ideological objective: helping Americans see the phenomenon of
contemporary national revolution--and, by extension, the
U.S. role as a counterrevolutionary agent--from a different perspective. How could the United States, the
country that "inaugurated the Age of Revolutions,"[4] the
country whose founding event has served as a model for
so many other nations, accept two centuries later an
imperialistic role?

It might be argued, of course, that prior history
has no bearing whatsoever on foreign policy. But there
are numerous indications that as recently as the Truman
era, and certainly under Roosevelt, American leaders
were deliberately self-conscious about the country's
anticolonial heritage.[5] Whether these concerns were
genuinely felt or simply viewed as domestic propaganda
considerations is impossible to determine. I doubt
that many Americans are really agonizing over their
international image and its consistency with the country's early revolutionary experience.[6] But at various
times, even during the Vietnam involvement, the issue
of U.S. "traditional values" has surfaced--for example,
in a speech by Senator Frank Church in December 1969,
which begins with a reference to some of the parallels
between the Vietnamese struggle and "our own struggle
for national independence" and ends with the observation that the "regenerative forces of protest and moral
reassertion" (concerning Vietnam) demonstrate that "we
are a people with a moral tradition, a people who dis-
criminate among their wars and who do not easily act
against their own traditional values."[7]

The American Revolution must be regarded as an
ideological "formative experience," obviously for Americans, but evidently for other people as well.[8] As the
central event in the founding myth of the United States,
the Revolution provided the "first new nation" (to
borrow a phrase from Seymour Martin Lipset) a gallery
of heroes, a national credo, and the basis for long-
standing traditions and values. To conjure with or
about the Revolution brings one quickly to the nerve
center of American consciousness. The Revolution's
propaganda potential, even today, remains high.

This is not to suggest that present-day leaders
have viewed revolution through the prism of the

American Revolution or that events in the eighteenth century can be adduced to "explain" outcomes in the twentieth. Indeed, at least since Graham Allison's illuminating study of "conceptual models and the Cuban missile crisis," students of international politics have exercised great caution in attempting to articulate "explanations" for foreign policy involvements such as Vietnam.[9] The search for "reasons why" the United States got involved in Vietnam may do violence to the nature of decision making in complex organizations. Instead of asking why, we perhaps must enquire how the process of involvement and escalation developed in the context of bureaucratic politics.

Allison has in a sense done for political science what Freud did long ago for psychology by exposing in a sophisticated formulation the unarticulated processes that make reasons into rationalizations. According to his critique of the "rational actor" model, any argument that takes the form "the reason why Americans intervened . . ." is immediately suspect as an explanation for U.S. behavior. Ultimately, foreign policy is as much the result of compromises attending bureaucratic infighting as it is the pursuit of a well-formulated rational objective. Despite this fact, despite the difficulty in distinguishing the rationale of foreign policy from the rationalizations in which it is enveloped, there still remains a residual importance in statements like "The U.S. was fighting in Vietnam to stop the naked aggressions of a hostile 'foreign' power." While this type of statement may have little bearing on the scientific explanation of involvement, it performs an essential service in the political community as a justification for involvement. And, undeniably, justification is a prime consideration in devising foreign policy propaganda. A given course or policy must be made to appear justifiable--morally, economically, or strategically--and preferably all three.

It is my contention that certain arguments justifying American counterrevolutionary involvement can be made to appear absurd and therefore worthless if the example of America's own revolution is explored. Particularly vulnerable is the assertion that the United States intervened in the interest of "national self-determination." To support my contention, we must develop a certain perspective on the American Revolution.

For good ideological reasons, early histories of the American Revolution deemphasized the internal conflicts dividing colonial society. The Revolution was portrayed as a heroic event that had widespread support

among the colonies. Like all wars for independence,
however, the American prototype featured bitter civil
conflict.[10] A recent study of the numerical strength
of American loyalists concludes that approximately
"19,000 loyalists formally took up arms in the service
of the Crown to suppress the American rebellion."[11]
Perhaps as many as sixty thousand loyalists were forced
into exile following the war. These expatriates were
drawn from a variety of social and ethnic groups, including rich and poor, powerful and powerless, recent
arrivals and third-generation native-born. The cleav-
age dividing loyalist from revolutionary ran right
through some families, pitting father against son and
brother against sister.

It is the "civil war" aspect of the American Revolution that provides an initial point of comparison to
the Vietnam case. We must be careful, however, to pursue the correct analogy. In the first instance, the
American war for independence from the British is analogous to the Vietnamese war for independence from the
French. Both events were catalyzed by an earlier distinct war in which the colonial powers were involved
(that is, the Seven Years' War and World War II). Following the war, many of the hated loyalist "collaborators" were exterminated or expelled. The winners
jubilantly took possession of the entire territory under
dispute, despite pockets of loyalist strength. The
losers withdrew entirely.

As everyone knows, the scenario described was not
carried to its logical conclusion in Vietnam, despite
the provision in the Geneva Agreement for an election
in 1956 that, it is generally accepted, would have
resulted in Ho Chi Minh becoming president of a unified
Vietnam. Instead, unification was aborted by the intervention of the United States, and a weak "loyalist"
regime was kept alive in the South by massive inputs
of American aid. For an eighteenth-century equivalent
of this outcome, we must hypothesize the creation of a
loyalist state in the southern colonies under the
tutelage, say, of France.[12] Such a settlement would
obviously have lacked legitimacy in the eyes of the
leaders of the new "revolutionary" country ("the
Northern United States"?). Frustration and disenchant-
ment would have resulted eventually (probably in about
ten to thirty years) in a new war, a war of liberation.
The "Northerners" would have invaded the French loyalist
state in the South to "liberate" their fellow countrymen.

What in fact did happen in America was not totally
dissimilar. The loyalists were not "set up" in the
southern colonies, nor did they form a coalition with

the revolutionaries. Attempted French intervention on
their behalf failed. Consequently, they were expelled
to Canada--at the time a virtual wilderness--settling
in the Maritime region and in what is now Ontario.
Thirty years later, however, the Americans fought a war
of liberation (the War of 1812) to "free" Canada and to
take over the remainder of the continent they "rightly"
deserved. After crossing the Detroit River into Canada,
General Hull, commander of the invading American forces,
issued a proclamation to the people offering them "the
invaluable blessings of Civil, Political, and Religious
Liberty" and informing them that they were to be "eman-
cipated from Tyranny and oppression and restored to the
dignified station of freeman."

     The analogue of this first expression of manifest
destiny in the wake of a colonial war for independence
can be found in the expansion of a highly nationalistic
North Vietnam into Laos and Cambodia. No virgin area
like Canada existed to which the Vietnamese loyalists
could be withdrawn to set up a barrier to Ho's expan-
sionist aims. The American defeat in the War of 1812
suggests that such a "solution" might have worked.
South Vietnam proved an unrealistic, and therefore un-
viable, functional equivalent of the Canadian solution.
It was in 1954 a loyalist state with no valid claim to
existence, because it had traditionally been part of
the greater Vietnamese whole. Twenty-one years later,
the "logic" of the Vietnamese Revolution had finally
fulfilled itself.

     So much for the structural comparison. I would
like now to pursue comparisons between U.S. involvement
in Vietnam in the 1960s and British involvement in the
American War for Independence, notwithstanding my earlier remarks about the "correct" analogy. (The similarities that will emerge from this comparison in my
view corroborate the interpretation of U.S. involvement
as an imperialistic adventure.)[13] The comparison will
examine both the dialogue and debate that surrounded
involvement in the war and the actual conduct of the
war itself.

     British involvement in what proved to be a success-
ful war of independence for the thirteen colonies
attracted widespread criticism in England from the outset. Even those who were conservative on domestic
policy issues--Edmund Burke most notably--voiced strong
objection to what was viewed as King George's War. The
critics articulated a variety of arguments. The war
was deemed a costly affair,[14] an ill-timed adventure
that was ultimately to shake the stock market and bring
about financial chaos.[15] In view of these financial

considerations, criticism of the war effort brought
merchants and country gentlemen into uneasy alliance
with radicals--the former for practical, the latter for
idealistic reasons.

Dorothy Mae Clark's comprehensive study, "British
Opinion and the American Revolution," turns up other
fascinating parallels. As the war developed, opposition
to it came from such subordinate public bodies as the
London Common Council, which refused to approve a
bounty system for enlisters, instead passing a resolution urging better peace terms.[16] (The analogy to the
actions of the Massachusetts legislature and of several
town councils is obvious.)

As occurred during the Vietnam War, there developed
considerable interchange and contagion between the revolutionaries and British radicals critical of the war.

> The history of British radicalism in the
> period of the American Revolution shows that
> the reformers in the two countries were a
> source of inspiration to each other. They
> corresponded with one another and exchanged
> philosophical ideas, and British radicals
> wrote pamphlets in defense of American claims.
> There was a general understanding and sympathy
> which linked the progressives in the two
> countries.[17]

Among other issues raised by critics were the familiar
concerns with parliamentary reform (too much power for
the "elected monarch") and the need to effect economy
in government. Indeed, a number of speeches made in
Parliament during the 1770s could, with appropriate
modernization of colloquialisms, have been uttered ver-
batim in Congress during the 1960s. Even as early as
1777, critics saw the British cause as terrifically
unpopular. Lord Camden thundered, "What part of America
is your own? Just as much as you occupy, or as you can
command with the mouths of your cannon."[18]

Parliamentary criticism of the war stemmed in part
from a sense of betrayal. The Lord North administration had from the outset attempted to convince Parliament that the "rebels" were disorganized, untrained,
unequipped, and poorly led.[19] Victory would come
quickly with a mere expenditure of more money and the
utilization of more men.[20] Two years later, however,
the critics had come to doubt the veracity of these
assurances of early victory.

> May 15, 1777. Mr. Hartley: "Surely the most
> obstinate partisan of the American War must

now begin to suspect his errors, and the de-
ceptions that have been put upon him. When
the war was first adopted in this House, the
cry was that the appearance of a few men would
soon annihilate all resistance in one campaign.--We are now in the third campaign!"

But the critics went largely unheeded. Their protests brought upon them accusations of disloyalty and
treachery from the administration. George III insisted
all along on the justice and wisdom of his cause, ex-
horting all loyal Englishmen to lend their fullest support. For this war represented an important test of
strength of the British Empire. Were the thirteen colonies to fall, other holdings might very well be lost as
well. The speech from the throne on October 31, 1776,
sternly warned that "if [the rebel leaders'] treason
be suffered to take root, much mischief must grow from
it, to the safety of my loyal colonies, to the commerce
of my kingdoms, and indeed to the present system of all
Europe."[21] If this early expression of the domino
theory seems anachronistic, it perhaps indicates a continuity between imperialist politics in the eighteenth
and the twentieth centuries.[22]

The dialectic of optimistic justification and critique continued throughout the war. The following
passage from the November 27, 1781, speech from the
throne indicates the effect that long-standing criticism
had on the rhetoric, if not the policies, of George III.
The speech ends with a phrase thought to have been invented by Richard Nixon.

In the prosecution of this great and important contest in which we are engaged, I retain a firm confidence in the protection of
Divine Providence, and a perfect conviction
of the justice of my cause; and I have no
doubt but that, by the concurrence and support of my parliament, by the valour of my
fleets and armies, and by a vigorous, animated and united exertion of the faculties
and resources of my people, I shall be enabled to restore the blessing of a safe and
honourable peace to all my dominions.[23]

Ultimately, of course, the shift in fortunes in America
effected a shift in the balance of power in Britain.
The "reformers" were able to move into positions where
they could negotiate for peace not in George's "safe
and honourable" terms, but more in line with the aspirations of the American revolutionaries.[24] The scenario
described above, in which Washington and his cohorts
obtained "the whole cake," was acted out despite

George III's bitter disillusionment. So personally crushed was the monarch that in March 1782 he took the extraordinary and unprecedented step of drafting a message of abdication:

> His Majesty during the twenty-one years He has sat on the Throne of Great Britain, has had no object so much at heart as the maintenance of the British Constitution, of which the difficulties He has at times met with from His scrupulous attachment to the Rights of Parliament are sufficient proofs.
>
> His Majesty is convinced that the sudden change of sentiments of one branch of the Legislature has totally incapacitated Him from either correlating the War with effect, or from obtaining any Peace but on conditions which would prove destructive to the Commerce as well as essential Rights of the British Nation.
>
> His Majesty therefore with much sorrow finds He can be of no further Utility to his native Country which drives Him to the painful step of quitting it for ever.
>
> In consequence of which Intention His Majesty resigns the Crown of Great Britain and the Dominions appertaining thereto to His Dearly Beloved Son and lawful Successor, George Prince of Wales, whose endeavors for the prosperity of the British Empire He hopes may prove more successful.[25]

The world would wait 186 years before another imperial ruler (again in March) would "abdicate" in the face of bitter opposition to his colonial war policies.

In summary, the rhetoric accompanying the conduct of the wars for America featured the following familiar features:
1. Assertion by the administration of a domino theory interpretation of the international consequences of "losing America";
2. A conspiracy theory interpretation of the origins of the war (Mr. Tuffnel expressed a widely held view when, in March 1775, he exclaimed, "Make no mistake, although this war was begun in America, it was planned in Paris!");
3. Repeated use of optimistic reports from the military on the progress of the war, reports designed at once to bolster confidence and to justify further escalation of inputs of men and materiel;

4. Criticism of the war from disparate groups in
    England, including those concerned with its dele-
    terious financial effects on the one hand and
    those ideologically identified with the American
    cause on the other;
5. Efforts by the administration to brand all critics
    as disloyal and treacherous, and the plaintive in-
    sistence that the war would quickly be won if only
    the country would unite behind the policies of the
    King;
6. Resort to "Americanization" of the war effort after
    the ignominious defeat of Burgoyne at Saratoga
    showed that this war would not be won as easily as
    early reports had indicated.

    As American military involvement in Vietnam was
drawing to a close, keen observers shifted attention
from the military to the political struggle, insisting
that the challenging question for the future was "Who
would win the peace?" and not "Who would win the war?"
Now, several years later, some critics are raising
questions about the ideological struggle at home: Who
will dominate the effort to construct and reconstruct
the history of U.S. involvement? Can Americans be
taught lessons about Vietnam that will not preclude
further imperialistic ventures abroad? According to
Noam Chomsky, this is the challenge that faces American
ideologists:

> Apologists for state violence understand very
> well that the general public has no real stake
> in imperial conquest and domination. The pub-
> lic costs of empire may run high, whatever the
> gains to dominant social and economic groups.
> Therefore the public must be aroused by jingo-
> ist appeals, or at least kept disciplined and
> submissive, if American force is to be readily
> available for global management.
>
>   Here lies the task for the intelligentsia.
> If it is determined that we must, say, invade
> the Persian Gulf for the benefit of mankind,
> then there must be no emotional or moral ob-
> jections from the unsophisticated masses, and
> surely no vulgar display of protest. The
> ideologists must guarantee that no "wrong
> lessons" are learned from the experience of
> the Indochina War and the resistance to it.[26]

    In pursuit of their ideological mission, those who
control what Comsky calls "the national institutions of
propaganda" have been careful to define the pedagogy of
Vietnam extremely narrowly, so as to exclude the drawing

of ideologically subversive lessons. Indeed, an editorial in the New York Times reduced the question to one of tactics: Could America have won (as the hawks insist) or was victory always impossible (the dove argument)?[27] Kept on this level, debate about the wisdom of American intervention could never possibly embrace "subversive" considerations of the fundamental morality of U.S. involvement or the socioeconomic forces of neoimperialism that seemed to make it inevitable.

This paper may serve as a contribution to the ideological struggle for the consciousness and understanding of the American people. By comparing U.S. involvement in Vietnam with foreign involvement in America's own revolution, I hope I have encouraged debate beyond the narrow issue of tactics to include a critical reassessment of the ideological implications of contemporary U.S. foreign policy and its relationship to the traditions that emerge from America's own revolutionary past.

NOTES

1. The voluminous literature on comparative revolutions includes early examples like Crane Brinton, Anatomy of Revolutions (1938), and more recent works like Thomas Greene's Comparative Revolutionary Movements (1973). For a review of more of this literature, see David V. J. Bell, Resistance and Revolution (Boston: Houghton Mifflin, 1973), especially chap. 7.

2. Ernest May, "Lessons" of the Past: The Use and Misuse of History in American Foreign Policy (New York: Oxford University Press, 1973), p. xi.

3. Cf. Richard B. Morris, The Emerging Nations and the American Revolution (New York: Harper & Row, 1970), pp. ix-x.

4. Ibid., p. x.

5. Leslie H. Gelb describes how post World War II policy toward Indochina was colored by "a residue of anticolonialism," but ultimately President Truman "decided that anti-Communism was more important than anticolonialism in Indochina" ("Vietnam: The System Worked," Foreign Policy, no. 3 [Summer 1971], pp. 155, 156).

6. Morris, (The Emerging Nations, pp. xi-xii) challenges his fellow citizens to choose which "image" is more consistent with America's "destiny" as an "exemplar" of liberty, revolution, and decolonization:

Which image do American prefer? Do they wish
the world to regard them as a nation with a
revolutionary tradition, sympathetic to colonies in their struggles against their imperial
rulers, tolerant of change and progress, and
dedicated to the principle of equality? Or
do they prefer the other image which America's
adversaries depict, that of a counterrevolutionary America, everywhere on the side of
urban elites seeking to stamp out the ardor
for change on the part of the peasantry,
against all national movements which seem to
have a socialist orientation . . . ?

"Images" notwithstanding, the U.S. military record is
heavily counterrevolutionary. Since 1798, America has
intervened in 148 internal wars, almost always against
the revolutionaries. See "Use of U.S. Armed Forces in
Foreign Countries," _Congressional_ _Record_, June 26, 1969,
S.6955-58.

7. Frank Church, "The Only Alternative--A Reply to the
President on Vietnam," _Congressional_ _Record_, December
19, 1969, S.17245-48.

8. "For too long have Americans been content to view
their revolution as a central experience in _their_
national life and to ignore the libertarian currents
that the event set off throughout the world" (Morse,
The _Emerging_ _Nations_, p. x).

9. See Graham Allison, _Essence_ _of_ _Decision_: _Explaining_
the _Cuban_ _Missile_ _Crisis_ (Boston: Little, Brown, 1971).

10. See Piers Mackesy, _The_ _War_ _for_ _America_ (Cambridge:
Harvard University Press, 1965), p. 4: "As a civil war
in America the struggle was often characterized by
atrocious cruelty between rebels and loyalists. . . ."

11. Paul H. Smith, "The American Loyalist: Notes on
Their Organization and Numerical Strength," _William_ _and_
Mary _Quarterly_, 25 (1968):259.

12. Incredibly, this outcome almost did occur in
America. France tried hard at the Versailles Peace
Talks to have the American loyalists reinstated so as
to capture American trade and keep the new United States
in a relatively weak position. For details, see David
V. J. Bell and Allan E. Goodman, "Vietnam and the
American Revolution," _Yale_ _Review_, 61 (Autumn 1971):26-
34. Included here are several paragraphs on the topic
that originally appeared in that article.

13. "Twenty-five years after the end of World War II,
the United States found itself an imperial power. Although the empire had emerged more by default than design, it was an empire of proportions unparalleled in
history:
    defense treaties with 42 nations
    3.5 million men under arms in 'peace-time';
    1.1 million soldiers stationed abroad (twice the
        present total of all other nations in the world
        combined);
    2200 military bases in 33 countries;
    a 25-year foreign aid bill of $150 billion;
    a 25-year defense bill of more than one trillion
        dollars;
    controlling more than half of all direct foreign
        investments;
    producing considerably more than half of the world's
        total manufactured products"

(Graham T. Allison, "Cool It: The Foreign Policy of
Young America," Foreign Policy, no. 1 [Winter 1970-71]:
p. 145). Note, however, that Arthur Schlesinger is
able to devote over 500 pages to the "Imperial Presi-
dency" without so much as a word about the American
empire. Such divorce of political from economic considerations is the bane of contemporary liberal
scholarship.

14. Indeed, the size of Britain's national debt, reduced from the all-time high of £132,716,049 in 1763
to the figure of £126,843,811 in 1775, nearly doubled
to £231,843,641 by 1783. Public Income and Expendi-
tures, 1688-1869 (House of Commons, July 29, 1869).

15. Probably intentionally exaggerating, the Earl of
Chatham said in 1777, "if an end is not put to this war,
there is an end to this country." Why? Because America
is a "double market" (i.e., in terms of both supply and
consumption) and there are innumerable "commercial advantages of these invaluable possessions." See Lords,
May 30, 1777, 17 George III, 316.

16. D. M. Clark, British Opinion and the American
Revolution (New Haven: Yale University Press, 1930),
p. 170.

17. Ibid., p. 175.

18. Lords, May 30, 1777, 17 George III, 339.

19. Cf. the comments before Parliament of Colonel
Grant (February 11, 1775): "I have served in America
and I know the Americans very well and I am certain they
will never dare face an English army, and do not possess

any of the qualifications of a good soldier."

The balloon of false optimism was deflated only
after the disastrous defeat of Burgoyne's army at Sara-
toga in October 1779. Following this event, hasty
efforts were made to start up "loyalist" regiments to
ensure that colonists would take over more of the burden of the fighting. This attempt to "Americanize"
the war for America anticipates by nearly 200 years the
policy of "Vietnamization" that followed the Tet offensive.

20. For a critical discussion of "the optimistic
reports constantly filed by the military on the progress
of the [Vietnamese] war," see Gelb, "Vietnam," pp. 161
ff.

21. Parliamentary History, vol. 18, 1774-1779 (London:
T. C. Hansard, 1813), p. 1366. Consider also a state-
ment made in the House on December 4, 1778, by a Mr.
Onslow: "The consequence of American independence will
be the loss of Newfoundland and then the Sugar Islands!"
(Ibid., vol. 19, p. 546).

22. For a discussion of the role the domino theory
played in American foreign policy toward Vietnam, see
Gelb, "Vietnam," pp. 140-44, and May, "Lessons" of the
Past, pp. 100 ff.

23. 22 George III, 637.

24. "Had it not been for the reformers, England might
not have made peace in 1783" (Clark, British Opinion
and the American Revolution, p. 180).

25. Sir John Fortescue, ed., Correspondence of King
George the Third, vol. 5, 1780-April 1782 (London:
Macmillan & Co., 1928), p. 425.

26. Noam Chomsky, "The Remaking of History," Ramparts,
August/September 1975, p. 30. Chomsky's interpretation
differs from Sheldon Wolin's discussion of "the politics of oblivion" in "The Meaning of Vietnam," New
York Review of Books, June 12, 1975, p. 23.

27. The editorial entitled "Vietnam Aftermath" spoke
of "lessons" in terms of a crisis of confidence in the
capacity of U.S. military power to achieve desired objectives. The editorial ends with an optimistic hope
that "the scars of Vietnam can bring new strength as
they heal, strength gathered in a clearer definition of
the priorities for the use of national power" (New
York Times, January 26, 1973). Presumably, future involvements will be more realistically planned and
executed.

Why Does the United States Prevent Social Change from Occurring in Latin America?

Mario Alberto Carrera Galindo
Translated by María A. Leal

THE SOCIOECONOMIC STRUCTURE OF THE UNITED STATES IN 1776

Since much has been written on this subject, I will state my viewpoint briefly. At the time of independence the United States possessed a peculiar type of socioeconomic structure, as it was moving from feudalism to capitalism. With independence, and the benefits and achievements that it brought, the society's capitalist nature became more clearly defined. Today the United States is the world's most faithful defender of capitalism, claiming it is the best and most just socioeconomic system. But even though it has attained capitalism's highest possibilities, and even though it has intervened frequently in other aspects of Latin American affairs, the United States has not attempted to impose a purely capitalist model upon Latin America. Is it in the U.S. interest that our countries maintain medieval characteristics at this stage of the twentieth century?

THE SOCIOECONOMIC STRUCTURE OF CENTRAL AMERICA IN 1821

The countries of Central America achieved independence from Spain on September 15, 1821. Mexico attempted immediately to appropriate the territory of Guatemala in the same imperialist way in which the Spaniards had conquered and colonized these lands. The attempt failed, and by 1823 Central America was free of Spain, Mexico, and every other nation that had tried to lay claim to its territory. Not long afterwards the states that formed the Federation of Central America dissolved their ties, converting the isthmus into five small parcels of land of little significance in economic and military terms to the rest of the world.

The peculiar characteristics of the Spanish con-
querors, our territorial smallness, the oppression of
our indigenous peoples, the division of the isthmus in
five parcels, the concentration of capital in the hands
of a few families, and, today, U.S. control of our af-
fairs--together these factors determine our socioeconomic structure. In reality, Central America has
not progressed very far since national independence in
1821. Our social structure was feudalistic then and
remains so today, 150 years later.

Some students of the American Revolution claim that
the historical event of 1776 did not constitute a real
structural change in U.S. society, while others affirm
the contrary. I would support the latter view. Capitalism was achieved almost immediately after independence. This, unfortunately, did not occur in Central
America. Rather than achieving independence, these
countries saw their governments simply change hands.
Evidence of this is that the same General Gabino Gaínza
who was the last Captain General appointed by the King
of Spain was also the first constitutional President of
the Federation of Central American Nations.

These reasons, however, are not sufficient to explain the failure of Central America to modify its
social structure in the 150 years since independence.
What, then, has held back the revolutionary process in
our nations? I would affirm that the greatest obstacle
to development in Central America has been the control
exercised by the United States over its governments.
Curiously, the United States, which has achieved more
socioeconomic progress within its own borders than any
other country in the Americas, has stood in the way of
such progress in other nations of the hemisphere.

THE REVOLUTIONS OF 1871 AND 1944 IN GUATEMALA

It must not be thought that our countries have not
made some effort to change their socioeconomic structure. In 1871, Generals Justo Rufino Barrios and
Miguel García Granados made such an effort in Guatemala.
Their achievements included educational reform; dis-
placement of religious power, which had rooted itself
deeply in the state; and the introduction of electricity,
railroads, and coffee production, which undoubtedly improved the living conditions for the middle and upper
classes. But the Indians, meanwhile, remained neglected,
for the modern achievements of civilized society hardly
took them into consideration. They were left in their
straw huts, without water, without electricity, on a
diet of beans and corn, without land, literacy, or
schooling. The introduction of electricity and the

railroad, as well as of banana cultivation by the United
Fruit Company some years later, brought with them direct
intervention by the United States in our business affairs and stagnation of our socioeconomic structure.

The years between 1871 and 1944 were hardly revolutionary ones for Guatemala. Of these seventy years,
thirty-five were characterized by authentic dictator-
ship. From 1898 to 1920, Manuel Estrada Cabrera was in
power; from 1930 to 1944, Jorge Ubico. Both presidents
are guilty of putting Guatemala through some of its
darkest hours. Secrecy and fear prevailed. No one can
deny that these presidents and their legacy of backwardness received full support from the United States and
the frequent advice of U.S. ambassadors with whom they
met continually.

Who indeed was responsible for the preservation of
our feudal structure well into the twentieth century?
Again the same list: (1) concentration of capital in
the hands of a few families; (2) enslavement of our
Indians; (3) dictators and president-kings, whose power
was nearly absolute in our country; and (4) foreign
capital, which was well served by the preservation of
feudalism in the countryside, where most of its investments were centered.

The government of General Jorge Ubico, like that
of Estrada Cabrera, was characterized by disregard of
constitutional principles and law. Ubico himself appointed the members of Congress (the highest law-making
authority in Guatemala) and used it to support his
reelection, time and again, in an arbitrary fashion.
There was no respect for citizens' rights or constitutional guarantees. As always, the Indians were by far
the worst afflicted. Ubico and Estrada Cabrera repressed and exploited them to the utmost; and during
their regimes, just as in the Middle Ages, private
jails were used to imprison them at the landowners'
request, without due process.

In 1944, Jorge Ubico was overthrown by a popular
movement that sprang from every stratum of Guatemalan
society. Young intellectuals rose to power, led by
Captain Jacobo Arbenz, Colonel Francisco Javier, and
Jorge Toriello. For the first time in Guatemalan history, the necessary forces were put into motion to
transform the feudal structures of Guatemalan society
that had prevailed since the colonial era.

There was nothing socialistic about the Revolution
of 1944, despite many claims to the contrary. It was
of a purely capitalist nature. Nevertheless, the
selfishness and power of the landowning class were such

that even the introduction of capitalist structures
proved too progressive. The agrarian reform, the most
progressive act of the 1944 revolution and the first
measure in Guatemala's history intended to benefit the
Indians, was harshly censured by the rich. This act
and the construction of a highway linking the capital
city with the Atlantic Ocean constituted the "sins" for
which President Arbenz was never pardoned. Of course,
that highway would have been detrimental to the interests of the railroad companies, which were based on
North American capital and whose most important activity was the transport of bananas cultivated by the
United Fruit Company in the fertile fringes of Guatemalan territory that extended along the highway's projected route. For these sins President Arbenz was
overthrown and the revolution was stamped out. With
the help of the United States, Castillo Armas invaded
the country in 1954, took power, and reversed the
achievements of the preceding ten years.

As we all know, the adoption of an agrarian reform
does not necessarily imply a socialist or communist
form of government. There are many kinds of agrarian
reforms. Moreover, the distribution of small parcels
of land to the landless without the abolition of private property is a process that has occurred in almost
every capitalist country. Nevertheless, this process
was prevented in Guatemala in 1954, not to repress a
communist movement as some claimed, but rather to maintain a socioeconomic structure similar to that of the
Middles Ages in Europe, an anachronism that favors
Guatemala's millionaire families as well as foreign
capital, since both benefit from cheap labor.

WORKERS IN CENTRAL AMERICA AND THE UNITED STATES

Why is it useful to maintain a feudalistic social
structure in Central America? It is best to go straight
to the point in answering this query: because wages
remain low, workers receive no benefits, especially in
the rural sector; and the less workers and peasants
earn, the fewer opportunities and the less free time
they will have to educate themselves. In this way
workers, living on the edge of misery, cannot become
conscious that they live in an unjust system that
enriches itself without contributing to those who make
up the forces of production.

The impact of the revolution of 1776 was strong
within the most powerful country of the world. Since
then, workers have made great progress in the area of
wages and social welfare. Though it may be denied that
a revolution is taking place in the United States, we

must admit that a strong progressive movement has
wrought justice for workers in their demands to the
wealthy owners of land and industry. Workers have been
supported and at times advised by intellectuals, writers, and students (such as philosopher Herbert Marcuse
and President John Kennedy), who have succeeded in modifying and, to some extent, socializing the now obsolete
structures of classical capitalism that arose after
1776.

Within its own borders, then, the United States
recognizes the necessity of modifying the social and
economic structure. Two Presidents, Lincoln and Kennedy, have given their lives in an attempt to obtain
greater social justice for their countrymen. And,
despite the attempts of most U.S. sociologists to prove
that capitalism will never be eliminated in their
nation, it is precisely because of its high level of
social development that the United States is destined
to change its social structure in search of a new and
lasting form of organization, if one accepts the idea
that history is dialectical and moves inexorably forward.

Marcuse has said that if change is to occur in the
United States, it must be led by the intellectual class,
since workers have attained such a favorable standard
of living (with television sets, cars, private homes,
and so on) that they are not interested in any movement that would transform the current structure of U.S.
society. Central American workers and peasants are
similarly unconcerned with organizing to change the
social structure, but this is due to their ignorance and
lack of civic awareness.

Who is responsible for the ignorance and fear of
Central American workers? Again, the old list: (1) a
handful of wealthy families; (2) the landowning class
in particular, which is content to see its peasants
half-clothed, undernourished, and able to earn only a
pittance; and (3) foreign capital, which, far from
seeking the social justice it upholds in its home country, behaves much like the native rich, adopting the
wage standards of the local area and helping to repress the slightest attempt by workers to seek higher
wages.

CONCLUSION

The American Revolution of 1776 undeniably had an
impact within the borders of the United States. Thanks
to its social justice, that nation has almost entirely
eliminated any movement toward a radical transformation

of capitalism. There is indeed a revolution within the
United States, a progressive sense and a desire to give
workers their due. But the major failure of the revolutionary impact of 1776 is that the United States behaves in a different and often contrary fashion in
response to Latin American demands for change. It
practices justice within its borders and selfishness
abroad. The North American revolution is for North
Americans, never for Latin Americans.

I close this discussion with a query to all the
participants in the New World Conference: Is the
United States exclusively worthy of revolution and progress? Will the impact of the U.S. Revolution--or of
any other revolution--never reach Latin American shores?

The Impact of the American Revolution in Two Brazilian Cities: Rio de Janeiro and São Paulo

Antônia Fernanda Pacca de Almeida Wright
Translated by María A. Leal

The subject of the United States began to be of interest in Brazil many years ago. Although literature about it had to be hidden away in the libraries of disloyal subjects,[1] it was a constant attraction in the years before independence and could even be heard on the lips of the future empress, Leopoldina, who declared: "In the manner of the United States [the country shall be administered by] and the ministry handed over to capable Brazilians."[2] And the subject remained at the center of discussion after the exile of Dom Pedro I, years later, in such places as the bookstore of Evaristo da Veiga[3] and the circles of restless patriots in the provinces.[4]

The discussion focused mainly on Jefferson, Franklin, and Washington, as well as on Jacksonian democracy. These American theorists and their approach to the problems of the New World became the order of the day. People increasingly began to emphasize the distinction between Old and New World values in Brazil, a distinction that did not always appear clear-cut in the individual behavior of some of these men, many of whom still belonged to the generation of the Enlightenment. This emphasis grew progressively stronger among those who came to power upon the opening of the General Assembly in 1826.

Ultimately, the American Revolution was one which, according to Benjamin Rush, did not end with the war of independence: "The American war is over, but this is far from being the case with the American Revolution."[5] It was still necessary to revolutionize the people, since many things had not yet undergone fundamental change. In the many local constitutions that preceded the Constitution of the United States, much of the old colonial charters was preserved in terms of form and spirit. Although many of these charters declared a government of the people, they themselves were rarely the result of a public referendum or convention. The juxtaposition of Old and New World values was evident both in these charters and in the states' debates over the American Constitution after 1787.[6] A further example of values from the Old World was Alexander Hamilton's proposal for a strongly defended national government, which many believed was based on the British model.[7] However, Hamilton asserted that his proposal was meant as a response to the unaccountability of the monarchy to the people, in opposition to the British model.[8]

Jefferson's ideas represented the antithesis of Federalist writings, particularly with respect to the behavior of the executive branch and the essence of representative government. Jefferson believed that power should be placed as much as possible in the hands of the people, but, as J. S. Mill commented in Representative Government, he expected popular government to abolish class privilege without at the same time depriving society of the leadership of gifted individuals.[9] Thus a whole complex of factors was involved in the forming of a national U.S. identity, some original and others resulting from a reformulation of pre-existing values in a New World context.

Many of the foregoing observations were relevant in the context of parliamentary debates in Brazil, such as the problem of executive responsibility and the question of the compatibility of certain political characteristics of English America with Brazilian reality. One particularly comparable issue, particularly in the period before independence, was the idea of "federating" metropolis and colony. This notion of Federalism was considered even by Jefferson, who imagined the construction of a "great republic" on the basis of smaller ones, that is, the states.[10] Nevertheless, both Hamilton and Jefferson eventually discarded the "Federalist" idea that it was possible for the rebel colonies to remain federated to England.

Close analysis of the constitutional debates in Brazil in 1823,[11] based on articles published in the Revérbero Constitucional Fluminense[12] and Correio Braziliense,[13] both liberal newspapers, reveals the plausibility of comparison with the United States. Hipólito José da Costa, the editor of the Correio, visited the United States and was delighted with what he saw long before settling in London, whence he sent news to Brazil of his trip to Philadelphia.[14] Later he condemned the attitude of the Royal Court, advising

Brazil "not to break its union until it became clear
that one part of the nation, the general government,
did not pay heed to the reasonable demands of the other
part."[15] Similarly, the Revérbero promoted the idea
that "the Portuguese of both worlds should be happy and
fraternally associated" and should "reconcile the general good of the nation."[16] In June 1822, Nicolau de
Campos Vergueiro wrote in Revérbero that the discontent
was aimed at "the European party, disconnected from
the country they inhabit and therefore disliked by the
Brazilians."[17] Finally, there was da Costa's passionate call to "direct our vision and our hearts to the
establishment of a Brazilian Assembly."[18] These words
were published in Revérbero on September 10, 1822, in
an article that clearly stated the proponent's demands:
liberty regulated by law; equality before the law;
representative monarchy; well-defined division of
powers; electoral, not hereditary, representation;
Catholic religion; and so forth. This article already
contained the outline of a radicalizing tendency in the
positions eventually adopted in Brazilian debates from
the time of the revolution.

In the United States, too, Jefferson and other
thinkers became progressively radicalized in their
positions as they defined their principles more clearly.
As noted above, Jefferson fought for the inviolability
of states' rights, while men such as Hamilton promoted
Federalism. But the idea of Federalism had its own
peculiar path in the development of these men's ideas,
beginning with acceptance of federation with England,
only to reject it later on.

Before looking more closely at the Brazilian press
of the independence period, one might consider what
the position of Portugal would have been in such a
Portuguese "system." How would Portugal have behaved
with respect to Brazil independent of the position of
the court? If the assembly had not reconvened after
the "liberal" revolution of 1820 in order to attempt
to recolonize Brazil, what political line would the
Portuguese court have adopted? Paulo Braga Menezes, in
a small study on the first Brazilian constitutions,
refers to two fundamental factors in this respect. Long
before the events discussed above, the king himself
legislated laws by authority of the Ordenações and the
Lei Mental in order to institute innovations that were
"adequate to the structure of a new world different
from that of Europe."[19] Menezes also mentions the
publication in 1821 of a literary and political newspaper called the Cidadão Literato, the first issue of
which contained an article entitled "Thoughts on the
Union of Portugal and Brazil." This article favored
the formation of a monarchy in Brazil under a free

constitution representing a treaty founded on common
interests. Such a constitution "will link these two
independent kingdoms with a tighter and more consistent
bond than that which has existed to date."[20] Echoing
the thoughts of this article was a document found in
the Imperial Museum: the Project for a Federative Pact
between the Brazilian Empire and the Kingdom of Portugal by Silvestre Pinheiro Machado, Minister of Foreign
Trade and War in Rio de Janeiro in 1821. Menezes also
refers to the possibility that Dom Pedro turned over
the same thoughts in his mind as he worked on the rough
drafts of amendments to the "constitutional project of
the Brazilian Empire" and the "constitutional charter
of the Portuguese monarchy."[21]

Following this line of thought, untimely action
by the court of Lisbon would have interrupted a clearly
evolving process that the Portuguese Crown had been
contemplating for some time. Dom João VI's astute perception of Brazilian reality no doubt underlay his policies and politics. But in the latter no consideration
of the necessary measures for the maintenance of union
among the provinces--that is, a centralizing power--
was present. Reorientation of these perceptions contributed to the sense of disaster surrounding the dramatic events of April 7 and sparked the idea in the
provinces that responsibility for independence belonged
to the Brazilians. Hence came the revival of interest
in the American experience upon this occasion as the
only respectable example of federation, in contrast with
the disorder and "sans culotterie" of the neighboring
republics that had arisen out of the old Spanish colonial empire.

Let us return now to the protest press. On April
7 the admirers of the United States spoke in moderation,
for the most part. The newspaper Novo Farol
Paulistano,[22] for example, carried the motto: "He who
disdains moderation rejects justice."[23] In that same
issue a letter signed by "one who knows them well"
expressed opposition to the rival Observador Constitucional, accusing its editors of being "revolutionaries
from the south" and "sans culottes."[24]

In a later issue the Farol defended foreign participation in provincial military defense, in reply to a
columnist for another publication: "Here in São Paulo
it is not a matter of defending our cause and our
liberty [illegible] . . . that foreigners are prevented
from contributing to these goals; and when it comes to
defending our cause and our liberty . . . we are no
better than the North Americans who also availed themselves of foreign assistance. The True São Paulo
Gentleman should also not be so sensitive as to feel

ashamed of that which caused no shame to Washington and
Lafayette."[25]   The comparison with the American Revolution is of special interest here.

Moving on to other examples, the Diário do Governo
and Aurora Fluminense were a continual source of articles for the provincial press.   From these articles it
seems clear that the writers possessed information
about the fall of Charles X as well as activities in
the United States since independence.   Countless examples of this nature can be found in the debate between
the Farol Paulistano and the Observador Constitucional
at the time of the first Brazilian attempt at self-
government, especially in the early period of the
Regency.[26]

On December 21, 1831, the Farol carried an article
from Man and America (O Homem e a América) criticizing
Portuguese influence in the government and characterizing American man as amenable to a sort of peaceful
rebellion.[27]   In issue 19 of Aurora (March 10, 1832)
Evaristo da Veiga wrote about the spirit of association
that prevailed in the world at the time, citing the
English companies as an example.   A superficial reading
might interpret this as clear evidence of an English
influence on da Veiga's thought.   However, Tocqueville
himself affirmed that nowhere in the world had the
spirit of association been practiced as much as in
North America.   It is also important to note that many
companies in England were structured as a reflection of
that nation's large maritime operation outside of Europe.
For this reason, many ideas thought to have originated
in England actually bore fruit in the United States.
This was the case with respect to certain doctrines
such as those of Jean Baptiste Say and Adam Smith,
which, while virtually ignored in England after a time,
were taken up by ardent believers on the other side of
the Atlantic at the beginning of the nineteenth century.

Number 47 of the Farol carried an article from
Aurora opposing the viewpoint of the editor of O Monitor,
who had called himself a "true federalist":   "Does he
perhaps fail to realize that the federal system is
guided by American principles?"[28]   This is a good example of the "local formula" prevailing in the mind of
the journalist.   Da Veiga's long article in Farol constituted a veritable "platform" of political thought
clearly endorsed by the newspaper.   Speaking up against
the extremists, he wrote:

> Our anarchists are merely servile plagiarists
> of the French revolutionaries of 1793, not of
> those who wanted a Republic founded on princi-
> ples of order, generous and honorable ideas

> pertaining to uplifted souls; but of those
> other revolutionaries who based liberty and
> the republic on the unchaining of all the
> passions of the least well educated classes
> of society, for the benefit of their leaders
> and plotters . . . who prescribed property,
> enlightenment, wealth, and sympathy of the
> heart to be domestic virtues. . . . Was
> Brazil designed for dear disciples of Marat?[29]

U.S. Consul William Wright found the above opinion
to be a common one among the journalists, deputies,
businessmen, and functionaries with whom he associated.
As an old resident of Rio, Wright had developed more
contacts than had his American colleagues. For this
reason his impressions about the Emperor in February,
1831, are worthy of note; the latter was "traveling
with the obvious objective of making friends in the
provinces," trying to forestall the growing crises.[30]
With great foresight of the events of April 7, which
he could have acquired only through contact with different political groups, Wright wrote on February 12:

> The opening of the next legislature will deter-
> mine the future. The imperial party admits
> that the Constitution needs to be modified;
> if not, the country will be ruined. Neverthe-
> less, the liberal party retorts: "Touch the
> Constitution and we will be prepared to
> resist." The liberal party will probably
> slough off on its opponents the task of fight-
> ing on behalf of the most controversial issues.
> Such an act will probably produce a revolution
> in the whole empire and it is believed that the
> liberal party will gain power thereby in all
> the provinces, with the possible exception of
> Rio de Janeiro, where the imperial party may
> predominate for a time. The inevitable con-
> sequence of a revolution in Brazil will be a
> state of anarchy that will last for years
> throughout the country.[31]

This piece by Wright reveals a very clear perception of the imminent political outcome. He refers to
the impasse between incipient political groupings,
which he calls the imperial party and the liberal party
(the opposition). Despite possible inaccuracies, the
identification as such of the political groupings was
a good approximation of the actual parliamentary debates.
Another interesting question is the figure of the
Emperor and his ministerial policy, which, aside from
the ruler's less liberal tendencies, are cited by Brazilian historians as fundamental causes of the events
of April 7. Judging from Wright's letter, however, the

substance of the issue was resolved in the assembly and
by way of electoral victory. The parties and their
voters came from more diversified social sectors than
has been thought until now. Their aspirations postponed since independence, many Brazilians no longer belonged to the "Emperor's party" by February 1831, particularly in the provinces, as Wright observed in
prophetic anticipation of the revolutions of the
Regency.

It is precisely on the basis of such aspirations
that the popular press sounded its protest. Wrote the
Voz Fluminense,

> Any country whose political administration
> is in the hands of foreigners is oppressed;
> this is a truth even more terrible if said
> foreigners are convicted criminals, actually
> pulled out of the galleys and jails of Eu-
> rope. . . . it is truly a day of anguish for
> us on which we have occasion to compare the
> fate of the Americans, of these United and
> still-to-be-United States, with our unfor-
> tunate vilification and misery. . . . Only
> political federation can save us.[32]

A Nova Luz Brasileira of October 26 called upon
soldiers not to "lend an ear to seduction by your lame
chieftains nor to your absolutist confessors." The common citizen was exhorted in these words: "The citizen
of the empire . . . is foremost among its constituting
authorities."[33] Nor were the incentives lacking for the
higher-ranking military to join the protestors, judging
by this passage from the Voz Fluminense: "The persecu-
tions do not cease; foreign officers are employed in
services that rightfully belong to zealous and patriotic
nationals."[34] It seems clear that the opposition's
satirists were well aware of the existence of an avid
public desiring political participation and being inex-
plicably excluded from power. In the Regency that
group would become more clear-cut and would carry weight.

Businessmen also shared the desire for political
independence since they yearned for an internal market
freed from the fetters of a foreign monarch. It is unfortunate that we do not possess enough of their correspondence for a study of their role in the fertile
decade of 1828 to 1838. However, we have some data
about their participation in certain Societies for the
Defense of Liberty and Independence. In the capitals
of São Paulo and Rio de Janeiro and in other cities of
the interior and the coast several of these societies
were established. The most detailed study of them has
just been initiated at the University of São Paulo,

beginning with the group based in Santos.[35] The professional distribution of the members of this society is revealed in table 1.

Table 1

Professional Distribution of the Members of the National Society for the Defense of Liberty and Independence of Santos

Professional Category	Number of Members
Administrators	2
Merchants	4
Craftsmen	13
Artists	3
Clerks	5
Clergy	3
Students	1
Customs officials	6
Public employees	6
Teaching	2
Magistrates	5
Businessmen	30
Businessmen, inadequately identified	10
Military	30
Small farmers	5

Source: Departamento de Arquivo do Estado de São Paulo, "Maços de População" (1831).

Combining the merchants and craftsmen with other groups engaged in business, there was a total of fifty-seven people engaged in business. Among the military, the second strongest group in the table, some also could be included with the business group since, according to the census, they also possessed businesses. It is evident, then, that businessmen formed the mainstay of this society, besides probably having financed its expenses.

In fact, businessmen throughout the country behaved similarly to those in Santos, placing great importance on order and moderation. This can be inferred from a statement by Feijó.* Defending the need to create a municipal guard to maintain public order, Feijó spoke of having to pacify the merchants: "six thousand proprietors and merchants each representing a family and property . . . have declared they will not tolerate more unrest, fear, discomfort and damages caused by the anarchists."[36]

---

*Then future Regent of Brazil [ed.].

At the beginning of the nineteenth century São
Paulo was coming into its own as a city. Having developed on the basis of the sugar cane industry and of
troop and land transport, São Paulo was an important
center of trade, despite its links to Rio de Janeiro by
way of coastal commerce.[37] It was more than a farmers'
town, especially after the establishment of a law
school, which attracted educated youth from the provinces and became a center of political interest. Visiting the province in 1839, Daniel P. Kidder observed
that the number of students had increased from 33 in
1828 to nearly 300 in 1830 and 1834.[38] The students
were an important influence on the political destiny of
the city and of the province.

Examination of the Farol Paulistano, official organ of the Society for the Defense of Independence of
São Paulo, does not corroborate Richard Morse's description of the period 1830-45 as characterized by "inde-
cision, failure and possible future promise."[39] According to the Farol, 200 students were among the members
of the society.[40] This represented a far cry from
"indecisive" political activity, especially considering
that the university had been in existence only five
years at the time (1831). In fact, the executive council of the society was composed almost entirely of law
students and graduates, as Augustin Wernet argues.[41]

Other members of the society included Antonio
Mariano de Azevedo Marques and Vicente Pires da Mota of
the Presidential Council of São Paulo province; future
deputies to the National Assembly; future presidents of
provinces and even regents and ministers of the empire;
and rural landowners, public employees, and entrepreneurs. After the abdication of Pedro I this latter
group took a politically more radical line, but eventually became more moderate.

Of those known in the press as "exalted liberals,"
few of the true extremists were inspired by the North
American model. The majority of writers for the Farol
and most of the members of the society neither approved
nor advanced extreme positions, but rather supported
reforms that would be possible only in a climate of
order and progress. They tended toward a moderate position, leaving street movements to other social strata.
The foremost political group was composed of men of
letters, responsible journalists, temporary and sometimes permanent military personnel, and public employees.
Moderation typified political aspirations in general,
along with fear of anarchy, even in view of the necessity
for economic and political reorientation and development.

The brothers Ernesto Antônio and Cornélio Ferreira França presented a proposal to federate Brazil purely and simply to the United States to the Chamber of Deputies on August 18, 1834. The curious proposal was composed of ten articles:

(1) Brazil and the United States will be federated in order mutually to defend themselves against external threats and assist each other in their internal development.

(2) The two nations will defend themselves with all their might, allocating the necessary resources to this end on a yearly basis.

(3) Each of the nations will have representatives in the National Assembly of the other.

(4) The products of each shall be received in the other in the same way as domestic products, tax-free.

(5) The two nations shall assist each other in establishing their institutions and economic activities each within the borders of the other.

(6) The citizens of each nation shall enjoy all the benefits of native citizens in both nations.

(7) Issues between the subjects of the two nations shall be decided on the basis of conciliation or by arbiters chosen by the two parties, or by a jury composed of citizens from each of the countries in equal numbers.

(8) The two nations shall be obligated to assist each other in the preservation and improvement of the national form of government in the event of any calamity that opposes said physical or moral improvement.

(9) The government of Brazil will seek to carry out this treaty of alliance for an indefinite period of time.

(10) Upon signing this treaty shall be presented to the General Assembly for final approval.

Palace of the Chamber of Deputies, August 18, 1834, [signed] Cornélio Ferreira França, Antônio Ferreira França, Ernesto Ferreira França, Antônio Fernandes da Silveira, João Barbosa Cordeiro, João Barbosa de Vasconcelos Pessoa, José Maria Ildefonso Jecome da Veiga Pessoa, Joaquim Teixeira Peixoto de Albuquerque, with some reservations.[42]

But the project was put off. Senhor Climaco,
calling for a vote against the project, stated that he
did not doubt the great benefit that might arise from
such an idea, but would vote against it "because I see
no way of obligating a nation to accept such an agreement." In recent research of the Annals of the Brazilian Parliament, I ascertained that the "extremist"
enthusiasm of the França brothers was an isolated gesture and did not represent a "political line" consis-
tently linked to the U.S. example. The same cannot be
said of statements in the Legislative Assembly from
1828 to 1838, particularly those of deputies Antônio
de Paula Souza and Francisco de Souza Martins of São
Paulo and of the mining interests represented by
Honório Hermeto Carneiro Leão, Custodio Dias, Antônio
Paulino Limpo de Abreu, and Bernardo Pereira de Vasconcelos.

In conclusion, it seems plausible that the example
of successful reformism in the United States provided a
clear alternative to those in control of the future of
the Regency.

NOTES

1. For more information on these libraries see E.
Frieiro, O Diabo na Livraria do Conego (Belo Horizonte,
1945). For a summary comparison of political ideas between the two countries see Nicia Vilela Luz, "A Monar-
quia Brasileira e as Repúblicas Americanas," Journal of
Inter-American Studies 3 (July 1966):358-70.

2. A. Fernanda Pacca de A. Wright, "Os Estados Unidos
e a Independência Brasileira," Anuário do Museu Imperial
33 (1974):69.

3. Paulo Pinheiro Chagas, Teófilo Otoni Ministro do
Povo (Rio de Janeiro: Livraria Editora Zelio Valverde,
1943), pp. 68-69.

4. Speech by Teófilo Otoni, Annals of Parliament, April
26 and May 10, 1838.

5. Oscar Handlin, The American People: A New History
(London: Hutchison, 1963), p. 177.

6. The Federalist by Hamilton, Jay, and Madison is composed of material contained in articles in the Daily
Advertiser of New York. The Brazilian edition was
translated anonymously in Ouro Preto with a note indicating that the translation was already completed in
1839 and was rapidly sold out. The translator of the
1896 edition is Teófilo Ribeiro. It was published by
Ouro Preto.

7.   Preface to The Federalist, in American State Papers, vol. 43, Great Books of the Western World, ed. R. M. Hutchins (Chicago: William Benton Publishers, 1952), p. 23.

8.   Ibid., p. 71.

9.   John Stuart Mill, Representative Government (1861), in ibid., pp. 327-442.

10.   John Dewey, ed., Thomas Jefferson: The Living Thoughts of Thomas Jefferson (New York, 1940), pp. 51-52.

11.   Anais da Assembléia Constituinte, 1823 (Rio de Janeiro: H. S. Pinto Printers, 1880). Interesting monographical work was done on this subject by doctoral student Dylva Moliterno, "A Constituinte de 1823" (Master's thesis, Universidade de São Paulo, 1974).

12.   Revérbero Constitucional Fluminense, vol. 8, January 1, 1822, pp. 86-89; May 28, 1822; September 3, 1822.

13.   Correio Braziliense, vol. 28, April 1822, pp. 442-47; June 1822, p. 697.

14.   Hipólito José da Costa, Diario de Minha Viagem a Filadélfia (Rio de Janeiro: Academia Brasileira de Letras, 1955).

15.   Correio Braziliense, vol. 28, April 1822, pp. 442-47.

16.   Revérbero, vol. 8, April 28, 1822, pp. 442-47.

17.   Ibid., June 10, 1822, pp. 181, 184, 185.

18.   Correio Braziliense, vol. 28, June 1822, p. 697.

19.   Paulo Braga Menezes, As Constituições Outorgadas ao Império do Brasil e ao Reino de Portugal (Rio de Janeiro: Ministério da Justiça, Arquivo Nacional, 1974), p. 8.

20.   Ibid., p. 10.

21.   Ibid.

22.   O Novo Farol Paulistano was founded in 1827 by José da Costa Carvalho, a law student in São Paulo. It was edited in large part by students from the academy, with the full support of Carlos Carneiro de Campos, professor of political economy and a follower of the

Catechism of Political Economy by Jean Baptiste Say.
See Daniel Pedro Muller, Ensaio d'um Quadro Estatístico
da Província de São Paulo (São Paulo: Secção de Obras
do Estado de São Paulo, 1927), p. 257.

23. Farol Paulistano, no. 22, October 19, 1831.

24. O Observador Constitucional was founded in 1829.
Its editor was Libero Badaró who was later assassinated,
provoking a major disturbance. Badaró was loved by the
students of the old academy of Largo São Francisco.

25. Farol Paulistano, no. 23, October 1831.

26. The debate can be followed in numbers 25 to 29,
October 1831; no. 30, November 16, 1831; no. 31, November 19, 1831; and no. 32, November 23, 1831.

27. Farol Paulistano, no. 20, December 21, 1831.

28. Farol Paulistano, no. 47, January 18, 1832.

29. Ibid., p. 86.

30. William Wright to Martin van Buren, February 12,
1831, Diplomatic Dispatches, National Archives, Washington, D.C.

31. Ibid.

32. Voz Fluminense, November 29, 1830. See also a
differing opinion based on the same material in Hamilton
Marques Monteiro, "Da Revolução de julho ao sete de
abril: O Papel da imprensa na abdicação de D. Pedro
I," Mensário do Arquivo Nacional, no. 5, May 1975.

33. A Nova Luz Brasileira, October 26, 1830.

34. Voz Fluminense, September 23, 1830.

35. Augustin Wernet, "Uma Associação Política da Época
Regencial: A Sociedade dos Defensores da Liberdade e
Independência Nacional dos Santos" (Master's thesis,
Universidade de São Paulo, 1973), pp. 150-56.

36. Transcripts from a proclamation in the Chamber
of Deputies, October 7, 1831, in Novelli Junior, Feijó,
um Paulista Velho, p. 138.

37. Maria Thereza Schorer Petrone, Lavoura Canavieira
em São Paulo, Expansão XX e Declínio, 1756-1851 (São
Paulo: Difusão Européia do Livro, 1968).

38. Daniel Paris Kidder, São Paulo in 1839: Original Sketches of Residence and Travels in Brazil; Historical and Geographical Notices of the Empire and Its Several Provinces (London: Wiley & Putnam; São Paulo: Sociedade Brasileira de Cultura Inglesa, 1969).

39. Richard Morse, Formação Histórica de São Paulo (São Paulo: Difusão do Livro, 1970).

40. Farol Paulistano, no. 479, April 26, 1831.

41. Our ex-student Augustin Wernet recently defended his doctoral thesis at the University of Sao Paulo. In this work, entitled "As Sociedades Políticas da Província de São Paulo na Primeira Metade do Período Regencial," he examines in detailed fashion the socioeconomic composition of the members of these societies in nearly forty towns.

42. Annals of the Chamber of Deputies in Anais do Parlamento Brasileiro, 1834 Session (Rio de Janeiro: Hipólito José Pinto e Cia. Printers, 1879), vol. 2, p. 241.

II. ARTS AND CULTURE IN THE AMERICAS

Mexican and North American Culture During the First Half of the Nineteenth Century

Jesús Valasco Márquez
Translated by **María A. Leal**

In order to consider the cultural development of a particular period or country it is necessary to define what we mean by <u>art</u> and <u>culture</u>. To attempt to define these concepts would be an enormous task in the context of this discussion, but I cannot avoid presenting at least a basic idea of these concepts before entering into the central theme.

Art and culture are not isolated phenomena; rather, they represent the ultimate expression of the social and economic conditions of the society in which they arise. Furthermore, the historical method is the only useful approach for studying cultural development, since culture, like the society that produces it, is an essentially dynamic process. These principles set the stage for a discussion of cultural development in Mexico and the United States during the first half of the nineteenth century. The ways in which cultural development expressed social and economic conditions in the respective societies will be analyzed and the two types of development compared. Of course, from a historical perspective any comparison is to a certain extent arbitrary, since history is made of concrete, unique facts. Nevertheless, tracing a parallel between two unique paths of development may shed light on each of them and may help to establish whether they had points in common, to determine what was truly original in each of them, and finally to analyze the influence of one upon the other.

When the United States emerged as a sovereign nation after a relatively short war of independence, it was organized on the basis of an original system of untried principles. In this sense the United States experienced a genuine revolution. Nevertheless, ways

of life continued unchanged, since the revolution had
no feudal society to overthrow and replace, nor did it
have to struggle against an institutionalized church.
At any rate, U.S. society at that time contained a sort
of aristocracy composed of landowners and businessmen
that maintained its position for many decades beyond the
struggle for independence. As a result, this group imposed its own tastes and ideals upon the people, producing an art and culture that satisfied its own needs.

During the years following the Revolution, North
Americans showed great interest in European culture.
They accepted England and were even proud to consider
themselves part of English tradition. France was also
admired for its accomplishments. At the same time,
however, U.S. intellectuals undertook a search for original forms, with the conviction that the United States,
having won political independence, had to demonstrate
its ability to create an equally independent culture.
Of course, the task was more easily contemplated than
done.

The notion of completely rejecting European teach-
ings was unacceptable to some Americans. Noah Webster,
probably the most enthusiastic nationalist of the period,
refused to view nationalism as cultural isolationism.
Therefore, neoclassicism continued to inspire U.S.
artists for a few decades, while intellectuals and
scientists were influenced by the Enlightenment. Behind
the ideas of Thomas Paine, Alexander Hamilton, James
Madison, Thomas Jefferson, Benjamin Franklin, John Adams,
and Joel Barlow were those of Locke, Hume, Hobbes, and
Montesquieu, as well as the Scottish "common sense"
philosophers. Likewise, the work of scientists such as
Palmer and Allen was based on theories established by
Newton. In poetry, Pope, Butler, Swift, Thompson, and
Young inspired such poets as Barlow, Dwight, Trumbull,
and Freneau. The British sentimentalists, especially
Richardson, were present in the novels of William Hill
Brown. In the same way the satirical novels of Swift
and Defoe greatly influenced those of Royal Tyler, while
Charles Brockden Brown imitated those of Walpole.

U.S. historians evolved an interpretation of colonial history as merely a series of events directed
toward the creation of a new nation. Nevertheless,
their works upheld the commonly accepted European notion
that underneath every historical phenomenon lay the general laws of nature.

At the time of the Revolution, American society had
attained a high level of sophistication, especially in
Charleston, Philadelphia, and New York. In these cities
the visual arts had not only been accepted, but

constituted a very important part of social life. But
in this case, as in others, Europe exercised a constant
influence. In theater, for example, London continued
to provide both the plays and the actors for American
productions. The United States had only two playwrights,
Royal Tyler and William Dunlap. Music followed a similar pattern; almost all the pieces composed and played
in the United States were created by composers who, if
not born in Europe, had at least been trained there.
Nevertheless, two important exceptions, Francis Hopkin-
son and William Billings, stand out.

Conditions throughout the colonial period were not
particularly favorable to the development of the plastic
arts. From colonial times to the end of the eighteenth
century, painting was considered "something frivolous,
of little use to society, and unworthy of being practiced by an individual capable of more transcendent
tasks," according to John Trumbull. But despite this
situation, there arose a group of first-rate painters
who had been born before the Revolution, including Benjamin West, John Singleton Copley, Charles Willson Peale,
Gilbert Stuart, and John Trumbull. But in this case,
as in literature, their works were rooted in the European tradition.

Of all art forms in the immediate postrevolutionary
period, sculpture showed the greatest dependence on
Europe. Most works were done by German, French, and
Italian artists. Giuseppe Franzoni and Giovanni Andrei,
the first two sculptors to work on the Capitol, were
imported, and by 1829 most American sculptors were
studying in Italian academies.

In contrast, architecture benefited greatly from
the Revolution. Immediately after the war there was
great demand for public buildings to house the new federal and state governments. An effort was made in construction to avoid the "Georgian" style, replacing it
with purely American forms. Thomas Jefferson and Benjamin Latrobe looked to Greece and Rome--the first
democracy and the first republic in history, respec-
tively--for inspiration, and under the influence of
Palladio and the French classicists, they created a
United States architectural style. Most federal government buildings were constructed in this style, which
was also adopted throughout the South. In New England,
in contrast, the federalist style, created by Charles
Bulfinch, prevailed, retaining British patterns to
which local modifications were added.

North American culture from 1776 to 1830 was
largely derived from and dependent upon Europe in general and England in particular. Most works were

influenced by colonialism, lack of confidence in native
tastes and ideas, and fear of not living up to "superior"
norms. Nevertheless, they became increasingly nationalist in spirit, gradually incorporating native materials and ideas.

Cultural colonialism is inevitable wherever economic
colonialism exists. After the War of 1812 the United
States began to move slowly, but firmly, toward economic
independence. The two political parties of the Jackson
era put forth nationalist economic programs. The marketing and transport revolutions were already in full
swing, and society experienced vertical as well as
horizontal mobility. Moreover, in the nineteenth century the middle class not only grew in numbers, but
rose to political power and dominance.

The restrictions of neoclassicism and the Enlightenment and their emphasis on permanent order did not
win acceptance in this restless society. Romanticist
ideas--that is, trust in human progress, acceptance of
the complexity of life, emphasis on individuals and
their feelings, and, above all, an organic notion of
the universe--agreed more with the aggressive, progressive spirit of the times.

North American culture undoubtedly continued to be
influenced by Europe, but increasingly less so. North
American romanticism was a much more constructive, individualist, and democratic movement than its European
counterpart. The opening up of the West, the discovery
of a common past, and the attraction of unbounded virgin
land were of far too much importance to be ignored by
the artists and intellectuals of the period.

The origins of transcendentalism were in Europe,
but there were no Emersons or Brownsons on the other
side of the Atlantic. Nearly all the discoveries in
the pure sciences between 1820 and 1870 were made in
Europe, but the United States made an overwhelming amount
of discoveries in the applied sciences. The concept of
"Yankee ingenuity," which today evokes universal respect, grew out of this period.

While Scott, Byron, and Keats exercised a definite
influence on U.S. poets, the New England Circle, in
particular Poe and Whitman, stood out in its own right.
Essayists such as Emerson and Thoreau and historians
such as Bancroft, Prescott, and Parkman achieved a high
level of sophistication, although their ideas may not
have been completely original. And even though Americans of the Jackson era were avid readers of Sir Walter
Scott, Dickens, Eliot, Austen, and Trollope, native
writers learned to exploit their nation's unique history,

geography, and society. Cooper and Irving marked the beginning of American literature per se, which reached one of its highest peaks with the works of Poe, Hawthorne, and Melville.

While the theater arts were dominated by the wealth of composers, playwrights, and actors from abroad, this did not impede the development of native forms to satisfy the tastes of the American middle class, which were by then considerably different from those of Europeans. In music, for example, there was a movement toward democracy that occurred nowhere else in the world; and in theater, forms became diversified and performances grew in number, thanks to the growth of urban centers.

Along with literature, painting was the most developed of the arts. Romanticism led painters in two directions, picturesque and naturalist. The former approach was adopted by William Sidney Mount, George Bingham, and Currier and Ives, the latter by the landscape painters of the Hudson River school. These two currents focused on the uniqueness of the American people and their natural surroundings, lending an indisputable originality to U.S. painting in this period.

Sculptors became less dependent on European masters after 1820, but never achieved complete autonomy. In the eyes of North Americans, the Greenough, Powers, and Crawford triumvirate was on a par with any group of European sculptors. Their work was certainly of high quality and their themes original insofar as they were inspired by U.S. history, but in general they continued to pay tribute to European masters.

The romantic movement in architecture was accompanied by a resurgence in old styles. Of all the "neos" that developed, the most popular was the neogothic, because it represented freedom of the imagination. North American architecture thus did not achieve the originality and grandeur of other art forms.

In sum, on the eve of the Civil War the United States had achieved a high level of originality and cultural independence. Whatever the debt that still existed to Europe, it was already leaving behind its original cultural colonialism and moving toward the construction of its own unique image.

Mexico, in contrast, acquired its political independence just when the United States was beginning to mature, that is, in the second decade of the nineteenth century. Mexican independence was not accompanied by the sort of favorable international climate that had welcomed U.S. independence. Moreover, eleven years of

struggle had devastated the economy, converting the
country into a fighting ground for U.S. and European
economic interests. Economic independence since then
has been more an ideal than a reality for Mexico.

Although during the war of independence there was
a great deal of participation by the lower classes, and
although most war leaders had professed programs for
social reform, in the end the Spanish (not Europeans, but
Creoles) remained in power. Virtually all politicians,
intellectuals, and scientists would come from this
group. Few individuals from other social classes would
have this opportunity, and those who did would have to
adopt the values of the ruling class. Thus, Mexican
culture during the first half of the nineteenth century
served and expressed the ideals of the Creole aristocracy. Within this group, however, there was internal
dissension between those who wished to prolong European
traditions and those who wished to create something new,
something truly Mexican. In politics these two forces
were expressed in the liberal-conservative opposition;
in art, in the opposition of classicist and romantic
forms; and in science, in the confrontation between
theorists and experimentalists.

In poetry, the transition from the neoclassical
forms of Rodríguez del Castillo and the Acadia group to
the romantic style lasted from 1821 to 1860. The romantic poets were further divided into two tendencies:
those who looked to the past, such as Carpio and Pesado,
and those who looked to the future, founding the Academy
of Letran under the direction of Lacuna. This group
was particularly influenced by Byron and the Spanish
poet Espronceda, but their themes--Mexican landscape
and history--lent them a certain originality.

Although few novels were written during the colonial period, the war of independence produced one of
the best satirical novels in Ibero-American literature,
El Periquillo Sarniento, by Joaquín Fernández Lizardi,
which portrays Mexican society in these years. But of
all literary forms, political literature had the
greatest intellectual following in Mexico. History was
particularly important as a tool for proving the validity of liberal and conservative viewpoints, and therefore the chief thinkers of both political tendencies
wrote history books. The most important of these were
José María Luis Mora and Lucas Alamán. In the same way,
philosophy was more a pragmatic discipline than a body
of theoretical knowledge and had deep roots in politics.

Mexican society had interests other than politics,
particularly in Mexico City, where a sophisticated element promoted the development of the theater. Thus,

Mexico had a number of important playwrights such as Gorostiza, Calderon, and Rodríguez Galvan.

After independence, critical demand arose for the development of a national style in literature and the plastic arts. The best response came from the painters. Without a doubt, Mexico already possessed a long tradition of indigenous painting, but it was nevertheless difficult to achieve total independence. The first generations of painters were unable to overcome established classicist influences after the reorganization of the Academy of San Carlos by the Catalan professor Pelegrín Clave, and even with all the support of the liberals, Juan Cordero was unable to shake off his Italian education and its religious themes. José María Velasco, who discovered the Mexican landscape toward the end of the century, was the only painter to achieve pictorial nationalism.

Sculpture and architecture remained undeveloped for lack of stimulation, as the constant economic crises of the period impeded the construction of monuments and buildings. Although scientific knowledge had advanced rapidly during the eighteenth century, it began to regress during the struggle for independence and was not to regain its former status until the end of the nineteenth century.

On the whole, then, Mexican culture during this period was just beginning to seek a national image, a goal that has not been fully realized until the present.

The question one may ask now is whether the cultural development of the two countries had anything in common. Certainly the necessity of creating a national culture was common to New World countries up to the nineteenth century. This necessity had never existed in Europe, where nations arose as independent political entities already possessing a certain degree of economic autonomy and thus a unique culture. In fact, today it is evident that some of these European countries have become satellites of their former colonies as a result of losing their previous economic independence. In this context, there is no doubt that both Mexico and the United States strove toward similar goals. Nevertheless, both countries were caught in the same contradiction: how to create something new without negating what they had thrived on for centuries. Thus, neither of them was able to develop a totally original culture, and both continued paying tribute to the ex-mother country and Europe in general.

At the same time, it is clear that both countries achieved a certain degree of originality--the United

States more than Mexico--and here they had something in
common. Insofar as the United States achieved a certain
degree of economic independence and developed a unique
society, it was able to develop a unique culture as well.
When this occurred, artists and intellectuals began to
take note of their surroundings and to discover that
the values of the common man, of immigrants and blacks,
were just as worthy as any others. The reality that
surrounded them, in short, became a source of inspiration, and in this way what had once existed as "subcultures" became simply "culture."

Something similar occurred in Mexico. On the
periphery of urban Creole culture there existed several
provincial and rural subcultures that developed without
fear of breaking with the past. Eventually these subcultures began to attract Mexican artists and intellectuals, and it is at this point that Mexican culture
per se began to develop. However, unlike the United
States, this phenomenon did not occur as early as the
first half of the nineteenth century. This leads us to
ask whether any type of influence was exercised by the
United States on Mexican culture.

The Mexican-American War of 1846-47 left Mexico
demoralized by defeat and the loss of half of its original territory. Immediately after the war Mexican intellectuals began to propose reconstruction and reform programs in order to resuscitate a seemingly dying country.
The United States played an important role in these
programs. Mexican conservatives based their programs
on a rejection of U.S. proposals, while the liberals
adopted the formula similia similibus curantur: to be
like the United States or to end up absorbed by it.
The liberals won the battle; and from then on, Mexican
intellectuals were forced to take stock of their surroundings in the same way in which U.S. southerners
did after the Civil War. Of course what the Mexicans
discovered was not at all like what the American
southerners would find; nevertheless, it was in its intentions that the United States made its influence felt.

In summary, it was not possible for Mexico to overcome cultural colonialism completely; in fact, it has
not been overcome completely yet. In most cases what
Mexicans have done is to superimpose other forms upon
indigenous and Spanish traditions or else to fall under
the influence of foreign currents. This is explained
by the fact that Mexican culture has not been rooted in
genuine economic independence.

The Role of Private Foundations in the Development of Art and Culture in Venezuela

Carmen Cecilia de Mayz
Translated by María A. Leal

BACKGROUND

The private sector in Venezuela has only recently become aware of the need to participate in the search for answers to the country's social, economic, and cultural problems. This new attitude was officially formulated in the International Executives Seminar held in Maracay, February 17-21, 1963. Private foundations pioneered this approach, in particular the Creole and Mendoza Foundations, which, together with the Venezuelan Executives Association, organized the 1963 seminar. The aims of these groups are best expressed in the words of a particpant, Dr. Eloy Anzola Montauban: "The firm is not merely a grouping of material and economic forces occasioned by circumstance; it is a human expression that must do good, in accordance with the hopes and feelings of those who comprise it and of the community in which it exists."[1] These notions, clearly indicating the importance of cultural development, conceive of man as a producer of spiritual, as well as material, goods.

The promotion and support of cultural activities in a systematic way has only recently been undertaken by the government. On April 4, 1936, the Department of Culture and Fine Arts was formed as a branch of the National Education Ministry. In 1938 the Workers' Cultural Service was formed within the Ministry of Labor and later became the Cultural and Social Welfare Bureau. In 1959 the Senate approved the formation of a committee to write legislation creating the National Institute of Culture and Fine Arts (INCIBA). President Betancourt gave executive approval for the law on April 8, 1960, and in 1964 an executive board was finally appointed for INCIBA. In 1975, President Andrés Pérez appointed a committee to prepare a new piece of cultural

legislation, which is still pending before Congress.
Its purpose would be to create a National Council on
Culture (CONAC).

Cultural policy is currently of great interest to
international bodies as a result of UNESCO's Inter-
governmental Conference on the Institutional, Administrative and Financial Aspects of Cultural Policies, held in
Venice, Italy, from August 24 to September 2, 1970.
Proclaiming the Cultural Decade, the conference spelled
out, first, recognition of the right to culture and the
state's obligation to provide the means for its exercise and, second, the notion of integral development.
Another key conference was the fifth meeting of the
Interamerican Cultural Council held in Maracay in February 1968 by the Organization of American States. This
meeting established the fundamental role of culture in
the development process: "Culture is not extraneous to
development, but rather should be considered as a factor
in the latter as well as a useful tool for American
integration."[2]

We can conclude, therefore, that a positive attitude toward integral social development is arising in
Venezuela as elsewhere.

Certain terms must be defined before analyzing our
results. Cultural development is the process of promoting all factors that promise to improve the cultural
level of a people, that is, their degree of access to
and participation in the cultural life of the community.
Culture is a pragmatic and utilitarian, rather than
theoretical, concept and therefore includes a wide range
of human endeavor. By foundation is meant a private,
nonprofit organization created to fulfill some public
service (social, artistic, scientific, or literary).
Cultural democratization denotes "the participation of
large sectors of the population substituting a foreign,
imported minority culture with a genuine, national culture of the people, based on national forms of expression."[3] This culture would aid in establishing and
strengthening a national identity prior to any social
or economic progress.

Lack of time has forced me to limit my investigation to a handful of private foundations, selected on
the following criteria: (1) diversity in the areas of
culture in which they work; (2) different budget limitations; (3) differences in the length of life of the
foundations; (4) location of a home base in Caracas.
The foundations selected were the Boulton Foundation,
the Caribbean Foundation for Science and Culture, the
Mendoza Foundation, the Neumann Foundation, and the
Planchart Foundation. My research has four objectives:

(1) to analyze the statutes and documents of the foundations as well as to conduct interviews with their executive personnel; (2) to determine their limitations in
providing opportunities for active participation by
the population; (3) to attempt to stimulate interest in
cultural affairs by segments of the private sector other
than the foundations; and (4) to evaluate the future of
national and international cultural exchange. Tables
1, 2, 3, and 4 are examples of the type of data collected.

FINDINGS AND RECOMMENDATIONS

Research showed that the private foundations have
made admirable progress in promoting culture, in accordance with the statutes and goals they set out for
themselves. The primary media for their efforts have
been publications, expositions, crafts, and conservation
work. Such methods promote public appreciation, stimulate individual creativity, and augment the level of
cultural exchange. However, greater progress could be
made by seeking solutions to the major problems detected through this study that relate to both the general policies of the foundations and the execution of
specific programs. In my judgment, there are two major
problems: the lack of a coordinating body among the
different foundations and the lack of concrete programs
to help achieve cultural democratization. My own
recommendations for solving these problems follow.

First, a federation or center of Venezuelan foundations, the function of which would be planning, representation, coordination, and information, should be
created. Rather than cause some loss of autonomy among
the individual foundations, this body would unite them
in more efficient and far-reaching activities. Centralized planning and coordination would improve the foundations' public image, as well as improve the scale of
their activities. A unified representation of the
foundations would serve to defend their legitimate
rights and interests and would assure that each foundation carried out its job. The foundations could work
together to meet some of the country's cultural needs;
and rather than compete with the public sector, they
should complement government activities on a national
scale. This would be their appropriate contribution to
development. Noncultural foundations would do well by
taking a similar approach. An interfoundation information service is vital in this scheme of things and
would (1) maintain a general directory of all the
foundations; (2) serve as a liaison between the different foundations, publicizing activities and helping
to prevent duplication of effort; (3) inform business

TABLE 1 Publications

Type of Publication	Boulton	Caribbean	Foundation Mendoza	Neumann	Planchart	Total
Reference works, documents	12		26			38
Pedagogical work		1	46			47
Research reports	34	1	6			41
Periodicals[a]	1		1	1		3
Other			6			6
Total	47	2	85	1	0	135

aThe Mendoza and Boulton Foundations worked together for a time on a quarterly journal on foundations in Venezuela, Fundaciones, now defunct

TABLE 2 Methods of Publication

Foundation	Distribution[a]	Number of Issues[b]	Selection of Authors Based on
Boulton	By exchange or donation to interested parties	Limited	Quality of work
Caribbean	By donation	Limited	Choice of the executive board
Mendoza	By donation and/or sale to certain parties	Limited	Contributions solicited from specialists in fields
Neumann		Limited	
Planchart		Limited	

[a] The problem of distributing quality publications in Venezuela should be investigated, for it affects all sectors of national life. Such a study could help to improve the distribution of published matter.

[b] The limited availability of publications in Venezuela is due to the high cost of printing. This problem is compounded for the foundations by the high degree of specialization of their publications.

TABLE 3　Expositions

Characteristics	Boulton (1950-75) Museo John Boulton	Foundation/Location			
		Caribbean (1974-75)	Mendoza (1951-71) Galería Mendoza	Neumann (1966-71) Taller Fundación Neumann	Planchart (1970-75) Quinta "El Cerrito"
Type	Permanent		Temporary	Temporary	Permanent
Number	1		227		1
Native artists	4		74		
Foreign artists	8		44		
Native and foreign collectives			45		

TABLE 4 Budgets, in official Venezuelan currency

	Boulton 1972	Caribbean 1974	Foundation/Year of Study Mendoza 1970	Neumann 1972	Planchart 1974
Size of budget	500,000	35,000	2,781,660	2,200,000	
Amount assigned to culture	500,000	35,000	349,239	396,000	
% of budget assigned to culture	100	100	12	18	

The Caribbean and Boulton Foundations are almost exclusively dedicated to publication programs. Boulton is also concerned with archival activities and the
conservation of historical monuments. The other foundations have varied programs, of which culture is only one element.

and the public of the foundations' work and thus improve their image; and (4) provide a link with similar centers or institutions abroad and perhaps maintain a library of related foreign documents and periodicals.

Second, in order to promote a democratization of culture, human and financial resources should be channeled into a "popular culture" plan. This defense of the nation's folklore is the best expression of nationalism that the foundations could make, since nowhere is the spirit of a nation more faithfully reflected than in popular culture. In this way an ever greater proportion of the population could participate in development. The development of crafts and the staging of public exhibitions of folklore on an increasing scale are examples of how this objective could be achieved. Regional decentralization, incorporating the provinces systematically into cultural affairs, would be a key aspect of democratization efforts. These programs could be carried out in conjunction with folklore research institutes (such as INIFEDEC) or university-level cultural departments.

NOTES

1. Eloy Anzola Montauban, "El desarrollo de Venezuela en función de sus habitantes," mimeo.

2. "La Cultura en Función del Desarrollo," document prepared for the General Secretariat of the Organization of American States, Fifth Reunion of the Interamerican Cultural Council, p. 1.

3. General Report of the Conferencia Intergubernamental sobre los Aspectos Institucionales, Administrativos y Financieros de las Políticas Culturales, p. 11.

BIBLIOGRAPHY

Books and Articles

Aguilar Gorrondona, José Luis. Derecho Civil (Caracas: Universidad Católica Andrés Bello, 1968).

Calelo, Hugo. Apuntes de Metodología (Caracas, 1975).

Fundación Eugenio Mendoza. Informe General 1951-1971 (Caracas: Cromotip, 1972).

_____. Sala de Exposiciones 1956-Caracas/1966 (Caracas: Cromotip, 1966).

Fundación John Boulton. Boletín Histórico, no. 37
    (Caracas: Italgráfica, 1975).

_____. Museo Fundación John Boulton--La Guaira (Cara-
    cas: Italgráfica, 1974).

Harvey, Edwin. Apuntes de la Asignatura Estado y Cul-
    tura (Caracas, 1975).

Mendoza de López, Antonieta. Fundaciones de América
    Latina (Caracas: Fundación Eugenio Mendoza,
    Cromotip, 1974).

_____. Fundaciones Privadas de Venezuela (Caracas:
    Fundación Eugenio Mendoza, Cromotip, 1974).

Seminario Internacional de Ejecutivos. La Responsabili-
    dad Empresarial en el Progreso Social de Vene-
    zuela (Caracas: Cromotip, 1963).

Tarre Murzi, Alfredo. El Estado y la Cultura (Caracas:
    Monte Avila Editores, 1972).

Documents

Código Civil de la República de Venezuela.

Constitución Nacional de la República de Venezuela.

Fundación Consejo de Arte y Cultura de la Ciudad de
    Caracas. Ante Proyecto y Proyecto de los Estatutos
    y del Acta Constitutiva.

Fundación Creole. Acta Constitutiva y Estatutos.

Fundación del Caribe para la Ciencia y la Cultura.
    Estatutos.

Fundación de Museo Arte Moderno. Acta Constitutiva y
    Estatutos.

Fundación John Boulton. Informe General.

Fundación Neumann. Informe General.

Fundación Planchart. Estatutos y Acta Constitutiva.
    Informe sobre la Residencia Caraballeda.

Fundateatros. Estatutos.

Ley del Impuesto sobre la Renta de la República de
    Venezuela.

OEA. "La Cultura en Función del Desarrollo." Documento
      del Secretario General para la Quinta Reunión del
      Consejo Interamericano Cultural, Maracay.

_____. "Proyecto Multinacional de Desarrollo de
      Archivos."

UNESCO. "Declaración Universal de Derechos Humanos."

_____. "Document de travail rédigé par le secrétariat--
      les droits culturels."

_____. "Informe Final de la Conferencia Interguberna-
      mental sobre las Políticas Culturales en Asia,"
      Yogyarkarta, 1973.

_____. "Informe Final de la Conferencia Interguberna-
      mental sobre las Políticas Culturales en Europa,"
      Helsinki, 1972.

_____. "Informe Final de la Conferencia sobre los
      Aspectos Institucionales Administrativos y Finan-
      cieros de las Políticas Culturales," Venecia, 1970.

On the Instrumental Use of the Mass Media in America for Purposes of Dependence

Antonio Pasquali

THE LATIN AMERICAN LACK OF CULTURAL HARMONY AND ITS CAUSES

For many vital aspects of Latin American culture, time seems to have stopped and the cycle of renewal given way to the eternization of stereotypes. Some forms of knowledge and of the aesthetic reflection of reality meekly follow the cosmopolitan flux of changes. In areas such as architecture, literature, arts, painting, and music, Latin America exhibits examples of universal or regional dimension, which become indicators of vitality and unmistakable signs of constant renewal. In other, less exclusive areas, the cultural panorama appears to have stagnated or to be detained by endogenous and exogenous forces--being the same as that of five, ten, or twenty years ago. Nearly all forms of popular, social, and collective culture that allow for industrialization, control, or transculturization processes have fallen into stasis, certainly more rapidly than in other parts of the world. The system allows, with a certain liberal outlook, progress of minority and elite cultural forms and also those of scarce social incidence, while it practices intolerance and terrorism in its control of popular national cultures, of industrialized knowledge, and of public opinion. The products of the upper layer do not circulate through the base and do not exalt it; those of the lower stratum are not perceived and do not vitalize the upper layer. It is a contemporary and "cultured" version of the divide et impera. The diffidence induced towards the intellectual by the comic strip and by television ends in true distrust; the systematic putting in parentheses of aboriginal and popular manifestations culminates in actual scorn. The discontinuity between forms of culture has levels of normalcy and critical levels. In

Latin America it reaches pathological proportions. The
excessive lack of harmony between basic potential and
superior activity implies a profound separation between
society and the individual.

These propositions, verifiable by segments and by
sectors, would require a multidisciplinary sociodynamic
analysis of regional culture in order to prove them
definitively. They are the result of empirical evidence
that is found in no other part of the world. The Latin
American imbalance between university and illiteracy,
between cultural dynamics and stagnation, exhibits sui
generis aspects that do not allow useful comparisons
with any other Third World reality. A primary cause of
this imbalance resides in a profound dysfunction in
communications, massively induced by a culture indus-
try--mainly radioelectric--that is hypertrophied and
lacks competition; it is a true owner of consciences
and director of behavior. At least, that is the hypothesis that I will try to demonstrate in the following
pages--a hypothese which is highly irritating to politicians and economists (accustomed to viewing social
communications as only a tangential aspect of economics
or politics), but which in the end becomes the only
theoretical and practical alternative to the economic
fatalism and unpredictability of a position of "revolution or nothing."

For the reasons just stated, those who produce,
store, or spread higher culture in Latin America deserve
to declare themselves reasonably satisfied (just think
of the boom in literature and painting of the last
decades). But those who theorize or pretend to influence the structural and social aspects of culture--and
I dare say these constitute a majority--have numerous
reasons to renounce the self-gratifying creation of
culture and to dedicate themselves to the difficult
task of planning, establishing policies, and attaining
cultural reform or revolution in its most varied aspects.

Much more of the Latin American culture could be
comprehended if the following were understood: a critical and negative reason predominates in the culture, for
anthropological and political-cultural interests override the seductions of a positivistic illuminism that
is uncritical, progressive, and developmental. And at
this moment in history, its predominance constitutes
the best contribution of the region to its own cultural
identity and to all the processes of cultural liberation taking place in the world. If our cultural attitude could be measured up against the double register
proposed decades ago by Mannheim, "ideology" versus
"utopia"--that is, positive-conservative thinking

versus negative-renovating thinking--one would detect
a strong preponderance of the utopian, possibilistic,
ethical, negative, and Dionysian views over the ideological, realistic-pragmatic, positive, and Apollonian
visions. Latin America is today a major world stage on
which the dependence-independence dialectics is taking
place, and thus an important site for the confrontation
between the instrumental, illuministic, dominating
reasoning and the critical, ethically tense, and liber-
ationist reasoning. A large portion of the Latin culture lives of and in this tension, depending on the
degree to which it is understood. Evidence of a strong
rupture between higher cultures, which are individualistic and cosmopolitan, and national, popular cultures--
the two in expansion and stagnation, respectively--
points to the therapeutic intent of that new critical,
utopian, and ethical point of view, in which reside
Latin America's highest hopes.

THREE ANALYTICAL HYPOTHESES

     I have pointed out (1) that the strong lack of
harmony between the elitist higher culture and the
national popular cultures (forty years ago we would have
employed the Schelerian terminology of national "spirit"
and "soul") constitutes one of the most notorious characteristics of the actual Latin American cultural
sociodynamics; and (2) that the major cause for this
lack of harmony seems to reside in an atrophy or a real
communicational underdevelopment, which in a massive
way affects the base culture, keeping it stagnated and
isolated from the other, higher culture. Further, its
causes are not only of a geographical and technological
nature, but--above all--an economic, political, and
global-dependence nature.

     The first proposition is highly verifiable, thanks
to the contribution of abundant sociological and sociocultural literature. To verify the second proposition,
which includes an explicit causal relationship, I shall
only put forth here, in a synthetic manner, three hypotheses and a final example. The rest, unfortunately,
must await another occasion.

The Sociologically Essential Character of Communications

     Economic determinism tends to consider the com-
munication/information processes as far removed from
the modes and forms of production. The mistake, while
typical of industrial age mentalities, minimizes unconsciously or intentionally the sociopolitical importance
of communication and excludes the fact that it may have
its own essence, laws, and consequences. But in

sociological terms, communication is a sine qua non for
all social forms, in all its modes and manners (human
beings physically living together but lacking communication do not constitute even the smallest social
protostructure).

The Greek word koinoonía, which expresses both
"community" and "communication," reflects fully the inherent similarity between the two concepts and functions.
The main corollary of this proposition is that the
modes, controls, and changes in the social communication processes are also the modes, controls, and
changes in the processes of community and coexistence.
In essential terms (as well as for subsequent functional
and practical needs), communication must be understood
as a basic, structural ingredient for living side by
side, since it denotes the real essence of living in a
community: the knowledge of one another. For this
reason the term should have its intrinsic, strong political sense restored to it. The platonic utopia of a
pacific coexistence, the hedonistic goal of a worldly
happiness, or the Kantian world of a perpetual peace--
all are based on a truly fulfilled and tranquil communication, free of competition, full of dialogue, complementarity, openness, and collaboration. The warlike
Hobbesian, repressive (socially and individually), and
isolating character of Western competitiveness has been
brilliantly analyzed--in this century--by the Frankfurt
philosophers, who pointed out that the authoritarianism
and the use of the other as an instrument was the result of a communicational maladjustment in the authoritarian's personality. In regions of the world--such as
Latin America--in which mass culture undergoes incredible distortions through the work of perverted and institutionalized communications authorities, the research
expert is shown the most acute pathological situations.
It allows him to recognize, by way of negatives, the
state of "well-being" of communications: that which it
should be and is not yet. It provides a frame of empirical references that intensify the relation between
communications and power; it supplies the best evidence
for the need to reject a satisfied positivism, which
accepts only what is and takes it as good.

The Result of the Expansion of Communication/Information:
A Qualitative Leap

If communication (bilateral, anthropological) and
information (unilateral, cybernetic) processes are inherent to the sociopolitical dimension, these processes
are not essentially propagandist or merchandising-
advertising phenomena, or privileged instruments of a
culture industry, or catalysts to economic process, or
forms of tertiary activity or services, or uncritical

stimulators of development and modernization--even
though in fact, and especially in many Latin American
countries, they do not serve any other purposes. As a
matter of fact, nearly all the communication and information technology has been and is being used with the
intent of domination and in spite of a gross lack of
knowledge of its own laws, its social consequences, and
its autonomous growth. Ever since the time of Socrates,
we have known that the existence or possession of an
instrument is not in itself bad; rather its use or misuse must be judged. Further, the neutrality intrinsic
to the instrument, once it is converted into an extension of a human capacity, will not necessarily remain.

In one of the most important documents written on
this topic in the last few years, Social Implications
of Computers/Telecommunication Systems (1975), author
A. B. Parker of Stanford points out the advent of an
"information society" as the only possible outcome of
the postindustrial era: in an advanced country, such
as the United States, the number of people employed in
the field of communications/information is higher than
the number of employees in the primary, secondary, and
tertiary sectors all together. (According to author
Parker, the P.T.E. evidence and statistics of personal
consumption for information goods demonstrate the predominance that these activities have reached in this
era.)

Assuming, with a certain probability, that this
societal form is extending rapidly--by imposition or by
spontaneous and transideological tendency--we may antic-
ipate many very important consequences, five of which
deserve mention.
1. If, in fact, the communication/information proces-
    ses have reached or are reaching the predominant
    dimensions described by Parker, then the centers of
    power, of authority, and of decision-making capacity
    are being displaced from their traditional poles
    (political, religious, industrial) and relocated in
    the new communication and information oligarchies.
2. This new "quaternary sector" of communication/
    information will tend necessarily to produce even
    more value added than the traditional third sector,
    which will always lack significant support in
    matter-energy, and the former will eventually accu-
    mulate more value added than any agricultural-
    extractive or industrial society ever dreamed of.
3. In geopolitical terms, it will generate an enormous
    concentration of real power within privileged
    societies, subduing even more the national economies
    dedicated to primary and secondary activities and
    reducing, perhaps even to an agent-patient relation-
    ship, the weak dialectics between development and

underdevelopment (therefore, relative national
autonomy in matters of communication/information
seems indispensable).

4. The quantitative expansion of communication/infor-
mation generates per se a qualitative leap from
competitiveness to sociability, but this intrinsic
spontaneity is distorted by the old authoritarian
forms. An economic, thus old-fashioned, control of
the new fourth sector will repress indefinitely its
essentially social and noncompetitive purpose. And
this perversion will be more dramatic on the periphery of systems, in developing countries that more
urgently need to socialize and remove from private
ownership their communication/information systems.

5. Information processes (telecommunications, computer-
ization, data storage, automation in production, and
so on) and communication processes (social communication media) should be studied separately and
should receive different treatments, a project that
might constitute the refinement of one of Parker's
theories. In dependent regions, for instance, an
atrophy in the capacity to inform can be easily detected. Also obvious is a contemporary infrastructural abnormal hypertrophy in mass media, which is
artificially induced by competitive, highly com-
mercialized systems, and results in disintegration,
deepening of class differences, and lack of interest
for national necessities (a case of extreme technological hypertrophy producing its opposite).

In summary, the analysis of our sociocultural
reality in terms of communication/information reveals
that, in the same way as industrial concentration nuclei
coexist in Latin America with preindustrialized poles
and large, marginal areas (even existing within the
same urban zone), there also coexists an evident lack
of information, typical of basic underdevelopment, with
an abnormally large development of social communications. The latter is more typical of a developed
"information society." But in this case it has been
imposed with the intention of achieving social, economic,
and political control and generates the already mentioned lack of coordination and rhythm between the forms
of culture.

The Law of Centrifugal Acceleration of Cultural Contamination

Students of media and development are working on
the theoretical and empirical foundation of a possible
new law of cultural sociodynamics, destined to explain
and measure situations of dependence within conditions
of underdevelopment: the law of centrifugal acceleration of cultural contamination.

Its premise would be the following. Given the near nonexistence of national groups that are culturally autarchic or self-sufficient in this technological era of simultaneous communication (within the civilized world), cultural dynamics on a worldwide scale seems to work as a system of high and low pressure in rapid exchange: the low cultural pressure zones tend to be rapidly "occupied" by high pressure systems. This is the end of the meteorological metaphor, because these "occupations" do not seem to be simple and spontaneous self-regulating mechanisms like those of the socio-cultural organism, which tend to restore an original balance. On the contrary, and based on a certain principle of "cultural ecology," a strong tendency to accumulate the waste products of the "high" zones in the "low" cultural identity zones, seems to be present, in the same way that this happens in industrial and commercial systems. The expansion of the capacity for communication/information causes the once peaceful and slow processes of cultural dissemination to become an instrument generating compulsive and controllable transculturizations (from which the functional principles can be detected).

In this respect our law would predict two outcomes: first, any culturally underdeveloped region with sufficient capacity for receiving and decodifying messages becomes the satellite of a more culturally dense development pole; and second, between both poles a process of centrifugal acceleration is generated, which tends to accumulate the waste and the most contaminated elements of the metropolitan cultural production precisely in the marginal periphery. The acceleration of the process is directly related to the cultural "distance." Lack of active or passive resistance, of "antibodies," or of suitable alternative in the periphery will facilitate and institutionalize these transculturization phenomena; in the end, fixed cultural-ideological-political processes of dependence result. Local "collaborators," acting as spontaneous or conscious agents of dependence, nearly always being more inflexible than the rulers themselves, collaborate in the final acceptance of the process.

This causal-centrifugal relationship from center to periphery is not, of course, the result of the industrial or information era, and one could find many historical examples of it in politics, law, historical philology, religion, arts, and economics. There have always existed a Palais de Justice and its Cayenne, a clever salesman and a naive buyer of terra incognita. However, this era of pragmatic rationalization and exponential growth, especially in communication/information, has enlarged the phenomenon, making it clearer.

If we were to consider, for instance, that a large
part of Latin America is today being made into a cultural satellite by the United States, and if we
attempt to apply this law to our social communication
panorama, we would at once find confirming evidence.
Latin America acutely lacks national and regional information systems (particularly in telecommunications
and data banks), thus preparing the way for a less re-
versible dependence than all previous ones. However,
the U.S.-inspired modernism, development, and diffusion
have installed in our peripheral region the powerful,
useless, and redundant "hardware" of mass communication,
nearly as costly as those systems of more highly developed countries, but scarcely contributing to specific
social or independent purposes.

The best known example of this situation is our
low-class huts and favelas showing television antennas;
however, here I propose another: our satellite-tracking
stations. Except for advantages in the field of telephone communications, these stations are to us the monuments to modernism and dependence, real-life monsters
with enormous ears, voiceless accelerators of serfdom.
In short, they represent examples of how an advanced
technology can act against true development and against
humans living together in equality. Our tracking stations broadcast a few minutes yearly, but they track
for thousands of hours; to make the situation worse,
each of our countries has to pay its own fee to the con-
sortium for the same program, since we do not possess
an interconnecting land microwave system. (In Europe,
for instance, one single station tracks and broadcasts
to the whole continental net.)

Regarding the accumulation in the Latin American
periphery of the most contaminating elements of the
metropolitan cultural industry, this aspect is barely
starting to be studied and measured in depth, but already there exist some elements on which to pass judgment. In television, where this phenomenon is more
visible, one could point not only to the process by
which competitive Latin American systems become economic
satellites of the competitive North American macrosystem,
but also to the larger peripheral contamination by way
of programming.

According to Nordenstrend and Varis ("La T.V.
circule-t-elle a sens unique?", Etudes UNESCO, no. 70
[1974]), our region has only 3 percent of all television
sets installed in the world, but receives approximately
35 percent of all North American programming exports,
that is, nearly 150,000 hours a year. This means that,
on an average, 45 percent of all regional programming
is North American. However, in Venezuela, for instance,

this percentage was higher, 52 percent as an average,
for many years (now this percentage has been partially
reduced by native soap operas); and the broadcasting of
commercials (1,313 as a daily average) was 61 percent
higher than the North American standard of advertising
on television. Naturally, the above-mentioned 45 percent of the imported programs represents, without a
shadow of doubt, the worst of North American production,
without any educational or cultural content, but merely
programming that entertains the most and sells the
easiest. What is the content of all this cheap programming? A psychologist from the Universidad Central de
Venezuela, Eduardo Santoro, researched the formation of
stereotypes induced by imported programming in children.
Among his findings of the remains of "centrifugal acceleration" were the following: (1) 63 percent of children
had absorbed foreign-language terms; (2) 86 percent of
children believed that the hero is a North American--or
82 percent believed he was at least English-speaking;
(3) only one in eighteen thought of the Chinese as good,
instead of bad; (4) the white man was considered better
than the black by eleven out of twelve children; (4)
the rich man was thought of as the "good guy" by 72
percent of children, the poor man as the "bad guy" by
41 percent.

THE PROGRESSION FROM ANALYTICAL PRINCIPLE TO CONCRETE
EXAMPLES

     The communication/information network is not a by-
product of the forms of production, but rather an essential element in the formation of the community and the
human political dimension. For this reason, its expansion or limitation favors or blocks an open and pacific
coexistence. In this case, it is the organ's function
that makes the organ what it is: the form and structure
of sociability derive from modes of communications with
the other.

     Quantitative growth of communication/information
has created a fourth sector predominant within the context of contemporary economics. This sector should
favor a spontaneous qualitative leap toward bilateral-
ism, cooperation, and sociability, but instead has
served to generate new concentrations of economic power,
or, simply, of power. Contemporary culture is intimately tied to communication processes, especially in underdeveloped regions. From a commercial, competitive, and
authoritarian use of communication/information power
derives a compulsive instrumentalization of culture
subject to a conservative ideology in which the mass
communication media act as a ruler's voice.

A unitary system originates between areas of high
and low cultural density, in which the former make
satellites of the latter, and within which system a law
of centrifugal acceleration operates, accumulating the
most contaminating messages and cultural products in
the periphery of such a system. This process, adequately induced and instrumentalized, turns underdevelopment
into dependence.

The three above mentioned concepts intend to be
only criteria or hypotheses (nonexclusive, of course) to
reach an analytical diagnosis of one of the most important and perverted aspects of Latin American culture:
social communications.

It could be argued, with certain justification,
that a methodological error is present in this work,
considering that such analytic criteria should have been
preceded by something similar to a descriptive diagnosis, which would allow the detection of congruence between the proposed analysis and reality. Such a diagnosis was not established because of the complexity of
such a description and because of the author's incom-
petence in covering so vast a subject. However, the
following description of two situations may give a concrete idea of the Latin American communicational panorama, of its influence on culture and the quality of
living together, and of the state of dependence in
which the region is maintained.

A REGIONAL CASE: LATIN AMERICAN BROADCASTING

Latin America is the only region in the world in
which broadcasting is almost totally controlled by private interprise, though many nations in the area pre-
serve it de jure for the public sector. (For instance,
among thirty countries with private, commercial television, two of them are found in North America, two in
Europe, nine in Asia and the South Pacific, one in
Africa, and sixteen in Latin America, this being the
only region, moreover, in which eight countries have
exclusively private television systems.) This is the
first important fact to bear in mind for the analysis
of implications between property and use of these media,
since public property tends to generate complementary
systems, while private property produces competitive
systems.

Do Latin Americans have the best television in
the world and, above all, the freest television, as
asserted by the slogans coming from interested parties?
My considered response is that Latin American broadcasting, on the whole, is one of the worst and most

useless--if not the worst--in the world, precisely because of its uncontrolled competitive character within
a commercial and private context. The system here is
inflexible--does not produce "antibodies"--and has created nothing resembling, for example, North American
NET.

Some of our countries appear in international
yearbooks as "mixed regimes." In the best case, such
regimes are fictions of a mix created by governments
when they establish a few weak stations which, through
so-called cultural programs, actually help the massive
and pervasive consumer-oriented output of private
broadcasting. One statistic and one episode will suf-
fice to corroborate the inauthenticity of the formula.
In Venezuelan radio broadcasting, private broadcasting
power is sixty-five times that of the public sector
(see Comisión Preparatoria del Consejo Nacional de la
Cultura, Proyecto RATELVE [Caracas, June 1975]). In
June 1974 part of the population of Recife, Brazil, was
not aware of the catastrophic inundations in the city
because the two commercial television networks, with
practically the total audience, decided not to inter-
rupt the broadcasting of their soap operas to announce
the emergency (see Rev. Veja, no. 366 [September 10,
1975]).

Latin American broadcasting, so uniform and internationally organized, stands as the supreme model for
the private radio and television industry acting without practically any constraints, without self-criticism,
or, in the words of Horkheimer and Adorno, in unbridled
positivism, unable to self-negate or self-constrain.
In an illiterate continent--with a low schooling rate,
sanitary problems, unequal wealth distribution and increasing poverty, exponential and ungoverned population
growth, underdevelopment in secondary and tertiary
sectors, and a depressing lack of cultural initiatives--
the programming pattern in broadcasting offers (with
minimal variation) the distribution shown in table 1.
Because of its exploitation and coverage criteria
(coverage is an excellent indicator), this kind of
broadcasting contributes to social disaggregation and
classism, contrary to national efforts to balance,
demographically and economically, the rural and the urban zones. Broadcasting is concentrated upon densely
populated areas where the largest purchasing power is
located, not offering service to territorially segre-
gated areas. In 1975--with the sole exception of
Cuba--no Latin American country had total coverage in
radio or television. In Venezuela, which can be considered the average case, radio had a theoretical
coverage of 84 percent of the population, while television purported to have 59 percent.

TABLE 1   Programming in Latin American Broadcasting

	Light music (chiefly imported from abroad)	Advertising	Live programs (mainly soap operas and news)
Radio	60-75%	20-38%	5-20%
	Movies and canned programs (chiefly imported from abroad)	Advertising	Live programs (mainly soap operas and news)
Tele-vision	40-55%	17-35%	15-25%

The programming pattern exacerbates the competitive system's trend to broadcast "omnibus" programs--accessible to every audience--neglecting real broadcasting needs of the various sociocultural strata in the population. This is due to the profit motive on the part of each station, everyone striving to reach the entire audience. Actually, so-called programming--practically identical in every station, even to similar time schedules--is just a musical or soap opera packaging for the easier introduction of the real message: advertising. Thus, Latin American broadcasting programs for the lowest social classes and, in any case, for an audience with almost infantile intelligence and sensitivity. The audience is reduced to the role of buyers, stimulated by a gigantic "banalization" process from which no one seems able to escape. (According to recent data, 45 percent of the Venezuelan audience for soap operas is composed of males from eighteen to forty-five years old.) The soap opera is the last successful invention of Latin American broadcasting to conceal reality, and its popularity is reaching almost irrational proportions in the whole continent, while any of the topics that could affect the advertisers' interests--even when they are of the highest social concern--are unnameable taboos. We know that in other competitive, nonperipheral systems, that is not true: you can advertise alcoholic beverages and broadcast a program on liver cirrhosis. In Latin America, such liberality is not allowed. That sort of broadcasting desocializes and sets apart the members of the human group, because it systematically avoids treating problems of the local or national community, at the same time neglecting priorities of development and limiting itself to inducing in every individual a personal dream of fictitious and intentionally stereotyped worlds. To be sure, the complex and delicate process of nationalization of steel and oil industries in Venezuela--which

required and requires strong moral commitment on the
part of the citizens--did not receive the slightest
support from local stations, which practically ignored
it.

Because of its economic power, because of its
tendency to engulf the remaining leisure activities in
a region with few alternatives, because of its abusive
accumulation of authority, Latin American broadcasting--
as the privileged branch of the culture and advertising
industries--exhibits today such a power and such an
arrogance that even political forces yield to it sometimes, not to mention the forces of cultural resistance.
It has been estimated that in Latin America $10 million
are invested daily in advertising, 60 percent of which
are channeled through radio and television. Of the
same $10 million, 60 percent, again, has originated in
North American and European multinational corporations.
Since broadcasting is in Latin America undoubtedly the
privileged channel--sometimes the only one--of popular
culture, one can infer that the only culture that is
massively distributed in the region is controlled by
the merchants and the ideologues of high consumption.
This, in turn, implies that the real ministries of our
popular culture are the advertisers (65 percent foreign)
and the advertising agencies (76 percent foreign--data
from Venezuela).

The national collaborators in this desocializing,
antinational, degrading, and consumer-oriented activity
are the private broadcasters, with or without the presence of foreign investment. (New regulations prohibit-
ing foreign capital in private broadcasting in Venezuela
did not produce _any_ changes in program content.) These
commercial broadcasting stations, controlling the only
significant part of radio and television in the sub-
continent, are affiliated to the Inter-American Association of Broadcasting (IAAB or AIR), which in article 1,
paragraph B, of its bylaws proclaims, "Commercial
broadcasting must be private and does not constitute a
public service." Their fidelity to this slogan--which
sounds today like a social and cultural catastrophe--
is immovable. In one of the resolutions of their
Twelfth General Ordinary Assembly (Montevideo, March 5,
1975), they approved the following self-explanatory
formulas:

> 6. that broadcasting . . . can only continue
>   to be useful and beneficial to the peoples
>   while depending upon private entities, spon-
>   taneous representatives of popular opin-
>   ion. . . .
> 7. that imposition by the State of programs of
>   a nationalist sort, besides implying

dangerous limitations, is against desirable competition in the media and constitutes an attempt against culture which
is and must be universal. (See C.L.E./XII
A.G.O./E.I.)

Fortunately, declarations in such a tone do not
pass with impunity today within a region where the contradiction between private broadcasting and social needs
is clearly recognized. For at least fifteen years,
sociocultural problems have been submitted to an increasingly defined planning process. Nowadays, there
are conscious sectors in practically every Latin American government--regardless of its political inclina-
tions--that are aware of the total lack of social
function on the part of broadcasters in the country and
also of the need to subject broadcasting to criteria of
concerted action.

Frustrated or reduced to isolated episodes,
"Teleducación," which only a decade ago seemed to be the
panacea for the most urgent regional needs, has become
a chimera (only project SERLA remains, still unapproved
by the regional governments). The glance of relevant
and mature planners now falls on the optimal and total
goal of issuing new national communication policies,
intended to rationalize media use in favor of maximum
social freedom and to adapt it to development priorities and the accelerated solution of the most pressing
needs (schooling, agriculture, community development,
population, health, and so on). Almost every Latin
American government foresees--though with different
degrees of clarity--the need to destroy the costly and
frustrating "Penelope's cloth" that is made by the
momentous educational and liberating public effort and
then unmade by the antieducation and colonization of
private broadcasting. Studies are being made--and
steps are being taken or planned--to remedy that situation in countries such as Argentina, Peru, Brazil,
Ecuador, Colombia, Venezuela, Costa Rica, and Mexico.

The most significant episode occurred when, in
November 1974, all the countries in the region solicited
from the Eighteenth UNESCO General Assembly (see resolution 4121) the promotion of an Inter-Governmental Conference on Communications Policies in Latin America,
getting its approval for 1975. (A similar one was
approved for Asia for 1977.) The aforementioned conference, thoroughly prepared with a conspicuous mass of
documents and thorough sectorial meetings, was not held
in 1975 for unknown reasons, though everyone hoped that
it would be held early in 1976. But it is indeed
known that the U.S. delegation was the only one to vote
in March 1975 for a proposal that practically eliminated

the Sub-General Direction of Communications of UNESCO, which was the department preparing the conference. It is also known that IAAB discussed the issue in its Montevideo meeting, protesting to UNESCO against the publishing of certain studies. (The Nordenstrend and Varis monograph, cited above, was considered a "war declaration.") At the same time the Interamerican Press Society (IPS) protested against a preliminary UNESCO meeting--scheduled for Quito in July 1975--in which the need to create national and regional news agencies for Latin America was discussed. (All the information concerning OPEC that is published in Venezuelan newspapers comes from agencies located in importing countries.)

This changing scenery, that fortunately leaves old immobilism behind, is bringing to light previously ignored facts. More and more Latin Americans are now aware that within the region--that fortress of private radioelectric enterprise--forty years of radio and twenty of television have demonstrated total incapacity of self-regulation and regeneration on the part of the private culture industry (in spite of innumerable "ethics codes"). They are also aware of the implications of continuing Latin American toleration and foreign subvention of an underdeveloped, polluting, and antinationalist broadcasting.

Each day, more and more people recognize the fallacious nature of self-conservation slogans proclaimed by broadcasters: those of the freedom of expression, the free flow of information, the so-called and somewhat obscene identification of democracy and advertising. Regional research on the effects of local broadcasting leave no room for intermediate or moderate stances. All "freedom of information" is concentrated within the oligarchic elites of information, contrasting with the social right to be informed; there is "free flow" only in a nonreversible direction going from the informer to the receptor; "democracy," as the free interplay of public opinion, is reduced to a mass opinion authoritatively manipulated with the help of imported engineering.

Fortunately, the increasingly tense relationship between the private culture industry and public planners is making evident a fact of the highest strategic relevance for the near future: the culture industry has wielded and will wield whatever weapons are necessary to maintain public broadcasting in underdevelopment. Lacking other alternatives, it sees in broadcasting the only potential for offering complementary services of real social interest in Latin America.

The meeting of Latin American governments for new
policies of communication would be the first of its
kind on the continent; hence arise its importance and
the opposition it has encountered among those who still
prefer the policy of not having policies. But the
trend to planning in communication and the tendency to
concerted action between broadcasting and public interest seem already irreversible in Latin America.

A NATIONAL CASE HISTORY: THE VENEZUELAN CONAC AND THE
RATELVE PROJECT

In July 1973, the political party Acción Democrática organized in Caracas a seminar of party members
and independents on problems concerning national culture, with the purpose of obtaining diagnoses and recommendations for a future cultural policy. During the
closing session of this seminar, Acción Democráticas's
candidate for President at that time, Carlos Andrés
Pérez, promised that should he be elected President,
his government would replace the existing inefficient
Instituto Nacional de Cultura y Bellas Artes (National
Institute for Culture and Fine Arts)--INCIBA--by a
National Council for Culture (CONAC), making the power
of cultural decision more democratic and providing it
with sufficient resources. Pérez emphasized that a
greater economic independence should be accompanied by
a greater power for self-determination (not autarchy)
in the ideological and cultural realms.

After the electoral victory of Acción Democrática,
the executive power created, in March 1974 by decree
number 18, the Committee for the Organization of CONAC.
Made up of twenty-five members of different political
trends, it was assigned the duty of preparing the bill
that would eventually create the council. This committee fulfilled its plan by July 1974; and in October 1974,
by decree number 491, the Executive named a Preparatory
Committee of eleven members, with the task of studying
the record of INCIBA, carrying out the corresponding
sectorial investigations, and contributing concrete
propositions for the new cultural policy. One of the
twenty investigations eventually presented specifically
covered the sector of radio and television; sixteen
communication specialists, high public officials from
the information sectors, representatives from universities, church officials, members of the armed forces,
and union leaders took part in this investigation.

The law creating the National Council for Culture
was finally passed by Congress in the first few days of
August 1975, and on August 29, 1975, it received executive approval and was published in the Official Gazette,

the same day that the oil nationalization act was passed. (I mention this act of carrying out promises made during an electoral campaign in order to point out, as an example to learn from, all the violent debates that occurred from its hopeful beginnings to its happy conclusion--debates that have been even more violent than those over the oil nationalization bill.)

In June 1975, when final debates started in Congress over the proposed bill, the Venezuelan Chamber of Radio and the Venezuelan Chamber of Television (the two unions split years ago due to internal strife) initiated a strong, well-organized public campaign against the proposed bill. Precise instructions were given to all the commercial television and radio stations: commercials against the CONAC were broadcast every five minutes; a special noontime program was sponsored by the two chambers, incorporating all the country's networks; several leaders, showmen, and popular television actors were mobilized to send out measages such as "Mothers, CONAC will forbid you to send your children to the schools of your choice" or "Young people, CONAC will take away your folklore, your radio and television." These messages and programs turned back the clock to the worst times of McCarthyism. The state, the message said, was preparing a law that would bring all mass media under its control; Soviet agents had infiltrated the presidential committees; the bill being discussed was a dictatorial instrument designed to bring an end to all democratic and republican freedom, of which these chambers were champions and defenders. A week later, these chambers were able to incorporate into their campaign a section of the Press Block, an organization that brings together all the printed publications in the country, and the attack assumed hysterical characteristics against individuals.

At the same time, these same chambers faithfully--following the resolutions reached at Montevideo--initiated an impressive series of conversations with congressmen, members of the cabinet, and the President himself. (A few months before, the advertising industry had obtained the overruling of a government effort to tax selectively the advertising of luxury goods.) At the beginning of their efforts, the chambers bitterly opposed many aspects of the bill, among them provision f, article 3, which holds the state responsible for "avoiding contrary and dependence effects which certain transculturization processes might engender." However, in realizing that their purpose would be easily identified by this attack, the chambers concentrated all the efforts against article 4, which stated:

In order that the State may guarantee the most
adequate public cultural services, all areas
relating to the following shall be considered
of priority interest: production; specialized
studies; promotion; research; increase, conservation, diffusion and enjoyment of painting
and sculpture, music, theater, dance and of
architectural, historical and anthropological
patrimonies; printing of cultural messages;
radio-electric and cinematographic messages.

According to private enterprise, this article was dia-
bolically destined to suppress freedom of expression in
Venezuela; in truth, it was trying to ensure, by stating
it as part of a law, the obligation of the state to
guarantee cultural services adequate to social needs.
If there had been any intent on the part of the committee drafting the bill to establish state control of the
culture industry, all that would have been necessary
would have been to transcribe the existing 1940 law and
1941 regulation, which state, "The establishment and
operation of all communication systems shall correspond
exclusively to the State. Radioelectric services shall
be under exclusive control of the State."

Private enterprise knew perfectly well that there
was no interventionist intent in this article, but it
was hoping to achieve two very definite purposes, which
I will cite for regional interest:
1. To blackmail political parties, including the one
   in power, with the implicit threat that if the
   status quo of broadcasting were in any way altered,
   there would be no microphones and cameras available
   to them for the next electoral campaign;
2. To destroy the sectorial report of CONAC (hardly
   ever mentioned by them) entitled "Design for a New
   Policy of Broadcasting for the Venezuelan Nation:
   The RATELVE Project." This project also does not
   suggest any kind of state control: the project
   studies it as one of four alternatives and reasonably discards it, proposing instead the establishment in Venezuela of an "authentic mixed system"
   that can offer the country a truly free selection
   between competitive private services and complementary public services.

These were the real reasons--in the opinion of the
best observers--that motivated the violent reaction of
the broadcasters, who in the end were able to modify
(insignificantly, in my opinion) article 4. However,
this incident serves to show, at least in Venezuela,
that the private broadcasting industry is willing to
carry out the worst abuses in order to maintain public
broadcasting in a condition of underdevelopment. (I

insist that public broadcasting is the only possible
alternative for Latin America, seeing the self-
regenerating incapacity shown by private enterprise.)
By assuming such attitudes, private enterprise is rejecting one of its own principles--that of free competi-
tion--and is stopping a true competitor from forcing it
to improve the quality of its program in order to maintain its audience. Analogous episodes have taken place
in Costa Rica' in order to discourage the government's
intention to improve broadcasting, while in Argentina
the broadcasting enterprises, in a joint effort with
the advertising sector, created an artificial reduction
in advertising expenditure in order to simulate an
economic recession and stop the nationalization of private television (a step later taken, anyhow). A few
years ago, in Venezuela, foreign film distributors, by
using similar practices, stopped the introduction to
Congress of a bill regulating the film industry by
moderately protecting local production and imposing
mandatory showing of national films (a measure adopted
by most countries).

What the cultural private broadcasting industry is
defending, in short, is a $100-million enterprise (in
a country of 12 million people), for which purpose it
needs to conserve monopolistic positions and obtain
legal support. These two incidents (or perhaps one two-
dimensional incident) can give an idea of how the mass-
culture manipulating system acts in Latin America, what
kind of dependence it establishes, and what difficulties
are confronted by anyone attempting to suggest changes,
even though these may be sensible and realistic.

Commercial broadcasting is the most penetrating
mass medium in this continent (indexes of all other
leisure-time activities are on the decline in most of
our countries); therefore, commercial broadcasting is
the strongest collaborator in the twofold process of
maintaining underdevelopment and converting it into
cultural dependence. The quality of coexistence between
individuals being profoundly conditioned by commercial
"hard sell" and by an incessant transculturization that
offers no alternatives; the undesirable accumulation of
authority in the local communication oligarchies per-
verting the power principle; the aid that such a system
gives to the mental dependence of peripheral areas and
to their accelerated cultural contamination--all these
conditions must be studied in depth in order to propose
several new policies that are truly adapted to real
social needs and do not merely offer disjointed, self-
defeating palliatives.

No more difficult task exists than that of demoti-
vating a previously conditioned and satisfied society

(Ulysses' companions, having been turned into pigs by
Circe, wish to continue receiving food suitable for animals; and the slaves in the Platonic cave try to kill
the bearer of truth). However, we have slowly learned
some things: to reject the seductions presented by
positivism and functionalism and to hold as false many
results of surveys and group dynamics, since communicational truth is far beyond preconditioned indexes. We
have also learned the futility of scapegoats, as this
only promotes further the unconscious complicity between victim and executioner.

I feel that the knowledge of being dependent and
acting as satellites does not confer upon us rights to
blame the contaminating metropolis for all our evils.
It is up to only ourselves to recover cultural dignity;
no one will help us, and all we can demand is respect
and no intervention as we seek our decisions.

Hierarchy and Equality:
A Structural Study of Two Carnivals

Roberto da Matta

INTRODUCTION

The goal of this paper is to analyze carnivals in
Brazil and the United States, concentrating on the Rio
de Janeiro and New Orleans carnivals in particular, as
important and revealing examples of ritual in complex
industrial societies. Comparisons of Brazil and the
United States are common, but usually focus on such
critical aspects of the societies as the political system, the constitution, the economy, and, above all,
their race relations. Here I intend to evaluate the
Brazilian and American carnivals in terms of what they
can reveal about social structure in these countries.
It is my opinion that these domains, generally considered less serious or even irrelevant by historians and
sociologists, are extremely revealing, for reasons I
shall explain.

To take an anthropological perspective on this subject implies that one must pay a good deal of attention
to seemingly unimportant aspects. Thus, rather than
study the history of the two carnivals, I shall focus
much more on their different usages of language and the
ways in which each society sets up its "disorder zone."
Likewise, I shall ignore statistical information in
favor of ideological aspects. And, finally, my comparison is based not on types, but on structural principles.
With this perspective I wish to distinguish a typological and/or functional analysis, in which the researcher
carefully compares things that he judges to be similar,
from an analysis based on contrast and opposition.
Typological or functional analysis would allow us to
compare the Rio carnival only with those of Trinidad
and the Dominican Republic. But seeking out structural
principles makes possible a comparison of carnivals in

Rio and New Orleans precisely because contrast is
involved.

CARNAVAL AND CARNIVAL

Comparison of the Rio and New Orleans carnivals
begins with an introduction to the categories by which
they may be analyzed. First, a few general points,
deriving from the American system of classification:

1. In Brazil as well as in the United States,
social events may be classified according to their
degree of predictability, to the extent to which they
are more or less part of a continuum of daily life, seen
as a routine. The word routine is appropriate to our
study because it denotes procedures, rules, "a sequence
of acts or procedures observed by force of habit"
(according to the Novo Dicionário da Língua Portuguesa).
In fact, it is enough to remove oneself from one's own
routine to become painfully aware of it, like a fish
out of water, running the risk of under- or over-
estimating what happens upon one's return to the former
situation. In other words, to step out of one's routine generates a ritualized attitude toward the world,
because one becomes suddenly so conscious that even the
purchase of a pack of cigarettes or a polite "excuse
me" becomes a difficult and risky undertaking. In the
same way, in a society different from ours, we become
conscious of the "good and normal order of things."

Thus, routines are part and parcel of the normal
world. In American and Brazilian culture, routines are
quite distinct from accidents, natural disasters, and
carnivals. Moreover, festivals, carnivals, ceremonies,
rites, and rituals are removed from daily routine in
more diverse ways than are accidents and natural disasters. Accident and disaster areas are places where
habits and normal procedures are suspended. But they
differ from festivals, rituals, rites, ceremonies,
conferences, and so forth in that the latter events are
planned, even though they are out of the ordinary. The
old definition of rite is a formula, a rule, a correct
way of doing things (see Fustel de Coulanges, 1945,
book 3, chap. 8). There is, therefore, a continuum
from routine to rite, for rites can be seen as mechanisms that serve to "tune up" daily routines. While a
routine is a habitual sequence of acts, a ritual is a
conscious, special sequence. But both are clearly
fundamental and useful in the social order. I shall
return to this theme later in this discussion. Meanwhile, I present two categories into which social events
generally may be divided: (1) those in which the unusual is constructed by society in a planned way, such

as ceremonies, festivals, rituals, and carnivals; and
(2) those in which the unusual escapes society's control
and which society is always trying to "resolve" or
"restrict."

2. Even though these notions may be taken as true
in general for both societies (Brazil and the United
States), the carnival is a special exception. In Brazil, carnaval has a special position in the realm of
the extraordinary. This realm consists of two opposing
subdivisions, ceremonies and solemnities on the one
hand and parties or festivals on the other. (I lack
corresponding information about the United States.) In
the first type of event, everything is formal--that is,
highly segregated--while in the second, everything is
informal and the emphasis is on social reunion and encounter. Formal events place different routines in a
certain hierarchy, reinforce them, and always require
the presence of an authority figure (civil, military,
or ecclesiastical) to legitimize the ritual. Moreover,
they are occasions in which Brazilian society tries
to universalize itself. The authorities present are
carefully distinguished, one from the other, according
to their position within a hierarchy that goes from the
most powerful and important to the least powerful and
important, with very elaborate steps in between. Thus,
according to the Brazilian ideology, each person has a
part in the ceremony.

In Brazil this is especially true in graduation
ceremonies. These events generally assume a formal
segregation according to the following types of person-
ages: (1) civil authorities who give conventional
civic speeches; (2) military and ecclesiastical authorities allied with the civil authorities and lending their
power and prestige to legitimize the occasion; (3) young
graduates who deliver fiery, stylized speeches; (4)
spectators who attend the drama, applauding the good
scenes--as though attending the theater--and sharing
definite expectations about each actor. At the end of
the ceremony, all the different groups mingle and congratulations are exchanged, the ritual having served as
a legitimate arena for the airing of radical opinions
in an atmosphere of tolerance and neutrality, much like
in parliaments and courts of justice.

Thus, in formal events there is opportunity for
encounter, but the emphasis is placed on the different
lines of power (and hierarchy) of society. The central
mechanism is <u>reinforcement</u> and the most salient social
principle is hierarchy, although the majority of rituals
try to show that each person has a place in society.
In fact, the very essence of a society is based on the
hierarchy and complmentarity of groups, persons, and
social positions (see Dumont, 1970).

Informal special events, of which carnaval is one,
are classified as parties. Parties or festivals in
Brazil provide contexts and places in which people play.
This is a complex category that merits explanation.
People play not in the sense of participating in a game
in which someone wins, but rather in the sense of
brincar (from the Latin vinculu), which connotes opening oneself up to others, that is, the original notion
of establishing a link with others and of crossing
barriers.

In carnaval play, as I have discussed elsewhere
(Da Matta, 1973), a great deal of self-inflicted bodily
abuse is involved. People run, leap, and sing, using
their bodies as a basic instrument of participation.
Thus the main social values at the carnaval in Rio are
based on equality and, as its complements, on anonymity
and inversion of the social order. Hence the exceptional
creativity of the carnaval, which, as Victor Turner
(1974) explains, is deeply related to peripheral areas
of social life that contain potential for alternative
action and behavior. In fact, public uproars are carnivals in Brazil, in the same way that revolutions are
ideologically perceived as one big carnival, with the
people laughing and singing in the streets and all
differences becoming dissolved in an ocean of individuals. In this sense, carnaval would mark the passage
from hierarchy to egalitarianism, with people being
transformed into individuals whose reputations are
safeguarded through anonymity.

3. But what does carnival signify in U.S. society?
Webster's New World Dictionary of the American Language
states: "a reveling festivity, an entertainment with
rides, side shows," and so on, that is, an amusement
park. The Encyclopaedia Britannica says of carnival:
"applies to a travelling amusement enterprise, including
rides such as merry-go-rounds and Ferris wheels, side-
shows and games of chance, which operate separately or
in conjunction with fairs and expositions. When combined with one of the latter, the carnival is distinguishable by the midway, a term used both for the
brightly illuminated area where the rides, shows, games
and refreshments are grouped and for a broad passageway
through which the patrons walk."

The American carnival is, thus, more of a place
than a party. That is, it is a specialized, well-
located event, a defined area where multiple encounters
between people and machines take place. Moreover,
these areas tend to be located on the outskirts of
towns, like the New Orleans carnival, which is located
on the last American frontier, the South--a changing,
but not yet egalitarian society, aristocratic and

hierarchical in its values, openly racist and internally
divided. With Mardi Gras, New Orleans brings together
its romanticized world and its marginalized elements
within its Latin boundaries, a type of France in
America, sensual, with verandas and open-air cafés that
encourage indolence, a place where sex is no longer
sinful and hierarchy is part of popular ideology. As
Edmonson (1956) indicates, it is this part of the
ideology that the carnival of New Orleans helps to pre-
serve.

As Max Gluckman (1962) shows, spatial specialization of the sort the American carnival represents is
typical of complex societies in which individualism and
egalitarianism in principle prevail. Life in these
societies is no longer synchronized.[1] This seems to be
a key concept in the sociology of modern society--as
opposed to tribal society, in which there are a multiplicity of social ties and a high degree of determinism,
as Gluckman (1962) and Lévi-Strauss (1962) show. In
tribal society, work is carried out collectively, as is
ritual. There is no place for the individual as a
social concept or, as Dumont (1970) writes, for the
individual as "an embodiment of humanity at large."

In tribal society, activities are not individualized, but synchronized. But in modern society, dominated by individualism, nothing is synchronized; syn-
chrony occurs only in rare moments. One of these is
during carnival, a universalizing ritual involving the
entire society (even the work that is done during carnival is related to it). In the American case this
synchronization would probably occur only in times of
large disasters or social upheavals. As Bellah (1967)
writes, with respect to rituals, perhaps only presidential inaugurations could produce synchronization,
since they link the individual to the family and the
family to the nation, but under the aegis of a civil
"religion." In other words, it would seem that only
the political sphere is able to synchronize that nation
of individuals (see Dumont, 1970a and 1970b).

The American carnival is, then, a place more than
a situation. In egalitarian and individualized societies, specific geographical locations may possess ideologies, social roles, and even objectives. Since they
are equal, competition exists and mutual relativization
becomes possible. Thence the difficulty of modern man
in perceiving his universe as a coherent whole; still,
a more profound analysis might reveal that many social
identities perceived as individualized and independent
are in fact related in complementary ways to others.
In this perspective, totalitarianism (like racism in
Dumont's view) could be seen as a way of resolving

the conflicts between an egalitarian ideology and an
effectively unequal and highly fragmented world.

THE TWO CARNIVALS: SOCIAL ORGANIZATION AND IDEOLOGY

    In an earlier work I compared the Rio carnaval
(taken as a model for Brazil) with the New Orleans carnival and tried to show that in Rio, the festivity was
typified by an ideology of "encounter and communion,
very clear-cut in the uninhibited meeting of sexes and
social classes" (Da Matta, 1973, p. 173).   And in order
to make this point more clearly, I tried to show how
the New Orleans carnival achieved just the opposite,
as Munro Edmonson (1956) writes in an article on this
American festivity.   He states:

> There can be little doubt that the main ideo-
> logical content of Carnival is aristocratic.
> The gorgeously clothed krewe masters ride their
> gaudy floats high above the profanum vulgus,
> carelessly and capriciously distributing their
> dime store largesse in response to cries of
> "Throw me something, Mister," from children
> and adults in the street below them.   Nor is
> the aristocratic motif of mock royalty restrict-
> ed to the parades; there is a very real and self-
> conscious ideology of exclusiveness to the mem-
> bership of the krewes, and the court ceremonial
> at the balls is very serious.   Nowhere more
> than in Carnival is the traditional prestige
> dominance of the Anglo-French upper class in
> New Orleans so clearly expressed.

    In order to understand these conclusions about the
carnivals in question, we will examine each one closely.

    The first interesting point is that the New Orleans
carnival is localized, while the Rio carnaval is generalized; that is, it is part not only of a city, but of
the entire country.   The New Orleans carnival is a
specialty of that city.   Another notable aspect is that
the Brazilian carnaval, even if it takes up only four
days, is perceived as a compact event: "It's carnaval
time!"   It is a special moment when anything can happen,
a period when the world is full of possibilities and is
no longer viewed in terms of ordinary social conditions.
Carnaval in Rio (and in Brazil) is, then a time for
attaining freedom and anonymity in social maneuvering
(see Da Matta, 1973, 1974).   In New Orleans, however,
carnival is in no sense compact.   It is divided in
phases that go from dances to parades, culminating in
the famous Mardi Gras, when the whole scene seems to
make sense and a better synchronization among these

activities is attained. Since the dances and parades
are separate activities, with all sorts of private
encounters in which the population is divided between
rich and poor and blacks and whites, the New Orleans
carnival is perceived as the exclusive thing of a certain class. Elements of anti-Semitic and anti-Italian
discrimination are also encouraged. All indications
are that in this carnival it is more difficult for an
ideology of integration and harmony to arise in a
healthy and peaceful meeting of social classes and
ethnic groups.

On the other hand, the New Orleans carnival is
based on upper-class organizations called krewes, some
founded as early as 1872, that determine the order of
the day at carnival time. Thus, groups participate in
carnival as corporate (or semicorporate) entities,
always emphasizing either the part of town they come
from, their race, their social position or school.
Moreover, the krewes are patterned after a common model
in the United States, with great emphasis on exclusive-
ness, for they are controlled by rich whites who belong
to the fanciest clubs in town. Thus, it is not surprising that in structure the krewes should resemble college fraternities, which are also exclusive and highly
discriminatory, or high-class clubs in New York or
Boston. Just as in the fraternities, whose names are
chosen from Greek letters (that is, from the classical,
aristocratic world of Athens), the language and etiquette of the krewes are those of royalty. Their
highly formal presentations always include a king, a
queen, dukes, and attendants, all dressed in formal
attire. As in a royal court, everything that goes on
within the krewes' orbit is controlled by them; for
example, their guests dance only in their dances. Moreover, the krewes' dramatic presentations are always
based on fantasy and folklore.

Since the krewes are exclusive, middle- and upper-
class blacks follow the appropriate patterns (equal, but
separate according to the American ideology of equality)
by organizing themselves in carnival clubs. But here,
the oppressed social group recreates the model of the
dominant society: instead of kings, the clubs have a
president, vice-president, secretary, business manager,
and dance captain. These clubs imitate the krewes,
even holding debutante and masquerade balls, but aristocratic language is completely absent. They would rather
recreate a bureaucratic structure in carnival, the
structure that rules them daily and is probably beyond
their reach.

Middle- and lower-class blacks also have corporate-
like clubs with descriptive names: Zulu Aid, Pleasure

Club, and so on (they are among the first to march in
the Mardi Gras parade). As Edmonson writes, the theme
of this parade is "a mock African motif to parody the
mock royalty of the white krewes and the pretensions of
society generally." Lower-class blacks also march in
the parade as Indians in "tribes" and singing tribal
songs. Likewise, "gangs" of blacks of the same social
class display their role as prostitutes, the "Gold
Diggers" and the "Baby Dolls."

Carnaval in Rio is organized in two segments,
street carnival and club carnival. Here, the carnival
clubs are middle-class organizations that open their
doors to the general public and charge an admission fee.
This applies to dances, luxury hotels, and the high
point of the Rio carnaval, the Municipal Theater Ball
sponsored by the State Secretariat of Tourism. In
street carnival people are grouped in blocks (formerly
representing different neighborhoods of the city) and
in samba schools. The latter constitute a structural
equivalent of the krewes, but with the following
differences.

First, the samba schools have a two-level system
of organization. An internal group determines the
internal order of the school as well as its artistic
functions (music, composers, and the like), while an
external group operates like a club. The internal
group can be more protective and exclusive in its activities than the external group, for the latter is oriented to attracting people from the South to join (see
Goldwasser, 1975, and Leopoldi, 1975).

Second, the samba schools also have a two-part
schedule according to a well-defined annual cycle.
During carnaval the main concern is the parade, in which
thousands of characters must get together to represent
a stereotypical play based on folkloric themes and
clever, refined, aristocratic language.[2] In this respect the parade is similar to the krewes parade.
During the rest of the year the samba schools have a
different purpose (see Leopoldi, 1975) and operate much
more like social clubs--excellent tourist attractions
and opportunites for members of the middle and upper
classes to fraternize with members of the so-called
dominated classes in "bohemian" activities.

Third, the samba schools thus follow a double pattern. On the one hand they are open, public clubs,
while on the other hand they are exclusive theatrical
associations with a great deal of consciousness about
origins, status, and race. The members of the schools
know that they are black and poor (the majority are
part of Rio's marginal labor force), but they are also

very aware that during carnaval they are the "doctors
of samba," the teachers. With this ideology they can
invert their position in the social structure, making
up for their social and economic inferiority with a
visible and indisputable superiority based on their
"instinctual" ability to do the samba, a feat that
Brazilians consider an innate privilege of blacks as a
social category.[3]

Krewes and samba schools are thus fundamental elements of the two carnivals, but with important differences. There is a certain redundancy about the krewes
because in the end the rich remain together, defined
and united by their social position and small numbers.
In the samba schools the cooperation among black slum-
dwellers indicates a high degree of organization that
comes as a surprise to middle-class people who tend to
view these blacks as oppressed. The paradox is that
the schools do not teach justice or social equality,
but samba. Thus, the status of these groups can be compensated for by excellence in carnival skills, in contrast with the daily routine that defines them as inferior. But here we have another fundamental problem,
because the social universe of the carnaval and the
samba schools seems to show that social position is not
determined along a single line, but along many axes.
Thus, a person can be poor, but clean; rich, but stupid;
powerful, but unhappy; unemployed, but expert at the
samba. There is also a paradoxical complementarity,
as I discussed above, which is likewise based on many
axes of hierarchy and is thus highly dynamic and compensatory. In Brazil, as relations between the samba
schools and the middle and upper classes suggest, there
is open admittance to the hierarchy, but it is based on
principles that vary from one situation to another.

Furthermore, it is important to note that the krewes
march according to a strict plan beginning with the
Krewe of Rex (the highest member of the hierarchy)
followed by the middle-class krewes, Orleanians and
Crescent City. In Rio, the samba schools march in
purely random order, determined by lottery, and their
hierarchy is established only at the end in a highly
tense and dramatic judging ceremony. The samba school
parade is thus a contest with winners and losers.

HIERARCHY AND EQUALITY IN CARNIVALS

Carnival in the two countries seems to confirm
everything that has been said about them from a comparative perspective, with the difference that in this case,
as in the case of race relations, Brazil comes out
ahead. The fact is that the really open, inclusive, and

"democratic" carnival would seem to be the Brazilian
one, while the American carnival is just the contrary.
This leads us to ask how it is possible to have an
aristocratic carnival in an egalitarian society and an
egalitarian carnival in a hierarchical, authoritarian
society. This seemingly obvious question presents some
basic problems.

There seems to be no doubt that carnival is a
ritual that applies the principle of inversion in consistent fashion. Comparison of the Rio and New Orleans
carnivals shows that it is impossible to study the event
without taking into account the problems and values of
daily life. Thus, in the United States, where an individualist and egalitarian ideology operates on a
daily basis, the inverted world of carnival allows an
open hierarchy of social groups to form. We might wonder if this is merely a metaphorical inversion that
occurs at carnival time or if it is really an everyday
occurrence that Americans are loath to admit. The only
difference is that carnival is a planned activity controlled by society. But in the American case it appears
to have a racist essence--in a society in which all
individuals have legal rights, color serves as an instrument of social differentiation.

My thesis is that it is precisely this hierarchy--
the fundamental basis of racial segregation in America--
that links such apparently separate phenomena as fraternities and the New Orleans carnival. But racism in
these events and organizations is really nothing more
than an attempt to reinstate a principle of differentiation in a context in which the official creed prohibits
it. And it is precisely because belief in equality is
so strong that hierarchy must be presented in so blatant
and perverse a manner.

The inversion that occurs in the Rio carnaval temporarily suspends the precise order of things, persons,
gestures, and categories in society, so that everything
is out of place. As a result carnaval is frequently
associated with "a grand illusion" or, for the more
political, "a true revolution." For a fleeting moment
carnaval transforms everyday hierarchy and authoritarianism into a magical equality.

Finally, we turn to the major symbols of the two
carnivals. In New Orleans, where daily life is centered on equality, the symbol of carnival is Rex, the
king, represented by a millionaire from a high-class
club or semisecret carnival society. In Rio de Janeiro
the symbol of carnaval is the malandro, or vagrant. In
fact, the malandro is neither within nor outside the
order of things; he lives in the interstices between
order and disorder, taking advantage of both.[4]

Who is the malandro, and what does he tell us about Brazilian society? He appears to offer precisely what the American king in New Orleans offers to his people, a chance to view the world upside down, if only for a brief moment. He presents a picture of moral relativity to Brazilian society. Our bourgeois individualist world is ordered along strict lines politically and economically, but the malandro says there are other dimensions, other lines: "I am poor, but I have my woman, the moonlight, and my guitar." This "relativization" of things is felt in the singing, dancing, fun, and joy that are left open to the malandros and are carefully judged at carnaval. These are undoubtedly mechanisms of compensation, but the malandro's world is full of potential and innovation. He occupies no single position; he is neither an exclusive function of the social order, nor a part of the forces of change. He occupies some middle ground and probably serves both sides. It is in this world that the people's creativity if fully exercised.

The same thing occurs in the samba schools, the centers of the malandro's contradictory world. Here we have various incongruous objectives. First is the school itself, generally located on a hill or in a suburb where poor, unemployed, and illiterate people live. These schools teach no skills for making a living, but rather teach life itself, as countless sambas and popular ideology would have it. Thus, anonymous "marginals" are transformed into samba teachers and "doctors" at carnaval time. They teach the middle and upper classes about the world of the malandro, built on having to survive on a paltry wage in a consumer society. They demonstrate the "power of the weak" by revealing their creativity, unparalleled organizational skills, and ability to recreate the social structure year after year. And they show, perhaps above all, the great paradox of the harmonization of unequal social groups, which could not exist without them as actors and audience. They represent, in a word, the multiplicity of vectors and zones of hierarchy that seem typical of urban and rural life in Brazil. For what is the mythical hero Pedro Malasartes, if not a "rural malandro" who cheats bosses and landowners and makes up for his lack of power through his unusual sagacity?[5]

It is not surprising, then, that during carnaval middle- and upper-class people (especially sophisticated intellectuals) leave town because they "can't stand carnaval" or the "transformation of the city into pandemonium." It is evident that this attitude expresses a reaction to loss of privilege during carnaval, a time when no one can carry on his daily business with the classical "Do you know whom you are speaking to?"

formula which, as I have tried to show elsewhere, transforms the individual into a person.

In an even more dramatic way, the rituals of the
Umbanda religion, particularly in Rio, reveal how these
same "structurally inferior" people can be transformed
into persons when possessed by the spirits of Indians
(índios), demons (preto-velhos), and spirits (pomba-
giras), allowing them to counsel their employers.[6] No
longer isolated beings and united to their guiding
spirits (that is, their astral godparents), they are
now the source of cures, wisdom, and mystical power.
This is when it becomes possible to invert the social
hierarchy.

Again, inversion does not mean eliminating hierarchy and inequality, but merely reallocating them temporarily. We see, then, that in studying the Brazilian
case it is possible to link phenomena so apparently distant as Umbanda rituals, which always seemed to belong
to the world of religion. It is easy to explain how
this inversion of roles became so quickly a part of
this universal domain. In oppressing free men, especially blacks, society did not manage to suppress their
mystical power. Thus in Umbanda it is the poor, and
especially poor women (doubly enslaved), aided by
spiritual entities also considered inferior, slaves
(pretos-velhos, or malandros-exus), prostitutes (pomba-
giras), or mestizos (índios), who cure without distinguishing between rich and poor. The ideology of charity,
love, and relinquishment of material interests, so fundamental in hierarchical societies such as India and
Brazil, is in fact the counterpart of inequality.

NOTES

1. I owe the idea of synchronization to José Sávio
Leopoldi, who wrote a detailed and imaginative thesis
about the samba schools (see Leopoldi, 1975).

2. See Baeta Neves, 1973, for a study of the meaning
of this language.

3. In the Brazilian world of ideas, the development of
the people is a central topic. Thus, there is the idea
that the three races contributed in different ways to
this development (and, of course, they continue to contribute). From the Indian came courage and love of
land and nature, but the Indian is weak and allergic to
work, although pure and innocent. From the black came
the brute force necessary for labor, but also indolence,
as shown in his innate love of dancing, rhythm, and
song. And, finally, from the Portuguese white we

inherited cultural values. On the other hand, the
white is always conceived in this myth as an adult man,
while Indians and blacks are seen as children (or women).
Miscegenation among these "races" produced some of the
typical traits of the Brazilian national character:
maliciousness, the malandro syndrome, the taste for
music and song, mysticism, inventiveness, etc. (see
Thales de Azevedo, 1966).

4. For a pioneer study of the malandro in our society,
see Antonio Candido, 1970. See also Da Matta, 1973,
and Fry and Howe, 1975.

5. I am preparing a study of Pedro Malasartes, with
his problems and paradoxes, as the myth of "rural
malandro." Also, the same could be said of Macunaíma,
our "hero without character," who structures the world
according to an absolute lack of logic, etiquette, and
discretion.

6. See Yvonne Velho, 1975, where these points are made
in more detailed fashion.

BIBLIOGRAPHY

Arendt, Hannah
   1975 (1951) Origens do Totalitarismo: O Anti-
        Semitismo. Rio: Editora Documentário

Azevedo, Thales de
   1966 Cultura e Situação Racial no Brasil. Rio:
        Editora Civilizacao Brasileira S.A.

Baeta Neves, Luiz Felipe
   1973 "A Imaginação Social dos Samba-Enredo," in
        Cadernos de Jornalismo e Comunicação. Rio:
        Edições Jornal do Brasil.

Bellah, Robert
   1967 "Civil Religion in America," in Deadalus, vol.
        96, no. 1, winter.

Candido, Antonio
   1970 "A Dialética da Malandragem," in Revista do
        Instituto de Estudos Brasileiros, no. 8. São
        Paulo: Universidade de São Paulo.

Cascudo, Luiz da Camara
   1967 Contos Tradicionais do Brasil. Rio: Edições
        de Ouro, no. 1443.

Da Matta, Roberto
    1971 "Les Présages Apinaye," in Échanges et Communi-
           cations: Mélanges Offerts à Claude Lévi-Strauss.
           Le Haye: Mouton.

    1973 "O Carnaval como um Rito de Passagem," in Ensaios
           de Antropologia Estrutural. Petrópolis: Vozes.

    1974 "Constraint and Licence. A Preliminary Study
           of Two Brazilians National Rituals," in Wenner-
           Gren Foundation for Anthropological Research,
           Symposium no. 64.

    1974a "Quanto Custa ser Índio no Brasil: Reflexões
           sobre o Problema da Identidade Etnica," Congresso
           Internacional de Americanistas, Simpósio sôbre
           Identidade Etnica, Mexico City.

De Coulanges, Fustel
    1945 A Cidade Antiga: Estudo sôbre o Culto, o Direito
           e Instituicões da Grécia e de Roma. Lisboa:
           Livraria Clássica Editora.

Degler, Carl
    1971 Neither Black nor White: Slavery and Race
           Relations in Brazil and the United States. New
           York: The Macmillan Co. Inc.

De Tocqueville, Alexis
    1956 (1835) Democracy in America. Mentor Books.

Douglas, Mary
    1966 Purity and Danger: An Analysis of Concepts of
           Pollution and Taboo. New York: Praeger.

    1970 "Introduction: Thirty Years after Witchcraft,
           Oracles and Magic," in Witchcraft Confessions
           & Accusations, ASA Monographs, no. 9. London:
           Tavistock Publications.

Dumont, Louis
    1970 Homo Hierarchicus: An Essay on the Caste System.
           The University of Chicago Press.

    1970a Religion, Politics and History in India: Col-
           lected Papers in Indian Sociology. Paris and
           the Hague: Mouton.

    1970b "Religion, Politics and Society in the Individ-
           ualistic Universe" (Henry Myers Lecture, 1970),
           in Proceedings of the Royal Anthropological
           Institute of Great Britain and Ireland for 1970.

Durkheim, E., and Mauss, Marcel
1963 (1903) Primitive Classifications. Chicago:
The University of Chicago Press.

Edmonson, Munro
1956 "New Orleans Carnival," in Caribbean Quarterly,
no. 3, 4:233-45.

Fry, Peter and Howe, Gary
1975 "Duas Respostas a Aflição: Umbanda e Pentecos-
talismo," in Debate e Crítica, no. 6, Julho de
1975, São Paulo.

Gillin, John
1955 "Ethos Components in Modern Latin American Culture," in American Anthropologist, 57:488-500.
Reprinted in Heath & Adams, Contemporary Cultures and Societies of Latin America. New
York: Random House, 1965.

Gluckman, Max
1962 "Les Rites de Passage," in Essays on the Ritual
of Social Relations, Max Gluckman, Ed., pp. 1-
52. Manchester: Manchester University Press.

1972 "Moral Crises: Magical and Secular Solutions,"
chap. 1 of The Allocation of Responsibility,
Max Gluckman, Ed. Manchester: Manchester
University Press.

Goffman, Erving
1959 (1975) The Presentation of Self in Everyday Life.
Doubleday. Tradução brasileira pela Editora
Vozes, 1975.

Goldwasser, Maria Júlia
1975 "O Palácio do Samba: Estudo Antropológico da
Escola de Samba Estação Primeira de Mangueira."
Dissertação de Mestrado apresentada ao Programa
de Pós-Graduação em Antropologia Social do
Museu Nacional, UFRJ.

Leopoldi, José Sávio
1975 "Escola de Samba, Ritual e Sociedade." Dissertação de Mestrado apresentada ao Programa de
Pos-Graduação em Antropologia Social do Museu
Nacional, UFRJ.

Lévi-Strauss, Claude
1962 La Pensée Sauvage. Paris: Plon.

Lewis, Ian
1963 "Dualism in Somali Notions of Power," Journal of
the Royal Anthropological Institute, vol. 93.

Mauss, Marcel
    1974 (1938) Antropologia e Sociologia, vol. 1. São
         Paulo: Editora Pedagógica e Universitaria Ltda
         & EDUSP.

Moore, Sally F.
    1972 "Legal Liability and Evolutionary Interpreta-
         tion: Some Aspects of Strict Liability, Self-
         Help and Collective Responsibility," chap. 2 of
         Gluckman, Ed., 1972.

Nakane, Chie
    1970 Japanese Society. Penguin Books.

    1974 "Sociological Significance of Ritual Behaviors,"
         in Wenner-Gren Foundation for Anthropological
         Research, Symposium no. 64.

Radcliffe-Brown, A. R.
    1956 Structure and Function in Primitive Society.
         London: Cohen & West. (Published in Portuguese
         by Editora Vozes, 1973.)

Turner, Victor
    1969 The Ritual Process: Structure and Anti-
         Structure. Chicago: Aldine. (Published in
         Portuguese by Editora Vozes, 1974.)

    1974 "Liminality, Play, Flow, and Ritual: Optational
         and Obligatory Forms and Genres," in Wenner-
         Gren Foundation for Anthropological Research,
         Symposium no. 64.

Velho, Yvonne Maggie A.
    1975 Guerra de Orixá: Um Estudo de Ritual e Con-
         flito. Rio: Zahar Editores.

Viveiros de Castro, Eduardo
    1974 "Devido Respeito," Programa de Pós-Graduação em
         Antropologia Social, Museu Nacional, UFRJ.

Folklore and Ethnomusicology in Latin America

Isabel Aretz
Translated by **María A. Leal**

INTRODUCTION

Folklore and ethnomusic are vital elements of Latin American culture, for most Latin Americans are heir to a traditional oral culture that permeates all aspects of creative and social life. The mountains and jungles of Latin America contain aboriginal cultures that have come into contact with our civilization, often at great cost to themselves. Groups of African descent have conserved their heritage in part, while the few Chinese and East Indian groups in existence retain their own traditional culture and may be studied, thus, not only in terms of their contribution to Creole culture, but also for what they can reveal about their societies of origin. Alongside the oral traditions of these cultures are the folk cultures that are the Creole product of European immigrants (Spanish for the most part; also Italian, French, English, and German) who intermarried with native and African peoples. These peoples, literate or not, have developed their own regional and even national cultures and share common traits throughout Latin America. Thus we may speak today of a Latin American culture. Its distinguishing features include patterns of friendship and <u>compadrazgo</u> (parent-godparent relations), mutual aid, certain beliefs, brotherhoods formed around the feasts of patron saints, devotional dances, musical counterpoint, all the ceremonies and feasts of the life cycle, craft techniques, and so on.

This world, rich in spiritual and cultural content, is today threatened by a lack of defensive policies to protect it from the overwhelming influence of modern communications media. Projecting a distorted image created by consumer society, the media provide illusions

of money making as the only worthwhile goal in life and
of a technology that is beyond the capacity of the local
culture to absorb. Thus the growth and expansion of
the media, uncontrolled by state or private cultural
associations, do not enrich the people's heritage, but
instead destroy it systematically. Transistor radios
play alongside peasants at work in the fields, while
television makes its way into more and more homes with
programs whose only purpose is to "entertain" the viewer
so that he will listen to the abundant commercial propaganda. The latter is preferably "sexy" or portrays
juvenile characters so that the child viewer himself
may become a product salesperson. Slogans are mouthed
even by educated people, and in all these programs good
music and theater are absent. Classical music has come
to be identified in the Venezuelan media with Holy Week
or the death of some important person, who may just as
well be a great man as a boxing champion. Here lies
the great importance of rescuing and studying folklore
and ethnomusic as well as preserving and reactivating
them in situ, disseminating them through all possible
means, applying them to education, and extending them
into the arts and crafts.

Creole writers and musicians understood early the
value of folkloric materials. Independence revolutions
throughout Latin America provided themes for many vernacular poets. Among these were the cielitos poets of
the South, who were generally semiliterates—such as the
Uruguayan Bartolomé Hidalgo (1788-1822), who printed
and sold his cielitos in Buenos Aires in 1820 in loose-
leaf form—and the gaucho poets—such as the Argentine
José Hernández (1834-1886), whose Martín Fierro (1872)
recreates the applied poetry of the gaucho in a work of
profound social and historical substance. In Venezuela,
General Ramón de la Plaza published in 1883 his "Essay
on Art in Venezuela," including two chapters on music
and indigenous studies and a musical appendix with
forty-four "national songs of Venezuela." In the same
year Samuel Lafone Quevedo began to write about folklore and customs in Argentina, while Juan B. Ambrosetti
(1865-1917) wrote his Supersticiones y Leyendas from
the Missionary Region, the Cachaquí valleys, and the
pampas, and Adán Quiroga (1864-1904) began to publish
his Folklore Calchaquí.

FOLKLOROLOGY

Specialized Studies

Specialized, methodical studies began in the early
part of this century and dealt mainly with literary
subjects. The few works I shall mention here are the

results not of casual encounters with popular poets,
but of the domestic travels of men and women dedicated
to the gathering of specific elements of traditional
oral culture. In our view traditional culture is folkloric when it pertains to civilized man, who partici-
pates in our major institutions and is therefore
bicultural, and it is ethnographic when it pertains to
groups who are not yet incorporated into our civilization and possess only an oral tradition. This distinction allows us to determine at what point elements of
aboriginal culture move into the folk world and at what
point aboriginal peoples have incorporated elements of
folk into their world.

    Among the researchers who had most contact with
folk and aboriginal peoples in the early days was the
Argentine Juan Alfonso Carrizo (1895-1957), who between
1926 and 1942 published his monumental collections of
songs from the Argentine Northwest. These books were
complemented by another entitled Antecedentes Medievales
de la Poesía Tradicional Argentina. Carrizo was essentially a hispanicist and was contemptuous of the works
of the gauchos, which by his time were already reaching
the northwest provinces. But to him is owed the establishment of the National Institute of Tradition, to
which he also donated his valuable library. Carrizo's
work was complemented in the Santiago region by Oreste
Di Lullo and in the Cuyana region by Juan Draghi Lucero.
Important collections in other countries include a book
by Manuel F. Zárate published by Decima y la Copla in
Panama and three volumes of Cantos del Folklore Boya-
cense (1949) by Joaquín R. Medina and José Vargas
Tamayo in Colombia.

    In Mexico a group project is now in progress that
utilizes a methodical classification system and excellent analysis. The first of five volumes in a series
titled Cancionero Folklorico de México, Coplas de Amor
Feliz, was published in 1975 by the Colegio de México
under the direction of Dr. Margit Frenk Alatorre.

    Collections of indigenous myths, stories, and leg-
ends include Taurón Panton (1964) by the Venezuelan P.
Cesáreo de Armellana; Watunna, Mitología Makiritare
(1970) by Marc de Civrieux; and the Geografía dos Mitos
Brasileiros by Basilio de Magalhaes (1947), author of
the pioneering study O Folk-lore no Brasil (1928). In
Paraguay, Carvalho Neto included twenty-three myths in
his book on Paraguayan folklore (1961).

    Anthologies of short stories got a good start in
Chile with the early work of Ramón A. Laval (1910).
Research begun by Yolando Pino Saavedra in 1948 resulted
in two thick volumes published in 1960. Brazilians

have done much work in this area, including Luis da
Cámara Cascudo, author of Cantos Tradicionais do Brasil.

In our opinion, studies of folk tales and literature in general should be based on recordings obtained
in situ, the only way to prevent distortions of the
original material. This has the double advantage of
preventing errors or omissions due to hasty penmanship,
while making phonetic studies possible.

Riddles are another important part of our brief
literary overview. In Argentina, Ismael Moya followed
on the footsteps of Roberto Lehmann-Nitsche with his
traditional riddles (1955). In Peru, Efraín Morote
Best published Nuestras Cien Primeras Adivinanzas (1950),
and in Chile José Santos González Vera collected his
Cuatrocientos Cuarenta y Cuatro Adivinanzas de la
Tradición Oral Chilena (1954). Other important collectors include the Puerto Rican Alden Mason, the Panaman-
ian Stanley L. Robe, and the Dominican Manuel Rueda.

Other aspects of folklore gradually came to be
studied by Latin American scholars. Miguel Acosta
Saignes studied housing in Venezuela, while Berta Coba-
hillas de Rodríguez has written about cooking in Puerto
Rico in El Puertorriqueno y Su Alimentación a través de
Su Historia (Siglos XVI al XIX) (1973). Students of
folk arts and crafts include the Argentine Augusto
Raul Cortázar, the Colombian Yolanda Mora de Jaramilo,
and the Mexican Rubin de la Borbolla, who has been involved in the phenomenal development of Mexico's arts
and crafts. Work has been done on ceramics in Chile
by Tomás Lago and others, while the development of
crafts in Bolivia, Peru, and Ecuador has been rapid. A
map of arts and crafts was designed in Guatemala ten
years ago by the National Department of Folk Art under
Ida Bremme de Santos. In Venezuela, I myself authored
a less well known book on Venezuelan folk art, not because it was my specialty, but because no one else at
the time was qualified to write a book on the subject.
The same is true of my volume El Traje del Venezolano.
Among the better-known studies of clothing habits are
those of Titú Palavecino of the Andean region and Dora
de Zárate of Panama.

Much more specialized literature exists with reference to social folklore as studies by folklorologists,
ethnomusicologists, sociologists, and anthropologists.
Countless studies have been done on Brazilian fiestas
and their attendant beliefs, dances, and music. Folk
calendars have been drawn up in Argentina, Bolivia,
Paraguay, Ecuador, Venezuela, Guatemala, and Mexico.
Folk and indigenous communities have been objects of
much study, particularly in Peru and Ecuador. Games

have been studied in many countries as well as customs, particularly those related to the life cycle.

Specialized studies of verbal communication include notable collections of popular proverbs, sayings, and idioms. Ismael Moya published his Estudio sobre los Materiales de la Colección de Folklore in Argentina (1944), while Luís Alberto Acuña in Colombia and Luisita Aguilera P. in Panama produced similar works.

Among the first students of folk medicine was the Argentine Tobías Rosenberg, who wrote between 1939 and 1951. In Brazil Mario de Andrade authored a double volume, A Medicina dos Excretos (1936 and 1956).

Few scholars have been able to specialize in magic and folk religions because of the complexity of the theme and the difficulty of gathering materials. Carvalho Neto has done a great deal of field work on magic in different countries. The foremost student of religion and spiritism is undoubtedly the Cuban Fernando Ortiz, author of such books as El Huracán (1947) and Historia de una Pelea Cubana contra los Demonios (1959). Another serious work is that of the Argentine Armando Vivante, Muerte, Magia y Religión (1953), which studies native euthanasia, the souls of purgatory, the "fear that kills," and ceremonial beans. Many studies have been done about African influences in Latin America, principally by Ortiz in Cuba and Arthur Ramos in Brazil.

Systematic Theoretical Studies

The first theoretical works on folklore appeared in Latin America after the founding of the London Folklore Society in 1878 and the publication of works by the Spaniard Antonio Machado y Alvares, Sr. (1881). Our theoreticians originated in many fields--for example, archaeology, linguistics, anthropology, sociology, literature, history, geography, music, teaching, and even law--often combining disciplines. Early theorizing in Latin America began at the turn of this century with the German linguist Rodolfo Lenz, who had lived in Chile since 1890. Lenz used the methods of R. F. Kaindl, also a German, and trained the first Chilean folklorologists. Eugenio Pereira Salas wrote a bibliographical guide to Chilean folklore in 1952. Studies of folklore and science began to be made known through the Archives of Chilean Folklore in 1954. At present Manuel Dannemann, sociologist and musician, is one of the most important folklorologists on the continent.

Starting in the 1940s, four folkloric theoreticians stand out in Argentina: José Imbelloni, an anthropologist and promoter of the Historico-Cultural School;

Carlos Vega, his disciple in anthropology; Ismael Moya, also a professor; and a man of the younger generation, Augusto Raul Cortázar (1911-1974). A doctor of juris- prudence, Cortázar performed important field work and did theoretical work as well. He forged his own path in 1944 with the publication of his essay "Hacia la Investigación Folklórica Integral," a response to the Spanish translation of A Scientific Theory of Culture by Bronislaw Malinowski in 1948. Cortázar advanced beyond Malinowski's work with the notion that synchronic studies of folklore should be followed up by diachronic studies; that is, the functional aspects of folklore should be studied in the light of the historical cir- cumstances that condition them and transform them into tradition.

Also in Argentina, Alfredo Povina published his Sociología del Folklore (1944), in which he maintained that folklore is the sociology of popular knowledge. Bruno Jacovella authored a brief, but useful, Manual- Guía para el Recolector in 1951. Among other brief, but informative, works by Jacovella are Los Conceptos Fun- damentales Clásicos del Folklore, presented to the International Folklore Conference in 1960, and an an- thology of recordings entitled "Las Canciones Folk- lóricas de la Argentina."

In Brazil, under the influence of Arthur Ramos (1903-1949), a school of interdisciplinary folklorolo- gists evolved and attained continental fame. Braulio do Nascimento published his Bibliografia do Folklore Brasileiro in 1971. In Uruguay two names are important, Ildefonso Pereda Valdés and Paulo de Carvalho Neto. The latter founded the Center of Folkloric Studies of Uru- guay in 1954. In Paraguay, according to Carvalho Neto, Eloy Farina Nuñez was the real precursor of folklorolo- gists with Mitos Guaraníes (1926) and Conceptos Estéti- cos. Farina Nuñez was followed by León Cadogan and Ramón Bejarano, who classified folkloric data in the famous tripartite division. Rigoberto Paredes, Julia Elena Fortún, and José Felipe Costas Arguedas were important in Bolivia, the latter particularly for his Diccionario del Folklore Boliviano.

Systematic work began in Peru in 1942 with the cre- ation of a chair in folklore at the University of Cuzco, through which Efraín Morote Best, as President of the Peruvian Folklore Society, published the Archivos Peruanos de Folklore and a Boletín, as well as his thesis, Elementos del Folklore (1950). He also pub- lished a Guía para la Recolección de Material Folklórico in 1951 and 1973 and numerous other works. The Biblio- grafía del Folklore Peruano was written by José María Arguedas (1960). Another important student of Peruvian

folklore is Mildred Merino de Zela, who has published
an article in Folklore Americano (1974).

While Ecuador does not possess major theoreticians,
Dario Guevara should be noted for Esquema Didáctico del
Folklore Ecuatoriano (1951) and Breve Ojeada sobre el
Desarrollo Científico del Folklore en el Ecuador (1955).
Carvalho is another important writer on Ecuador, author
of the Diccionario del Folklore Ecuatoriano (1964).
Andrés Pardo Tovar of Colombia authored a monograph
entitled Hacia una Labor Tecnificada en el Campo del
Folclor (1953), while Octavio Marulanda published his
Folklore y Cultura General (1973).

The first important study of folklore emerged in
Venezuela in Contribuciones al Folklore Venezolano by
Aristides Rojas (1907). But it was not until 1939, when
Dr. Eloy González taught the first folklore course at
the Pedagogical Institute, that the field began to
develop. Six years later, Tulio López Ramírez published
Estudios y Perspectivas de Nuestro Folklore. Meanwhile,
the poet Rafael Olivares Figueroa undertook literary
research in folklore, later becoming a professor of
folklore at the Central University of Venezuela. In
the same period another poet, Juan Liscano, began field
work and founded the National Folklore Research Service
in 1946, later to become the National Folklore Institute
under Luis Felipe Ramón y Rivera. Liscano also published a book, Folklore y Cultura, which deals with
theory.

Among other works by Ramón y Rivera are his three
volumes, written with my collaboration, on a general
study of a Venezuelan state, Folklore Tachirense (1961-
63). He has also been in charge of the Boletín del
Instituto de Folklore (1953-64), replaced in 1968 by
the Revista Venezolana de Folklore. In 1956 I published the Manual de Folklore Venezolano and in 1962
founded a chair in folklore at the Pedagogical Institute in Caracas. I have just published my Guía Clasifi-
catoria de la Cultura Oral Tradicional, which is part
of the first volume of the Biblioteca INIDEF series and
contains nine works by Latin American folklorologists.
Like the Revista INIDEF, the Biblioteca is a publication of the Interamerican Institute of Ethnomusicology
and Folklore. In creating INIDEF, the Organization of
American States brought together various Latin American
experts in Caracas and out of that meeting published
the Charter of American Folklore (OAS, Washington, D.C.,
1972).

Also in Venezuela, the Central University's Institute of Anthropology and History has published its
Archivos Venezolanos de Folklore since 1952 and is
presently putting together an Anuario.

Theoretical work on folklore in Panama includes
Breviario de Folklore by Manuel F. Zárata (1958). In
Guatemala the foundation of the Center for Folkloric
Studies in 1967 at the University of San Carlos was a
key event. The most important Guatemalan folklorolo-
gist is Roberto Díaz Castillo, and another important
scholar is Celso Lara, editor of the journal Folklore
Americano.

The study of folklore in Mexico began with the
work of the Mendozas. The Folkloric Society of Mexico
has been active since 1945. Among its publications is
Aportaciones a la Investigación Folklórica de México
(1953) in the series Cultura Mexicana. Vicente Mendoza's work focused on literature and music, while his
wife, Virginia Rivera de Mendoza, is noted for Mujeres
Folkloristas (1967). Anthropologist Gabriel Moedano
Navarro made his contribution to folklorology with the
article entitled "El Folklore come Disciplina Antro-
pológica" (1963). Mexican studies focus on the nature
of "Mexicanness," examining folklore in light of its
profound social significance, and they take an interdisciplinary approach, emphasizing the "lore" and rejecting the concepts of "folk" and a "folk community."

ETHNOMUSICOLOGY

Early Works

This discipline existed in Latin America long before it had a name, with two important scholars,
Vicente Mendoza in Mexico and Carlos Vega in Argentina.
Mendoza collected and studied indigenous and folk music
as well as prehispanic instruments and musical compo-
sitions. Among his many publications were El Romance
Español y el Corrido Mexicano (1939), La Décima en
México (1947), Música Indígena Otomí (1950-51), Panorama de la Música Tradicional de México (1956), and
numerous articles. Because he had an excellent ear
for transcribing music, he left behind few recordings.
Carlos Vega, undoubtedly one of the most prolific Latin
American ethnomusicologists, is remembered for his
scientific approach. Among his many works are the well-
documented Danzas y Canciones Argentinas (1936); Frase-
ología (1941), in which he proposes a systematic method
for transcribing musical ideas; Panorama de la Música
Popular Argentina (1944), in which he establishes different families of music called "cancioneros"; Los
Instrumentos Musicales Aborígenes y Criollos de la Argentina (1946), and Las Danzas Populares Argentinas
(1952).

I myself was active in Argentina in the Institue of Musicology from 1940 to 1950. Four works grew out of my work there on Argentine folk music, as well as a student workbook: Música Tradicional Argentina, Tucumán (1946); El Folklore Musical Argentina (1952); Costumbres Tradicionales Argentinas (1954); and Música Tradicional de la Rioja (unpublished thesis).

In the Dominican Republic, Edna Garrido was the first to collect folk music in record form, from 1944 to 1948. In Brazil the Discoteca São Paulo, founded by Mario de Andrade, at one time contained one of the lar- gest record collections of folk songs. Andrade authored many works, including Música de Feiticaria no Brasil (1963). Luis Heitor Correa de Azevedo did a great deal of field work in Ceará, Minas Gerais, Goias, and Rio Grande do Sul from 1942 to 1946. The Library of Con- gress in Washington contains a complete copy of his recordings, while INIDEF in Venezuela contains a partial copy. Another fine researcher and musician is Rossini Tavares de Lima, whose works include Folguedos Populares do Brasil (1962) and Folclore das Festas Ciclicas (1971), containing general studies of fiestas and dramatic dances.

The best work on Bolivian music to date is Margari- ta D'Harcourt, La Musique des Aymara sur les Hauts Plateaux Boliviens (1959), based on recordings by Louis Girault. Raul and Margarita D'Harcourt, La Musique des Incas et Ses Survivances (Paris, 1925), and Rodolfo Holzmann, Panorama de la Música Tradicional del Peru (1966), are the best publications on Peruvian folk music. The earliest works on Cuban folk music dealt with musical instruments, such as those by Israel Cas- tellanos. Fernando Ortiz, Los Instrumentos de la Música Afrocubana, is an important five-volume work. Argeliers León, María Teresa Linares de León, and Odilio Urfé did important work based on recordings obtained in the field. With these researchers we may begin to speak of ethnomusicology, the study of music in culture.

Contemporary Works

Ethnomusicology in Latin American consists of syn- chronic and diachronic studies. The synchronic approach allows us to know the present in terms of the processes of change and acculturation and sometimes cultural destruction, analyzing their causes. The diachronic approach focuses on origins--native, European, African, and Asian--and attempts to delineate stages of mestizaje, or the mixing of different cultures. Latin American ethnomusicology is centered in large part at the Insti- tuto Interamericano de Etnomusicología y Folklore (INIDEF) in Venezuela, which is also the Multinational

Center of the Regional Program of Cultural Development
of the Organization of American States and, as such,
the only institution at present that offers courses on
a regular basis to American scholarship students.
INIDEF contains an archive of ethnomusicology and folklore with one thousand tapes from all over Latin America
obtained in the field under the Multinational Plans, a
small library, a collection of five hundred aboriginal
and folk instruments, and seven thousand slides, photo-
graphs, and documentary films. It produces two publications, Revista INIDEF and Biblioteca INIDEF.

        At INIDEF we study music in its musical, folklor-
ological, and anthropological aspects, emphasizing the
oral traditions since it is our goal to increase knowledge about our Latin American heritage. Studies of
change and sociological studies are considered complementary, but not essential, for they are symptomatic of
situations and of contact that can help destroy native
cultures. Folk and aboriginal music is distorted and
destroyed by communications media, which tend to broadcast a high proportion of bad music, silencing the
voices of rural people, and by missionaries who forbid
the Indians to make their own music or who teach them
other kinds of music. As Latin Americans we are concerned with stemming the erosive tide that could lead
to a loss of our own cultural identity.

        L. F. Ramón y Rivera has written eight books on
Venezuelan ethnomusic: La Polifonía Popular de Vene-
zuela (1949); El Joropo (1953); Cantos de Trabajo del
Pueblo Venezolano (1949); Música Indígena, Folklórica
y Popular de Venezuela (1963); La Música Folklórica de
Venezuela (1969); La Música Afrovenezolana (1971); La
Canción Venezolana (1972); and La Música Popular de
Venezuela (1976). For my part, I have written three
books on the subject: Los Cantos Navidenos en el Folk-
lore Venezolano (1962); El Tamunanque (1970); and
Instrumentos Musicales de Venezuela (1967). My Historia
de la Etnomusicología en América Latina is forthcoming.

APPLICATIONS OF FOLKLORE

        The necessity of preserving the musical heritage
of a large segment of the population in the face of
erosive pressure by the media has called for conscious-
ness-raising activity among those responsible for its
study and dissemination. An important objective is to
promote folk music in the schools so that all children
may learn about, practice, and even recreate traditional
music. This would be no stranger than teaching traditional European songs and would provide a unifying bond
among children in the rural areas where folk and

aboriginal music is practiced spontaneously. Songs, instruments, traditional poetry, dance, popular theater, clothing, and tools could be taught along with the appropriate explanations to put them into context. The selection of topics should be made on the basis of their intrinsic value and in accordance with the age of the students.

The study of material folklore in Latin America accords a special place to handicrafts, and the fabrication of musical instruments is of particular interest to ethnomusicologists. We believe that well-developed and well-promoted handicrafts can become an important source of income for folk and aboriginal peoples.

Other applications of folklore can occur through its use or incorporation in the creative arts and crafts. A composer, for example, may be interested in the musical phenomenology of a specific culture--its musical instruments, special techniques, combinations of sounds, and the like--while a choreographer may be interested in its dances and their particular symbolism. A craftsman may be interested in different designs, materials, and decoration involved in certain types of furniture, while a writer may want to know about folk people's myths, tales, customs, ideas, experiences, or modes of expression. These are among the concerns of Latin American folkloric institutes.

In conclusion, I recognize that it is difficult-- if not impossible--to present a synthesis of folkloric and ethnomusicological studies in Latin America, so large is the number of scholars at work and so numerous their publications, while the work of countless others remains unpublished.

Censorship and Best Sellers: Some Considerations About Conformism in Literature

Walnice Nogueira Galvão

Let us acknowledge that Jorge Amado and Érico Veríssimo are two solitary voices crying out, in this sudden wilderness, against the restrictions on freedom of expression in Brazil. Authors of middlebrow fiction, these writers make their living by exercise of their craft rather than from employment in some government department, as is the case with the great majority of Latin American writers. Nevertheless, they have made highly dignified and courageous declarations, openly and publicly. Could it be that the freedom to express opposition to the restrictions imposed on freedom of expression is in some way related, on the one hand, to the ability to make a living independently from the state, and, on the other, to what is written?

This independence, if intimately associated with the professionalization of a writer, collides with coercive official norms that are not those of the liberal democratic systems apparently predominant in the world; but it is an independence born of liberal democracy and owing its origin to timeworn traditions. Making a living from the exercise of one's craft as a writer and desiring to protect that craft's autonomy are things that rest, of course, on the idea of free enterprise. However, restrictive norms are inconvenient for those very people whose interests they defend--newspaper proprietors, film and television producers, or publishers. But here let us take care not to confuse freedom of the press and freedom of enterprise. This confusion exists and frequently gives rise to ironical snickers when its hidden side of poetic vengeance is unveiled: in a system that protects private enterprise, the very owners of the enterprises may become the protesting victims of censorship. In the case before us, it is perhaps unnecessary to dwell on the somewhat notorious sociopolitical aspects of the problem; I would prefer to attempt to draw some internal inferences from what is written when a writer is economically independent in these conditions.

Being an independent writer apparently implies, in certain historical situations, a more flexible relation with the state and a more dependent one with the market--an exception to the rule among Brazilian writers, who have been for centuries employees of the state. Hence arises this paradoxical equation according to which being able to express an opinion in favor of freedom of expression means being the most governed by the taste prevailing in the market. If a writer is governed by the taste prevailing in the market, his work cannot go against that taste, either in form or in ideas. It cannot be new; it is old before it is born. It should be stressed, however, that I am not interested here in discussing the prestige of novelty as novelty, a theoretical and aesthetic argument that has been harped on so intensely in recent years that it must be linked to the extraordinary acceleration in processes of change characteristic of the second half of this century. Running parallel with the planned obsolescense that production imposes on consumers of material goods, the overrating of novelty at a theoretical level must be the ideological correlative of headlong change.

Fiction that is governed by the taste of the market at large cannot innovate, for innovation makes a text difficult to read and thus reduces it to circulating among a small group of initiated readers. Only the passage of time permits the extraction of stylistic traits, or "stylemes," from the new: these can then be transmitted to wider circles of consumers by means of absorption and propagation in works of secondary importance, television programs, or advertisements until the point at which their intrinsic innovative quality is lost, and they can be quietly digested. If Machado de Assis, our great nineteenth-century novelist, had not previously provided his plot's basic triangle situation of cunning couple exploiting ingenuous provincial millionaire, and if Guimaraes Rosa had not more recently performed an extraordinary renovation of language and an introduction of fantasy, then The Colonel and the Werewolf by José Candido de Carvalho would not have been written, nor would it have become a best seller. Fiction written for the market taste has to remain in the old discourse of realism so characteristic of best sellers, where the narrative flows on without hooks to catch or entangle the reader's attention within either the diction itself or the subject of the narration, which must not be politically compromising. Neither the themes nor the writing should be problematic, as

opposed to what the best contemporary literature does
everywhere. Fluent diction and a plot full of traps to
provide suspense: such is the recipe for success.

There can be no innovation, not only in terms of
formal resources, but even in ideas; the creation of new
ideas with an old form, or of new forms with old ideas,
has, indeed, yet to be seen. For this reason, the
critical function of literature is muzzled, and there
can be no proposition of transcending what is wrong
with the present moment; whatever element of criticism
there may be is prevented from reaching beyond the
framework of the existing system, literary or otherwise. There may be a mild form of criticism that col-
laborates toward perfecting the system and correcting
its lesser defects in order that it might function more
smoothly. But there must be not a single criticism
that suggests exchanging the system for another, nor
even an admission that the system itself is the wrong
one, that its defects are necessary--not accidental--
ones.

Even the small degree of "social criticism" that
exists in this type of literature is obligatory. Does
not one of the many best-selling novels by José Mauro
de Vasconcelos recount how life is miserable for the
poverty-stricken children of Brazil? From such a life
it is possible to make a miraculous and individual
escape, thanks to a millionaire who takes a liking to
us (which in a few words is what happens in his book)
or thanks to a specific gift at the lowest level of
human talent, promoted by the machinery of big business
and the state, as in the case of some soccer player or
other. The whole of best-selling literature is progressive, in the worst sense of the word: without a pinch--
but not more than a pinch--of humanitarian ideas, no
best seller can catch on. It is sufficient to cite the
science fiction books that have achieved huge sales in
recent years by, for example, Ray Bradbury, whose
Fahrenheit 451 made a big hit and was later adapted for
French cinema; by Arthur Clarke, who also contributed
to Stanley Kubrick's 2001--A Space Odyssey, which broke
box-office records the whole world over; and by Isaac
Asimov and Robert Heinlein. Or we may consider the
new swinging type of detective story, such as Ed McBain's
enormous series about the Eighty-seventh District of
Isola City, an obvious metamorphosis of New York; or
the one by Harry Kellerman, whose detective-cum-rabbi,
going to bed late or waking up early, is not only
Jewish but religious; or the Shaft series, about a
black detective; or the bunch of women that E. V.
Cunningham used for the leading characters and titles
of his books. The oppressed are hoisted to the level
of heroes, whether they are women, blacks, or Jews.

Even beyond the detective thriller and science fiction, this formula remains constant, as can be seen from the success of Arthur Hailey's architectonic-institutional sequence, including Airport, Hotel, and Hospital.

Obscure names to the adepts of highbrow culture: soon they will have a moldy smell and no one will even be able to identify them any more. Today, so long after the explosion of the 1960s, would Ian Fleming's James Bond still be acceptable, in all his snobbish racism?

Cartoon strips are undergoing a similar modification. Such traditional heroes as Batman, Superman, or Scrooge and other Walt Disney characters who used to be ostensibly "sordid agents of Yankee imperialism" are now becoming progressive. The new European cartoons--Guido Crepax's sophisticated Valentina, Wollinsky's Paulette, even the Russian Oktobriana--are incredibly advanced. In a more popular line, the list includes Goscinny and Uderzo's Astérix, as well as Goscinny and Tabary's Iznogud. In all of them we find the same pokes at pollution, ecological destruction, military-police repression, property speculation, administrative corruption, trade union manipulation, consumerism, and racial oppression.

Among the new Americans, those who come closest to the Europeans referred to--with highly anarchical, uninhibited, and innovative strips--are the creators of cartoons that began as part of the "underground": some more intellectual, such as Jules Feiffer; others somewhat less so, such as Charles Schultz, the creator of Peanuts, or the extraordinary Robert Crumb. As is widely know, the latter is the author of a cartoon feature film, Fritz the Cat (distributed in Europe and the United States, but not in Brazil): in a supremely disrespectful and hence hilarious manner, the film examines the blind alleys into which the most advanced progressive thinking is marching, by claiming to oppose society's institutions or to dribble past their clutching tentacles.

In societies reasonably open to cultural debate, the progressive ingredient in best sellers, whether fiction writing, film, or cartoon strips, is a matter of course, and it may even go as far as its own self-criticism. As for us in Brazil, the years come and go and yet another novel by Jorge Amado, the writer whose latest book is the object of this analysis, awaits us, reiterating the usual mannerisms, and merely sharpening his utensils for the worst. His books are becoming more and more voluminous, which means not only higher

prices, but, consequently, a higher percentage for the
author on the sale of every copy. There are more and
more obviously repeated passages; it is easy to see
that there are three or four versions of the same episode written for selection and refinement into one
final version, which never appears; yet the three or
four preliminary ones appear as they flowed from his
typewriter. There is less and less artistic elaboration, while the mythology of Bahia--a Brazilian state
that Jorge Amado has made into an infallible personal
formula--is more and more reinforced: typical local
food and sugar-cane brandy, beaches and coconut trees,
candomblé and mulatto girls, blacks and fishing boats,
colonels and prostitutes, sex and violence.

The latest exploit, War-Weary Tereza Batista* is a
462-page sample of all that is worst in best-selling
literature and in ourselves. The avidity with which
the book is read is equal only to the irritation it
provokes. Jung was right to remind us that a certain
kind of literary work--and he speaks of high-quality
works--is always rejected by the public "unless it
unleashes the crudest reactions."

Jorge Amado's progressive banner is populism, the
glorification of the "people," which justifies whatever
atrocity his fiction may perpetrate. Everything good
comes from the people, and thus all characters are
caricatures. The only exceptions are the colonel, a
rich and well-bred man, and the people's representative,
a mulatto prostitute--a couple that reveals the writer's
classist and sexist point of view. Who embodies the
virtues of the people--and, in this case, the obvious
implication is "the unflinching resistance of the
oppressed Brazilian people," used in spite of being an
obsolete cliché--but Tereza, the incorruptible prostitute? Thus far, no objections: if a prostitute is not
an industrial worker, nor is the majority of her country's population. As to the Colonel, Tereza's influence
will make him into a virtuous man, thus demonstrating
that a class alliance is viable and that the enemy is
the petite bourgeoisie.

And Tereza herself never falters: she is the only
unfailingly virtuous character in the book. If we cast
our minds back to the paupers of Brecht and Buñuel, we
are inclined to believe that Jorge Amado must be trying
to be funny. In his novel it is as if the ethics of
misery were quite different and a virtuous pauper did

---

*Free translation of Tereza Batista Cansada de Guerra
(São Paulo: Ed. Martins, 1972). All translations within the text are the author's.

not die of hunger; the idealization of misery loses
nothing to the idealization of slavery in the work of
our renowned sociologist Gilberto Freyre. The structure of the fiction is constantly interrupted to give
way to abstract and polemical statements on the subject
of misery; in Tereza's life, however, this misery never
appears in a concrete form. She is, in fact, a moral
being, just like one of Balzac's opulent duchesses; on
the cold and cruel scene of the upper circles of
nineteenth-century French society, where everybody
devours everybody else, such a character appears from
time to time. And Balzac points out the condition--
necessary, but not sufficient, since it appears only as
an exception--in which a moral being can emerge: on
top of a big heap of money.

Tereza, a one-dimensional stereotype, acts in a
disinterested and altruistic way, all devotion to her
neighbor. We are reminded of Defoe's Moll Flanders, and
the comparison is distressing. Moll Flanders, writing
her memoirs at the age of sixty, is a model of flexibility guided by the need to survive. She is born out
of wedlock in the dungeons of Newgate prison and separated from her mother, who is deported to the American
colonies. She roams the country with a band of gypsies
until the age of three. She lives in an orphanage,
where she learns a craft: her greatest fear is that of
becoming a domestic servant. Then she moves to live
with a family where she is seduced by and falls in love
with the oldest son, who abandons her. She marries
five times, once with her own brother, by whom she has
children. She subsists for years on end as a thief and
prostitute. She has to abandon the children she con-
ceives through various men. She is caught thieving and
sent to Newgate, where she is condemned to death. Thanks
to a priest who leads her to conversion and repentance,
her sentence is commuted to exile in the New World,
where she goes with one of her husbands, a highwayman
she had met up with again in prison. Finally, a wealthy
landowner in Virginia, she achieves a reconciliation
with her son, the fruit of incest, who had remained
there. Such is the life of Defoe's heroine.

As a character, she achieves greatness, as did the
author who invented her, because she is a complex human
being, a mixture of practical shrewdness (otherwise how
could she survive?) and conventional sentiments, those
dominant in the ideology of the society in which she
lives. When she soars on the wings of the most dazzling
passion, she hides away some money or property for some
emergency without telling her loved one. If she has to
abandon a child in order to survive, she weeps and
laments, but abandons it in the end. Seduced by one of
the brothers of the family she lived with, she falls in

love with him, yet marries the other one, who shuts his
eyes to her inferior social position; and, though with
a heavy sense of guilt, she never confesses her previous
affair, which would invalidate this marriage and the
consequent position she has acquired. This does not
prevent her, however, from being a kind-hearted person,
kind to others and equally prompt to perceive kindness
on the part of others. She is capable of the vilest
transactions: a fighter who never flees the lists,
unless flight can mean the chance to go on living.

Not Jorge Amado's Tereza: Tereza is all of one
piece, a Don Quixote endowed with mental health and
deprived of Sancho Panza, as if such a character had
become acceptable since Cervantes so many centuries ago
wrote his derisive criticism of the hero in fiction.
She is even endowed with political consciousness, to
the point of leading civic movements for the protection
of the needy and resistance against repression. Among
other exploits, this citizen of the underdeveloped
polis, like Lysistrata, leads a strike of the same kind
in the prostitution zone. If Sartre's prostitute is
respectful, this one is respectable. The problem of
literary construction that has to be faced as a result
of stereotyping and artistic falsifying of this magnitude is no small one: how to give verisimilitude to
the actions of such a character, in a repetitive novel
based on the worst formulas of watered-down realism?

The solution has already been exploited by Jorge
Amado in previous works. Every turning point in the
plot, when there is one--for instance, how will Tereza
and her unarmed fellow prostitutes be able to take on
the police?--has a supernatural denouement. The orixás
(African divinities) of Bahia intervene ex machina, and
everything comes right at the end; this is a frequent
occurrence. Whether it be virtue in peril, a menace to
the good-hearted, or the weak and just against the
strong and unjust, the reader may raise his eyes to the
heavens: some friendly orixá will appear to resolve the
impasse; for, just like author and reader, the orixás,
too, are on the side of the oppressed. As the writing
is ambiguous, it permits its audience to read it as
materialist; but the other--supernatural--reading, which
is presented as metaphorical, is also the lyrical one,
where the author shows in pièces de résistance that he
knows how to be poetic when he wants to.

Here is an example, chosen among many. A woman
goes to consult the priestess of the African religion
about Tereza's plan to resist the police, who are in
the process of evicting them from the houses where they
live and practice their profession; she also wants to
know if Tereza is acting in good faith. The African

divinity appears and gives counsel through his priestess: "And the girl Tereza--is she trustworthy? The
answer was categorical: absolutely. Warrior, daughter
of Iansã, behind her Ogum Peixe Marinho sees an old man
with a staff and white beard: it is Lemba di Lê in
person, called Oxalá by the Yoruba faithful." Soon the
police make a raid on the houses and all are arrested--
but Tereza manages to escape into the street. The
policeman nicknamed Dogfish, her personal enemy, tries
to stop her, but the two of them are separated by an
old man: "From where does he appear, this old man who
hides her from the eyes of Dogfish? An imposing old
man, in a white linen suit, a Panama hat and a gold-
embossed walking cane." Through rapid feints, Tereza
slips away and disappears. "Dogfish and another policeman search for her in vain--where did the wretched woman
get to? The old man has vanished too, without a trace.
What old man? . . . No one has seen an old man, not
before, nor now, nor since" (pp. 395-98). The mobilization of indirect discourse, as in the passages quoted
here, is the basis for the ambiguity that makes possible
the two readings, according to the reader's preference:
if he aligns with the irrationalist progressives, he
will feel satisfied; if he takes sides with the ration-
alist progressives, he will put the supernatural element
down to the author's "lyricism." One way or the other,
the correct position, the correct line of the author
and reader alike, is saved.

This stylistic weapon, free indirect discourse,
which Jorge Amado so well knows how to use, allows his
writing to be irresponsible. For in this way the source
of the narration is not a narrator, but some mysterious
voice flowing from an unknown source. Sometimes, in
short passages of two or three pages printed in italics,
the narrator is identified at the end. Of course in
these cases it is always a real and living person--some
fashionable, famous, and folkloric figure from the
mythology of Bahia--such as Mãe Menininha do Gantois,
Cuíca de Santo Amaro, or Camafeu de Oxossi. Such passages are passed off as personal testimony, but there
is no change in the style: it is the same free indirect
discourse that governs the entire novel.

But where Jorge Amado surpasses himself in the
present work, winning out over such other illustrious
writers of ours as Cassandra Rios and Adelaide Carraro
(specialists in obscene trash), and even such classics
of pornography as the Victorians, is in the titillation
of the reader. He has been working in this line for a
long time, but to keep the reader's interest he has had
to renew it incessantly and has resorted to it more and
more heavily. Having passed through various degrees of
intensity, the present peak is no longer mere pornography

but a leap forward into the dubious regions of perversion. The touchstone in this case is sadism. About
one-third of the entire book is dedicated to describing
the intimate relations between Tereza and the sadistic
Captain Justiniano, who keeps her locked up in a bedroom, flogs her with a cat-o'-nine tails and a strap
with a metal buckle, and burns the soles of her feet
with a boiling-hot flatiron. The initial scene in
these relations--the rape, of course--alone occupies
four pages. It should be remembered that Tereza is only
twelve years of age, which adds pedophilia to the
sadism. Furthermore, it is difficult to ignore a certain amount of admiration for the exceptional deeds performed by the captain who, having wrestled a whole night
before managing to rape Tereza, suffering scratches,
burns from a lantern flame, and a kick in his strategic
area, remains nonetheless at full capacity and--I
quote--"a complete male forever erect" (p. 114).

     In milder episodes, such as when Tereza meets
Daniel and with him learns the joys of love, ten pages
are consecrated to a single night. Detail follows upon
detail: none of the manuals so common nowadays in this
era of sexual liberation would probably be so meticu-
lous. Each kind of caress, each recess of the body,
every possible combination, each vocal manifestation,
every movement, and every smell--they all have their
place. Moreover, they can be found spread out through
the whole of the novel, though they are especially concentrated in these two exemplary passages. This option
for pornographic detail makes the reader into a voyeur
and the characters into exhibitionists, which accom-
plishment completes no small list of perversions:
sadism, pedophilia, voyeurism, and exhibitionism. It
would not be inappropriate to beg forgiveness of the
Marquis de Sade, in whose works the practice of perversion constituted, at the very least, an object of
existential meditation.

     It is here that we arrive at a delicate point:
the treatment of the prostitute as the central character.
There is apparently nothing more progressive than hoist-
ing one of society's most destitute creatures up to
this position of eminence. The image of the prostitute
as a woman with infinite sexual capacity traditionally
makes frequent appearances in the fantasies of imaginary
life. We may cite as an example Fellini's abundant
gallery of prostitutes. For previous generations she
played the part of initiator of men into the mysteries
of sex, the result being very often a preferential fix-
ation for them. For married women, she represents the
model of maximum polygamy that contrasts with their
own obligatory monogamy; thus, if she is an enemy to
the extent that she is a threat to the husband's

fidelity (even though she is simultaneously a guarantee
of the institution of marriage), she is also an object
of envy inasmuch as the hypothetical richness of sexual
experience is forbidden to wives. Yet it is rare indeed to find any knowledge of what the prostitute
thinks of herself, of her condition, of other women, of
men, and of the world. Research about prostitution is
seldom carried out by women; the majority of those
studies that do exist are authored by men, whether consisting of clinical material that appears indirectly
via the psychosexual deviations of male clients, as for
example in the case of Krafft-Ebing's or Freud's work,
or via journalistic writing. Recently the women's
liberation movements have taken investigations a step
forward, even to the point of recording the personal
testimony of the prostitutes themselves. As a further
advance in the attempt to clarify the question and to
incorporate this clarification into the movement, the
first feminist congress on prostitution was held in
the United States in December 1971, including the participation of prostitutes.

      I shall try to analyze Jorge Amado's prostitute by
joining the available threads, whether those of fiction
writing, clinical cases, research work, or personal
accounts, in an effort to understand the question. One
more necessary difficulty may be added here, already
confessed by Virginia Woolf in The Death of a Moth,
although her times were more repressive in this respect:
when writing, the flow of inspiration risked being
interrupted if it happened to run onto some meditation
or fantasy concerning the writer's own body or sex.
The profile of the prostitute common to all these
sources seems to contain one clear element that some of
them endeavor to overcome: the contours of a dominant
male representation. It gratifies men to think of prostitutes as an eternally available and accessible source
of pleasure; they are the only women who may not say
no and thus possess the lowest possible degree of liberty in their contacts with the opposite sex. The gesture
of giving money and the act of payment introduce a mercantile relationship and reduce to a commodity what
should be enjoyable. At the same time, from the woman's
point of view, receiving money is the remuneration of
her labor, but it is also degradation: she was bought;
it was no choice of hers. The degradation exists for
both parties, given that the other desires something he
will only obtain if he resorts to the crudest and most
brutal form of persuasion--money. Sexual seduction
ranges over various levels, from the use of class position (revealed through external signs such as cars,
clothes, good manners, and educated, mundane small talk)
to the well-known promises of jobs and administrative
posts, eternal love, and even marriage. In the act of

paying the money, a power relation is set up, in which
the power--though in different shades--is on both sides:
both are dominant and dominated, both are degraded.
Hence the extreme rarity, though they do exist, of prostitutes with some consciousness of their condition.
Furthermore, they compete with their fellow prostitutes
to obtain the favors of their men, given that a larger
clientele is a source of more money and prestige, better survival, and a greater share of power. To win the
exceptional favors of men, they have to be more of a
prostitute, that is, more docile and more prepared to
play the roles in which men cast them, to give the
caresses men desire, to refine the dramatization of the
pleasure they simulate.

It is in the most extreme cases that this relation
becomes transparent. I refer to those prostitutes who
specialize in flagellation, about whom there is ample
material in the clinical classics. There is nothing so
classic, however--though it is just as routine, perfectly integrated into everyday life and so-called normali-
ty--about the personal testimony of the Parisian girl,
Jackie, published in an issue of Les Temps Modernes of
late 1972. There we can observe how the exercise of
the power within the prostitue's reach attains its maximum: she is paid by men to flagellate them, making
them pay the price of her own degradation with this
same gesture, a payment she exacts in the concrete form
of the act of beating and wounding. Of course, if we
consider the world of imagination it is more in Buñuel
than in Fellini, with his self-complacent view of prostitutes, that we can find something approaching these
murky, but revealing, situations.

Sometimes the threatening, dangerous side of the
prostitute is perceived. It is no coincidence that the
mysterious case of Jack the Ripper occurred at the time
of Queen Victoria. In the space of a few short weeks,
five prostitutes were murdered and dismembered by a
criminal whose identity was never discovered. This gesture illuminates Victorian morality in action, stretched
to the limit; in other words, it is the prostitute's
very physical person that must be exterminated because
it represents the correlative of the family institution,
a frightening sexual potency, a presentiment of obscure
debts that may one day have to be paid.

Occasionally some prostitute or other with more
consciousness of her condition recognizes its inherent
alienation. She can perceive both the degradation to
which she is subjected and the degradation to which she
submits the other, thereby extracting the few moments of
revenge for her own condition, as well as the sensations
of power, that she is able to obtain. The majority,

however, are quite unconscious of all this and perform
the role, in all its alienation, that society has con-
ferred upon them. Nevertheless, the burden is excessive; body and soul exact their revenge beyond the
sphere of consciousness, as the high incidence of frigidity and lesbianism among prostitutes indicates.
Frigidity points to an inner rejection of the possibility to enjoy sex; lesbianism, to the only way out of
the commodity relationship, signifying a free choice
and the recovery of the sexual relation as something
that is not a commodity.

Against this background, Jorge Amado's prostitute
assumes the proportions of one of Latin America's most
remarkable products of the male chauvinist imagination:
Tereza Batista is the ideal woman of every progressive
man with money in his wallet. A prostitute, a pretty,
warm-hearted, welcoming woman of good character, and,
above all, a mulatto--this latter quality being the
product of an erotic fantasy that predominates in all
peoples with slavery in their past. Alongside this,
she is conscious of her situation, shows her solidarity
with her professional companions to the point of defending them in physical combat with men, is politicized, and ends up by earning a marriage for love's
sake. She possesses not only all the characteristics
of an absolutely alienated and unconscious prostitute,
but also those--only those which interest male chauvin-
ism--of a highly conscious one.

The prowess of Jorge Amado has now reunited and
reinforced the discoveries of his previous books. The
prostitute who wanders pleasantly through all of them
has now become the leading character and title; their
joyful eroticism has crossed the frontiers of perversion; the mythology of Bahia is reiterated, and free
indirect discourse shrewdly manipulated. Jorge Amado,
in short, has produced the kitsch version of himself.
His own conception of literature is expressed by one of
the male characters in his book making expert use of
indirect discourse: let us not lose time with writing
that "does not give us a hard-on or a good laugh" (p.
303). Such is the sum of Jorge Amado's aesthetic ideas,
and here is his latest book, War-Weary Tereza Batista,
to confirm it.

Contemporary North American Literary Primitivism: *Deliverance* and *Surfacing*

Evelyn J. Hinz

"They tell me that this is the kind of thing that gets hold of middle-class householders every once in a while," observes Bobby Trippe, in James Dickey's Deliverance, concerning a canoe trip that he and three other businessmen are planning to make through a yet wild section of northern Georgia.[1] If we judge by the popularity of Deliverance, which is structured as the narrative of that adventure, an entire nation--and not merely bored suburbanites--has simultaneously been seized with the same impulse; and if we judge by the equally phenomenal success of Margaret Atwood's Surfacing, a Canadian novel with a similarly "primitivistic" theme, the impulse is not exclusive to the United States, but endemic to all of North America in the 1970s.

There are, of course, interesting differences between the primitivism of Deliverance and that of Surfacing, and my ultimate concern in this study is whether these differences should be attributed to the different sexes of the writers in question, to their different nationalities, or to both. That is, does the type of primitivism that Dickey depicts derive from the fact that he is a man or from the fact that he is an American? Does the type of primitivism that Atwood espouses derive from the fact that she is a woman or from the fact that she is a Canadian? Or, finally, do the two come together in the sense that the American psyche is

Note: I am indebted to the Killam Foundation for financial assistance in the form of a Post Doctoral Research Scholarship that facilitated my research during the years 1973-75.

characteristically masculine in its orientation and the Canadian psyche characteristically feminine?

What I also hope to demonstrate, however, is that the tendency to categorize immediately in this manner, the tendency to stress chauvinistic and sexist distinctions, and the tendency to seek the origins of art in the peculiarities of the artist are all aspects of the major problem of modern times that Dickey and Atwood are concerned with exploring. Furthermore, what we are dealing with in the case of Deliverance and Surfacing is not two isolated novels linked only by reason of a basic theme, nor even simply two novels of the same period, but rather two primitivistic works that have almost simultaneously emerged out of the ostensibly progress-oriented ethos of the 1970s; Deliverance was published in 1970, Surfacing in 1972. Hence before, or by way of preparing for, a discussion of the cultural significance of Deliverance and Surfacing in an ethnological frame of reference, it is important to consider their cultural significance in a topical sense. That is, to what should we attribute the manifestation of the primitivistic impulse in these two works in the first place? What does it mean, in terms of general cultural history, that the 1970s should be marked by the strong reappearance of primitivistic literature? What is there about the contemporary ethos that should inspire two artists, of different sexes and nationalities, and both of them internationally famous poets, to turn to the writing of primitivistic fiction?

How one answers these questions depends to a great extent upon how one defines primitivism, although, as both Dickey and Atwood suggest through the structuring of their novels, all possible definitions are finally reducible to one, and all explanations that fail to recognize this common denominator constitute a compounding of the problem that the true primitivist is out to correct.

Both Deliverance and Surfacing, for example, begin with the "weekend in the country" syndrome that Bobby Trippe sees as constituting the primitivistic impulse. The initial setting in Deliverance is the familiar suburban bar, where four middle-class types have met at noon in the middle of the week; two of them are at first doubtful about concurring with the ringleader's suggestion that they spend the upcoming weekend in the wilds, but both agree after reminders of the impending dullness of their afternoon's work and upon condition that they can take certain amenities with them--a guitar, in the case of Drew Ballinger, and liquor, in the case of Bobby Trippe. Surfacing similarly begins with three city-dwellers accompanying a fourth, the nameless

female narrator of the novel, on a trip to an island in
northern Quebec, the site of the narrator's childhood.
The ostensible purpose of this trip, as far as the narrator is concerned, is to check on a report that her
father is missing and to discover what has happened to
him; for the others, the trip is an excuse to get away
from the city and, specifically, for Anna to do some
sunbathing and for the other two, David and Joe, to do
some fishing and capture some scenes for a film they
are making. Like Drew and Bobby, the narrator's companions have also brought along some "creature comforts"--
beer, pot, and a transistor radio.

From a conventional point of view, then, what primitivism involves is getting away for a while. And what
works like Deliverance and Surfacing seem designed to
do is to provide a living-room experience of the wild,
for the impulse to get away and the popularity of such
fiction are traceable to nothing more serious than the
ennui that universally afflicts urban residents and the
dissatisfaction that perversely manifests itself in
highly civilized cultures. As Dickey and Atwood see it,
however, the tendency to define primitivism in this way,
the inability to recognize the incongruities inherent
in the desire to return to nature equipped with all the
artificial amenities of the city, is symptomatic of the
utter decadence of modern North American civilization
and its total dependence upon technology. And consequently, the type of "exotic" or academic primitivism
of the opening of Deliverance and Surfacing sets the
stage for the more serious and practical kind of primitivism that Lewis and the narrator's father in Surfacing
represent.

Primitivism for these two stems from a feeling
that civilization has or is about to collapse and that
the thinking man's solution is to get out while he can
or to prepare himself to withstand the cataclysm when
it comes.

As Lewis and Ed drive to Oree, the point of departure for the last look at the wilds that will soon be
destroyed by technology, for example, Lewis attempts to
explain that his concern with physical fitness is not
merely a case of "narcissistic" fanaticism, just as his
interest in the people of these parts is not merely
anthropological. "I just believe," he tells Ed, "that
the whole thing is going to be reduced to the human
body, once and for all. I want to be ready." And when
Ed asks him, "What whole thing?" Lewis replies, "The
human race thing. I think the machines are going to
fail, the political systems are going to fail, and a
few men are going to take to the hills and start over"
(p. 40). Relatively speaking, the narrraor's father in

Surfacing is one of the "few" who have taken to the
hills and attempted to begin again. An amateur scien-
tist--part botanist, part geologist, part cultural his-
torian--the father sought an island refuge for his family during the cataclysm of World War II, training himself and his family to survive under conditions that
reflected "not the settled farm life of his own father
but that of the earliest ones who had arrived when
there was nothing but forests and no ideologies but the
ones they brought with them."[2] A freethinker, the
father did not believe in a traditional God, but in the
"reason and benevolent order" (p. 190) of man and the
universe, both of which he could not find in the city.

     If such primitivism sounds very much like a modern-
ized version of eighteenth-century attitudes and problems, Atwood and Dickey have succeeded in their intention, though one could hardly miss the point, given the
specific allusions that both make. As Lewis waxes enthusiastic about returning to the wilds, Ed Gentry
attempts to check him with the question, "What's the
life up there, now? . . . I mean, before you take to
the mountains and set up the Kingdom of Sensibility?"
(p. 43). Similarly, the narrator's father is a combination Robinson Crusoe-Rousseau-Shaftesbury-"mute,
inglorious Milton," who believes that "with the proper
guide books you could do everything yourself" and whose
library consists of "the King James Bible which he said
he enjoyed for its literary qualities, a complete
Robert Burns, Boswell's Life, Thompson's Seasons, se-
lections from Goldsmith and Cowper. He admired what he
called the eighteenth century rationalists: he thought
of them as men who had avoided the corruptions of the
Industrial Revolution and learned the secret of the
golden mean, the balanced life, he was sure they all
practiced organic farming" (p. 38). To complete this
suggestion of the eighteenth-century shadow that lies
behind the primitivism I have been discussing thus far,
Atwood also has David and Joe, teachers of adult education, define themselves as the "new Renaissance men"
who teach themselves what they need to learn (p. 10),
while Dickey gives Drew a deformed little boy named
"Pope" and has Drew discover the Wordsworthian untutored
genius in the idiot child, Lonnie. Finally, the narrator summarizes the neoclassical, preromantic ethos perfectly in her observation on the first night of their
"return to nature": "A little beer, a little pot, some
jokes, a little political chitchat, the golden mean"
(p. 39).

     Where the primitivism of the eighteenth century
had its climax, however, was in the French Revolution,
and consequent to the primitivism of the supporting
characters in Deliverance and Surfacing, we have the

primitivism of the two protagonists. In the case of
Dickey's novel, this primitivism manifests itself in
the transformation of Ed Gentry from an apathetic
businessman, who at the outset could not kill a deer,
into a dispassionate killer. In the case of Surfacing
it takes the form of the transformation of the narrator
from a seemingly cool, liberated woman, who prior to the
beginning of the novel had reasonably agreed to have an
abortion, into an obsessed maniac who indulges in an
orgy of destruction, slashing every civilized object
within her reach, and who ruthlessly uses a male com-
panion to beget a child. Whereas the primitivism of
the other characters was signaled by its conscious and
voluntary qualities, the primitivism of these two protagonists is characterized by its unconscious and in-
voluntary qualities. Ed Gentry is not, like Lewis,
out to prove himself or to reorient himself; indeed, at
the outset he ridicules Lewis's notions to this effect,
emphasizing that his philosophy is "sliding": "I don't
have any dreams of a new society. I'll take what I've
got" (p. 46). Similarly, unlike her companions, Atwood's narrator does not regard the task of checking on
her father's disappearance as an excuse to get away
from the city and routine, but as a duty that has taken
her away from her work, which accordingly she has
brought along and engages in while the others are fishing and sunbathing. Whereas the primitivism of Lewis
and the father stemmed from a reasoned belief that something was wrong, the primitivism of Ed and the narrator
is totally unpremeditated; whereas the primitivism of
the former types consisted in a conscious reaction
against impending collapse, the primitivism of the latter takes the very form of such a collapse.

      With the two protagonists, then, we get a new per-
spective on Bobby Trippe's definition of the primitivistic impulse as something "that gets hold of middle-
class householders every once in a while." For if in
the case of the conventional characters, the emphasis
should fall on "middle-class," in the case of Ed Gentry
and Surfacing's narrator the emphasis falls upon "gets
hold." In turn, we also get a new perspective on the
cultural significance of Deliverance and Surfacing.
For if we find the correlatives for the type of primitivism practiced by the conventional characters in such
things as physical fitness programs, health food diets,
ecological measures, and interest in aboriginal cultures
and wild life, we find the counterparts of the primitivism of the protagonists in the increasing incidence of
fanaticism, violence, apparently motiveless vandalism,
and mental disturbances that seem to constitute an
alternate to the back-to-nature trend of modern North
America. If we also, finally, are encouraged--by the
parallels that Dickey and Atwood draw between the

primitivism of Lewis and the father and that of the
eighteenth century--to see in such a trend the imminence
of the new "Reign of Terror," then we are also given the
opportunity to recognize the forces lying behind such
cultural upheavals and the possibility of changing the
outcome by correcting the cause.

As I have noted, what causes the behavior of the
two protagonists is not political, or social, or economic, or intellectual; neither is determined or motivated by any principles at stake. Nor can their
behavior really be traced to any personal cause. While
the abortion experience of the narrator has been trau-
matic, there is no reasonable connection between this
experience and the objects upon which she vents her
violence; if it were merely the question of the child,
from the beginning of the novel both of her male companions would have been only too glad to be obliging.
Similarly, if Ed Gentry has a practical reason for killing the mountaineer, there is nothing in his personal
background to account for the emergence of the killer
instinct and no psychological way of accounting for
the strength and stamina he exhibits in his pursuit.
As both Dickey and Atwood suggest, then, there is some
force beyond the individuals that is in operation in
either case, some inexplicable force that is using them
as means to an end.

And what this end is, paradoxically, is the physical and psychological survival of the protagonists by
means of a destruction of the ideologies upon which
Lewis and the father had based their theories of survival. Ed Gentry, who is unprepared and out of shape,
survives to protect the physically broken Lewis from
the natural world he had extolled as the necessary
ingredient for a new beginning; he survives by disproving Lewis's belief that survival is in man's hands and
that it depends upon man's foresight, well-trained body,
and discipline. Similarly, the narrator, who exhibits
the "failure of reason" that her passivist father saw
exemplified in Hitler and in World War I, survives
while three possibilities are held out for the fate of
her father: either that he has gone irrevocably mad,
that he has drowned in an attempt to photograph the
submerged rock paintings of the Great Canadian Shield,
or that he has become the victim of the various arche-
ologists and surveyors with whom he has been in touch.
The narrator survives, in other words, by disproving
her father's belief that irrationality is something
outside, that violence is political in its origins, and
that withdrawal and return to nature are the solutions.
Both protagonists, finally, survive by disproving the
idea that the life force is a material thing subject to
man's control, and both survive to disprove the idea

that the irrational is a purely iconoclastic force,
which is antagonistic to all forms of civilization and
asserts itself only in times of psychological or cultural crisis.

In contrast to the typical novel of violence,
Deliverance and Surfacing do not end with the protagonists' having come to their senses and looking back
upon their experiences as nightmare or catharsis; rather
both novels end with the protagonists' being firmly in
touch with the irrational force they have encountered.
The only change is that whereas previously it manifested
itself as an external force that took control over their
conscious selves, it now has become internalized and
works through their consciousness; whereas previously
it took a destructive form, it now takes a creative one.
Thus, whereas previously Ed Gentry was "possessed" by
the thing that "gets hold of middle-class householders,"
at the conclusion of Deliverance he possesses it: "The
river and everything I remembered about it became a
possession to me, a personal, private possession, as
nothing else in my life ever had. Now it ran nowhere
but in my head, but there it ran as though immortally."
Then shifting the locus, he goes on: "The river under-
lies, in one way or another, everything I do. It is
always finding a way to serve me, from my archery to
some of my recent ads and to the new collages I have
been attempting for my friends" (p. 234). Similarly, at
the conclusion of Surfacing the narrator emerges from
the madness that has overtaken her not to repudiate
what she has done, but to cling to it and nurture it:
"I re-enter my own time. But I bring with me from the
distant past five nights ago the time-traveller, the
primeaval one who will have to learn, shape of a gold-
fish in my belly, undergoing its watery changes. Word
furrows potential already in its proto-brain, untravel-
led paths. No god and perhaps real, even that is un-
certain; I can't know yet, it's too early. But I
assume it; if I die it dies, if I starve it starves
with me. It might be the first one, the first true
human; it must be born, allowed" (p. 191).

Finally, in contrast to the creativity and new beginning that thus characterize the "irrational" primitivism of the protagonists, the rational primitivism of
Lewis and the narrator's father results in nothing productive: Lewis returns to take up archery once more and
Zen; the father never returns. What the primitivism of
Lewis and the father really accomplishes is to precipitate the eruption of the destructive direction that the
irrational takes when it is imposed upon; if the destructive behavior of the protagonists is something
occasioned by a force beyond their control, it is also
occasioned, as the structure of Deliverance and

Surfacing suggests, by the decision of Lewis and the
father to return to nature.

   The point that Dickey and Atwood are trying to
make, then, is precisely the point that Otto Rank attempted to make in Beyond Psychology, a series of essays
that he wrote in an effort to diagnose the cultural upheavals of his time--the period between the two world
wars.

   Arguing that whatever human nature is capable of
must by definition be regarded as natural, and observing
the extent to which emotional reaction is independent
of the will of the individual and the prior factor in
all of his decisions, Rank came to the conclusion that
this irrational, impersonal, and autonomous force was
the cornerstone of human existence. Further, he determined that the confusions of his time were directly
related to the fact that Western ideologies are structured upon the belief that the rational is the norm in
human nature, the criterion of what is natural, and concomitantly that all behavior which is not rational is
unnatural. This emphasis upon the rational, in turn,
Rank diagnosed as a fear of those forces which lie beyond conscious thought and control, a fear incidentally
that he saw manifested not only in technological and
sociological attempts to regulate and order human existence, but also more subtly in the various attempts to
rationalize the irrational--the tendency in psychology
to define irrational behavior in terms of the repressed
personal consciousness, or the tendency on the part of
the historians and cultural analysts to ascribe the
emergence of mass movements and social change to ideological and political causes. Finally, insofar as the
irrational is the cornerstone of human existence,
attempts to subject it to rational control, to eradicate
it from human behavior, really constitute a life-denying
tendency; and conversely in rebellions against excessive
rationalism is to be found a life-asserting force.
Accordingly, in the incidence of irrational behavior in
a rationally oriented culture Rank saw a paradoxical
moral that he expressed in terms of a plea for a recognition of the creative potential of the irrational and
a veiled warning of the destructive form it would take
if its determining role were not recognized: "We still
have to learn, it seems, that life, in order to maintain itself, must revolt every so often against man's
ceaseless attempts to master its irrational forces with
his mind."[3]

   The extent to which the 1970s are characterized by
man's attempt to master the universe is too obvious to
require comment, just as the key incidents that Dickey
and Atwood use to symbolize technological control are

rather patent: the building of the dam at Aintry in
Deliverance; the narrator's abortion in Surfacing.   The
extent to which this attempt at mastery may be our un-
doing is something of which we may be becoming aware,
as Dickey and Atwood demonstrate in the concern of Lewis
and the father with ecological measures and survival
tactics.   The extent to which we still have much to
learn, however, as both writers also demonstrate, is
the extent to which we focus upon technology as the
villain, refusing to recognize the subtler forms that
man's attempt at mastery takes.

Dickey and Atwood illustrate in numerous ways man's
attempt to master nature and the forms that such mastery
can take, but the best example for the purposes of summary is to be found in the dramatic opening of Deliverance.   In the diction of the first paragraph, if we
attend to it carefully, there are simultaneously evoked
the image of a surgeon general lecturing on the condition of a patient about to undergo an exploratory; an
intelligence expert outlining a plan of attack on a
primitive village; a sex educationist defining the location of various erogenous zones in the female anatomy;
an editor of a large publishing firm demanding cuts and
changes in a script; a psychiatrist recommending ster-
ilization of a straitjacket case; a jaded, impotent, or
puritanical millionaire methodically indulging in
mechanical, exhibitionistic, and debasing foreplay upon
a woman whom he cannot possess or who has failed to
live up to his idealistic expectations; and finally
Noah and his three sons speculating on the outcome of
the Flood.   And perhaps the best summary of what we have
to look forward to if we persist in such attempts to
exert control over life forces is to be found in the
Atwood's narrator's observation, after she has hunted
through her brain in vain to find an "emotion that
would coincide" with what the word love was supposed to
mean, and after she has turned away from searching for
direct clues to her father's whereabouts to the family
album: "It was no longer his death but my own that concerned me; perhaps I would be able to tell when the
changes occurred by the differences in my former faces,
alive up to a year, a day, then frozen.   The duchess at
the French court before the Revolution, who stopped
laughing or crying so that her skin would never wrinkle,
it worked, she died immortal" (p. 107).   We will die
beautiful, in other words, and become famous for our
discoveries of how human nature can be improved.   But
we will die, and our attempts to rise above time will
occasion nature's revenge.

If the primitivism of Deliverance and Surfacing
goes beyond ecological or survivalist protest against
technology--and indeed sees in modern man's attempt to

return to nature a compounding of the problem of technological take-over, so also does it go beyond a mere
protest against excessive rationalism. What lies behind rationalism, as we have observed in the case of
Lewis and the narrator's father, is a fear of death or
a desire to rise above time, on the one hand, and a lack
of belief in any system beyond man, on the other. As
Rank puts it, and as the connection of deism and
eighteenth-century early romantic primitivism suggests,
rationalism is really a secular replacement for religion, born of the desire for immortality, the desire to
divorce that which can decay from that which cannot.
As a religion, however, rationalism lacks the major
characteristic of religion, which is the ability to
command emotional response; hence the irrational element, which we have defined as the force that impels
us, has no communal outlets and so becomes a disunifying
factor or a tool in the hands of political leader or
propagandist who gives it outlet in terms of a "cause,"
while the misplaced religious element is apparent in
the extent to which such a cause takes the form of a
crusade. The major function of these North American
primitivists, accordingly, is first to point out the
fact that the old religious symbols are dead and then
to discover new ones that are humanly--rather than
politically--vital, universal rather than local. In
short, what the primitivist is concerned with is what
James Baird calls "cultural failure"--the "loss of a
regnant and commanding authority in religious symbolism," which consequently leads to the loss of reverence
for all objects that a culture has earlier regarded as
sacred.[4]

One of the major ways in which Dickey and Atwood
illustrate cultural failure or the loss of commanding
religious symbolism in North America is through the use
of Christographic expletives, while the unobtrusiveness
of such usage subtly proves the point they are making.
"Who made it, Christ, think of the work," says Anna in
Surfacing of the "Bottle Villa," which the narrator
goes on to describe as "a preposterous monument to some
quirkish person" (p. 11). Or again, "Oh Christ, you
have to do that about everything, don't you?" she
retorts to a pun by David on the narrator's suggestion
that he can use his own rod for fishing (p. 63), while
as she watches the narrator fix a live frog on the hook
of her fishing line, she exclaims, "God you're cold-
blooded." One purpose here is to suggest what lies
behind such blasphemous language--the loss of any emotional connotations in the word God, deriving from the
fact that religion has become a cold-blooded or intellectual abstraction. Finally--though certainly not the
last of the examples one could provide--as the narrator
lies with Joe in one bedroom, she overhears David and

Anna in theirs:

> Anna breathing, a fast panic sound as though
> she was running; then her voice began, not like
> her real voice but twisted as her face must
> have been, a desperate beggar's whine, please
> please. I put the pillow over my head, I
> didn't want to listen, I wanted it to be through
> but it kept on, Shut up I whispered but she
> wouldn't. She was praying to herself, it was
> as if David wasn't there at all. Jesus jesus
> oh yes please jesus. Then something different,
> not a word but pure pain, clear as water, an
> animal's at the moment the trap closes (p. 82).

The wordless cry of pain that follows Anna's verbal in-
vocation of the redeemer may result from the agony of
ecstasy, but it may also be a modern cry from the cross,
deriving from the fact that the cross no longer means
anything and implying in this sense that the individual
is alone.

Dickey's purpose is also to suggest that God has
become routine. But Dickey does not simply depend upon
the reader's sensitivity to his puns. As Ed Gentry
outlines the situation to Bobby after the killing of
Drew and the crippling of Lewis, Bobby expostulates,
"Jesus Christ Almighty!" Replies Ed, "Yes, you might
say that. As Lewis might say, 'Come on, Jesus boy,
walk on down to us over that white water. But if you
don't, we've got to do whatever there is to do'" (p.
130). As Ed sees it at this point, calling upon God is
as pointless as calling for mama, appealing to the elements, or putting Lewis on a rock and doing a rain dance
around him to cut down the visibility, which latter form
of primitive evocation he then goes on to ridicule as
well: "But if we got rain, we couldn't get out through
it, and Lewis would probably die of exposure" (p. 131).

When religious symbols lose their potency, so also
do national and social ones, which are formed in a
traditional religious ethos, a point that Atwood makes
very subtly in a typical anarchic and blasphemous interchange. David begins the conversation with the one
great symbol that used to be evocative of the New World
and was applied generally to this continent, the symbol
of America itself: "If only we could kick out the
fascist pig Yanks and the capitalists this would be a
neat country," he observes; "But then, who would be
left?" Anna's reply is "Oh Christ," and though she goes
on to add "don't get going on that," the expletive has
accomplished its function of suggesting that Christ is
no longer to be found among Canadians or Americans.
The idea that a redeemer could be found if one got rid

of the old symbols is one that intrigues the narrator:
"How? . . . How would you kick them out?" And with
David's answer another symbol is shown to be no longer
sacred: "Organize the beavers . . . chew them to
pieces. . . . You heard about the latest national
flag? Nine beavers pissing on a frog" (p. 39). And
when national symbols and emblems go, there is nothing
for the individual to believe in, and only one's friends,
or rather casual acquaintances--the narrator has known
Anna for two months--to cling to: "It's old and shoddy
but I laugh anyway," says the narrator of the joke;
"still I'm glad they're with me, I wouldn't want to be
here alone; at any moment the loss, vacancy, will over-
take me, they ward it off" (p. 39).

When religious symbols lose their potency, so also
do all rituals that originally had a religious sanction
degenerate into purely social and meaningless formality.
This is Dickey's point in repeatedly describing as
"games" those exercises by which Lewis attempts to
discipline himself as well as his purpose in demonstrating that such games do not work toward the ends for
which they were designed. This is also his point in
choosing four middle-aged men as his characters and
forcing them to undergo a violent initiation in the
wilds, as well as his purpose in having Bobby Trippe
scream and fail the ordeal. Finally, this is also his
point in emphasizing the role of golf and football in
North America; modern man does not have to go to the
wilds to satisfy his appetite for violence, nor is there
any lack of organized violence. What is lacking is the
religious sanction for such activity, the loss of the
totemic sense that one becomes a part of what one
destroys.

If the primitivist's first function is to illustrate cultural failure, his task does not end there,
however, as it does for the satirist, for example, or
for the "wasteland" artists like T. S. Eliot or James
Joyce. Having illustrated cultural failure, the primitivistic artist must forge new symbols, new not in the
sense that they are original constructs of the artist's
imagination--the private symbolism of poets like
Wallace Stevens, for example--but new in the sense that
they are not an attempt to revitalize decadent Christian
symbolism--as Thomas Mann and numerous others have
attempted to revitalize biblical stories by making
them relevant or giving them a modern form. And how he
accomplishes this task, according to Baird, is by
searching for a culture evidencing the kind of commanding religous symbolism that his own has lost and then
by wedding this prototypic symbolism to his own, or
"autotypic," experience. In this way, he returns with
a new symbolic idiom, one which is organic to his own

culture and hence able to speak without affectation to
the reading audience of that culture, but also one which
is sufficiently foreign to the religious conventions of
that culture to avoid eliciting the conditioned response
or lack of response to religious symbolism.

As Baird sees it, this search for a prototypic culture should involve a physical journey, specifically
to the Orient, the return to the Orient being the imagined return to the source of religion. I do not have a
log of Dickey's and Atwood's travels, nor need we have
one, as in this particular case we are dealing with two
artists who have created artistic protagonists. And
while a complete study of the primitivism of the two
novels would have to incorporate the autotype, for the
moment we are concerned with the log they have provided
for their surrogates. Ed Gentry and Atwood's narrator
do make physical journeys, but the direction is essentially north rather than east, while the oriental
aspect in each novel is associated with the failed
primitivists: Surfacing begins with Anna's palm reading, Deliverance ends with Lewis's turning to Zen.
Similarly, the primitivistic types that both protagonists experience in their geographically atavistic
trips are historical throwbacks, as both artists make
quite clear. Claude, in Surfacing, whom David appreci-
ates as the real thing and tries to communicate with
through Hemingway terminology, is a clod--as much a
parody of the yokel as David becomes a parody of the
primitivist; the mountain men whom Ed encounters in
Deliverance are not bootleggers defending their still
or their own ethical code, but depraved and degenerate
products of the civilization that Bobby Trippe's
bachelorhood symbolizes. At the same time there is a
distinct "depression" quality about these ersatz primi-
tives, which leads us to suspect that Dickey and Atwood
are also parodying the type of chronological primitivism that informs the attempted rejuvenation of the prohibition era and the nostalgia for the Dust Bowl ethos
reflected in contemporary music and the open road
syndrome.

In any case, the culture represented by Claude and
by the mountaineers who rape Bobby is certainly not one
which reflects sacred communal values, and what Dickey
and Atwood seem to be arguing is that no such prototypic society exists in the modern world. Chronological
primitivism in a geographical sense is, as D. H. Lawrence had discovered, a fruitless venture. At the same
time, however, this idea--that a return to nature or
the primitive must be an empirical thing--is symptomatic
of what Mircea Eliade would call modern man's orientation to history and loss of the primitive sense of connection with the cosmos or the numenal world, just as

the idea that the culture must be a human one is symptomatic of his loss of a totemic sense of connection
with the natural world. Hence while both Ed Gentry and
the narrator of Surfacing do make physical journeys,
the physical journey is also a psychological one, a
journey into the unconscious, as both authors emphasize
through the sense of suspended time or dream that
characterizes the activities of the protagonists, as
well as through the submergence in the depths of water
that characterizes the physical trip itself. Unlike
Lewis, who views the building of the dam at Aintry as
symbolic of the fact that a return to nature will soon
be an impossibility in the modern world, and unlike
the characters in Surfacing, who regard technology as
irrevocably divorcing man from his past and roots,
Dickey and Atwood realize, like Leslie Fiedler, that
there is a way back "available even in our atomized
culture," which is an extension not of the way consciously sought by eighteenth-century primitivists, but
"of the way instinctively sought by the Romantics, down
through the personality of the poet, past his particular
foibles and eccentricities, to his unconscious core,
where he becomes one with us all in the presence of our
ancient Gods, the protagonists of fables we think we
no longer believe."5

    Now because the journey in Deliverance and Surfac-
ing is a psychological one, the characters who come to
represent the primitive mentality are the protagonists
themselves, and in their activities and relationship
with the natural world is to be found the religious
quality that characterizes the prototypic culture.
That is, the situation in both novels is one wherein
the conscious self of each protagonist, the artist
searching for a prototypic culture, observes its unconscious self, the representative of a prototypic culture.
For example, at the point at which the psychological
journey begins in Deliverance, Ed Gentry becomes aware
of a different self; as he explains to Bobby what he
intends to do, concluding with the phrase, "Look up
yonder," he observes: "I liked hearing the sound of my
voice in the mountain speech, especially in the dark;
it sounded like somebody who knew where he was and knew
what he was doing. I thought of Drew and the albino
boy picking and singing in the filling station" (p.
131). Whereas the rapist and Lonnie represent the decadence of a once symbolically vital culture, Ed Gentry's
other self becomes the representative of the true kind.
Similarly, the narrator in Surfacing, after she admits
the truth of the abortion--the point at which she stops
being split in terms of her attempt to repress a personal problem, as well as the point at which she stops
looking for the rock paintings or concrete artifacts
and evidence of the geographical location of a once

primitive culture--her self becomes the primitive from
her conscious perspective. She returns after the lake
episode to the island: "There was no one in the cabin.
It was different, larger, as though I hadn't been there
for a long time; the half of me which had begun to
return was not yet used to it" (p. 148). Hence, whereas in the older form of the primitivistic novel the
creation of new religious symbolism follows an experience with a truly primitive culture, in these novels
the experience of the prototypic culture and the formulation of a new symbolic idiom occur simultaneously.

     In the case of Surfacing, what this new symbolism
consists of is essentially the use of an ecological
metaphor for the myth of the dying God, which is specifically presented in terms of a contrast to a technological symbol of the cross. "Overhead a plane, so
far up I could hardly hear it, threading the cities
together with its trail of smoke; an x in the sky,
unsacred crucifix" (p. 140). Following this suggestion
of the artificial community that the technological
cross signifies, the narrator then describes one of the
victims of technology, the heron, who at the same time
however becomes the symbol of redemption. "The shape
of the heron flying above us the first evening we
fished, legs and neck outstretched, wings outspread, a
bluegrey cross, and the other heron or was it the same
one, hanging wrecked from the tree. Whether it died
willingly, consented, whether Christ died willingly,
anything that suffers and dies instead of us is
Christ." Finally, the killing of the god is reunited
once more with the cannibalistic banquet that formed
the ritual for the primitive: "The animals die that
we may live, they are substitute people, hunters in the
fall killing deer, that is Christ also. And we eat
them, out of cans or otherwise; we are eaters of death,
dead Christ-flesh resurrecting inside us, granting us
life. Canned Spam, canned Jesus, even the plants must
be Christ" (p. 140). What Atwood has done, in short,
is to take Christ off the tree and present him as a
tree; she has taken a symbol for the freedom of the
soul, the flight of a bird, and made the bird itself a
soul. What she has done is to turn the language of
survival and ecology into a new mode of religious
expression.

     In Deliverance, Dickey similarly provides a new
symbol for the brotherhood of man that lies behind the
theological doctrine of the mystical body and the principle of agape and atonement. As Gentry stalks his
prey, he becomes psychologically at one with his victim, experiencing a mystical type of communion with the
other, which culminates in the final sighting of the
man: "We were closed together, and the feeling of a

peculiar type of intimacy increased, for he was shut
within a frame, all of my making" (p. 165). As both
the idea of Gentry's omnipotence and his simultaneous
dependence on the death of the mountaineer suggest,
Gentry is herein a type of God the Father who requires
the death of his son in atonement for man's transgres-
sion. Similarly, what is being evoked is the Abraham-
Isaac situation, which Lewis had earlier narrated to
Gentry in the form of the story of the father who had
sent his boy out into the night and the forest to find
Lewis's friend. "Son, go find that man" is the epi-
graph for that story, and Lewis's purpose in telling it
is to suggest that this dependability arises from the
mountain life: "The kind of life that guarantees it.
That fellow wasn't commanding his son against his will.
The boy just knew what to do. He walked out into the
dark" (pp. 44-45). Hence Gentry is at once the god
and the son of god, as is also the mountaineer: "Die,
I thought, my God, die, die," prays Gentry as he watches the wounded man bleeding in a position of prayer,
while the effect of the shooting incident results in
Ed's acquisition of the wounds of Christ, the cut palms
and the wound in the side. In short, as Christ's death
guaranteed that man was not to be eternally alienated
from God, so the purpose of the primitivistic artist is
to bring man back into a new relationship with the
divine.

Having identified cultural decadence and the loss
of religious symbolism as the major impetus behind the
primitivistic impulse in Dickey and Atwood, we can now
see clearly why it would have perverted the ultimate
significance of Deliverance and Surfacing to have begun
with a consideration of the sexual and national differences they may reflect. But having established such
a basic context and observed the striking similarities
between them, we can now safely observe certain contrasts, and rather speedily, since many of the things
that might have looked like differences before will
probably no longer appear as such.

Most of the differences between the two novels can
best be outlined by way of a Jungian analysis of the
respective protagonists and their situations, which,
given the essentially nonpolitical and religious character of Jungian premises, possibly suggests that these
differences are really means to the same end we have
just defined. In simplified terms, Jung's theories are
based upon a recognition of the difference between the
masculine and feminine psyches, but also a recognition
of the bisexuality of each individual psyche. As he
puts it, man is by nature oriented towards logos, or
rationality, in his consciousness, while his unconscious
is oriented to the complementary eros, or irrational

factor; woman, conversely, is by her nature oriented
to eros in her consciousness, while in her unconscious
she carries the complementary quality that we have
identified with the male, the logos potential. This
unconscious other self, as it were, Jung defines for
the male as the _anima_ and for the female as the _animus_,
the anima (the muse) being the force that encourages
creativity and exploration of the unknown and strange
on the part of man and the animus being the force that
encourages woman to be purposeful in her activities,
clear, strong, and decisive in her thinking. To the
extent that man and woman respectively recognize this
other self, they exist as integrated human beings in
themselves and in harmony with each other--the man
recognizing the woman as the other part of himself, the
woman recognizing the man as the other part of herself.
To the extent that man and woman deny their other selves,
they become their own worst enemies as well as those of
the opposite sex. It is the latter situation--the
factors that occasion it, the forms it takes, the solution to it--that Dickey and Atwood are concerned with
exploring in the characterizations of their protagonists. The common way in which both of them symbolize
this divorce between the conscious and the unconscious
self is in the fact that both protagonists do not
dream: "There was something about me that usually kept
me from dreaming, or maybe kept me from remembering
what I had dreamed," observes Ed Gentry (p. 27). "I
used to have dreams but I don't any longer," reflects
Atwood's narrator (p. 43).

Specifically, in the character of Ed Gentry we are
presented with a man who is totally oriented to logos,
as Dickey suggests, on the one hand, by Ed's inertia
and feeling of inconsequence and, on the other, by his
"power" poses: "I went into the office and hung up my
coat, and for a second put my hand down on the drawing
board, as though posing for a house-ad: Vice-President
Gentry makes important decision" (p. 18). Typically, a
man encounters his anima in terms of a woman upon whom
he projects it, but in the world of Ed's acquaintances
there do not seem to be any women capable of embodying
these qualities: Ed is married to a woman he regards
as his "buddy," and their love life--she is a nurse à
la Hemingway--consists in the "practical approach to
sex" (p. 29). Similarly, his secretary is the efficient
"Wilma"; and as he walks to his office, he observes the
other representative American types:

> almost all secretaries and file clerks, young
> and semi-young and middle-aged, and their hair
> styles, piled and shellacked and swirled and
> horned, and almost every one stiff, filled me
> with desolation. I kept looking for a decent

> ass and spotted one in a beige skirt, but
> when the girl turned her barren, gum-chewing
> face toward me, it was all over.   (p. 17)

Dickey here defines the vicious circle that leads to
Ed's final male chauvinistic complaint; not being in
tune with his anima, Ed regards women purely as sex objects.   But one of the reasons he is not in tune with
his anima is the logos orientation of American culture
that has encouraged women to downplay their eros.   The
anima, however, refuses to be ignored, and hence, where
Ed encounters it, appropriately, is in one of the prime
examples of man's attempt to capitalize upon the feminine, in the seminude model for the "Kitt's Britches"
ad: "There was a peculiar spot, a kind of tan slice in
her left eye, and it hit me with, I knew right away,
strong powers; it was not only recallable, but would
come back of itself" (p. 21).

Ed encounters this force of eros or the anima most
dramatically in his ascent up the cliff, where at one
point he comes to rest in a crevice that is at once
both womb and tomb, while at another point he becomes
the lover of the earth in the very primitive sense of
both terms: "I would begin to try to inch upward a
again, moving with the most intimate motions of my body,
motions I had never dared use with Martha, or with any
other woman.   Fear and a kind of enormous moon-blazing
sexuality lifted me, millimeter by millimeter" (p. 151).
Thus after being totally reduced to dependency upon the
eros he derided, Gentry is finally permitted to become
the lover; and instead of battling against the cliff as
he had previously, he now joins with the earth under
the moon in a hierogamous or sacred marriage with the
Great Mother and White Goddess, the two faces of eros.[6]

Having become the earth's lover is not sufficient,
however; he must also prove his fidelity and recognize
the creative direction of her destructive tendencies,
and this he does in the killing of the mountaineer--
more precisely, killing what the mountaineer symbolizes
is the type of refusal to admit one's mortality, one's
inability to rise above time.   To the extent that this
is Lewis's problem, Gentry is also figuratively killing
Lewis and his rigidly logos mentality.   Also, the jerky
motions of the dead man's head, says Gentry, irritated
him "more than the set of Thad's secretary's--Wilma's--
mouth and her tiresome, hectoring personality posing as
duty" (p. 174).   What is also being destroyed here,
then, is the masculine woman.   The association of Bobby
Trippe with the necessity for the murder suggests that
the type of effeminacy or masculine perversion of the
feminine characteristics that he epitomizes is also
under attack, just as is the homosexual sadism of the
other mountaineer.

And finally, Drew Ballinger and another very
important character are also brought into the picture.
As Ed returns, after the trip, and is trying to "get
the story together," he observes that it is more than
a matter of getting the facts straight--or corrected,
as the case may be: "But back of the story was the
reason for the story, and the woods and the river, and
all that had happened. There must be some way for me
to get used to the idea that I had buried three men in
two days, and that I had killed one of them. I had
never seen a dead man in my life, except a brief glance
at my father in his coffin" (p. 196). Drew, as we have
noticed, was characterized by his ethical absolutism,
so we can see why eros should mark him out as an object; that Ed's father should be mentioned in this context is also symbolically explicable in terms of the
fact that his death is associated with the coffin or
artificial burial--in contrast to the burial of the
other three. But is is also possible that Dickey
brings the father in at this point as a kind of all-
inclusive symbol of the American logos-oriented culture
of which Ed was a product and against which in the name
of eros he has rebelled. Specifically, at the end of
the novel the sheriff (played by Dickey himself in the
film) turns to Ed and says: "You damned fucking ape.
. . . Who on earth was your father, boy?" Ed's mono-
syllabic reply is "Tarzan" (p. 225).

Atwood's narrator in Surfacing has also been the
product of a logos or masculine education and consequently, like Ed, experiences the tension that such a
domination of the unconscious involves. But to the
extent that the consciousness of woman is oriented to
eros, she suffers doubly. Whereas Ed suffered the
denial of the eros qualities of his unconscious, she
must suffer the derogation of her consciousness in itself, as a result of which her animus has been forced to
become her consciousness. Hence she has no consciousness of her own, just as she has no accessible unconscious. This provides one of the reasons why she is
nameless; she has no identity. As a result of her
logos education and, furthermore, her lack of emotional
education, she makes the worst possible choice of
lovers, selecting a man who is anything but a lover in
any erotic sense of the term; in addition, he is a male
chauvinist perfectionist who persuades her to give up
her creative work and become a commercial illustrator
instead. In turn, this so-called husband, who is also
a respectable citizen, encourages her to abort the child
she has "accidentally" conceived--as he quaintly, but
quite logically, puts it, since he believed she was
practicing contraception. Faced with the trauma that
such an incident occasioned, finally, she is unable
to give expression to her feminine feelings of outrage,

since by virtue of her father's values such behavior would be unacceptable.

At the same time that Atwood presents her narrator as a woman who is a victim of logos, however, she also presents her as a woman who is capitalizing upon her weakness, who refuses to admit her animus potential and the strength it involves. Throughout the early part of the novel, as she reminisces about her childhood, for example, we discover that she long before the abortion saw herself in a passive role and at moments of crisis always took the path of least resistance and nearest escape. Similarly, if at the beginning of the novel she advances the theory that it was her decision to end the "marriage" as a way of protecting herself from the fact of the abortion, then as her psychological journey progresses (and as the above example suggests), she sees the abortion as something that was done to her. Refusing to admit her own animus or capability of taking control, in other words, she projects this masculine aspect in an extreme form upon her associates, particularly males, and upon her environment, particularly such man-made things as politics, technology, and language.

Finally, the one incident that the narrator repeatedly associates with the abortion is the death of her mother; and the mother as we come to see her is the epitome of the woman who is reconciled to her animus, who acts with strength and compassion, who is totally capable of taking control--she confronts an approaching bear, for example--but who is also utterly maternal and natural. What the abortion symbolizes, then, is not merely the death of motherhood, but the death of this kind of mother.

Hence, the narrator's first problem is to admit her responsibility for the abortion, which she does when in diving, while attempting to discover the historical past--the submerged rock paintings--she encounters the image out of her personal past, the long oval trailing arms: "Whatever it is, part of myself or a separate creature, I killed it. It wasn't a child but it could have been one, I didn't allow it" (p. 143). Her second problem is to admit her complicity in the violence and victimization that she had projected respectively upon the Germans, then upon the Americans, then upon the problem of language, which she partly does through direct admission and partly through indulgence in the orgy of destruction that I noted earlier. At last she must expiate for her crime against motherhood in the sense in which we have defined it. This she does by acting as the initiator of sexual intercourse with Joe, by insisting that the act be performed outside

on the ground and in the light of the moon, and by
demanding that it be a procreative rather than merely a
sensual encounter: "I'm impatient, pleasure is redundant, the animals don't have pleasure. I guide him into
me, it's the right season, I hurry" (p. 161). And as
a result of this encounter, she emerges not as a woman
looking for a god, but as a woman who has become the
mother of a god, a Dionysian rather than an Apollonian
one.

While Dickey, then, is specifically concerned with
a masculine problem and Atwood with a feminine one,
both novels must be characterized as explorations of
these problems rather than as reflections of them. Perhaps this is also the best way to consider the question
of whether the differences we have been exploring can
be seen to derive from the nationalities of the writers
in question. What Dickey is depicting in Deliverance is
assuredly his own American ethos and its cultural history. I earlier mentioned the eighteenth century and
the French Revolution as historical prototypes for the
primitivism of Lewis, for example, and what we should
now notice is that it was also the eighteenth century
that gave rise to the American Revolution, while it was
the albeit biblical primitivism of the Puritans that
occasioned the founding of the United States of Amer-
ica.7 Similarly, we should notice that Lewis Metlock
together with Ed Gentry may be seen as types of Lewis
and Clark, the great American explorers. Finally, in
the situation of Ed Gentry, the primitive, drawing his
arrow upon the unsuspecting mountaineer we have an icon
out of the period of the great Indian battles. In the
same way, to the extent that Atwood's novel depicts few
such classic prototypes, while others like General Wolfe
are ridiculed by characters like David, she too is
providing a distinctly regional setting. Clearly too,
Dickey himself is characterizing America as an essentially masculine and patriarchal society, while it is
Atwood's central thesis in Survival that Canada is
characterized by the "victim" syndrome. Once again we
recall that the united colonies of America achieved
their independence through a rebellion against a
"father" figure, whereas Canada came to her own under a
female ruler, the Great Mother, Queen Victoria, and has
generally displayed passivism in its foreign policies.
Both Deliverance and Surfacing, then, do respectively
reflect masculine and feminine, United States and
Canadian, attitudes, and both seem to suggest that
there is a connection between the two. Both also,
however, reflect a questioning of these attitudes and a
criticism of the traditions that have given rise to
them. Thus, one must finally define Deliverance as
simultaneously indicative of typical masculine American
attitudes and at the same time--to the extent that

Dickey is a male American--as not. A similar judgment
must be made in the case of Surfacing. What really
seems to be the defining characteristic of both works
is their suggestion that specifically sexual and national differences are minor issues in comparison with
the major cultural problem that we share in common,
citizens of the United States and Canada, masculine and
feminine, North Americans.

NOTES

1. James Dickey, Deliverance (New York, 1971), p. 8.
All further page references will be to this Dell edition
and will be identified within the text in parentheses.

2. Margaret Atwood, Surfacing (Don Mills 1973), p.
59. All further page references will be to this Paper-
jacks edition and will be identified within the text in
parentheses.

3. Otto Rank, Beyond Psychology (New York, 1958), p.
18.

4. James Baird, Ishmael (New York, 1960), p. 16.

5. Leslie Fiedler, "Archetype and Signature," in
William Phillips, ed., Art and Psychoanalysis (New York,
1975), pp. 471-72.

6. For a full discussion of the concept of hierogamy,
see my essay, "Hierogamy vs Wedlock: Types of Marriage
Plots and their Relationship to Genres of Prose Fiction," PMLA (forthcoming).

7. For a fuller discussion of this idea, see John J.
Teunissen and Evelyn J. Hinz, "Roger Williams, St. Paul,
and American Primitivism," Canadian Review of American
Studies 4 (Fall 1973):121-36; and in a nineteenth-
century context, see our "Poe, Pym, and Primitivism,"
SSF (forthcoming).

The Impact of the American Film Industry on Quebec Society and Its Cinema

Michel Brûlé

> "When they go to the Cinema, Canadians seem
> quite satisfied with the foreign feature
> films that are offered to them and two-
> thirds of revenues go back overseas" (Georges-
> Emile Lapalme, extract from the first annual
> report (1968-69) of the Société de Dével-
> oppement de l'Industrie Cinématographique
> Canadienne).

DEUS EX CINEMA

It is as easy--or as difficult--for a sociologist
from Quebec to demonstrate the impact of the American
film industry on the cinema in Quebec or, even more
broadly speaking, on the whole of cultural life in Quebec (taking the terms in the anthropological sense), as
it is for a Catholic to demonstrate the existence of
God. God has, furthermore, one point in common with
the American film industry, since they are both a trin-
ity--the film industry comprising producers, distributors, and exhibitors. Like God, the film industry is
everywhere and nowhere; it is very discreet and prefers
the shadows of the wings to the brilliance of the lime-
lights. A great deal of tenacity is required if one is
to have an accurate view of the multiple aspects of its
workings and of its many-directional branches; it is,
therefore, extremely difficult to analyze its impact.

In general, I would say that as far as the cinema
is concerned, the situation of Canada in relation to
the United States is special since Canada is considered
to be fully integrated into the American domestic market. In a forthcoming article, Thomas H. Guback writes,
"The book value of American direct private investment

abroad (largely branches and subsidiaries of American firms) in 1950 was reported to be $11.8 billion. A provisional figure for 1973 set the value at $107.3 billion of which $28.0 billion was in Canada, twice as much as American investment in the world two decades earlier."[1]

This type of relationship between Canada and the United States applies to a great many activities, but that is not our immediate subject in this paper. As for the position of Quebec in relation to Canada, and even more so in relation to the United States, it has a certain characteristic that we all are familiar with: although Quebec is in majority French-speaking, that does not in any way prevent it from being economically directed by the English-speaking population. In other words, Quebec is under economic and cultural domination.

The following two extracts from the newspapers are quite clear and require no additional comment.

La Presse, Wednesday, August 6, 1975:

Ottawa--The two most important cinema franchises in the country, Famous Players and Odeon Theatres, have agreed to present Canadian feature films four weeks per year in each of their theatres and to increase their investments in the production of Canadian films. The Secretary of State, M. Hugh Faulkner, made it clear yesterday that the sum of $1.7 million that the two chains agreed to invest in production will be added to the approximately $3 million that are invested each year by the Canadian Corporation for the Development of the Cinematographic Industry, itself a government organization.
    In a press conference, the Minister also announced that a new regulation concerning income taxes will allow everybody investing in the production of Canadian films to deduct the totality of their investments. According to the Minister, this is a measure that should stimulate the indigenous cinema industry.

Le Jour, Wednesday, August 6, 1975:

. . . This agreement between Famous Players and Odeon on the one hand and the Secretary of State on the other is valid for a period of one year and it does not have the full force of law. . . . The new regulation

concerning income taxes is retroactive to
November 18, 1974.

YESTERDAY AND TODAY

The breakdown of this subject has always been one
of the main problems of the sociologist who wishes to
deal properly with the relationships between the American and the Quebec cinema.

It is said that to deal with such a subject, the
first thing to do is to have all pertinent data at one's
finger tips. Since we wish to deal with the period
from 1945 to 1975, we must, first, retrace the extent
to which the American film industry is implanted in
Canada in general and in Quebec in particular, from
three points of view, that is, production, distribution,
and consumption, second, have at our disposition the
data concerning the situation of the French Canadian/
Quebec cinema industry for the same period.[2] With that
data we would know whether the American cinema was or
is still dominant and--an important goal for us--be
able to measure in some way the extent of this domination. This procedure would give us a quantitative
image of the situation.

From the point of view of production, in 1945 two
feature films had been filmed in Quebec. They were
A la croisée des chemins made by J.-M. Poitevin and
Père Chopin made by Fédor Ozep, a Russian, naturalized
in France, who worked in Quebec. No American film was
produced in Canada or in Quebec. From the point of
view of distribution networks, there were a few independent cinemas and the small chain called France-Film,
all the other cinemas being controlled by Anglo-American
capital. As for the theatres, they were, as they are
today, generally the property of the Americans and the
English. The largest theatres in Quebec and in Montreal
belonged to foreigners. It is true that France-Films
owned a few cinemas, and there were a few independents,
but one could hardly speak about a situation of competition. Thus, in practical terms, the films available
in Quebec were entirely American. Because of the war,
America was the only country to possess a flourishing
industry, and in any case films from European countries
did not reach us.

If we examine the situation of the 1970s, we can
say that it strangely resembles the situation that prevailed thirty years ago. The distribution networks are
still American, the exhibitors are also American, and
even the independents obtain their supplies in most
cases from American distributors. As for production,

there is no link between Quebec and the United States.
Quebec has, however, developed its own film industry,
small if we compare it to the industry that is controlled directly or indirectly by American capital, but
large if we take account of the population of Quebec,
which is about 6 million.

Nonetheless, in a certain way, we cannot affirm
that the American film industry has been damaging for
us. At least I do not think that we were very con-
scious--prior to the 1960s--of the hold it had over us.
It was there and it was "normal," just as normal as the
strong position of Anglo-American capital in our economy, just as normal as the exploitation of our natural
resources by American multinational corporations.

UNQUESTIONABLE TRUTHS

For the purpose of this study, it seems to be of
secondary importance to know whether the American film
industry's power over Quebec can be quantified as 68.3
percent or 72.1 percent. I do not deny the importance
and the relevance of a search for empirical data and
the translation of these data into figures. But whatever the statistics that are obtained, it will always
be necessary to interpret them to a certain extent and
in a certain direction--which is precisely why the
breakdown of the subject and the point of view of the
researcher are important.

My analysis, however it may be evaluated, is based
on unquestionable facts: (1) the Quebec cinema is not
an autonomous industry; (2) the Quebec cinema depends
on exhibitors and distributors who are not from Quebec;
(3) the Quebec cinema relies on capital that comes from
outside Quebec for its production (at least in the
short term); and (4) this "non-Quebecer" who controls
our cinema at these three levels in generally American.
Finally one can add, without any doubt, that the Quebec
cinema-goer has seen and continues to see more films
coming from the United States (or produced with American capital) than from any other source, including the
European Common Market.

This situation is not new; it has always existed.
The only thing that has changed is the awareness (or
perhaps one should say the beginning of an awareness)
of the professionals and the spectators concerning this
domination. Further, this situation is not particularly
original, since we find ourselves in a situation resembling that of many Third World and industrially advanced
countries.

Obviously, this domination has an important economic impact, since it has been estimated that $50 million leave the country because of it. It is therefore certain that we are contributing significantly to finance the American cinema industry and at the same time to finance our own domination. It is a process that is well known by now, a kind of endless chain that makes the rich countries richer, while the poor countries get poorer and poorer.

SCYLLA AND CHARYBDIS

But it is not necessarily the effects that can be expressed in percentages that are the most damaging. We can therefore put forward two propositions, two hypotheses which, despite their apparent contradiction, seem to me to be correct. I believe that if American exhibitors, distributors, and producers decided to invest massively and significantly in the Quebec cinema industry, there would be no structural change in that industry. There would quite simply be more money and so less unemployment. On the other hand, it seems to me equally correct to put forward the opposite statement and to suggest that the situation would be a hundred times worse than the one we know today.

First hypothesis: there would be no structural change because already an important part of our cinema is conditioned in its way of seeing things by the American cinema, that is, by the Hollywood or neo-Hollywood type. The reason for this state of affairs is that since the beginning of cinema, the industry that has been dominant worldwide is the American one, and it has operated like a multinational or transnational business all along.

Second hypothesis: the situation would be worse because the few pockets of resistance against the American type of cinema would be rapidly wiped out, and there would be no objective possibility of developing an alternative cinema. The professionals and producers of the other cinema--if they continue to persevere-- would have to take to the bush and operate as a true underground.

A SHORT HISTORY OF THE CINEMA

The cinema is the only art born out of the Industrial Revolution; it is an art that has grown out of a technique. We must remember the origins of this form of amusement, of this curiosity that has grown out of optics and chemistry, has followed the rise of the middle classes, and has become, together with the novel, the great art of the middle and educated classes. After the initial, hesitant competition between Europe and the United States, it soon became clear that the United States was becoming dominant from the point of view of both technique and economics. We now know that it was after World War I--and indeed because of it--that the American cinema gained an irreversible advantage over all the other national film industries, an advantage that increased after World War II. Because of their know-how and their financial resources, both of which encouraged the brain drain, the Americans were soon able to assert themselves and impose one kind of cinema--their kind.

The great victory of the middle classes was to dominate humanity as if they were Humanity and to convince everybody--sometimes by force and sometimes by trickery, but always through exploitation--that they alone represented the true Man, that their values coincided exactly with the very laws of human nature. In the same way, the American succeeded in convincing the middle classes in general that they alone incarnated the ideal of this man that we call Middle-Class Man. The American way of life has become a norm for mankind. Whether it be in industry, in technology, or in science (including the science of war), the Americans have dominated the world and are still dominating it. It is hardly astonishing, therefore, that its films fill 60 percent of the screens throughout the world. Were the situation to be otherwise, it would be problematic; the situation as it is can be explained.

Furthermore, we are beginning to recognize the importance of the film image on people's value scales. The magnates of the American film industry and the politicians quickly realized the power of the image, and more than anyone else they grasped the impact of the "innocent image."[3] In a sense, there is no film that is more political than the film intended to amuse (if we accept the hypothesis that the objective of politics is to depoliticize the masses). Propaganda is the arm of the weak; the strong behave as if the political question had been solved once and for all. One does not make an educational film to show that social classes do not exist any more; instead one hears the story of someone who--through his determination, his individual courage, and his qualities--reached an enviable situation (of richness and power). Give them bread and circuses, said the caesars. Give them popcorn and images, say the rulers from Hollywood.

It is on a worldwide scale, including Eastern countries, that the problem of the impact of American films

can be posed. The cinema, as a medium, has become
American. The Americans won the battle of the cinema
because they set up a financial strategy that enabled
them to induce consumers and producers--whatever their
country--to finance the American enterprise and, at the
same time, to create a vacuum concerning sociopolitical
realities. This double process is called imperialism,
an amusing, agreeable, and, in a number of cases, high-
quality imperialism. Even war is beautiful in techni-
color on a giant screen.

A SHORT HISTORY OF QUEBEC

      Quebec had a culture when the cinema was born; it
had a culture when foreign capital began to concern itself with our cheap labor and our cheaper raw materials;
it had a culture but it did not know it. What does one
need to know about one's own culture, one's own traditions, one's own vision of the world, when one is among
friends? It is not necessary here to go back to the
Great Flood, particularly as our Flood was not very
long ago.

      Our Flood was called the conquest (1760), and some
people pretend that our Noah's ark was the church. Maybe I would have had a different opinion about things if
I had lived at that period, but since we have left it
behind, let us accept in good grace what the others
called "the priest-ridden province." Some of our
essayists have been offended by this situation; perhaps
they forgot that the clergy was ours and that to deny
it is more political than befits an analytical sociologist. When the other, the Britisher, arrived, he was
the conqueror and he acted as such; that is, he took
charge of the levers of command and he commanded in his
way. We should realize that he was not like us. He
spoke English, he did not believe in the Holy Virgin,
and he did not confess in the presence of a priest; in
any case, his priests were married. Furthermore, he
was different because of some natural gifts (they could
not be gifts of God since God was French--at least at
that time). Among the gifts that he had received from
nature, this other person had two gifts that he exploited at our cost. He had the ability to command and he
was good at business; in other words, he was a materialist.

      Faced with this situation against which there was
no appeal, we defined ourselves in other terms. We
plunged body and soul (soul above all) into cultural
and spiritual matters (spiritual above all); we spoke
the most beautiful language in the world; and more even
than the Jews (since they crucified Christ) we were the

people chosen by God. Our main mission was to evange-
lize the rest of the world, particularly the United
States, since we were the only Roman Catholics on the
continent (the Britisher was, of course, a Protestant).
We took shelter therefore in culture, the fine arts,
and the finer professions, leaving to the others the
fields of technology, science, and business.

Because this split seemed to suit the other, we
could each grow in our own directions, but the two lines
were absolutely not parallel.[4] Since the country could
not support them, our country folk took exile in the
cities and abroad, that is, in the United States.
First they went into manufacturing and the secondary
industries, then into the service industries. As all
industry belonged to Anglo-Saxon capital, our people
found that their culture had no meaning outside the
privacy of their homes. The whole of economic life
took place within the rules of one culture, and the
rest of life was controlled by another culture, without
any true exchange between these two worlds. My colleague Guy Rocher has explained this very clearly:

> One can say that Quebec was living through a
> strange contradiction in the first part of
> the twentieth century; it was adopting the
> social structures of an industrial civiliza-
> tion, but it was preserving the mentality,
> the spirit and the values of a pre-industrial
> society. There are very few other examples
> of societies which--while becoming industri-
> alized--have faced up to such a radical split
> between social structures and culture.[5]

This social schizophrenia lasted up to the end of
the 1950s. I agree entirely with Rocher's analysis,
and, like him, I believe that one must look beyond a
simple statement about the dichotomy between social
structures and culture to see what were the goings-on
that enabled the dramatic split in our social life to
be bearable. I think that some cultural products, and
particularly the cinema, played a very significant role
in the successful adaptation of our culture to North
American society.

ILLEGITIMACY AND DIFFERENCES

Let us turn to the essential data. There are about
5 million French-speaking people in North America, that
is, about 3 percent of the population of this northern
part of the continent. Generally we all come from a
rural Catholic setting; and during the twentieth century
we have been projected into an industrial civilization

that we are helping to build, but of which we are not
the prime movers. We are doers, and we come together
only after work. Our culture is a question of free
time or, one might say, of nonworking time. There is
no dramatic suspense in my story since you know that we
survived and that we have continued to be different.
At the same time this difference is not the same as the
difference that we can detect in the Frenchmen from
France (nor even in the Latin Americans) because, whatever one says, we are not French (nor English). We are
North Americans speaking French. Let us call this our
illegitimacy, but it is an illegitimacy that we are
proud of. We keep our distances, at least as much from
the French as from the Americans. In fact, if the
Americans ate better (that is to say, like us), if they
would only stop thinking all the time that the biggest
is the best, we would feel more at ease with them than
with our much vaunted cousins from France (who are now
trying to explain America to us--to us, of all people).

So we are French-speaking people in America. And
I fully agree with Rocher when he writes that "another
element of recent cultural evolution is the impregnation
of Quebec by the American civilization."[6]

The French Canadian of the 1970s, like the French
Canadian of the 1940s, has scarcely any direct contact
with the United States. Certainly he gladly spends his
vacations by the sea near Cape Cod or even in Florida
during winter, but more often than not, he meets other
French Canadians on vacation, like himself, and scarcely
meets the Americans with whom he is staying. No, it is
not through these brief stops in Maine, in Florida, or
in New York that the Quebecer discovers the United
States and the value scales of the American culture.
It is in his own home, sitting in front of his television, listening to the radio, or going to the cinema.
Like all inhabitants of the industrially advanced countries moving towards the postindustrial era, the French
Canadian is imbued with the rhythms of technology, and
he has been persuaded without realizing it that productivity and performance were the two sources of natural
progress and of civilization.

To keep pace with the Americans, the Quebecer does
not need to speak or read English or even to have set
foot in the United States. First the radio with its
rhythms and its songs, the words of which were incom-
prehensible to the majority of the population, then the
cinema, and finally the television integrated the Quebecer into the American world. But I was going to
forget publicity; it is so prevalent that we do not see
it any more; we breathe it like the air. And yet its
power is proportional to its nonvisibility.

After having worked all day, all week at a speed,
to a standard, and within an organization built up
according to the American model, the Quebecer rests
from his labor, letting himself be impregnated by productions that are created on the other side of the
frontier. And so, Johnny Quebecer, who had probably
never left his village or his country town (or even his
neighborhood if he was living in Montreal), relaxes in
front of images of New York or Chicago or Texas or the
Grand Canyon full of Indians. Close to his St. Lawrence,
he walks on the banks of the Mississippi to the strum-
ming of banjos.

This sketch describes, not so much the impact, but
the impacts that American films have had on the mass of
cinema spectators, whether they were simple consumers
or well-informed film-goers, and the impacts on the
craftsmen of the Quebec film industry--for it must be
understood that what is valid for the public at large
is also valid for the craftsman.

APPRENTICESHIP

Through the cinema the Quebecer met a value scale
that was not his own.[7] He learned the importance of
success (defined as succeeding over an antagonistic competition). He was told about the virtues of money, the
number-one index of social success, and of the value of
an individual (and thus of societies: since we are
living a free-enterprise economic regime, what is good
for the individual can hardly be bad for society as a
whole). This is the way that the Quebecer was sold on
the merits of free enterprise, and if industry has succeeded in implanting the notion of productivity as an
absolute end, the cinema, as perniciously as advertising,
took charge of the second aspect of the economic development of American society: consumerism.

Nobody can deny the impact of exhibiting the American style of living as seen and corrected by Hollywood
and its subsidiaries. By making spectacular the standard of living of a certain America and projecting it
throughout the world, by idealizing the thousand and one
details that make up this high standard of living, the
film industry has forced on the world a unit of measure
by which each individual measures his well-being and
compares his position with this ideal.

The latent function of showing the American way of
life in this way was the greatest publicity operation
ever undertaken . . . and it succeeded. Coca-Cola and
General Motors can bear witness! Obviously, we can see
that this marketing of the American way of life took

place to the detriment of national ways of living. It
is sufficient to read the criticisms and the accounts
of our first feature film of the 1940s to realize the
pleasure, the pride, and the fascination that the
Quebecer felt when he saw on the screen his own country
life, his own customs, and his own way of behaving.

In this vein, we can read about the release of La
Forteresse: ". . . this film was completely filmed in
the studios of Saint-Hyacinthe, in the city of Quebec
and at the Montmorency Falls. . . . Our beautiful
French Canada and the Montmorency Falls are revealed to
the whole world by the film La Forteresse."[8]

A FRENCH CANADIAN DREAM

An exhaustive study of press cuttings of the period
of our first dramatic films showed clearly the type of
reactions that we had. On the one hand, as I have just
mentioned, we reacted with pleasure and pride to see
finally on the screen the countrysides of our home, to
see the customs and behavior that were ours, and to
hear a language that was also ours (by opposition to
English--obviously--but also by opposition to the
exotic French that we were hearing from Paris).

We can see, therefore, a true film of our own;
a rough but expressive language is spoken, the
images do not seek for virtuosity but for a
simple realism. It is exactly what was necessary and what the general public will appreciate. We like the film precisely because it
is not trying to be dazzling, to be striking,
or to imitate Hollywood or Paris (Léon Franque,
La Presse, January 29, 1949).

There can be no doubt that this statement by (and
about) the Canadian cinema (as it was called at that
time) was also a denial of the American and European
cinema. On the other hand, it would be dishonest to
overlook the fascination that the Hollywood cinema exercises over our understanding of what a film industry
should be. The unbeatable model was the American film
industry, which is why we were trying above all to build
up an industry that could rival Hollywood. To create a
French Canadian Hollywood, that was our most secret
desire.

We were, therefore, extremely ambivalent. We
wanted to see our own reality, our world, and not the
world of the United States or of France, but we also
wanted a product resembling that which came to us from
those two countries. It was a failure, because once

the effect of curiosity had worn off, producers found
themselves with a subproduct of the American or European
film industry. That is obviously not the only reason
for the failure of this beginning of a film industry,
but it is also obvious that the public who are formed--
indeed, conditioned--by American films did not find in
the Quebec film that which they had learned to see in
the American films. The Quebec film industry believed
that it could rival the foreign films by injecting
local content, without touching the form of the product.
But the distinctly provincial nature of the problem
areas being treated meant that it was difficult (or
even quite impossible) to export these films. Furthermore, even if we had produced exportable films, we
would have had to deal with foreign distributors and
exhibitors. Knowing what we know today about the monopolistic American control over the cinema industry as a
whole, it is obvious that such an undertaking could not
succeed.

Nonetheless, the relative success that the first
movies filmed in Quebec did obtain was attributable to
the kind of curiosity with which we look at a family
photograph album. And the same phenomenon occurred
again during the 1960s when, after a fifteen-year
blackout, Quebec films reappeared on our screens.

One of the most severe criticisms that we can
level at the American film industry implanted in Quebec
is that it prevented (or at least slowed down and inhibited) the expression of a self-image in the cinema. The
self-image that a people can see in the cinema is far
more than a simple reflection. One forgets too easily
that the image is a project or a construct, in the same
way as the story that is told by the film, because of
the nature of the cinema as a medium. Any film is an
interpretation of an existing reality and includes the
intention to exist in its own right. I would go so far
as to say that a film translates less of that which
exists already and more of that which men want to come
about or to maintain. In other words, a film is a kind
of project about the future. This is what the Quebecers
have been deprived of--until quite recently. Since
1960, popular songs have achieved an extraordinary feat
in singing about Quebec society and its social ideals,
yet the cinema has been essentially paralyzed in its
attempts at producing images and dreams for the people
of this country. There is a cinema working in this
direction, but we must recognize that this is a minority
and that it has not yet succeeded in implanting itself
on the commercial circuits.

SOME VIOLENCE

Without wishing to add one more chapter to the hundreds of papers and articles devoted to the theme of
violence in the cinema, I may point out here that violence has occupied and continues to occupy a predominant
place on the screen. American films have succeeded in
creating an esthetic of violence and in forcing on the
world its understanding of violence; this is a certain
type of violence, namely, a physical and spectacular
violence that takes place nearly always at the level of
the individual. It is hardly ever a question of economic, social, or political violence that touches man in
his soul and his very reason for living. When, excep-
tionally, we find this kind of violence, one individual
comes out of the shadow, leads his own battle, and
succeeds alone in overcoming the forces of evil. For
historical, socioeconomic, and cultural reasons, violence in the United States has undergone a general
development and a considerable extension; we must note
that even if American films show a great deal of violence, it does not reveal the structural antagonism
that exists between social classes--a concept which,
incidentally, is not often examined by American sociology.
American violence in the cinema seems to me, therefore,
to reflect a certain ideology, and, like any ideological
discourse, this violence is an interpretation of society
and aims at a certain kind of existence for that society.

This type of violence proposed by American films
was quite foreign to French Canadian experience, and
even today, despite a certain increase in the rate of
crime, we cannot assert that we experience the same
violence that rules over nearly all the greater American cities. Canada as such and Quebec in particular
are "retarded" concerning the phenomenon of urban violence. Even in this respect, we are different. I am
not able to measure or evaluate the impact of cinematographic violence on Quebec society, and that is not my
objective. One thing is certain, however: the violence
that is shown in American films is, largely speaking,
disconnected from the Quebec spectators' experience.

One could pass in review all sectors of life and
show that what the spectator receives does not correspond to his cultural experience. Even if this statement is fundamentally exact, it is nonetheless true that
American films have exercised on French Canadians a
veritable educational role. Even if there are no studies on the subject, I readily believe that the cinema
has significantly contributed to bringing Quebecers
into contact with urban and industrial problems: in
this regard (whatever value judgment one may put on this
form of initiation) American films reached home to

people, posing problems for them which they had perhaps
not yet had to resolve, but which would soon arise in
any industrially advanced country. It is not a question of forecasting or of chance. Since technology is
essentially American, it is inevitable that sooner or
later all those who participate in industrial development should know similar problems. How the American
cinema has played a role that I must call pernicious is
that, having posed the problem, it imposes its own
solutions and its own responses--and that imposition is
pernicious even though we may understand those solutions
and those responses.

CHECKMATE TO THE FRENCH CANADIAN HOLLYWOOD

        Since the reality of the impacts of the American
cinema are extremely complex, we must, I believe, come
back to the end of the 1940s to try to sketch a kind of
phenomenological description of what happened when a
national film industry suddenly entered into competition with a monopolistic foreign industry. I will try,
very schematically, to outline the situation in the
following way.

        It is obvious that before the first Canadian films
were made, there were only foreign films, of which the
great majority came from the United States. The American film industry filled the need; indeed, one can
easily say that the American cinema was quite simply
the cinema and that generations of Quebecers were initiated to the seventh art through it.

        But lo, films made here arrived on the market with
their local actors, their local images, their local
speech and stories "made in Quebec." The way this
"here" was represented was--both by naivete and by lack
of skill--somewhat rough, somewhat out of perspective,
we must admit. These films seemed in certain ways to
be squinting at a past that we must call traditional.
As for the actors, they were inevitably making their
first films, and they came for the most part from radio
and theatre. In contrast, there was the American cinema, with actors who did not come from here, but who,
thanks to publicity and the star system, were quite as
well known as local actors. As for the scenarios, they
have little to do with the immediate problems of French
Canadians. Nonetheless, let me put forward the imaginary hypothesis that all film-goers were immediately to
leave the American cinema for a certain time and to rush
into the theatres where Quebec films were being projected.

The first reaction to this new cinema would be a reaction of curiosity and of pride. The public could finally see its stars (known by their voices, which had been heard for years in radio novels). Also there was the countryside--the critics in any case had underlined this "happening"; at last one could see the Montmorency Falls and our beautiful Laurentians. As for the story that the film told, attention was first drawn to the folklore aspects, the illustrations of our customs and ways of behaving. The story was generally simple and lent itself to picturesque scenes. Critics, for their part, strongly emphasized the birth of a new industry and forecast the creation of a French-speaking Holly-wood. It was said that each new film was better than the preceding ones and that progress was slowly but surely being made towards the American "ideal." At the beginning of the 1950s and in the following years, new critics, who had been brought up in the schooling of the ciné-clubs, looked down their noses at the products of the period and, to be frank, were ashamed of them because they could not bear comparison with the Euro-pean or American films. This bald judgment about the films of the period is still held today; it is "good taste" to make fun of the films of that period.

However, a serious analysis of those films leads to much subtler conclusions, even opposite ones. Work that I have carried out on the subject of these films shows that they were telling about the transition from a traditional society to an industrial society, and they were very precisely dealing with the absurd value scales of a society that was cut off from new economic structures. But it seems that the reaction was stronger to the apparent content, which seemed to be better un-derstood than the structural content behind it. These films, in reality, borrowed the decor and the trappings of a traditional ideology in order to criticize it seriously, in a way that allowed no appeal. This led, I believe, to a misunderstanding, and these films seemed to be a defense, or at best an illustration, of Catholic French Canada, 1890-style.

Once curiosity had been satisfied--that is, after having marveled at the Montmorency Falls, after having seen and recognized local talents and followed with the greatest interest a story that took place, in 90 percent of the cases, in a rural or semirural setting--the spec-tators recognized that something was lacking. Specif-ically, they recognized--in a degraded and handicraft form--a product that they had already consumed in its "authentic" version: grandiose decors, professional actors used to the camera (and not to the radio, as was the case here), stories constructed by specialists, experienced librettists, and so forth. Furthermore--

and this is, I believe, the most important feature--the American film was not without relevance to the experience of the industrial worker in an urban setting. Béla Balazs said in effect that the cinema as an art was the product of a capitalist-industrial society.[9] Like Balazs, I believe that the prototype was made in Hollywood. Westerns say as much about our industrialization and urbanization as do "whodunits."

In other words, while the American cinema was speaking about the city and the industrial milieu, the Quebec film of the period 1943-53 was still casting back to the "true life" of the Quebecer, even if it was to denigrate it. But this true life was already of the past; its roots were nourished only by the discourses of the former elite, and it revived within the family circle only at the festive season. What the modern spectator of 1949 saw on the screen was linked to a bygone set of problems, problems that had yet to be liquidated culturally. The culture was dragging its feet; it had not yet acquired the new rhythms of the economic life of the wartime or the postwar period.

On the other hand, the American cinema did not represent the true life of the French Canadian, either. It may have looked like it, but it did not sound like it. The world that the American film showed was not yet the reality of the Quebecers even though they felt obscurely, through their experience at work and their experience of an economic life subordinated to technology, that their life would come to resemble more and more closely the life that they glimpsed on the screens of the Famous Players.

So we have on the one hand culture, a culture that was a bit faded and out of date, and on the other hand an economic structure, something that had achieved full growth. Between that which was not yet quite dead and something else which was not quite a reality of the day, Johnny Quebecer could not find his "today" in the cinema. So in 1952, he hastened to buy a television set and tried to justify his investment by spending hours looking at it; after all, television is a medium that reflects the "today."

MOVEMENT FROM MORALITY TO ECONOMICS

The people in the cinema industry were doubly hurt by the backlash of the American and European presence. They were influenced, just like everybody else, and yet they had to live with this foreign reality precisely because they were the craftsmen of the cinema industry. I emphasize the word foreign because it is only recently

(in the last twelve years or so at the most) that the
cinema technicians became aware that their industry and
its films were foreign to them.[10]

Let me outline rapidly the most visible consequences of the implanting of the American film industry
in Quebec. By the most visible consequences, I mean
the fact that the great majority of cinema circuits are
directly or indirectly controlled by Americans and that
the Americans were never interested in distributing or
featuring films made here. Even the Canadian government's film agency, the National Film Board (NFB), has
to pass through Columbia Pictures to distribute its
films. As for the investments in production, they are
so marginal and recent that they are hardly worth
talking about.

The growth to maturity of the Quebec cinema tech-
nician can be summed up in the following way.[11] First
of all there was a stage of his education in the ciné-
clubs and the first cinema magazines. Different cinematographic techniques were discussed from a didactic
point of view, and criticism was featured; it was an
impressionist and moralizing criticism as well. Cinema
and real life were unconsciously confused; moral judg-
ments made about films should have been made about true
happenings or about real people. Nonetheless, this
work experience, in the setting of the ciné-clubs, contributed enormously to developing a certain taste--even
a certain passion for anything cinematographic.

At the end of the 1950s and the beginning of the
1960s, we noticed that several of the militants of the
earlier period had been integrated into different sections of cinematographic production, notably within the
National Film Board. Their place was taken up by teams
of young aficionados of the screen, most of them university students. This second phase was particularly
characterized by the attention that was paid to Quebec
films (English or French) coming from the NFB. It was
an extremely dynamic period, in which each short film
that came out of the NFB was analyzed and feverishly
discussed. However, the great discourse of that period
was censorship. Quebec is well known for having had
an extremely severe censor. The epoch of quiet revolution had begun, and all sectors of social life in Quebec, with its new liberal government, were trying to
make up for the time lag accumulated during the many
years of rule by former Prime Minister Duplessis.
There was a gap between what people had become and the
politico-legal framework within which they had to live.
The great battle of censorship was an important one in
the history of the cinema, but it was also, on the
scale of society as a whole, a kind of historical

turning point. The censor's office was a kind of
bastion of conservatism and puritanism. It was particularly around French films that the battle was fought.[12]
The battle fought over censorship drained off a considerable amount of intellectual energy.

The third phase was centered on the need for a
broadly based law or, in other terms, on the need for
the government to intervene and to pass laws in this
particular sector of the culture industry. This phase,
which lasted twelve years or so, just ended with the
passage of a general law in 1975.

This struggle to ensure that the state intervened
to protect and favor the growth of a cinema industry was
based on studies in which the cinema people had to analyze their situation objectively. While doing this
work, they were able to show the extent of the American
imperialism in the domain of the cinema and to demonstrate the total dependence of Quebec. We must remember, however, that this activity in the field of the
cinema coincided with similar initiatives starting in
different sectors of socioeconomic activities. In
other words, the work that the craftsmen of the cinema
were undertaking was synchronized with happenings in
the whole of Quebec society. In retrospect, it is easy
to note that a great many analyses revolved around
themes of alienation and colonization of the Quebec
people--themes that are dominant in certain critical
analyses in Quebec. This period, roughly speaking,
reaches from 1964 to today, when we can really begin to
speak about a Quebec cinema industry. During these
years, about 250 feature films have been produced--most
of them since 1968, the year in which the Société de
développement de l'industrie cinématographique canadi-
enne (SDICC) started to function.[13]

Production was organized around private and public
initiatives. But neither the public sector nor the
private sector is monolithic. In these two sectors, we
find art films and essentially commercial films. This
can be explained by the fact that Quebec society is
small, that there is a great deal of interaction
between artists, and that the NFB never really had a
policy concerning feature films.

OPTIMISM DESPITE IT ALL

The Quebec film industry was characterized up until
the present by a continuing reference to problems that
Quebec society experiences as a totality. This is true
for the most commercial of our films and even more so
for art films. Evidently, reference to Quebec society

as an entity are not uniformly deep nor uniformly rich,
but there is a kind of organic cultural link between
artistic producers and the Quebec cinema. My colleague
Marcel Rioux likes to say that Quebec is closely knit;
in fact, the distinction between the commercial and the
art cinema is artificial, even if each of us thinks
that we understand the distinction that we are trying
to make in using the terms.[14] All films are commercial;
all cinema has to fit into a microindustrial circuit.
At the present time, the larger the budget of a film,
the stronger are the links that tie the craftsmen of
the cinema to capital and the more the product risks
being politically influenced by the vested interests
of the providers of the money (who for their part have
only one objective--namely, to maintain the stability
of a system that gives them a great many advantages).
That is why it is important to recognize where the
capital comes from. When the money comes from the
state, the emphasis is placed on the protection of the
system; when it comes from the private sector, the
emphasis is placed on profit. As for a crown corporation like the SDICC, its role is mixed because the
corporation has to play openly in both arenas at the
same time. One has only to analyze the questionnaire
that must be filled out by the adjudicators (who evaluate scenarios proposed to the SDICC) to realize what
kind of film is hoped for and highly valued by the
SDICC. It is a film with a story emphasizing the psychology of people and the universality of sentiments.
And when the question of the environment comes up, it
is not society, nor the classes that struggle in that
society that are referred to, but instead the anachro-
nisms or technical errors that should be avoided. It
is obvious that the financiers of the Quebec cinema
(or the Canadian one, for that matter) have modeled
their criteria on their ideal of a cinema industry,
namely, the American industry.

When we know that it is almost impossible to make
a film without turning to this corporation, we realize
at once how much pressure is exercised on the Quebec
cinema industry. Like all the other industries, it is
called upon to play the role of cultural tranquilizer
and at the same time to provide a means of escape for
the leisure society (live now, pay later--at 22 percent
per annum) in which, to survive, people are advised to
stimulate themselves with a sex film, to frighten themselves with a horror film, or to tickle themselves with
a comic. Anything except reality!

However, despite it all, I am optimistic because,
up until now, the marginality of Quebecers compared to
the ensemble of North American society has always
helped them and has protected them from the crudest

contradictions of that society. I am also optimistic because art always exercises a highly critical function in our industrial society.

NOTES

1. Thomas H. Cuback, "Derrière les ombres sur l'écran: Le cinéma américain en tant qu'industrie" [Behind the shadows of the screen: The American cinema as an industry], in Sociologie et Sociétés (published by Presses de l'Université de Montréal), special number devoted to the relationships between cinema and society.

2. Originally the name "Canadian cinema" was used; then, in about 1960, "French Canadian cinema"; and finally, in about 1968, "Quebec cinema."

3. By "innocent image" I mean that which seems to be pure amusement, without any message, without any "content."

4. The other person was first of all the Britisher from England, but he was also the American. Indeed, one can say that since World War II, it was primarily the American who took the control of our economy.

5. Guy Rocher, Le Québec en mutation (Montreal: H.M.H., 1973), p. 18.

6. Ibid., p. 26.

7. This is a rapid way of describing the situation. Obviously, I do not believe that the cinema is the only bridge between American society and our own.

8. Dorchester (Sainte-Marie-de-Beauce), May 11, 1949.

9. See Theory of the Film: Character and Growth of a New Art (London: Dennis Dobson Ltd., 1950).

10. By cinema technicians I mean not only film editors, cameramen, and sound engineers, but also producers. Time has shown that a number of cinema technicians turned to producing after having acquired their experience with other activities.

11. I use the word maturity because we must not forget that our oldest cinema technicians, with a few exceptions, are not yet fifty years old.

12. Le Rideau Cramoisi by Alexander Astruc and particularly Hiroshima mon Amour by Resnais, among others, were pretexts for these great battles.

13. This crown corporation is, as its name indicates,
mandated to give financial help for the production of
Canadian films. Its budget in 1968 was $10 million.

14. Marcel Rioux, La Question du Québec (Paris:
Seghers, 1969), and Les Québécois (Paris: Editions du
Seuil, 1974).

Hamburger Stand: Industrialization and the Fast-Food Phenomenon

Bruce A. Lohof

In 1936, Charlie Chaplin unveiled one of the more famous of his satirical commentaries on life in the United States in the twentieth century. Modern Times, he called it--the movie and the century--and his protagonist was a factory worker who, standing at his station beside an assembly line, tightening a perpetual sequence of bolts, each with a single turn of a single wrench, monotonously abetted the replication of some standardized product. The movie was not named "best of the year" (an honor that went, instead, to a now forgotten film, The Great Ziegfeld), but its setting did have a certain recognizable madness, which explains, one supposes, why Chaplin's imagery has since become a cultural cliché.

The helpless pawn of standardized industrial forces was no Chaplinesque invention, of course. Historians who viewed Modern Times knew its protagonist well. A century before Chaplin's birth, the hand-loom weavers of England had succumbed to Richard Arkwright's power looms, even as their fellows in a myriad other callings had sooner or later fallen to a similar turn of events. And the same circumstances that Chaplin now attacked with pathos and satire had, in all seriousness, been confronted a hundred years earlier by the namesakes of Ned Ludd. Indeed, so compelling and so ubiquitous had been the narrative that Chaplin's themes--the subordination of the skilled artisan to the sophisticated mechanism and the replacement of the unique item by the uniform product--became major leitmotifs in the history of the Industrial Revolution.

The times have changed, now, and many millions of us live in cultures that have moved through secondary and tertiary revolutions into what has often been

characterized as a postindustrial condition. Still,
the dichotomies of artisan-versus-mechanism and unique-
versus standardized, so central to the Industrial Revolution, are extant here and there as indicators of cultural progression. One such place, for instance, is
suggested by Modern Times itself. For, as aficionados
will recall, Chaplin had his masochistically submissive
protagonist actually suggest that the mechanisms of the
factory might be further augmented by a feeding machine
that would oblige the workers to eat without loss to
the company through downtime.[1] The suggested machine,
thought too complicated to be feasible, was rejected by
management. But the most cursory glance at the postindustrial landscape--with franchised eateries standing
cheek by jowl along every city's neon strip--suggests
that it need not have been. A handful of internationally recognized trademarks, with thousands of individual
eateries snuggled beneath them, gives evidence of the
mechanical feasibility--not to mention the large-scale
profitability--of feeding machines. The Industrial
Revolution, in short, has finally come to fast food,
and it would be well for us to examine its advent.
For, in so doing, we may recapture, in our own time,
the processes by which industrialization occurs. We
may also find in the fast-food industry an indicator of
a given culture's industrial condition. And, finally,
we may learn something about the impact that industrialization's imperatives have had upon our individual cultures, many of which, quite literally, take much of
their sustenance in the form of the machine-made hamburger.

The preindustrial history of the fast-food phenomenon disappears somewhere into the diner (this Americanism of nineteenth-century vintage), initially a railroad
car especially equipped for the preparation and serving
of food and, subsequently, a derailed facsimile that
follows its calling in a single location. But perhaps
a more recognizable form of preindustrialism in fast
food is the greasy spoon (a colloquialism with roots
apparently as deep as the 1920s), that franchised or
company-owned edifice of the postwar period, that Royal
Castle or White Castle or White Tower or Toddle House,
et cetera ad nauseam, that continues to punctuate the
cityscape. A faithful representative of this genre is
found in any one of the hundred-or-so Royal Castle restaurants in existence at this writing. Owned by a
Miami-based firm, Royal Castle System, Inc., this
greasy spoon and its fellows account for some $21 million
in sales each year.[2] In financial as well as symbolic
terms, then, it can stand as an archetype of preindustrialism in fast food.

Architecturally, our sample may conform to any one of the four types that the Royal Castle System has constructed since its inception in 1938. Type D, the earliest of the four, is a rectangle of approximately thirty-five by forty feet, its forward corner being indented into a front entrance and its interior featuring a counter flanked on one side by a row of stools and on the other by a galley-style kitchen (see figure 1). Type DD, in turn, is simply a type D structure, augmented by a smaller module of approximately eighteen by twenty-six feet that is fitted for table service (see figure 2). Or, our archetype might be a J structure, a slightly smaller building--approximately twenty-eight feet by forty feet--whose exterior is dominated by an illumined facade across the roof line, but whose interior is very similar to that of type D (see figure 3). And, finally, there is the K type, a square of approximately thirty-five feet, whose exterior features an exaggerated hip roof (see figure 4). Inside, the K departs from the greasy-spoon tradition by obscuring the kitchen behind a partition, with only a service passage joining preparation and serving areas.[3]

Whatever its call letter, however, our type conforms to what John Kouwenhoven and others have called the "vernacular tradition," for each of that tradition's characteristics--"economy, simplicity, and flexibility"--are in clear evidence.[4] Each of the types was designed for economical maintenance, with tile floors, concrete and glass walls, and either porcelain enamel or aluminum fixtures. Each--with, perhaps, the exception of the K and its excessive roof line--is free of meaningless ornamentation. And each is an invention in the broadest sense, an architectural contrivance that can be replicated over and over again without modification in design and can be placed down wherever a fast-food eatery is needed. Indeed, certain of the types--specifically, D and DD, are so flexible that they are properly thought of as a series of modules--basic structural elements--that can be horizontally "stacked" to produce a variety of restaurant types with only a small repertoire of modules.[5]

The door to a busy Royal Castle restaurant is an entrance upon an animated collage. Here a derelict dozes in his coffee; here a nurse, fresh from a night's sleep, breakfasts on bacon and eggs before reporting to work; here a cabbie, weary from a night on the streets, relaxes over a hamburger; here a nondescript couple consumes any of the fifty-odd other itmes appearing on the Royal Castle menu. The establishment, in short, is a jostle of apparently disparate activities, each in pursuit of its separate agenda.

Lending unity and coherence to this jostle, however, is the presence of the artisan-in-residence, the
fry cook (yet another colloquialism, this, apparently,
of unknown origin). He is the common denominator among
these unshared agendas because he--usually with single-
handed dexterity--has taken each order and has prepared
and served its contents. More important, he stands as
the artisan in the classic sense of that term, for he
has undergone an apprenticeship and is now able to
exercise special skills and to manipulate specific tools
in the pursuit of an applied art. His education is of
the crudest and most basic sort: on-the-job. Experience, then, rather than some more formal order of training, accounts for his expertise. His workbench, so to
speak, is the galley kitchen, stretching from grill
to ice maker, with coffee urns and soup warmers, toast-
ers and waffle irons, griddles and sinks, all strate-
gically interspersed (see figure 5). Scattered across
his galley is an array of tools with names as arcane
and functions as specialized as those of the tanner or
the carpenter. Finally, his product--mean fare, to be
sure--plays ham and eggs to the chef's soufflé, even as
the anonymous gargoyle plays to Michelangelo's Pietà,
even as, in more general terms, the product of any
artisan plays to the more sophisticated, but nevertheless similar, product of his artistic counterpart.[6]

As surely, then, as the hand-loom weaver was the
central character in textile production before the introduction of the power loom; as surely, also, as the
cooper was the central character in the barrel-making
process before the advent of the mass-produced steel
drum; as surely, in short, as the artisan class as a
whole served as the mainspring of preindustrial fabri-
cation--so the fry cook is the central character in
this archetype of preindustrial fast food, the greasy
spoon.

Down the road, however, is a new central character
housed in a new variety of structures. Down the road,
also, is a new and standardized product; the industrialized hamburger.

The Burger King Corporation is a subsidiary of the
Pillsbury Corporation, which operates or licenses nearly
fifteen hundred fast-food restaurants in thirty-nine of
the United States and a half-dozen foreign countries.
Its sales, as this writing, exceed $600 million annually,
making it one of the largest fast-food firms in the
world.[7] And each of its fifteen hundred stores is the
home of the industrialized hamburger.

Like the preindustrial Royal Castle System, the Burger King Corporation has constructed four distinct store types in the two decades of its existence, and our sample restaurant might conform to any one of these. The Walk-up, whose appellation has obvious origins, is the earliest of the types, a single rectangle whose interior contains equipment for the preparation of food, but lacks a seating area, rest-room facilities, or other amenities that ordinarily pertain to a restaurant (see figure 6). The Handlebar store, so named because of its dominant roof-line decoration, is a slightly larger structure of approximately forty-five by fifty feet. Reminiscent of the stacking relationship that is shared by the Royal Castle System's D and DD buildings, the Handlebar is little more than a Walk-up that, in keeping with the flexibility of the vernacular tradition, has been augmented by a seating area (see figure 7).

For the past ten years, however, Burger King stores have invariably conformed to either the Red Roof or the Natural Finish types, and our sample structure will probably be one of these (see figures 8-9). Rectangles of forty-five by fifty feet to fifty by fifty-five feet, depending upon the desired seating capacity, Red Roof and Natural Finish are distinguishable from Handlebar, as well as from each other, by their distinctive decors. Gone is the earlier handlebar logo, and in its place is either a red mansard roof line or a nature motif, with cedar shakes, brickwork walls, and warm color schemes. Architecturally, however, little has changed. As before, food preparation and seating areas lie side by side within rectangular boxes.[8]

Indeed, these current Burger King types are similar not only to their antecedents, the Handlebar and the Walk-up: they are reminiscent as well of the Royal Castle System's greasy-spoon architecture, for they, too, illustrate the vernacular tradition. Hence, our eye is caught by that familiar economy of maintenance and simplicity of design. We notice, again, the flexibility and replicability of the structure. And, finally, we notice in the Burger King store, no less than anywhere else within the tradition, a vernacular reliance upon the horizontal stacking of modules. Hiding behind a different logo, then, and clothed in a different wardrobe of motifs is the same vernacular tradition.

As our attention turns away from architecture and back to the processes of cookery, however, we cannot help noticing that the greasy spoon's artisan-in-residence, the fry cook, is conspicuous by his absence. Neither can we ignore his replacement, which is a

remarkable facsimile of Charlie Chaplin's feeding machine. Accordingly, as feeding machinery replaces artisan, we are obliged to come to terms with the other
dichotomy of industrialization: the replacement of the
unique with the uniform. We are, in short, obliged to
come to terms with the industrialized hamburger.

Like the other machines we find in the world of
industrialization, the Burger King Corporation's hamburger machine--or line-up, as it is referred to in the
trade--rationalizes the construction of its product.
The process is first separated into its discrete tasks.
Each of these tasks is then relegated to a station,
mechanical or manual, that has been designed for its
particular purpose. Finally, each of these stations is
given its appropriate place along the assembly line.

The line-up begins with a broiling mechanism.
Moving along endless-grate conveyors, buns of bread and
patties of meat travel at precise speeds through intense
temperatures (see figures 10-12). When properly cooked,
these patties and buns fall from their endless grates
and descend small chutes, where the one is sandwiched
within the other (see figure 13). These sandwiches can
then be moved to the next station, a preparation table,
where a variety of condiments are applied as prescribed
by the customer (see figure 14). Here the hamburger
is completed, packaged, and sent forward to the point of
sale.[9]

The Burger King line-up is, of course, no more
sophisticated than its product makes necessary. But
students of, say Oliver Evans's eighteenth-century mill
at Redclay Creek or Henry Ford's twentieth-century
plant at River Rouge will, nevertheless, recognize its
mechanical essence. As Siegfried Giedion has written:
"Mechanizing production means dissecting work into its
component operations. . . . in manufacturing complex
products such as the automobile [or, as we see, relatively simple products such as the hamburger sandwich],
this division goes together with re-assembly."[10]

Remembering the preindustrial nature of our sample
Royal Castle restaurant, we are now struck by the industrial milieu of the Burger King line-up. The basic
elements of the factory have obviously been introduced
to the fast-food phenomenon. Moreover, this introduction has brought with it other inevitable changes.
First, the advent of the feeding machine has meant the
possibility--some would say the dulling certainty--of
a standardized, recognized product. "Burger King," one
commentator has written, "wants the food it serves in
New York to be as identical as humanly possible to that
served in New Mexico or New Orleans."[11] And industrialization alone makes such conformity possible.

Concomitantly, the advent of mechanization means the demise of the artisan--in this case, the demise of the fry cook. Standing in the place of the artisan, his careful skills, and his arcane gally is the glistening metal line-up and its inexperienced attendants. The Burger King Corporation claims that a single hamburger machine represents an investment in excess of $40 thousand. It also claims that its average restaurant employee is an unskilled teenager who will work for the prevailing minimum wage and will last, perhaps, four months on the job.[12] What other data could better illustrate the replacement of the experienced artisan and his tools with the sophisticated machine and its callow caretakers? In fast food, as elsewhere, the truth of Giedion's title is inescapable: Mechanization takes command!

But what do they all mean, these fifteen hundred Burger King stores, these hundred-or-so Royal Castle greasy spoons, and their thousands upon thousands of fellow fast-food eateries that, albeit under competing logos, punctuate the landscape? Surely, no gothic cathedrals, these. Surely, no mighty engines of awesome sophistication or power are found within them. What lessons, then, are there here that we should contemplate this apparent trivia?

First, we can look to the architecture of the fast-food phenomenon to find a ready example of the vernacular tradition. And though, as aesthetes, we may be put off by the vulgarity of the tradition, we cannot, as students of culture, ignore its ubiquity. Vernacular architecture is all around us. If it is not a Burger King for the refueling of our stomachs, it is a gasoline station for the refueling of our automobiles or a chain-operated motel for the resuscitation of our travel-weary bodies or a tract home for the renewal of our world-weary families. Inspirational as we might find the architecture of a Wright or a Sullivan or a Pei, it is the vernacular tradition in which we live our lives. And the economy, simplicty, and flexibility of that tradition are nowhere more evident than in the houses of fast food.

Second, we can look into the bowels of the fast-food phenomenon to find an ongoing example of what it has meant to make an industrial revolution. And, for students of industrialization who live, as most of us do, in industrialized cultures, such examples are as rare as they are useful. Here, in comparing the greasy spoon with the home of the industrial hamburger, one finds all of those aspects of mechanization that students from before Adam Smith to after Siegfried

Giedion have explained to us. Here, moreover, we find
the imperatives of mechanization: first, the standardized product, in this case, the industrialized hamburger; and, second--to return all the way back to the seat
of Charlie Chaplin's malaise--the subordination of the
skilled artisan to the sophisticated machine.

Those are the lessons--technological and cultural--
of the industrialized hamburger.

NOTES

1. Modern Times, United Artists Corporation, 1936.
Cf. Siegfried Giedion, Mechanization Takes Command (New
York, 1948), pp. 124-26.

2. Interview with Nancy Bailey, public relations officer, Royal Castle System, Inc., March 28, 1975. Also,
see Dun & Bradstreet, Million Dollar Directory, 1975
(New York, 1974), p. 1960.

3. These architectural observations are based upon the
above-cited Bailey interview, as well as upon on-site
investigations that were conducted in April-May 1975.

4. John A. Kouwenhoven, Made in America (Garden City,
N.Y., 1948), p. 41.

5. The stacking characteristic of vernacular architecture is most apparent in service station design. See,
for instance, Bruce A. Lohof, "The Service Station in
America: The Evolution of a Vernacular Form," Industrial Archaeology 11 (Spring 1974):1-13.

6. These observations are based, in part, upon a series
of interviews with Royal Castle restaurant employees
that were conducted in April-May 1975.

7. Interview with Donna Nichol, public relations officer, Burger King Corporation, May 27, 1975. Also, see
Dun & Bradstreet, Directory, pp. 321-22; "The Hamburger
that Conquered the Country," Time, September 17, 1973,
p. 84; and Jan Cook, "The Hungry Fight for the Fast-
Food Dollar," Tropic, February 16, 1975, p. 6.

8. These architectural observations are based, in part,
upon an interview with Jack Meyer, architectural and
engineering officer, Burger King Corporation, February
28, 1973.

9. These observations are based, in part, upon an interview with Ray Taweel, management operations training
officer, Burger King Corporation, September 4, 1974.

10.   Giedion, <u>Mechanization</u> <u>Takes</u> <u>Command</u>, pp. 31-32.

11.   Cook, "Fight for the Fast-Food Dollar," p. 7.

12.   Ibid.

FIGURE 1

FIGURE 2

FIGURE 3

FIGURE 4

FIGURE 5

FIGURE 6

FIGURE 7

FIGURE 8

FIGURE 9

FIGURE 10

FIGURE 11

FIGURE 12

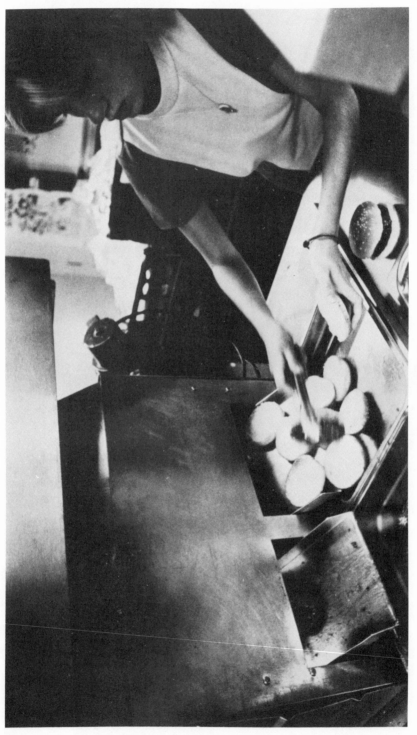

FIGURE 13

FIGURE 14

III. THE UNITED STATES AND THE HEMISPHERE: SPECIAL PROBLEMS

The Commonwealth Caribbean in U.S. Foreign Policy: A Caribbean Perspective

Basil A. Ince

INTRODUCTION

The postwar decolonization process began for the English-speaking territories in the Caribbean in the early 1960s and has not yet run its full course. Some of the territories have been formally decolonized; others have been partially decolonized; and at least one of them remains a crown colony. This paper addresses itself to the foreign policy of the United States toward those territories now commonly called the Commonwealth Caribbean.[1] Although I plan to cover the period from 1962 to the present, there may be good reason to refer to events prior to 1962, when the first Commonwealth Caribbean states became independent.

The United States and the Commonwealth Caribbean belong to the Pan American system and both are English-speaking, but similarities between them end there. Although the social and cultural differences are patently evident to those familiar with both areas, it is the sharp distinction between them in power, economic and political, that is most significant. Relationships between them have been asymmetrical in nature, with the United States playing the role of the dominant power. Indeed, Latin America has served as a subordinate system playing an inferior role to the United States. The Caribbean forms a subsystem of the Latin American subordinate system and, like Latin America, also regards the United States as the validation power for the hemisphere.

Note: I am thankful to Leslie Manigat, who kindly read the entire article and made incisive comments.

Once British paramountcy in Latin America had declined toward the end of the nineteenth century, it was
simply a matter of time before the United States asserted its dominance over what later was to be called the
Commonwealth Caribbean. Four U.S. actions might be
taken as indicative of American dominance. The first
occurred in 1895, when the United States demanded that
Britain arbitrate in the Guyana-Venezuela boundary dispute, and the next in 1940, when the United States
signed leased-bases agreements with Britain that virtually ignored the rights of the islands' inhabitants.
American clandestine behavior and political influence
were the main catalysts in the delay of Guyanese independence in the 1960s, while the appearance of U.S.
warships just outside Trinidad's territorial waters in
1970 was a grim reminder that the English-speaking territories were not exempt from the type of "visits" frequently paid by U.S. forces to the non-English-speaking
territories of the Caribbean.

This paper is divided roughly into four sections.
Section one treats the international relations of the
period 1962 to the present with special reference to
U.S. foreign policy toward Latin America and the Caribbean. Section two views the Commonwealth Caribbean
states as penetrated societies and examines the various
forms of penetration by the dominant power in the hemisphere. The third section assesses the interests of
both parties in their relationship; and the concluding
section analyzes prospects for the future with emphasis
on a new relationship characterized by interdependence
rather than asymmetry.

INTERNATIONAL RELATIONS, 1962 TO THE PRESENT

The beginning of the 1960s was a time of ferment
in international relations. Cracks appeared in old
alliances, decolonization picked up speed, and the
United States attacked what it perceived as communist
offensives in various parts of the globe. De Gaulle,
bent on moving France to the leadership of Europe,
which in turn would be strong enough to stand up to
the United States, offended U.S. leaders and threatened
the Atlantic partnership. On the other hand, the Sino-
Soviet quarrel for ideological leadership in the communist world became more pronounced as China became
more hostile.

Countries emerging from colonial tutelage added to
continued friction in the international system. Indo-
nesia was on the verge of independence from the Nether-
lands, while Algeria emerged as a republic after seven

years of war with France. The Belgians fled from the
Congo in haste, leaving the country in turmoil as rival
groups, encouraged by cold war leaders, fought among
themselves for power.

The major threat to the "free world," as far as
the United States was concerned, was the spread of
communism. Thus, it became increasingly involved in
fighting what it considered to be communist subversion
in Vietnam. The United States was quite disturbed by
Cuba's communist regime and used its influence to have
Cuba barred from participation in the OAS in January
1962. In October of that year, the Cuban Missile Crisis
demonstrated how far the United States was prepared to
go to prevent missiles from being placed within its
defense perimeter. Indeed, the idea of a communist
menace was so paramount in U.S. thought that the nation's leaders measured success in foreign policy by
victories against the communists. President Kennedy
himself declared at the end of 1962: "If it were not
for us the Communists would be dominant in the world
today, and because of us, we are in a strong position.
Now I think it is a pretty good record for a country
with six per cent of the world's population, which is
very reluctant to take on these burdens."[2]

This anticommunist penchant led the Kennedy Congress to approve a record peacetime military expenditure of $49.7 billion with additional military-related
appropriations of $51.6 billion. Military might was
the cornerstone of U.S. foreign policy. A former Chairman of the Senate Foreign Relations Committee, J. William Fulbright of Arkansas, was later to disagree with
this emphasis: "To equate security and the quantity of
arms can only drag us into an accelerating arms race,
lead to a rise in international tension and accordingly,
to a decline in security. Nor is it out of the question
that we might possess overwhelming military superiority
and still face erosion of our power and influence in
the world."[3] Security-consciousness on the part of the
United States was particularly acute if the threat lay
within the Western hemisphere. Every president from
Kennedy to Ford was quick to respond to the communist
threat in this hemisphere, and the Alliance for Progress
was a weapon primarily devoted to fighting it. The in-
vasion of the Dominican Republic under orders from
President Johnson was intended, according to U.S. officials, to prevent "another Cuba on our doorstep."
President Nixon voiced support for the anti-Castro policy years after, and today Cuba remains outside the pale
of East-West détente.

During this period the United States and the Soviet Union sought adherents to their respective camps, giving recently decolonized states an opportunity to play an important role in world affairs. While continuing to push for total decolonization, these states began to recognize that to be decolonized and poor led to a multiplicity of domestic problems. Adopting a posture of nonalignment in an attempt to hold themselves aloof from the cold war concerns of the superpowers, they employed the United Nations as a forum for seeking solutions to their problems. As a result, the West, led by the United States, lost its automatic voting majority in the United Nations and began to use phrases such as "tyranny of the majority" and to cry plaintively that the new states were "against the West."

In Latin America, bilateral aid with strings attached often engendered resentment during the 1960s. Military intervention, a historical American tradition in Latin America, was imposed on the Dominican Republic in 1965, and the OAS was manipulated to suit American interests. The prestige of that institution fell to rock bottom.[4]

Despite the opportunity to play a role in world politics afforded by the bipolar competition of the cold war, by the early 1960s the nonaligned nations had declined in prestige and were playing a decreasing role in world politics. Soviet-American détente had been declared, and the rigid bipolar structure of world power, which for many historians ended in 1962 with the Cuban Missile Crisis, became a muted bipolar one. In any case, the Third World states declined in importance during the 1960s because, according to one scholar, "there has been little effort on their part to revise their immediate post-independence view of the world and to evolve an understanding of the changed structure of world politics."[5]

The United States emerged from the 1960s with balance of payment problems and foreign policies which, in Morgenthau's words, "have become obsolete. . . . the United States has been unable to devise new policies capable of dealing successfully with the issues of a different age."[6] The economies of Western Europe and Japan had become powerful. The nonaligned nations, having lost their influence in the 1960s, began to make themselves felt on the world scene as they shifted their tactics at Lusaka in 1970 and began to concentrate on economic issues. Cooperation among oil-producing countries was later to sharpen divisions between the industrialized world and Third World nations, which began to press for structural changes in the international economic system.

In assessing the new world situation, President
Nixon proposed a doctrine of shared responsibilities.
As he stated in a report to Congress, "This doctrine
was central to our approach to major allies in the
Atlantic and Pacific. But it also shaped our attitude
toward those in Latin America, Asia and Africa with
whom we were working on formal alliance or friendship."7
Nixon further described this doctrine as a "deliberate
policy of restraint, encouraging others to furnish concepts as well as reasons for hemispheric development."
With regard to Latin America, this theme was to be repeated in various phrases, such as "reduction of our
visibility," "accommodation to diversity," or "lower[ing]
our profile in the Hemisphere."

The greater part of U.S. aid to Latin America, formerly conveyed through bilateral channels, was to flow
through multilateral organizations such as the Inter-
American Development Bank, the World Bank, and the
United Nations Development Program. The Nixon report
stated: "It is politically easier for a country to
accept assistance from an international bank or other
organization than from one country. And international
organizations can impose strict conditions for loans on
economic grounds without opening the door to charges of
political 'meddling.'"8

U.S. foreign policy for the 1970s is clear and un-
equivocal. President Ford's policy toward the developing nations and Latin America was essentially the same
as Nixon's. In a 1975 address to the Annual Meeting of
the International Monetary Fund, President Ford reiterated that "the U.S. stands ready to help all nations
[combat the global recessions] but Washington alone cannot solve the world's economic problems."9 Ford was
eminently correct. However, he failed to see that although the United States cannot solve all the problems
of the developing nations, it could contribute a great
deal more to their solution by responding positively to
the developing nations' demands for a new international
economic order than by offering strong resistance to
them.10

Thus, it is in the context of a fluctuating
environment in international relations that I shall
examine U.S. Caribbean policy since 1960.

THE COMMONWEALTH CARIBBEAN AS PENETRATED STATES

When the Commonwealth Caribbean states began to
achieve independence, it was evident that the United
States would loom large in their foreign relations.
This is not to say that the United States deliberately

set out to play a dominant role in the lives of these
states, but that, as a matter of course, it entered
into a relationship with them as new actors in the
international community. The mere existence of a
superpower in the hemisphere was sufficient for the
new states to look with awe upon the United States.
Even more awesome, from the perspective of the new
international actors, was the knowledge that the giant
had had and continued to have strong interests in the
Caribbean. The former mother country, anxious to be
rid of them and hastening to attend to its own problems,
had created a power vacuum. Noting this waning of
British power in the Caribbean, one U.S. scholar wrote:

> Power is intolerant of a vacuum. . . . by some
> natural law of the international process, not
> so much by conscious design as by the nature
> of power itself, other influence, that of the
> dollar area and of the United States in partic-
> ular, is coming to replace it, thereby serving
> existing interests of the United States and
> creating new ones as well.[11]

That the United States is important to all the independent Caribbean Commonwealth polities is exemplified
by the fact that on the attainment of independence, they
all immediately established diplomatic relations with
that country. Even tiny Grenada, for whom the burden
of external relations is most onerous, opened an embassy
in Washington. This was not an easy decision for a
state of Grenada's resources, for as Paul Hammond has
noted, "One of the major questions about foreign policy
concerns the level of effort: How much should the State
extract from the internal political system in order to
pursue its external objectives?"[12] In the case of
Grenada, the Prime Minister had said prior to independence that his country had a shortage of economic capa-
bilities and that foreign aid would be welcomed.

The introduction of foreign aid on a bilateral
basis opens the receiver state to penetration from the
donor states. One way in which a prospective receiver
state can avoid this sort of economic penetration is
to insist that aid be channeled through an international
organization. It is my belief, however, that even aid
channeled through an international organization can be
penetrative. After all, technical assistants, although
they become international civil servants when employed
by an international organization, remain citizens of
a particular country and frequently work for the welfare
of their country whenever possible. This is one reason
that states do all in their power to place their citizens in key positions in international organizations.

Mindful of this, some governments have requested that
experts from other developing countries be sent by
international organizations in preference to experts
from the developed countries.

It is pertinent at this time to define the concept
of penetration, since it is pivotal in clarifying the
relationship between the United States and the Commonwealth Caribbean states. According to Rosenau, "a penetrated political system is one in which non-members of
a national society participate directly and authoritatively, through actions taken jointly with the society's
members, in either the allocation of its values or the
mobilization of support on behalf of its goods."13
Different methods of penetrating a state--economic,
military, and cultural--may lead, jointly or singly, to
political penetration. The line between military and
cultural forms of penetration, on the one hand, and
political penetration, on the other, is a thin one.
It is even thinner between political and economic forms
of penetration. With this in mind, we may consider
U.S.-Caribbean relationships in the light of economic
and political penetration.

Economic Penetration

The importance of the United States in Caribbean
affairs began prior to independence. American bauxite
companies had established themselves in Jamaica as early
as 1946 and even earlier in Guyana, when the Demerara
Bauxite Company (Demba), formed by American and Canadian
aluminium interests, began operations in 1916. Some indication of the extent to which Jamaican bauxite was
controlled by foreign interests can be seen from the
earnings North American companies made in 1960--approxi-
mately $105 million. From this sum the Jamaican govern-
ment received $22 million in royalties and taxes. In
Guyana the government received less than one-quarter of
bauxite earnings. Moreover, many of these bauxite companies brought unsavory racial practices with them and
were the cause of poor social conditions for the work-
ers.14 The U.S.-Caribbean bauxite relationship spawned
a series of articles by UWI economist Norman Girvan, who
advocated change.

With the rise of economic nationalism in the Commonwealth Caribbean states, the Guyanese and Jamaican
governments began to act on behalf of the welfare of
their citizens. In Guyana the Canadian-owned company
Demba, a subsidiary of Alcan Aluminium, was nationalized,
and in Jamaica the Michael Manley government placed a
production levy on bauxite companies operating there.
This brought in some $175 million by May 1975. This new

arrangement, which does not entail nationalization, has
been protested by the multinational corporations that
have sought arbitration from the World Bank regarding
investment disputes. Guyana, impressed with the Jamaican action, followed suit at the time and yet made
plans to nationalize the Reynolds company.

Just prior to the decision to nationalize Demba,
which had substantial U.S. investor interest, the
Guyanese government had applied for a $5.4 million loan
from the World Bank to assist in the construction of
seawalls or dikes to prevent the flooding of coastal
areas. Although the loan was technically sound, the
U.S. Executive Director of the bank abstained from
voting on the application. The U.S. Undersecretary
of the Treasury warned developing countries to "tread
very lightly" in nationalizing foreign corporations,
while two aluminium officials in the United States lob-
bied within the State Department to put pressure on
the Guyanese government.[16] The Undersecretary of State
admitted that the days of gunboat diplomacy and direct
intervention were over, but suggested:

> There is an appropriate place for a policy
> where the US Government can support the ac-
> tivities of its nationals abroad through a
> fair and balanced policy of deterrents, in-
> dicating that there are economic costs in-
> volved in expropriation for the host country,
> and that if they seek to pursue their policy
> the cost will be incurred.[17]

A U.S. scholar, testifying on United States Caribbean
policy before the House Subcommittee on Inter-American
Affairs, noted that there was some difficulty in curb-
ing the habits of American multinationals, "but if
there were a will in Washington, there might be a
way."[18] Evidently the will is nonexistent, as evidenced by CIA involvement in the ITT affair in Chile,
which led to the eventual downfall of the Allende
government. It was not surprising, therefore, that
a journalist writing in a Trinidad newspaper asked
whether Manley was "about to be hit with the kind of
pressure that led to the overthrow of President Salvador
Allende of Chile."[19] He was referring to the vigorous
opposition by American bauxite companies to the Jamaican
government's new production levy.

While in 1971-72 crude attempts on behalf of
foreign interests would not have had much effect on
Guyana's future economic foreign policy, in the era
prior to independence Guyana had to display more caution in its foreign economic policy initiatives. Guyana
achieved independence with the blessing of the United

States, which had successfully thwarted Jagan's attempt
to lead the country. Immediately following independence, the aid that the Jagan regime had been unable
to obtain flowed into Guyana. The Guyanese government,
desiring not to offend the United States, circumscribed
its trading patterns to suit the latter's interests.
This action led Jagan to declare, "In keeping with US
world-wide diplomatic pressure for the isolation and
blockade of Cuba and China, the coalition government
has abandoned trade with Cuba and placed serious restrictions on the importation of less costly goods from
the socialist countries."[20]

The United States was similarly able to influence
the foreign policy of Jamaica and Trinidad and Tobago,
particularly in the pre-1970 period. In Trinidad, U.S.
investment had begun to displace British investment in
petroleum by the 1950s. By the early 1960s Texaco was
a powerful and influential multinational in the country.
For example, in 1964 the government agreed to borrow
nearly $9 million from Texaco, to be repaid in U.S.
currency. An opposition member in the House indicated
that the loan would do more for the U.S. export program than for the development program of Trinidad since
the loan was to be used "solely for purchases in the
U.S.A." He drew the obvious conclusion that any government that found itself in such a position was suscepti-
ble to pressure and could not "dare to call itself independent."[21] Four years before, there had been other
strong indications that the United States would play
an influential role in Trinidad's politics. The Trinidad Prime Minister, retreating from his earlier nationalist stance on the return of the U.S.-leased Chaguaramas
base to the people of Trinidad and Tobago, decided to
negotiate with the Americans. A Trinidad scholar considered the Prime Minister's negotiations over the base
to be a sellout.[22] Two additional telltale signs that
linked Trinidad's future economic development with the
United States were the Prime Minister's "West of the
Iron Curtain" speech in May 1960 and his expressed desire, some five months later, that his country join
the OAS. It was after Williams's speech in 1960 that
a U.S. official remarked, "we knew we could do business
with him."[23]

Sizable U.S. interests in bauxite and petroleum and
smaller ones in banking (Chase Manhattan) and bananas
(United Fruit Company) add up to make U.S. business a
force to be reckoned with in the internal politics of
the Commonwealth Caribbean States. In addition, the
United States provides a sizable market for sugar from
the area. In fact, the overall economic relationship
with the Caribbean is not a disadvantageous one for the
United States. The report of the U.S. Secretary of

State for 1972 stated with respect to the Commonwealth
Caribbean that it "proved again to be a fast growing
market for US products [U.S. exports here trebled in
the 1960-71 period] as well as a source of vital US
imports, particularly bauxite, alumina and petroleum."[24]
Loans and other forms of assistance to the Commonwealth
Caribbean states in recent years seem to be strengthening the economic bonds between the United States and
these countries (see tables 1 and 2).

Even if Caribbean mineral exports have gained in
importance in recent time, the United States still holds
the upper hand in the economic exchange. Barbados and
Jamaica, once tied to the sterling bloc, have now moved
over to the dollar camp, and there is speculation in
Trinidad and Tobago about when that country will follow.
While Britain remains economically important to the
Commonwealth Caribbean states, the tremendous growth in
importance of the United States cannot be denied.

Political Influence and Penetration

In spite of détente with the Soviet Union and
China, there was to be no thawing of U.S. relations
with Cuba. As early as 1970, at a meeting of the
Inter-American Economic and Social Council in Caracas,
the Trinidad Prime Minister began to talk about the
reintegration of Cuba into the hemisphere. In December
1972 the four then independent Commonwealth Caribbean
states established diplomatic relations with Cuba in
a bold move. The United States expressed its dis-
pleasure at this action, labeling the move by the Commonwealth Caribbean states a "violation of hemisphere
sanctions against Cuba." A few months later the
United States drastically reduced the Caribbean's
sugar quota by more than 176 tons, saying that the
Caribbean states had not met their quota for the last
two years. Yet two Latin nations that had violated
their trade agreements with the United States were
awarded their full quotas. In short, the United States
was not applying the same treatment across the board to
all its defaulters. This led a local newspaper's editorial writer to wonder if this was "Uncle Sam's sweet
way of telling us we should not be so friendly with
Cuba."[25] In time, the United States found it possible
to restore the Caribbean quota, but it had made its
point clearly: "Our sugar market will not be open for
those who establish diplomatic relations with our
enemies."

Clandestine activity or subversion is a technique
employed by the U.S. government to topple governments
unfriendly to it or to ensure that political parties
not in accord with U.S. political ideology do not get

Table 1. FOREIGN ASSISTANCE ACT ECONOMIC PROGRAMS, FISCAL YEARS 1971-73
(In Thousands of Dollars)

	TOTAL			DEVELOPMENT LOANS			TECHNICAL ASSISTANCE			POPULATION		
	1971	1972	1973	1971	1972	1973	1971	1972	1973	1971	1972	1973
Guyana	1,250	12,500	10,100	-	11,300	9,000	1,250	1,200	1,100	-	-	-
Jamaica	20,937	1,218	10,849	20,000	-	10,000	357	426	400	580	792	449

Source: Program Agency for International Development, U.S. Department of State,
U.S. Foreign Aid in Latin America, Proposed Fiscal Year 1973 (Washington, D.C.:
U.S. Government Printing Office, 1972).

Table 2.
DISTRIBUTION OF U.S. AND MULTILATERAL DEVELOPMENT ASSISTANCE TO LATIN AMERICA, 1961-70
(In Millions of Dollars)

	Inter-American Development Loans Ordinary Capital	FSO	Social Progress Trust Fund Loans	World Bank Loans	International Development Association Loans	International Finance Corporation Loans
Guyana	-	-	-	8.8	5.1	-
Jamaica	-	10.9	-	46.4	-	3.1
Trinidad	-	8.9	-	46.4	-	-

Source: Development Assistance to Latin America, 1961-70 (Washington, D.C.:
U.S. Government Printing Office, 1971).

into power. Caribbean governments in the last few
years have complained often about subversive activities
by foreign agents. The case of U.S. subversion in
Guyana is well known,[26] as is the role of labor unions
in American foreign policy.[27] In 1972 the Trinidad
government expelled a U.S. trade union organizer after
objecting to the manner in which foreign missions selected recipients of travel and student grants and
sponsored visits without consulting it.

Territorial disputes, relics of colonial times,
have remained to bedevil the two mainland countries of
the Caribbean. The border dispute between Guyana and
Venezuela has been temporarily settled by the Protocol
of Port of Spain, while the Belize-Guatemala dispute
prevents Belize from advancing to independence. Since
the United States has a stake in both of these disputes,
final solutions could hardly be reached without its
blessing. If a Marxist regime were to come to power in
Guyana, it is unlikely that the United States would sit
by idly. Indeed, Venezuela could be encouraged to ac-
tivate its claim to five-eighths of Guyana's territory
at that time. In the Belize-Guatemala case, the United
States probably would not object to Guatemala's absorption of Belize, since Guatemala is one of its client
states and would continue to protect U.S. interests
there. While the United States may appear aloof in
these situations, it could opt for outright intervention, should its vital interests appear in jeopardy.
A U.S. scholar has justified his country's intervention
in the Caribbean "to preempt the crisis situation before the Communists have an opportunity fully to exploit
its possibilities."[28] In any case, the possibility of
seeing what he labels "preemptive intervention" is more
likely to materialize in Guyana than in Belize. While
these disputes appear dormant, their eruption in the
future remains a possibility.

Military and Cultural Penetration

The U.S. military is not without influence in the
Commonwealth Caribbean states. However, given the small
size of the military in these nations (because there is
no potential foreign enemy, except in Guyana) and the
relative proximity of the United States, there has been
no need for military penetration of the area.

In Trinidad the Chaguaramas base provided the focus
of the nationalist movement against the United States in
1956, but since an agreement was concluded in 1967, all
that remains in Trinidad is a U.S. navigational aids
station. In 1970, Trinidad purchased light infantry
weapons from the United States in the face of the
military-cum-black-power revolt. Meanwhile, there

seemed to be some military penetration in Jamaica
and Guyana. Jamaica signed an agreement with the
United States in 1963 for the latter country to furnish defense materials and defense services. Under the
arrangement, the Jamaican government had to "permit continuous observation and review by, and furnish necessary
information to, representatives of the Government of the
United States with regard to the use of such defence
articles and services."[29] Thus there was ample opportunity for penetration of Jamaica's military by the
United States.

In Guyana an agreement was signed, giving the
United States the right to erect military installations
at Atkinson Field and Makouria, to land military equipment and personnel, and to fly over Guyanese territory.
In addition, the United States would train and equip
the Guyanese police force. These situations certainly
provided U.S. military officers with access to information about Guyanese politics. In light of this, the
opposition leader charged that "the government does not
practice what it preaches. For public consumption at
home and abroad, it says one thing, but does the opposite. While it claims to be non-aligned it is completely tied to the West, particularly the USA. Washington
dictates our foreign policy."[30] Caribbean military ties
with the United States have by no means excluded military arrangements with other countries. For example,
Jamaica entered into an agreement in 1964 with the
United Kingdom to assist in the staffing, administration, and training of its armed forces, while the UK was
in command of Guyana's military and security forces up
to 1967. However, U.S. military ties with these countries are immensely more important than the British support because, first, the Caribbean is protected from
external aggression by the Rio Pact and, second, Britain
would be only too glad to let the United States play an
active military role in the Caribbean, should that become necessary.

In addition to political, economic, and military
forms of penetration, U.S. cultural penetration has
affected the Commonwealth Caribbean. The Caribbean's
proximity to the United States and the diffusion of
radio, newspaper, and television media have played a
decisive role in this process. The Peace Corps is one
form of cultural penetration that existed in all the
independent Commonwealth Caribbean states. In August
1971, Guyana asked the U.S. government to phase out its
operations there. The news media facilitated the adoption and spread of lifestyles and values alien to the
area, an unhealthy situation for Caribbean leaders attempting to foster Caribbean nationalism.

In examining the various forms of penetration by
the United States, we quickly note that the direction
of penetration runs vertically from north to south.
Also apparent is the virtual absence of reverse penetration. While Caribbean bauxite, petroleum, sugar,
and bananas are important to the United States, it
could do without its Caribbean supplies of these goods
without hardship. (Bauxite may be the only exception.)
In contrast, the loss of the U.S. market in all these
products would present Caribbean economies with serious
problems. It is with this in mind that we may consider
the mutual interests of the United States and the Commonwealth Caribbean states.

MUTUAL INTERESTS OF THE UNITED STATES AND THE CARIBBEAN

U.S. security interests in the Caribbean are easily
grasped when viewed in light of the United States' continuing goal of predominance in the Western hemisphere.
The report of the Secretary of State on U.S. foreign
policy for the year 1969-70 expresses these interests
in very precise terms: "We have an important security
interest in the area, and, with the agreement of the
governments concerned, we maintain military and scientific installations in several of the smaller islands."[31]
Before the House Subcommittee on Inter-American Affairs,
Caribbean expert Robert Crassweller testified to the
same effect:

> In military terms, the region is significant
> for the underwater surveillance systems that
> the United States operates there, systems
> vital to the physical protection of the
> southern latitudes that are the weakest link
> in this country's antisubmarine defenses.
> The area also serves as a base for naval and
> air components necessary to back up the work
> of the underwater surveillance elements.[32]

Nevertheless, maintenance of a military presence is
not the end-all of U.S. policy in the Caribbean. Crassweller himself writes that "the American strategic
presence at selected points in the Caribbean region is
itself a psychological and symbolic reality of very high
importance."[33] The psychological and symbolic effect
of its presence in the Caribbean is important for the
United States insofar as the Caribbean is an important
component in the overall equation of the world balance
of power. What else can Crassweller mean when he writes
that "a nation that has fought two wars on the far side
of the Pacific in the past two decades for the purpose
(in the last analysis) of protecting the balance of
power in Asia can hardly assume a stance of indifference

while equilibrium is put to hazard"?[34] Crassweller
spells this out more clearly in his testimony before
a House subcommittee on U.S. national interests in the
Caribbean: "The first consists of the relationship between the Caribbean and the worldwide global interests
of the United States. . . . I suspect that [it] is
equally, or even more, important in terms of advancing
or hindering America's worldwide objectives."[35]

        In addition to strong security interest in the
Caribbean, the United States has a substantial economic
interest in the area. There is some $25 billion worth
of investment in the Caribbean, and the area also provides an annual market for about $1.5 billion worth of
U.S. products. The following figures supply a picture
of U.S. direct investment in the Commonwealth Caribbean
area for 1968.[36] While the total for the entire area
(including Puerto Rico, Dutch and French territories,
and some Spanish-speaking countries) amounted to almost
$5.4 billion (U.S.), investment in the Commonwealth
Caribbean amounted to nearly $1.1 billion. The break-
down was as follows: Barbados, $3 million; Belize, $5
million; Guyana, $50 million; Jamaica, $500 million;
and Trinidad and Tobago, $500 million. For comparative
purposes it should be noted that the total trade of
three Latin American Republics (Venezuela, $2.6 billion;
Mexico, $1.5 billion; and Colombia, $0.6 billion)
amounted to $4.7 billion dollars. Thus, U.S. trade
with the smaller territories compares very favorably.

        The United States also had a favorable balance of
trade with these Caribbean states according to 1968
figures. In that year the United States imported $2.9
billion worth of products from the area and exported
$3.1 billion worth of products to it, resulting in a
balance of $123.5 million in the United States' favor.
Table 3 breaks down trade figures for the United States,
several Commonwealth Caribbean states, and--for comparative purposes--three large Latin American countries.

        Caribbean trade in 1968 constituted 44 percent of
Latin American exports to the United States, while
Caribbean imports from the United States made up 43 percent of the Latin American total. These figures indicate a substantial economic relationship between the
United States and the Caribbean as a whole. Moreover,
U.S. trade with the Commonwealth Caribbean has continued
to increase. In sum, while the economic importance of
the Commonwealth Caribbean is not overwhelming in terms
of U.S. worldwide investments and trade, the latter's
economic interest in the area is evident.

Table 3.   U.S./LATIN AMERICAN TRADE, 1968
(In Millions of Dollars)

	EXPORTS TO U.S.	IMPORTS FROM U.S.
Barbados	5.9	14.5
British Honduras	6.7	8.0
Guyana	34.0	22.7
Jamaica	137.8	146.9
Trinidad and Tobago	213.3	61.7
Entire Caribbean area	2,935.2	3,058.7
Venezuela, Colombia, Mexico	2,083.9	2,338.7

Source: Richard Crassweller, The Caribbean Community
(New York: Praeger, 1972), pp. 46-47.

        Conversely, the importance of the United States to
the Caribbean is also obvious. All Caribbean states
welcome investment and loans from the larger nation.
The difference now is that they try to win more favorable terms of trade, thereby erasing the unequal
treaties of the past. They are relatively poor countries with burgeoning populations and little land space
(with the exception of Guyana). Moreover, unemployment
rates are high, contributing a great deal to social unrest in the area. The Caribbean states believe the
United States could alleviate this situation by opening
its doors to immigrants from the region on a fairly
liberal basis.

        Thus, economically and militarily the United States
is vastly stronger than the Commonwealth Caribbean
states. The disparity in power between them is so great
that we can only describe their relationship as asymmetrical.

PROPOSALS FOR U.S. POLICY TOWARD THE COMMONWEALTH
CARIBBEAN STATES

        The change in world attitudes toward colonialism
and the achievement of independence by former colonies
in the Third World during the 1960s are compelling the
United States to devise new foreign policies. In the
past, its policy toward the Commonwealth Caribbean

states was either to neglect them along with the rest of Latin America or to treat them still as appendages of Britain. Thus, as a first step in the revision of its policy the United States should recognize these countries as the distinct entities that they are-- a subsystem of the Latin American subordinate system. U.S. policy must recognize that although there are many similarities between the Commonwealth Caribbean states, on the one hand, and the non-English-speaking Latin American countries, on the other, there exist enough cultural and stylistic differences between them to warrant separate consideration for each group.

Any U.S. policy toward the Commonwealth Caribbean states must recognize the Caribbean in its new form-- that is, as a group of states whose internal problems are causing considerable social ferment and are compelling their leaders to look for more radical solutions to socioeconomic dilemmas. U.S. policy revisions must not come on the heels of an immediate crisis, only to peter out very soon thereafter, but must represent a long-term commitment to this region that the United States professes to be crucial to its security. This commitment must show a serious concern for the population of the area as a whole, not merely regarding the islands as sunny tourist spots.

A forward-looking policy must support all progressive policies of the region's leaders and constitute a well-thought-out plan leading to a Caribbean community of both English-speaking and non-English-speaking nations. However, such support would not give the United States the right to intervene in the internal affairs of the Caribbean states. The U.S. predisposition to intervene in the area must be eradicated. It must exercise self-discipline to change its former ways. For example, the United States must not become involved in territorial disputes in the region. Particularly objectionable to Caribbean progressives would be U.S. intervention on behalf of tottering and discredited Caribbean regimes.

The Caribbean has a history of unemployment and underemployment in addition to rapid population growth. The United States should liberalize its immigration policies so that some of the social discontent could be siphoned off, thereby minimizing instability in the region. The United States could easily absorb immigrants from the Caribbean, since the size and wealth of the former would easily bear what would be just a few extra people in comparison to immigration from other parts of the world. In the area of investment, the United States must regulate the behavior of its multinationals in the Caribbean and try to infuse them with

a sense of social responsibility for the area in which
they operate: ITT performance in Chile should not become the norm for the Caribbean area. The calm of the
region would be enhanced if these companies did not believe that a 500 percent profit must be carted away to
the north. The United States has already begun to mul-
tilateralize aid to Latin America. This policy should
be accentuated in the Caribbean so that the United
States can avoid the taint of political maneuvering
that accompanies bilateral aid.

The United States should liberalize its trade relations with the area and maintain an open market policy
for Caribbean agricultural products, such as sugar.
There should be no reason why U.S. trade policies should
run counter to the interests of Third World countries
(including the Caribbean states). Europe and Japan,
now in competition with the United States for markets
throughout the globe, offer markets, credits, and advice that fully rival the latter's. Testifying before
the Subcommittee on Inter-American Affairs, treating
the entire question of trade references for Latin America and the Caribbean, C. Fred Bergsten pointed out the
negative aspects of U.S. policy toward the Third World,
in comparison to the European and Japanese: "Our
foreign aid has declined while the aid of other donors
has risen. Our trade barriers have risen while the
barriers of others have declined. . . . We have tried
to bilateralize multilateral aid by blocking international loans to countries which have expropriated US
firms even when they have provided compensation."[37]
This approach toward the Third World should be changed
entirely, and there is no better place to begin such
change than the Caribbean.

What if the United States were to implement all the
policy recommendations advanced in this paper? Would
this mean that the asymmetrical relationship between
the United States and the Caribbean states would be
transformed into one of interdependence? This is hardly
likely. The traditional elements of national power do
not permit it. Even the possession of bauxite, which
the Caribbean has in sufficient quantity and for which
there is not likely to be any substitute, would not
swing the relationship to one of interdependence.[38] It
is more meaningful to talk of interdependence when we
speak of the United States and the Third World. Only
by acting politically and economically in concert with
the rest of the Third World can the Caribbean begin to
experience a collective relationship of interdependence.
Of course, there is no assurance that Third World countries would cooperate with one another on all occasions.[39]
While positive U.S. action on these recommendations
would not ensure the happiness of the Caribbean peoples,

at least it would allow them to live with a modicum of dignity that would not be inimical to the interests of the United States. For their part, Caribbean leaders would have to ensure that any benefits derived from such action would be spread equitably among the masses.

NOTES

1. In this article the Commonwealth Caribbean refers to those English-speaking areas, independent and dependent, that aspired to become politically and economically unified. It must be admitted that they did not pursue this goal with equal zeal. They include the independent countries of Jamaica, Trinidad and Tobago, Barbados, Grenada, the Associated States, and, on the mainland, Guyana and Belize.

2. Richard P. Stebbins, The U.S. in World Affairs, 1962 (New York: Harper & Row, for the Council on Foreign Relations, 1963), p. 7.

3. J. William Fulbright, Old Myths and New Realities (New York: Random House, 1964), pp. 49-50.

4. See, for example, Jerome Slater, "The Decline of the OAS," International Journal 24 (Summer 1969): 497-506.

5. Sisir Gupta, "The Third World and the Great Powers," The Annals, Vol. 386 (November 1969): 55.

6. Hans Morgenthau, A New Foreign Policy for the United States (London: Pall Mall Press, 1969), p. 1.

7. U.S. Foreign Policy for the 1970's: A Report by President Richard Nixon to the Congress (Washington, D.C.: U.S. Government Printing Office, 1971), p. 8.

8. Ibid., p. 125.

9. Herald Tribune (International Edition), September 2, 1975.

10. Ibid., September 4, 1975.

11. Robert Crassweller, The Caribbean Community: Changing Societies and U.S. Policy (New York: Praeger, 1972), p. 48.

12. Paul Y. Hammond, "The Political Order and the Burden of External Relations," in World Politics XIX (1966-67): 443-64.

13.   James N. Rosenau, "Pre-Theories and Theories of
Foreign Policy," in James N. Rosenau, ed., The Scientific Study of Foreign Policy (New York: Free Press,
1971), pp. 127-28.

14.   See, for example, H. J. M. Hubbard, Race and
Guyana (Georgetown, Guyana: H. J. M. Hubbard, 1969),
p. 25, and C. H. Grant, "Company Towns in the Caribbean:
A Preliminary Analysis of Christenburg, Weismer-
MacKenzie," Caribbean Studies 11 (April 1971): 55-56.

15.   See, for example, The Caribbean Bauxite Industry
(St. Augustine, Trinidad: University of the West Indies,
Institute of Social and Economic Research, 1967); "The
Denationalization of Caribbean Bauxite: Alcoa in Guyana,"
New World Quarterly, vol. 5, no. 3 (1971); "The Guyana-
Alcan Conflict and the Nationalization of Demba," New
World Quarterly, vol. 5, no.4 (1971); "Multinational
Corporations and Dependent Underdevelopment in Mineral
Export Economics," Social and Economic Studies, December
1970; Why We Need to Nationalize Bauxite, and How, New
World Jamaica Pamphlet no. 6, 1971; and "Regional Inte-
gration vs Company Integration in the Utilization of
Caribbean Bauxite," in Sybil Lewis and Thomas G. Mathews,
eds., Caribbean Integration: Papers on Social, Political
and Economic Integration (Rio Piedras, P.R.: Institute
of Caribbean Studies, 1967), pp. 101-18.

16.   See I. Litvak and C. Maule, "Nationalism in the
Caribbean Bauxite Industry," International Affairs 51
(January 1975): 55.

17.   Program Agency for International Development, U.S.
Department of State, U.S. Foreign Aid in Latin America,
Proposed Fiscal Year 1973 (Washington, D.C.: U.S.
Government Printing Office, 1972), p. 118.

18.   Dante B. Fascell, "Toward a New Caribbean Policy
for the United States," in Hearings before the Subcommittee on Inter-American Affairs of the Committee on
Foreign Affairs, House of Representatives, 93d Congress,
2d session, U.S. Caribbean Policy, pt. 1, September 19
and 21, 1973 (Washington, D.C.: U.S. Government Printing Office, 1974), p. 105. Hereinafter cited as
Hearings: U.S. Caribbean Policy.

19.   Express, June 30, 1974.

20.   Roy Preiswerk, ed., Documents on International Relations in the Caribbean (Rio Piedras, Institute of
Caribbean Studies, 1970), p. 63.

21.   Hansard (House of Representatives), vol. 4, December 4, 1964, col. 453.

22. Lloyd Best, "From Chaguaramas to Slavery?" New World Quarterly, vol. 1 (1965), pp. 43-70.

23. Quoted in Ivor Oxaal, Black Intellectuals Come to Power: The Rise of Creole Nationalism in Trinidad and Tobago (Cambridge, Mass.: Schenkman Publishing, 1968), p. 134.

24. U.S. Foreign Policy, 1972: A Report of the Secretary of State (Washington, D.C.: Department of State Publication, 1973), p. 428.

25. Express, October 17, 1973.

26. See Stanley Meisler, "The Dubious Role of AFL-CIO Meddling in Latin America," Nation 198, 7 (February 10, 1964). New York Times, February 23, 1967; June 10, 1963; and July 10, 1963. Times (London), June 29, 1963. Sunday Times (London), April 16, 1967. Philip Reno, The Ordeal of British Guyana (New York: Monthly Review Press, 1964), chaps. 4-6. Arthur Schlesinger, Jr., A Thousand Days: John F. Kennedy in the White House (New York: Fawcett Crest, 1967), chap. 15, "Sabotage and Subversion." Basil Ince, Decolonization and Conflict in the United Nations: Guyana's Struggle for Independence (Cambridge, Mass.: Schenkman Publishing, 1974), chap. 2.

27. See, for example, Ronald Radosh, American Labor and U.S. Foreign Policy (New York: Random House, 1969). Serafino Romnaldi, Presidents and Peons: Recollections of a Labor Ambassador in Latin America (New York: Funk and Wagnalls, 1967).

28. John Plank, "The Caribbean: Intervention, When and How," Foreign Affairs 44, 1 (October 1965): 45.

29. See par. 6 of Agreement Between Jamaica and the United States of America Providing for the Furnishing of Defence Articles and Defence Services to the Government of Jamaica, June 6, 1963, in Preiswerk, p. 647.

30. Cheddi Jagan, "A Review of Guyana's Foreign Policy," International Affairs Quarterly 4 (1967).

31. U.S. Foreign Policy, 1969-70: A Report of the Secretary of State (Washington, D.C.: U.S. Department of State, 1971), p. 116.

32. Hearings: U.S. Caribbean Policy, pp. 31-32.

33. Ibid., p. 32 (emphasis added).

34. Crassweller, The Caribbean Community, p. 58.

35. Hearings: U.S. Caribbean Policy, pp. 31-32.

36. Figures taken from Crassweller, The Caribbean Community, pp. 44-47.

37. Hearings before the Subcommittee on Inter-American Affairs of the Committee on Foreign Affairs, House of Representatives, 93d Congress, 1st session, Trade Preferences: Latin American and the Caribbean, June 25 and 26, 1972 (Washington, D.C.: U.S. Department of State, 1973).

38. C. Fred Bergsten, "The Threat is Real," Foreign Policy, no. 14 (Spring 1974), p. 88.

39. For reasons, see Mikdashi Zuhayr, "Collusion Could Work," Foreign Policy, no. 14 (Spring 1974), p. 59.

War, Cold War, and Canadian Dependency

J. L. Granatstein

Said Pierre Trudeau, the Prime Minister of Canada,
in a speech in Washington on March 25, 1969,

> Americans should never underestimate the con-
> stant pressure on Canada which the mere pres-
> ence of the United States has produced. We're
> a different people from you and we're a dif-
> ferent people partly because of you. . . .
> Living next to you is in some ways like sleep-
> ing with an elephant. No matter how friendly
> and even-tempered is the beast . . . one is
> affected by every twitch and grunt. . . . It
> should not therefore be expected that this
> kind of nation, this Canada, should project
> itself . . . as a mirror image of the United
> States.

Every Canadian would agree with Trudeau about the
constant pressure exerted by the overwhelming presence
of the United States; and all would laugh knowingly at
his comparison with the difficulties in sharing the
elephant's bed. But many might quarrel with Trudeau's
easy assurances that Canadians are different than Americans, that they do not project a mirror image of citizens of the United States. That is the way it should
be, not necessarily the way it is. In fact, the search
for the differences, the quest for the elusive Canadian
identity, is one that has obsessed Canadians for decades,
from the very achievement of confederation in 1867. And
although Canadians cover themselves with maple leaf
patches and deliberately flaunt themselves as Canadians--
not Americans--when they travel abroad, that very act of
asserting national identity is probably more "American"
in style than "Canadian."

The differences between the two countries that inhabit the top part of the North American continent are
really rather minimal. Canada is a parliamentary democracy, still attached to the Commonwealth, still showing
Elizabeth II on its stamps and coins. But presidential
leadership is very much in the style of Pierre Trudeau,
and the monarchy is an anachronism to all but the most
fossilized Canadians. The British tie no longer exists
in any meaningful fashion, a clear reflection of the
collapse of British power and a reflection, too, of
growing links with the United States. About all that
differentiates Canadians from their powerful neighbors
to the south are some interesting regional accents.

Still, as one Canadian politician put it, "the
Americans are our best friends whether we like it or
not." That perfect malapropism assesses the relationship almost exactly. There is an enormous pool of af-
fection and regard for the people of the United States
that is mixed with fear, envy, and dislike for the
power, luxury, and waste exercised and enjoyed by the
richest nation on earth. Canadians know that they
should not want to be like Americans, but they do.

This pressure to emulate the United States has had
distorting effects on Canada, a country of just 23 million people, located cheek by jowl with a giant ten
times its size, twenty times its power. The fragile
blossom of Canadian culture, for example, has been
choked by the hardier and more colorful variety from
the south. Canadian magazines constitute only one in
seven of those read in the country, while Time and
Reader's Digest alone have 23 percent of total magazine
circulation. Almost 85 percent of the sales volume of
book publishing concerns is controlled by foreign--
largely American--subsidiaries.[1] And with most of the
population within easy reach of the border, television,
too, is pervasively American. Even the Canadian Broadcasting Corporation, owned and operated by the government, shows more American shows than Canadian, more
American trash than Canadian. Painting, sculpture, the
performing arts--all are dominated by American trends,
methods, and cult figures. Even university education
is very heavily influenced by the substantial numbers
of American academics teaching in Canada.

There are, as a result, precious few areas that
Canadians culturally can call their own. Only one of
significance needs to be mentioned, and that, of course,
is French Canada. French-speaking Canadians are insulated by language from the worst excesses of their English-speaking compatriots, and the cultural life of
Quebec remains distinctive and vibrant. But that is a
double-edged sword. The separatist instincts of French

Canada are encouraged and enhanced by this distinctive-
ness and by the success in withstanding the more overt
pressures of Americanization. The resultant strains on
confederation increase with each passing year.

But no more than the rest of Canada, Quebec cannot
be insulated from the economic pressures of American-
based multinational enterprises. The United States
effectively owns Canada. Data prepared by the Canadian
government itself show that non-Canadian firms control
99.7 percent of petroleum and coal products production,
87 percent of transport equipment production, 55 percent
of primary metals production, 72 percent of machinery
production, and 64 percent of electrical equipment production.[2] In virtually every segment of the economy,
control lies outside Canada. And the situation, despite
feeble efforts by the Canadian government to control it,
worsens year by year. The possibility of true independence seems to be slipping irretrievably out of reach.

How did Canada get into this position? This is obviously a huge topic, far beyond the scope of a brief
paper. But some tentative answers can be raised, some
suggestions ventured. This paper will focus on the impact of three wars on Canadian-American relations: the
Great War (1914-18), World War II (1939-45), and the
cold war.

Canada sought to create a domestic manufacturing
industry in the first years after confederation. The
"national policy" of tariff protection was begun in the
1870s, and within two generations a reasonably healthy
industrial base had been established, based mainly in
Quebec and Ontario and consisting in substantial part
of American-owned branch plants. These industries
served the home market, and only rarely did the Dominion's manufactured goods find markets abroad. Canada's
foreign exchange came as it always had from the export
of staples--wheat, fish, lumber, and minerals--and the
money for development was imported from abroad, mainly
from Great Britain in the early years.

This system worked adequately enough when Canada
commanded good prices for its staples in the metropolis,
but it failed lamentably when times were hard or when
European markets became glutted with raw materials.
Similarly, so long as capital remained plentiful in
London, so long as the squires and merchants of Britain
stayed satisfied with a 3 percent return on relatively
stable Canadian securities, there was no shortage of
investment money. The coming of war in 1914 ended this
happy system.

The Great War marked the beginning of the end for
Britain as a great power; for Canada it signaled the
coming transformation from a British to an American
satellite.   This was most clear in economic terms.
The war placed such demands on British financial resources that in 1915 Canada was forced, almost for the
first time, to turn to the New York market for capital.
In that year 42 percent of Canadian bond issues were
financed in New York, and the next year the percentage
rose higher still, to 65 percent.   Before the war, by
comparison, Britain had always supplied between 50 and
80 percent of Canadian capital requirements.[3]

The real crisis came in 1917, when the United
States entered the war and closed its money markets.
Canada's industrial development seemed on the verge of
disaster and its munitions production threatened with
collapse, particularly as Britain by this stage was so
over-extended that it was seeking aid from Canada,
rather than offering assistance.   In this crisis the
Canadian approach--one that would be employed time and
again in the future--was significant.

Essentially, the Canadian Minister of Finance, Sir
Thomas White, recognized the reality of Canada's new
situation.   Canada had to get financial help from the
United States, White recognized, and at the very least
permission to borrow enough to cover Canada's adverse
trade balance with the United States.   On the other
hand, White saw the dangers in borrowing directly from
the United States government as other Allies were doing.
They all had an ocean to separate them from America;
Canada, however, shared a long border.   "We shall have
to pay a fairly stiff rate of interest," White wrote of
his efforts to borrow on the New York market, "but I
believe I would rather do this than borrow directly
from the Government of the United States even at a
lower rate of interest.   In other words," he concluded,
"I would rather we should 'hoe our own road.'"[4]

That was a good principle, but it would be honored
more in the breach than the observance as the war went
on.   Most of Canada's coal and iron ore, for example,
had always come from the United States.   But the war
created scarcities in the United States, and American
officials needed every ton of ore that could be found
for the factories of Detroit and Gary.   The only solution possible for Canada was to act like a regional lob-
by in Washington, to create a Canadian War Mission there
to interview officials, to press Canada's case.   That
case was a strong one: Canada had been in the war for
two and one-half years and had suffered high casualties
at the front while simultaneously exerting itself in the
production of munitions and food.   In addition, Canadians

shrewdly stressed the relatively small proportion of the
total available supplies that they required, and they
cautioned against the creation of duplicate facilities.
Above all, they relied on the friendship and goodwill
that existed between the two English-speaking nations
of North America. Their success was marked. At no
time did Canada suffer from severe shortages of coal
or iron. Canada received exemption from the decisions
that all foreign purchases in the United States had to
pass through a centralized purchasing commission and
that all loans to Allies had to be spent in the United
States. More even than this, the U.S. Treasury permitted the Allies to use American loans for the purchase
of goods in Canada, and Canadian manufacturers were allowed to compete for scarce American supplies on an
equal footing with domestic industry. And when British
orders for munitions began to dry up with Britain's
financial resources, American orders in Canada filled
the gap.[5]

The war sped the process of continental integration. Canada had undergone an accelerated development
as a result of the war, and this development could have
been financed only from U.S. sources. To get this
necessary capital and the necessary war orders, Canadians had to stress their similarities to Americans, their
contribution, their dependency. Canada sought and won
exemption from American regulations designed to control
relations with foreign states. The irony of this state
of affairs is that the conservative government that won
these special considerations in Washington had been
elected in 1911 on a platform that rejected reciprocity
in trade with the United States, one that virtually
called the liberal government traitorous for its dealings with the United States.

A further irony is that the war demonstrated that
Canadians had ample capital to finance their own industrial growth. When the government hesitantly ventured
into borrowing money from its own people in the first
war loan of November 1915, it regarded the idea as
dubious in the extreme. "No loan of even five million
dollars had ever before been subscribed in Canada," the
Finance Minister later wrote, "and a war issue of less
than twenty-five millions would have been hardly worth
while."[6] To everyone's astonishment, the first loan
produced $100 million; the second, $200 million; and
the third, $250 million. And in three great Victory
Loan drives in 1917, 1918, and 1919, the government
secured the staggering total of $1.7 billion, a huge
sum indeed for a small nation of 8 million people.[7]
Once the crisis of war had passed, however, the money
went back into the banks or under mattresses, and
Canadian industry continued to be financed abroad,

most of the capital now coming from the United States
rather than Britain. By 1939, American investment in
Canada amounted to $4.15 billion, fully 60 percent of
the total foreign capital invested in the country.[8]

        World War II reinforced the trends started in the
Great War. More important still, the demands of the
longer and more mechanized 1939 war were such that institutionalization of Canadian-American defense and
economic cooperation seemed necessary.

        The Canadian problem in World War II was almost
exactly the same as in the earlier conflict. Canada's
prewar surplus of trade served neatly to balance the
deficit with the United States.[9] But the war stopped
the convertibility of sterling at the same time that
it increased the British demand for food, minerals,
and munitions from Canada. To meet the United Kingdom's
requirements, Canada had to import more from the United
States, leading to a situation that saw Canada fall into
ever greater financial difficulties as its war effort
increased. By the beginning of 1941, despite strict
exchange and import controls and despite very high
taxation of its citizens, Canada had reached a very
dangerous stage in its economic war.[10]

        The answer, as in 1917-18, was to turn to the
United States for help. Once again, Canadians had to
rely on the goodwill of Washington, on the sense of
shared interest in the cause, something that American
neutrality scarcely interfered with at all. Indeed,
in August 1940, when Britain's survival seemed in doubt,
Canada and the United States had entered into an unprecedented defense arrangement and had set up the
Permanent Joint Board on Defense to plan for and coordinate the security of North America.[11] Now, as
Canada's economy buckled under the strain of war,
economic integration seemed the answer.

        The result was the Hyde Park Declaration of April
20, 1941, the product of "a grand Sunday" spent at Hyde
Park by Prime Minister Mackenzie King and President
Franklin Roosevelt. The declaration aimed to meet
Canada's substantial trade deficit with the United
States by increasing American purchases of raw materials
in Canada; at the same time the purchases Canada had to
make in the United States to produce munitions for Britain came under the British account under the Lend-Lease
agreement. At a stroke, Canada's crisis ended. The
United States would spend an additional $200-300 million
each year in Canada, adding substantially to Canada's
holdings of U.S. dollars; but those holdings would not
have to be depleted by Canadian purchases on Britain's

account. It was an ideal solution, and when King returned to Ottawa from his meeting with Roosevelt, his
Cabinet colleagues hailed him as Canada's savior.[12]

There was some truth in that description. The
Hyde Park Declaration, for example, permitted Canada
itself to avoid the necessity of seeking Lend-Lease
aid from the United States, something Canadian officials
desperately sought to avoid. It was one thing for Britain to take such aid, for Britain was a long distance
from America. If Lend-Lease were ever accepted, feared
senior officials in the Department of Finance, Washington might insist on a radical revision of tariffs after
the war.[13] Equally important, Canada was not taking
something for nothing. The main assistance required was
that the United States agree to buy more goods in Canada. The United States needed the raw materials, and
Canada could supply them. Hyde Park seemed a good bargain for everyone, one that saved the Canadian bacon
and one that essentially cost the United States nothing--
thus having the virtue in a shrewd President's eyes that
it did not have to pass Congress.

There were added benefits, too. Before Lend-Lease
had been accepted by the administration and the Senate,
Britain had been forced to demonstrate that it was
stripped of its investments in the United States.
As a result, a few well-publicized liquidations were
staged. But Canadians, too, had investments in the
United States, estimates of their value running from
$200 million to over $1 billion. By not discussing
this question, Hyde Park left the Canadian holdings
intact, thus providing what Finance Department officials
saw as a useful cushion and a counterbalance against the
pressures that could be exerted as a result of American
investment in Canada.[14]

What did Canada give up at Hyde Park? At the time
it seemed that nothing whatsoever had been lost. But
unhidden and unconcealed in the declaration's anodyne
phrases were the seeds of present Canadian difficulties.
The President and the Prime Minister, claimed the Declaration,

> discussed measures by which the most prompt
> and effective utilization might be made of
> the productive facilities of North America
> for the purpose both of local and hemisphere
> defense. . . . It was agreed as a general
> principle that in mobilizing the resources
> of this continent each country should provide
> the other with the defense articles which it
> is best able to produce . . . and that pro-
> duction programmes should be coordinated to
> this end.[15]

There it was--the virtual coordination of the two countries' economies.

Was this imposed on a reluctant Canada by a shrewd
American President? Not at all. The Hyde Park Declaration as adopted was almost entirely the product of Canadian drafting.[16] Canada sought this coordination of
economies and sought it deliberately. If the two were
coordinated, if the two were inextricably linked together, Canadian financial problems would cease. There
would be no shortages of dollars or crucial materiel.
There would be greater influence in Washington for the
dominion. The war would be won in less time and at less
cost. And Canada would do its part to drag a still reluctant United States into a tighter relationship with
the belligerent Allies. The real and potential gains
from Hyde Park far outweighed the long-term implications
that few even considered. The declaration was Mackenzie King's triumph, a victory that secured Canadian
economic stability and fostered its independence. Or
so it seemed in April 1941.

Hyde Park and the events it set in train had important consequences. For example, Adolf A. Berle,
the Assistant Secretary of State, had been involved
in discussions with Canadian officials who, in March
1941, even before Hyde Park, were proposing economic
integration. "But the rest of it goes much further,"
the corporate theorist and former brain truster noted
happily of his conversations with Hugh Keenleyside of
the Department of External Affairs. "Keenleyside
realizes this is now one continent and one economy;
that we shall have to be integrated as to finance,
trade routes, and pretty much everything else; and
in this I so thoroughly agree with him that it is
refreshing."[17] The result of these talks was the
establishment in the summer of 1941 of Joint Economic
Committees, charged with planning for the integration
and coordination of the two nations' economies.

As it happened, the Joint Economic Committees never
amounted to much in themselves, except symbolically.
Most of their work was absorbed by a Canadian-American
Materials Coordination Committee that linked the Department of Munitions and Supply in Ottawa with its American
counterpart under Donald Nelson in Washington.[18] The
establishment of the Anglo-American Combined Boards in
1942 and the eventual--and difficult--working out of a
place for Canada on some of them furthered the cooperation across the forty-ninth parallel.[19]

Still, Canada and the United States were separate
countries; and despite the vastly more complex links
between them, the changing course of the war soon began

to create strains. In April and May 1941, for example, the military conversations on the Permanent Joint Board on Defense became heated. The American military began seeking strategic and tactical control of the Canadian forces in the event of a war that would see the United States join with the Allies against the Axis. This was a fundamental matter to Canada, one that involved the whole question of sovereignty and autonomy. Britain had never been conceded tactical control of the Canadian army in two world wars; to concede it to Washington on questions involving the defense of Canadian soil would have been politically disastrous and supremely foolish. After long dispute and substantial acrimony the result was agreement for the "coordination of the military effort of the United States and Canada [to] be effected by mutual cooperation," something vastly different than the original proposals.[20] That the American military would suggest such a course at all was the surprise.

That scheme was only one sign of a new and hard American attitude. Another was the refusal of Washington to permit Canada to establish a military mission, a situation that was complicated by Britain's desire to combine Commonwealth representation in the American capital. Only after the Prime Minister himself made extraordinary representations, and only after a year of frustration, did Canada succeed in its aim.[21]

These problems were the outward sign of the change in American official thinking from a concern with hemispheric matters to globalism. The panicky mood that had gripped Washington (and Ottawa) in the spring and summer of 1940 was gone, and, as Lend-Lease symbolized, America recognized its interests to be broad indeed. Canada had been very important when the hemisphere was the concern; it was insignificant on a global scale, only an appendage of limited importance. Unfortunately for the Canadian government, it had made arrangements of permanent significance on the assumption that the U.S. concerns would remain the same. King and Roosevelt would still meet regularly and talk over problems in the friendliest of fashions, but the President could no longer spare time for serious consideration of Canada's place. The realities had intervened; Pearl Harbor would make the new situation permanent.

The Canadian government had to grapple with the new situation as well as it could. Norman Robertson, the senior official in the Department of External Affairs, told Prime Minister Mackenzie King that Canadians "have tended to take it for granted" that tha United States "will always regard Canadian interests as a close second to their own and appreciably ahead of those of any third country." Now this was no longer the

case, while the United States was still "inclined to
take Canadian concurrence and support entirely for
granted." Equally important was the American shift
in the perception of power. Before the war, Robertson
said, the United States had believed it could save the
world by "its example, by minding its own business,
pursuing a fair and friendly policy toward its neigh-
bours." But this era was over, and "we can see the
United States turning everywhere to more direct and
forceful methods of exerting its influence." The result was a "new appreciation of the enormous strategic
importance and strength of the United States" and a new
sense of "manifest destiny," all of which implied "quite
an important modification of the special relationship in
which Canada has hitherto stood with regard to the
United States."[22] In other words, Canada would have
to watch its step more closely than ever before in all
dealings with Washington.

With the Japanese threat in the Pacific--particular-
ly after the Japanese army occupied islands in the Aleu-
tian chain off Alaska--Canadian-American relations at
once became closer and more cautious. The Alaska highway was constructed by U.S. Army engineers, linking
Edmonton, Alberta, with Alaska. Airfields, oil pipe-
lines, and a host of installations of every type were
planted in Canada, and upwards of fifteen thousand
American servicemen took up residence in Canada, part
of what was jocularly known as the "army of occupation."[23]

But it was no joke to Mackenzie King, disturbed by
what he perceived as a possible American intention to
retain control of northern Canada. The Alaska highway,
he told the British High Commissioner in Ottawa, "was
less intended for protection against the Japanese than
as one of the fingers of the hand which America is
placing more or less over the whole of the Western
hemisphere." This worry led eventually to the appointment of a special government representative in the
northwest, charged with representing the Canadian
government in all dealings with the visitors and
especially instructed to ensure that Canadian rights
were in no way infringed. And it was also government
policy to pay for as much as possible during the war
and to buy every installation, including several of
no use, after the war.[25] In the end there were no
lingering elements of control and only a few elements
of resentment, but many Canadians believed it had been
a damn near run. The Canadian disinterest in the north,
an endemic and continuing feature of national policy,
had almost resulted in a loss of effective control.

There were a host of other difficulties with
Washington, some trivial, some important, but in spite

of them there was a feeling in Canada that the United States was henceforth going to be the major influence on the world--and on Canada. At a meeting of the Canadian Institute of International Affairs in 1945, its membership consisting of virtually everyone in the country with any interest in world affairs, this theme was evident. The British High Commission's observer at the meeting was disturbed at this:

> There was a high degree of acceptance of the proposition that Canada's future alignment would be with the United States, and only secondarily with the British Commonwealth. . . . [A U.S. State Department speaker] said that Canada's views and wishes exerted an influence on the United States administration out of all proportion to Canadian power, and added that on commercial policy Canada already enjoyed a consideration accorded to great powers alone. The enormous gratitude of the company at this remark could not be concealed, and it apparently occurred to no one that it might be a bit exaggerated and of questionable validity in relation to the future.[26]

Nor was this optimism about American consideration and benevolence limited to those outside government. Two senior civil servants who had spent the war in Washington waxed rhapsodic on their experiences:

> There has been the open exchange of confidence . . . the warm welcome, the freedom from formality, the plain speaking, and the all-pervading friendship. Neither is it easy to enumerate the conditions which made the high degree of co-operation possible. Co-operation was, of course, a sensible course to follow. It stood on its own merits. However, common-sense is not always able to prevail over sovereignty, and self-interest, and special national interests. That the course was followed, or at least adopted so readily and successfully, is due in part to the friendly disposition that existed, attributable no doubt to our common background of language and culture, and to the close trade and industrial relationship: in part it is due to the fact that our approach to problems is similar.[27]

Canadians and Americans, the message ran, were just the same.

    World War II, therefore, ended with extraordinarily
close personal, economic, and military relationships
across the border. An array of committees and joint
bodies had sprung up to coordinate the economies in
the common cause, and their work had generally eased
problems and enhanced productivity and prosperity.
Against this, however, was a concern, not widely shared
as yet, that the new power and aggressiveness of the
United States posed potential threats to Canadian autonomy. The war had changed many things.

    Some things remained the same. After the war
Europe was prostrate, Britain devastated economically.
If Canada wished to restore its traditional markets
abroad, it would have to loan its trading partners
the money to buy Canadian products and foodstuffs.
As a result, Canada loaned Britain $1.25 billion in
1946, a huge sum more than double the total prewar
federal budget and one-third of the American loan
made for the same reasons at the same time. Another
$500 million in loans went to other European countries.[28]
This was generous and necessary. But when the effect
of the loans was combined with the impact resulting from
a postwar orgy of consumer spending, much of it on goods
imported from the United States, the result was the collapse of Canada's U.S. dollar holdings. In May 1946,
Canada had more than $6 billion; in April 1947 this had
fallen to $700 million; and on November 30, 1947, the
holdings had dropped further to $480 million. The
Canadian government imposed a series of measures to
reduce imports drastically and to curtail tourist
travel;[29] in addition--exactly as it had in the Great
War and World War II--Canada turned to Washington for
aid.

    Again the United States proffered it. In the first
place, the restrictions imposed by the dominion were
cleared with official Washington in advance and accepted,
albeit grudgingly. This was important, for Canada had
signed the General Agreement on Trade and Tariffs (GATT)
in Geneva on November 17, 1947, the very day the restrictive measures were revealed. And as the restrictions were clearly directed against the import of American goods, there was an open violation of the GATT provisions before the ink on the treaty was dry. By ac-
quiescing, the United States relieved Canada's fears of
reprisal and permitted the necessary steps that aided
the nation's recovery.

    More important still, the provisions of the Marshall
Plan, then still being worked out in Washington, were
interpreted liberally by American officials, permitting
Canada to reap substantial benefits. Not that Canada

itself wanted or received aid. On the contrary, Canada
was treated just as it had been during both world wars,
almost as if it were the United States. European recipients of American largesse could buy Canadian goods
and use their credits to pay for them. By April 1949,
$706 million had come to Canada by this route; and
coupled with the effect of the restrictionist measures
and an increase in the export of Canadian raw materials
to the United States, this had helped to restore Canada's dollar balances.[30] Once again, Uncle Sam had come
to the rescue. The reasons were simple generosity, a
recognition that Canada's problems had largely come
about because it had given too much aid to Europe, and
some guile. The United States could not let Canada go
down the economic drain, if only because of the huge
amount of American investment there. Nor did it want
to be seen as the solitary provider of aid to Europe,
a state of affairs that caused problems with Congress
and that led to charges of imperialism abroad. It was
better to share both kudos and blame with another country. For its part, Canada would repay this generosity
by being one of the most loyal of American client states
through all the cold war years. Through the formation
of NATO, through Korea, through the 1950s and into the
1960s, Canadian policy generally followed the American
lead. And Canadian firms benefited greatly from contracts placed in Canada under defense-production sharing
agreements, contracts that helped create the incredible
boom in the first half of the 1950s.

In more recent years, the United States also extended aid to Canada. In 1963, for example, the Kennedy
administration introduced proposals for an interest
equalization tax that would have sharply reduced the
flow of investment capital into Canada. Inevitably,
a high-level delegation flew from Ottawa to Washington
to seek an exemption, and after careful consideration
the Canadian claims were recognized. The same thing
happened in 1965 with the voluntary cooperation program
and in 1968 with the mandatory direct investment guide-
lines. Invariably, Canada's pleas for special treatment
met with a sympathetic response. Again and again the
Canadians would point to the similarities between the
two countries; the cooperation in war and cold war would
be stressed; and the "undefended border" clichés would
be dusted off.

The irony of all this is that by the 1960s there
was a growing feeling in Canada that American investment
was already too high, that American influence on governmental decisions was too pronounced. The American programs that tried to restrict foreign investment offered
Canada a chance, had the Canadian government not spurned
it, to move toward economic independence and probably

toward political independence as well.   To be fair, the
pressures on the government were severe.   Businessmen
and stock exchange presidents demanded action, the
markets plummeted, and the newspapers warned of havoc
to Canadian living standards.   The success of Canadian
governments in playing "exemptionalism" with the United
States may have effectively foreclosed the option of
independence.

The politicians, officials, and businessmen who
made the policy must bear the responsibility for it.
They have been Liberal and Conservative, free trader
and protectionist; they did not believe they were
selling their country down the river.   In every case,
from the Great War to the present, they acted in response to great pressures and in a fashion that seemed
to them to meet Canada's needs.   In the Great War, they
managed to keep industry working by filling the short-
fall in British orders with American; in the Second
World War, they integrated the economy of the continent
in an attempt to keep employment up and to win the war
in the fastest and most economical way; in the cold war,
they maintained this integration because it conveyed
palpable benefits to the Canadian people in the form
of jobs and prosperity.   For the politicians, not un-
naturally, prosperity meant happy voters.   Prosperity
also meant economic success, and Canada raised its
living standards to a level just below that of the
United States.   Unfortunately, that high standard was
paid for out of the country's natural resources and
without heed enough for the future.

As the beneficiary of Canada's resources, the
United States has never responded to Canadian pleas
out of simple benevolence, although that cannot be
discounted totally. Within its borders, Canada held
a huge, potentially hostage, branch-plant industrial
complex, and no American government could lightly write
that off.   In addition, Canada was the largest market
for American goods, the greatest repository for American
foreign investment.   The dominion, as well, sat on the
strategic northern approaches to the American heartland,
a factor of increasing importance from the 1940s onward.
And most important, the costs of helping Canada have
been minimal in relative terms.   Those costs were a
small price to pay for the gain of welding Canada firmly
within America's hemispheric economic and political
sphere of influence.

Moreover, as Arnold Heeney, one of Canada's senior
diplomats, admitted undiplomatically in his posthumous
memoirs, "In my experience of Canadian-American negotiations, which stretches over thirty years, Canadian dele-
gations have, in most cases, been outmanoeuvered by

those on the US side of the table." That is a striking
statement, made no less so by his equally frank admission that "in the Canadian situation there is no alternative to partnership with the United States."[31]

As we have seen, it has been war and cold war that
created the problems leading to Canada's present economic integration into the American system. Paradoxically,
however, the Vietnam War, a war that Canada fortuitously
managed to avoid, fostered the development of Canadian
nationalism. Canadian war industry prospered with
American orders, but the Canadian people, increasingly
appalled by the effects of American policy and by the
war-induced strains on the American polity, began to
look inward. Under this new pressure Ottawa has hesitantly begun to look at the influence exerted by $50
billion of foreign capital, and the present Liberal
government has created a limp-wristed foreign investment review board with the power, seldom exercised, to
block foreign take-overs of Canadian companies, as well
as the Canada Development Corporation (CDC), which is
charged with using public and private funds to buy control back in certain key sectors of the economy. The
CDC, for example, recently captured control of Texas
Gulf Co., a major producer of minerals in Canada. (That
coup led to American complaints about foreign take-overs,
complaints that Canadians heard in a wry mood.)

Such measures are undoubtedly too little and too
late. About all that can save Canada, given the inability or unwillingness of its governments to act effectively, is firm American action. Only if the United States
decides to prohibit further exemptions for Canada can
the dominion hope to regain its autonomy. Washington
will have to do it; for if the past is any guide,
Canadian politicians will always be in Washington
seeking special treatment.

NOTES

1. Paul Audley, "A Very Grave Prognosis," Journal of
Canadian Studies 10 (May 1975): 3.

2. The Gray Report (Toronto, 1971), p. 31, table 3.
This confidential report on foreign investment was
secured and published by the Canadian Forum in December
1970 and subsequently published in book form.

3. Robert Cuff and J. L. Granatstein, Canadian-American
Relations in Wartime: From the Great War to the Cold
War (Toronto, 1975), p. 154.

4. White to G. E. Foster, April 28, 1917, Public
Archives of Canada, W. T. White Papers, vol. 18.

5. Cuff and Granatstein, Canadian-American Relations,
chap. 3 and pp. 155-56.

6. Sir Thomas White, The Story of Canada's War Finance
(Montreal, 1921), p. 22.

7. Ibid., p. 59.

8. M. C. Urquhart and K. Buckley, eds., Historical
Statistics of Canada (Toronto, 1965), p. 169.

9. Ibid., pp. 181-82.

10. J. L. Granatstein and R. D. Cuff, "The Hyde Park
Declaration, 1941: Origins and Significance," Canadian
Historical Review 55 (March 1974): 62 ff.

11. J. L. Granatstein, Canada's War: The Politics of
the Mackenzie King Government, 1939-45 (Toronto, 1975),
pp. 127 ff.

12. Granatstein and Cuff, "Hyde Park," p. 74.

13. Phillips to Treasury, February 4 and March 4, 1941,
Public Record Office (London), Foreign Office Records,
FO 371/28792 and FO 371/28795; R. W. James, Wartime
Economic Cooperation (Toronto, 1949), p. 32.

14. Urquhart and Buckley, Historical Statistics of
Canada, p. 168; W. C. Clark to King, April 9, 1941,
Public Archives of Canada, W. L. M. King Papers,
f. 288018; Phillips to Treasury, March 4, 1941,
FO 371/28795.

15. Granatstein and Cuff, "Hyde Park," pp. 79-80.

16. Ibid., p. 73.

17. B. B. Berle and T. B. Jacobs, eds., Navigating the
Rapids, 1918-1971: From the Papers of Adolf A. Berle
(New York, 1973), pp. 365-66.

18. James, Wartime Economic Cooperation, p. 228.

19. Granatstein, Canada's War, pp. 295 ff.

20. Ibid., pp. 131-32.

21. Ibid., pp. 147-48.

22. Memo for King, December 22, 1941, Public Archives of Canada, Department of External Affairs Records, vol. 810, file 614.

23. James Eayrs, In Defence of Canada, vol. 3, Peacemaking and Deterrence (Toronto, 1972), pp. 349-50.

24. Diary, March 21, 1942, King Papers.

25. Granatstein, Canada's War, p. 323.

26. "Notes on Annual Conference . . . ," attached to Holmes to Stephenson, June 15, 1945, Foreign Office Records, FO 371/50365.

27. S. D. Pierce and A. F. W. Plumptre, "Canada's Relations with War-Time Agencies in Washington," Canadian Journal of Economics and Political Science 11 (1945): 410-11.

28. Cuff and Granatstein, Canadian-American Relations, pp. 140-41.

29. Kenneth Wilson, "Dollar Famine," Behind the Headlines 7 (1948): 7.

30. R. A. Spencer, Canada in World Affairs, 1946-49 (Toronto, 1959), p. 236.

31. A. D. P. Heeney, The Things That Are Caesar's: The Memoirs of a Canadian Public Servant (Toronto, 1972), pp. 198, 201.

U.S.-Latin American Relations
in a Changing International Framework

Luciano Tomassini

Much has been written about U.S.-Latin American relations. Bearing this in mind, I do not intend in this
paper to provide new thoughts or to make new contributions to the scholarly analysis that has already been
made. What I will try to do is to look at this old
topic in the light of new developments. In doing so
we will no longer consider U.S.-Latin American relations
within a narrow hemispheric framework, nor as a special
but fatalistic case of old imperialism, but just as a
very important field for both U.S. and Latin American
foreign policy under changing international and regional
conditions.

As a consequence of the great transformation experienced by Western societies from the early days of
the Industrial Revolution to the emergence of the new
industrial state, focus on labor relations at the workshop level shifted toward pressures from both capitalists and workers to influence the state and to shape
public policies, each in their own favor. Confrontation
of interests was still there--maybe a little changed--
but what has completely changed was the stage at which
these interests could be promoted.

It is my contention in this paper that traditional
U.S.-Latin American relations have moved into a new
stage, which is no longer hemispheric but worldwide,
and must be considered from a world perspective. Hence,
inter-American relations no longer form a self-contained
system, but a dependent variable--dependent upon other
international and regional factors--which interacts and
changes very rapidly.

This approach will allow us to escape the trap of
considering inter-American relations (1) as a completely

isolated phenomenon, (2) as a continuation or amendment of past trends within the system, or (3) as a particular application of a general theory of imperialism.

In what follows I will make a brief account of the evolution of inter-American relations up to 1970. Then I will describe some changes in the international system that are bound to affect the relations between the developed and the less developed countries in general and between the United States and Latin America in particular. In the first section, I present the main changes that can be noticed in Latin America, taking into account both intra- and extra-regional relations. In the following section I reach some conclusions about U.S.-Latin American relations. I finally emphasize some issues that may be of paramount importance for the future of inter-American affairs.

LATIN AMERICAN INTERNATIONAL RELATIONS BEFORE AND AFTER 1970

Ever since the end of World War II, the international relations of Latin America were determined by a fundamental event: the outbreak of the cold war between the victors of this earlier contest.

In 1940, U.S. Secretary of State Cordell Hull had already tried to ensure the "active neutrality" of Latin American countries with regard to the armed conflict. One should recall that until the war was well under way, the traditional ties between Europe and the Latin American countries, the strong influence of Germany (and, to a lesser extent, Italy) in some of them, and the existence of profascist movements in several countries of the region tended to encourage the expression of their loyalties. During this period, the Axis powers as well as the Allies competed to obtain the cooperation of Latin American countries, or at least to prevent the enemy from taking advantage of it. On the other hand, in the conflict raised between the Western powers and the Soviet Union at the end of the war, the alignment of the Latin American countries with the former was unquestionable, due to their adherence to the values of Western civilization, the existence of conservative governments in many of them, and the determination of the United States to intervene in protection of hemispheric security. The Inter-American Treaty of Reciprocal Assistance--signed in 1947 and noted for serving as a pattern for those of NATO, CENTO, and SEATO--and the establishment of the OAS in the following year gave a formal framework to this strong alignment within the hemisphere. This same alignment was expressed within the scope of the United Nations, in which, by that time,

Latin American votes supported the U.S. positions in
confrontations with the Soviet Union.

In fact, in the period of time between the Conference of Chapultepec on War and Peace in 1945 and
the Ninth Conference of American States held in Bogota
in 1948, Latin America became fully integrated with the
security area of the Western world.[1]

The U.S. position consisted in assigning top priority to European reconstruction. Where a second priority
could be foreseen, it would be related to the rearrange-
ment of Far East affairs. These were the two critical
regions from the cold war viewpoint. The United States
could not cooperate simultaneously with the European
reconstruction and the maintenance of security in East
Asia, on one hand, and with the development of the Third
World, on the other. In the case of Latin America, this
position was supported by the healthy situation of monetary reserves with which the countries of the region had
emerged from the war. In any event, if these countries
faced economic problems, they could satisfactorily solve
them by attracting private capital. As far as Latin
American countries were concerned, they never ceased to
emphasize the importance of their economic problems.
Having had to sell their products in a controlled market
during the war, they had then to replace their depreci-
ated equipment, buying new capital goods in a free
market. In the Rio de Janeiro conference, Argentina,
Cuba, Chile, and Mexico had already stated the need to
discuss problems of economic cooperation. The Cuban
representative even proposed that the provisions of the
Rio de Janeiro Treaty would ban "economic threats and
aggressions."[2] In answer to these claims, the Inter-
American Economic and Social Council was asked to prepare a proposal on the basis of which the Ninth Conference of American States would call an economic conference in the second half of 1948. This meeting was
not convened.

The only opportunity for having such a meeting
occurred at the time of the Tenth Conference of American
States, held in Caracas in March 1954. The aim of the
meeting was to obtain a joint declaration of Latin
American countries to the effect that the establishment
of a government controlled by a Communist party in any
country on the continent represented a threat to hemispheric security and, consequently, would legitimize
joint action, according to the provisions of the Rio de
Janeiro Treaty. The purpose of this resolution was to
provide a cover-up for the already planned intervention
against the regime of Colonel Jacobo Arbenz in Guatemala.
The Secretary of State, John Foster Dulles, represented
the United States on that occasion. The resolution was

approved, but it required that the previously promised
economic conference take place.

The conference was held in Quitandinha, Brazil, in
November 1954 within the framework of the Inter-American
Economic and Social Council (IA-ECOSOC). The main ideas
elaborated by the United Nations Economic Committee for
Latin America (ECLA) at the end of the previous decade
were presented under the leadership of its Executive
Secretary, Dr. Raúl Prebisch. The preliminary works
carried out by ECLA for the Quitandinha conference were
channeled through a committee of experts whose president
was Chilean Senator Eduardo Frei Montalva and whose rap-
porteur was Colombian economist Carlos Lleras Restrepo.
The major thesis that would largely inspire the development policies of Latin American countries in forthcoming
years included the need for a strong program of external
cooperation, principally by adoption of measures to
stabilize raw material prices and the establishment of
an inter-American development fund. During the meeting
the U.S. position, represented by the Treasury Secretary,
George Humphrey, prevailed. Although it tended to base
the solution of development problems on the attraction
of foreign private capital by means of adequate external
policies, those proposals were the basis from which the
inter-American system would be renewed some years later.

Once again it was necessary to wait for the right
moment. In this case, the opportunity was provided by
visits to Latin American countries made by the Vice-
President of the United States and, subsequently, by
the Undersecretary of State for Latin America, Roy
Rubottom, and the Secretary of State, John Foster Dulles,
to Brazilian President Juscelino Kubitschek in 1958.
On this last interview, the Brazilian President insisted
that the restlessness and violence that had broken out
in some countries of the region could not be attacked
with security measures, as they were the expression of
a deeper uneasiness, which had its roots in the economic
and social conditions of the majority of the population.
He proposed the launching of a huge cooperative development program, which on that occasion was called the
Panamerican Operation.[3]

The statements of the Panamerican Operation were
to be analyzed in a meeting of foreign affairs ministers
held in Washington in September 1958. The meeting was
preceded by an announcement made at a special session
of the IA-ECOSOC by the Undersecretary of State, Douglas
Dillon, that the United States was ready to participate
in a regional financial organization, together with
measures tending to ensure the adhesion of the United
States to the International Coffee Agreement.[4] The Conference of Foreign Affairs Ministers established the

so-called Committee of 21, in charge of implementing
the Panamerican Operation. These steps, together with
Fidel Castro's entrance into Havana in January 1959,[5]
represented the beginning of a change in inter-American
relations, a change that would lead to the Alliance for
Progress.

To what extent did the Alliance for Progress mark
a change in inter-American relations? Of course, it
changed neither the adherence of Latin America to the
Western hemisphere nor its position in the international
system. On the contrary, within the context of hemispheric relations the Alliance for Progress meant,
first, that the United States granted its neighbors
south of the Rio Grande a priority that they did not
enjoy before. Second, the United States decided to
face the solution of the economic and social problems
plaguing the region instead of giving preference to
considerations of hemispheric security. And third, in
that huge development cooperation program the United
States assumed many of the concepts and aspirations of
the Latin American countries themselves.

These characteristics are explained if we look at
the background of the Alliance for Progress. Initially,
two groups took part in its preparation. One was a
group of U.S. statesmen and scholars gathered by Adolf
Berle at President Kennedy's request, including several
liberals such as Lincoln Gordon, Robert Alexander, and
Arthur Whitaker. The other group was formed by some
close associates of Puerto Rico's Governor, Luis Muñoz
Marin, with whom Berle had been in contact for many
years; among them were Arturo Morales Carrion and
Teodoro Moscoso. The speech by which President Kennedy
launched the Alliance for Progress on March 13, 1961,
was based on the ideas of the report prepared by this
task force, as well as on the proposals of a group of
nine eminent Latin Americans that was assembled for
this purpose by José Antonio Mayobre, then Venezuelan
Ambassador to the United States, in response to a personal request from President Kennedy himself. This
last group included the directors of the main regional
agencies, such as Raúl Prebisch, ECLA Executive Secretary; Felipe Herrera, Inter-American Development Bank
(IDB) President; and Jorge Sol Castellanos, IA-ECOSOC
Executive Secretary.

These groups, in some manner, interpreted the main
democratic and progressive trends that by then actively
influenced their countries' policies--either within the
government or through the opposition--and their major
leaders, such as Rómulo Betancourt, Alberto Lleras
Camargo, José Figueres, Victor Raúl Haya de la Torre,
and Eduardo Frei Montalva.

Thus, the Alliance for Progress could incorporate most of the proposals for which the most progressive groups in Latin America had struggled. The alliance proposed an "utmost effort" decade to promote the development of Latin American countries. Its platform recognized many needs:

1. To give new momentum to the industrialization process and, in general, to the diversification of Latin American economies;

2. To remove the archaic rural structures of these countries by means of effective land reforms;

3. To promote social development through massive housing, health, and educational programs;

4. To promote strongly scientific and technological development by means of modernization of Latin American universities and technical assistance programs;

5. To promote the establishment of national planning systems that would give coherence to the development policies of Latin American countries;

6. To encourage the process of economic integration for the countries of the region with the aim of expanding their markets;

7. To move the United States to cooperate with the programs of price stabilization for Latin America's commodities, by examining existing problems, case by case;

8. To launch a wide program of financial cooperation, beginning with a contribution from the United States of $500 million through a Social Progress Trust Fund.

For the purposes of this paper, I am not so much concerned with evaluating the results obtained by the Alliance for Progress as with raising the question of whether the two premises on which this operation was based are still in force or not. First, it was assumed that there existed reform-oriented movements or political regimes, relatively homogeneous, in a significant number of Latin American countries. The second premise claimed the existence of a "natural harmony of interests" between the United States and Latin America, evidenced by the fact that the alliance incorporated most of the proposals launched by the aforementioned reformist movements.

The fact is that at the end of the past decade these conditions were beginning to lose effect; new factors were appearing on both the international and regional stages. Consequently, a fundamental alteration was occurring in the pattern that had governed international relations of these countries during the past twenty-five years.

A CHANGING INTERNATIONAL FRAMEWORK

One of the main features of the current pattern of
international relations is the top priority given to
economic issues in national foreign policies and international negotiations. As a result of that, the politically neutral economic order assumed in the past
ceased to work that way, and international economic
affairs became increasingly politicized. The "two
track" system in which politicians dealt with highly
sensitive political affairs while technical officers
took care of the economic ones within a frame of indisputable international regulations (as Richard Cooper
characterized it[6]) seems now completely out of touch
with reality. In the world today, economic policy is
more and more foreign policy.

This is a consequence of a combination of circumstances: first, the long-standing trend toward a
greater intervention of the state in every aspect of
national life and the strengthening and proliferation
of governmental social and economic goals that can be
seen everywhere, in less developed--as well as in de-
veloped--countries; second, the expansion of transnational relations stimulated by the emergence of new
transnational actors, the growing interdependence of
national economies, and the improvement of international
finance, transportation, travel, and communication;
third, the transformation of the international economic
order from a system based on stable and widely accepted
rules of the game, within which economic transactions
did not require political decisions, to a new situation
in which the basic assumptions, institutions, and rules
of the game are called into question and in which a new
international economic order is actively sought.[7]

This state of affairs has resulted in two major
changes bearing strong implications for developing
countries.

One is the decreasing relevance of security targets
vis-à-vis economic considerations in the foreign policy
of the great powers. During the last decade the bipolar
world arising from World War II gradually became a poly-
centric one, as a consequence of the Sino-Soviet conflict, the nuclear parity achieved by the great powers,
the growing economic and technological interdependence
among nations, the emergence of new power centers in
the international economy, and the relative decline of
the international decision-making leverage of the United
States.

All this has brought a sharp devaluation of military resources in world politics and has weakened the

trend to resort to force as the traditional way to settle international disputes, at least in the nonsocialist
world.   Given the current international atmosphere, the
multilateral intervention in Suez in 1956 and the U.S.
intervention in the Dominican Republic in 1965 may prove
to be the last cases of overt military intervention in
a strict sense, while the American debacle in Indochina
should most probably be the last case of massive military involvement, in broader sense.   The greater margin
of security achieved by the great powers as a result of
nuclear parity and the high costs of military involvement with conventional weapons have made increasingly
improbable the use of force by major military powers
and have contributed to dispel the fears of military
intervention among weaker states.   That is why not one
of the oil-exporting countries took seriously the mass
media speculations and the covert official warnings
about a military solution for the oil dispute.

Besides that, as the threat of force faded, the
great powers have seemed to favor using economic pressures as alternative weapons to excessive influence in
the world arena.   The facts that economic pressures are
a subtler and more elusive expedient and that economic
resources are at least slightly less concentrated than
military power make it possible for less developed
countries (LDCs) to emulate the monopolistic practices
of industrial nations (as illustrated by the case of
producers' associations) or even to retaliate in the
same economic field (as OPEC countries did in 1973).
We have already seen one good example of how this new
economic weaponry can spread and to some extent be
shared by less developed countries: while in 1971 the
United States linked trade and monetary negotiations
against the wish of their industrial partners in order
to get a better monetary agreement, in 1975 the OPEC
and Third World countries insisted at the Paris dialogue
that a link be established between oil, raw materials,
finance, and international assistance, against the will
of the industrial countries.

At the same time, while security affairs lose importance, a broad new set of social and economic targets
rises in the international agenda--among them economic
welfare, political autonomy, cultural identity, and
international status--thus setting the stage for a
process in which the less developed countries can better
express their basic interests.

The policy of détente, to which this wider margin
of security gave place, provided for greater fluidity
in the international system.   This new international
permissiveness enabled less developed countries to
strengthen their bargaining position vis-à-vis

industrialized countries, to promote diversification of their foreign relations, and to seek at least some degree of autonomy in international affairs.[8]

The second change that may influence the opportunities open to the developing countries is linked with recent trends in the field of natural resources and raw materials.

The development models followed by the industrial countries have led to a deep crisis, whose overt expression is that mixed situation called stagflation, but whose underlying causes are to be found in their wasteful patterns of consumption, their high production costs, an accelerated rate of technological obsolescence, the careless use of depredatory technologies, the overload of the ecosystem's absorptive capacity, and the fast depletion of world natural resources. The crisis has raised doubts about the validity of the assumption that it is possible to achieve indefinite economic progress and has revealed the existence of limits to economic growth.

The prospects of world scarcity dominate and shape the current economic outlook. A survey conducted in the United States during the summer of 1974 showed widespread concern over the quality of the environment and the availability of natural resources: 64 percent of the public believed that "sooner or later world population and economic growth have to be regulated to avoid serious shortages." The feelings expressed in some quarters at the beginning of the energy crisis--that oil would be the exception[9]--may prove to be purely wishful thinking. In fact, the predictions made in 1973, on economic grounds, that such a strategic product as oil was not to be linked to other raw materials was revised in 1975 through a political decision by linking them together in the forthcoming Paris dialogue. In the meantime, transactions encompassing a growing rate of primary and even manufactured products has been transferred from a buyers' market to a sellers' market, and shortages and bottlenecks at various stages of the production process--along with high production costs due to the lifestyles of contemporary industrial societies-- stand as the main factor behind current inflationary trends instead of excessive aggregate demand, by which inflation was explained in the past.

As a consequence, a growing concern over "economic security" may have supplanted the traditional concern for economic growth. However, some trade-offs will be needed in the industrial countries between steps taken to achieve economic security and measures intended to fight inflation: the first may assure supply at

stabilized--but higher--prices, as Japan and several
European countries arranged in the case of oil. These
factors lead to a new policy of scarcity in international relations, which may significantly benefit developing
countries.

The combined effects of détente and scarcity are
producing a shift from the emphasis on East-West relations, characterizing the postwar period, toward North-
South relations. This may presumably lead to deep
changes in the power relations between these two groups
of countries as a result of some demographic, political,
and economic factors that are becoming increasingly important within the present international economic situation.

The great powers have realized the need for a
prompt agreement between the two blocs in order to
regulate their clashes and conflicts in a steady manner,
as was the case in Helsinki. Such an agreement provides
an encouraging promise of peace, but, at the same time,
makes it possible for the superpowers to restructure
relations within each bloc under their hegemony.

However, the trend toward change in power relations
between the two groups seems irreversible. First of
all, by the end of this century industrialized countries
will make up only 10 percent of the world population,
a fact that raises serious doubts as to whether such
a minority will be able to maintain its economic and
political control over the international system.
Second, industrialized nations are becoming increasingly
dependent on natural resources available in the LDCs,
whereas the latter will most likely continue struggling
to win control over their resources and will go on joining forces in defense of their products and markets, as
shown by the OPEC experience. In the third place, it
seems inevitable that sooner or later the developed
countries will require the expansion of Third World
markets to allow for the continued growth of their own
industrial apparatus; they may even have to consider
the relocation of industries on a global basis in the
search for comparative advantages arising from the
availability of natural and human resources and the
environmental capacity to absorb pollution.

The trend to reevaluate the relatively scarce resources available in Third World countries leads to the
conclusion that the struggle of LDCs to improve their
participation in the international system can neither
solely nor principally concentrate on securing concessions from the industrialized countries. The experiences of the last decade--fully illustrated by lucid and
eminent reports, such as those of Pearson, Prebisch,

Jackson, and Peterson--left a generalized feeling of
disappointment in light of the excessive trust placed
on foreign aid as well as on the possibility of achieving the transfer of real resources from industrialized
countries to LDCs in adequate amounts and conditions.
The expansion of cooperation among developing countries
could be part of the answer to these feelings.

The first UN team of experts that discussed the
measures to be adopted in favor of LDCs met in 1950.
This group reached some simple conclusions and a clear
prescription on which international action should be
based.   The basic obstacle faced by LDCs was lack of
capital and technical skills.   As those factors can
be neither improvised nor built up in the short run,
they had to be obtained abroad.   However, development
costs were in fact so high that unexpectedly large
volumes of capital and technology had to be imported.
If, as recommended by the experts, the LDCs wished to
increase their production by 2.5 percent per year, they
had to make a net annual investment of \$19 billion.
Nonetheless, the poor countries would have been unable
to raise more than half that amount, even after making
the greatest internal sacrifices to increase their
savings rates.   Therefore, about \$10 billion would have
to be obtained abroad.   Since the United States was, at
the time, the only potential supplier of financial resources, this would have meant the transference of approximately 4 percent of its gross national product
(GNP); for this reason the formula prescribed by the
UN experts twenty-five years ago contrasts ironically
with the frustrated efforts of industrialized countries
as a whole to achieve the goal established by United
Nations Conference on Trade and Development (UNCTAD):
to transfer 1 percent of their GNP to developing countries.   In fact the transference has never exceeded
0.5 percent and has been declining to 0.3 percent in
recent years.

Since then, however, the national income of Third
World countries has increased at an average annual rate
of 4.5 percent, almost twice that proposed by the United
Nations in 1950, despite the fact that foreign aid received during those twenty-five years was only one-tenth
of that foreseen by the experts.   This might show that
the internal resources of Third World countries represented a force roughly twenty times stronger than that
originally estimated to foster their own development,
as well as prove the fragility of the hopes placed on
foreign aid.[10]

The foregoing was possible in spite of the fact
that during that period the LDCs followed development
patterns that experience proved to be quite inadequate.

These patterns were mainly concerned with the growth of
the GNP. It was assumed that high GNP growth rates
would bring about increased levels of income and would
ensure full employment. After one or two decades,
theoreticians and practitioners of development are not
sure whether in fact high rates of growth lead to a reduction of massive poverty and unemployment, even in
those countries whose economic performance has been
more successful. Such was the case during the last
decade, for instance, of Pakistan and Colombia, where
it was possible to recognize that, following a long
period of growth of over 6 percent per annum, unemployment problems had become substantially worse. Similarly,
in Brazil and Mexico, there is currently a growing and
encouraging concern over income distribution, despite
a high rate of growth during the last several years.

Developing countries have been applying foreign-
imposed and generally unsuitable concepts, priorities,
economic policies, evaluation standards, and value systems. It is not surprising, then, that some of these
countries have now decided to review their development
strategies. This has brought about an increasing diversification of the roads to development and a quest
for new targets and development values. A new pattern
based on a more equal distribution of income and consumption would tend to modify the composition of GNP
and the technologies needed to generate it, thus improving the utilization of local resources and achieving
a better balance between external cooperation and domestic efforts.

In other words, as an experienced economist stated
a few years ago, an attempt is being made to place the
concept of development on its own feet and to shift the
emphasis from its quantitative aspects--mainly related
to the growth of the GNP--to the qualitative ones, related to the lifestyles of these societies and to the
fulfillment of human needs.[11] The fact that China,
which contains almost one-fourth of the world's population, has chosen this road is significant, especially
because this country will spread its experiences to
other developing countries as its participation in
international affairs increases.

Should this occur, it would exert considerable influence on the adoption of new forms of international
cooperation, by reducing the degree of foreign dependence of LDCs and by encouraging cooperation between
Third World nations. In other words, the stress formerly placed on cooperation between central and peripheral
countries, particularly in the financial field, is being
displaced by the quest for a new international economic
order to secure a better and fairer participation for

LDCs and by the search for new development strategies
substantially based on individual and collective self-
reliance among the LDCs.

THE NEW LATIN AMERICAN SETTING

These trends at the international level, which
open the way for a more autonomous development of the
countries of the Third World, have special significance
to Latin America because of its previous evolution.
From the beginning of this decade, this evolution has
been characterized by sustained economic growth, increasing experience in handling the development process,
and a generalized trend toward economic nationalism.

One may note three characteristics of particular
importance for the future relations between the United
States and Latin America: the institutionalization of
economic growth, at least when considering the region
as a whole; the intensification of cooperation among
the countries of the area; and the increasing coordination of the Latin American countries' foreign economic
policies.

Above all, it may be said that during the last fifteen years the economic development of the region has
been institutionalized at a fast rate, which in the last
years has widely exceeded 6 percent per annum. During
this time the secondary sector has grown at a faster
rate, 8 percent per annum. Between 1960 and 1970 the
share of manufactures in total Latin American exports
increased from a 3.1 percent to 9.3 percent; this trend
continued during recent years. In 1975, the GNP of the
region exceeded $200 billion, and its per capita income
exceeded $650. Among the eighteen strategic products
to which the UNCTAD's integral program refers, fourteen
are of interest to Latin America, which is assuming an
active role in the existing producers' associations
(OPEC) and is promoting the creation of new ones (Union
of Banana Producer Countries).

To the foregoing I must add the fact of a more
comfortable financial situation. The international
reserves of Latin America as a whole have exceeded
$20 billion. Growth indicators have determined that
Latin America is gradually becoming a good risk in
international capital markets, whereby at least the
more developed countries of the region have already
had access to new nonconcessional financing sources.
The net flow of private external resources received
by Latin America rose from $652 million during the
period 1961-65 to approximately $3,700 million in
1972 and 1973. Furthermore, Latin America's successful

experience with export diversification and the potential
improvement of the terms of trade for its traditional
products in an era of scarcity allow us to predict a
more stable flow of resources in foreign currency.

This does not mean that Latin America needs no
external aid, as some people contend, but that its role
in the framework of the external economic relations of
the region has changed. Global indicators still hide
deep unbalanced conditions. While a few countries are
far advanced in their industrialization and import substitution process, others continue to rely substantially
on primary production and the external sector. In 1972
and 1973, excluding Brazil, the growth rate in the rest
of Latin America amounted to about 5.5 percent on average (it reaches 6.6 percent if Brazil is included).
The attainment of these growth rates does not seem to
have alleviated the unemployment and underemployment
problems, and it may have even heightened the unequal
income distribution, which, according to some reports,
in Latin America not only is worse than that found in
industrialized economies, but even compares unfavorably
with many developing countries in Asia.

In addition to these structural imbalances, there
exist pressures derived from higher oil import prices,
which in 1975 forced many Latin American countries to
employ between 10 and 25 percent of export revenues to
pay those additional costs. Yet, this same situation
has served to reveal to what extent Latin America is
now forced to seek solutions to its main problems beyond the hemispheric framework and increasingly to resort to regional cooperation and the international
community.

A second manifestation of this trend is the remarkable intensification of cooperation among Latin American
countries, experienced through a variety of actions and
instruments that generally exceed provisions contained
in the existing formal integration agreements.

It has been a long time since the world economy
turned from internationalization of trade to internationalization of production, as shown by the fact
that during the 1960s foreign control of industrial
companies based in developing countries increased by
10 percent per annum--that is, almost three times faster
than the growth of their economies--and that production
of the transnational corporations' subsidiaries since
1970 is considerably larger than the world trade value.
Latin America does not escape this trend, as indicated
by the increasing number of multinational investment
projects promoted among two or more Latin American
countries. Those initiatives respond, in some cases,

to the need to complement the managerial or technological ability of two or more countries, generally at different levels of development; in other cases, as in the
joint exploitation of natural resources, they are based
on the need to secure their supply or the participation
of those countries more able to develop them. Among
other examples, we must recall the agreements signed by
Brazil and Bolivia for exploitation of iron and marketing of natural gas from the latter; the multinational
hydroelectric projects of Itaipú, Salto Grande, and
Yaciretá-Apipé in the River Plate basin; the studies
carried out for the installation of an aluminium plant
to exploit Jamaican and Guyanese bauxite, with the
eventual participation of Mexico and Venezuela; as
well as the possibility of attracting multinational
investments to Honduras with the purpose of developing
its forestry resources in order to service an expanded
market. As a consequence of the application of joint
industrial planning within the frame of the Cartagena
Agreement, up to the time this was written the programs
corresponding to the metal-mechanic and the petro-
chemical sectors have been approved, and the automotive
industry program is in the process of approval. Recent
studies show that, in wider or more restricted geographical scope, there are interesting possibilities
for joint action in the electric, nuclear, petroleum,
plastic, fertilizers, steel, and transportation
(especially metropolitan) sectors.

All this has brought along a renewed interest for
trade expansion among the area's countries, within the
framework of existing schemes or by new bilateral or
multinational agreements. Such ideas are particularly
promising in the exchange of technology and capital
goods among countries. There is a belief that Latin
American countries have a considerable asset of technology that, as a consequence of a long-standing process
of adaptation and practical application, is no longer
protected by the international license system and is
therefore free for use by local companies. Thus the
countries of the region are paying more and more attention to technology available from national companies,
public as well as private, mainly at the plant level or
in the hands of the engineers of the firms themselves.
Another field worth observing is the regional market of
capital goods that in the countries of the Latin American Free Trade Association (LAFTA) presently amounts to
over $6 billion. Studies show the feasibility of a
Latin American multinational trading company of capital
goods, designed to contribute (1) to the development of
local industry and local engineering of equipment goods
by expanding its markets; (2) to regional integration,
complementation, and specialization of the production
of capital goods; (3) to an increase in its international

competitiveness; and (4) to the guarantee of a more
favorable supply from the viewpoint of regional buyers.
A decisive factor would be the concerted utilization
of the investment capacity of the Latin American public
sector, whose acquisitions of equipment are concentrated
on a small number of activities; they relate to extraction, refining, and distribution of oil, generation and
distribution of electric power, public transportation,
and the steel industry, all of which are characterized
by a growth rate higher than that of the GNP and by
huge projects.

At the same time, the Latin American countries
have made some progress in the field of financial cooperation, particularly due to the clever allocation of
Venezuelan financial surpluses. Worth mentioning here
are several actions: the agreements concluded by Venezuela with the Central American countries for financing
their oil imports and for retaining their coffee harvest
in order to protect coffee prices in the international
markets; the establishment of a $500-million trust fund
under IDB administration for financing projects in
relatively less developed countries; the acquisition
of bonds of the International Bank for Reconstruction
and Development (IBRD); and the opening of an Andean
Development Corporation (ADC) line of credit for $60
million to finance integration projects in the sub-
region.

A third manifestation of this process can be seen
in the trend toward an increasing coordination of the
foreign economic policies of Latin American countries
vis-à-vis third nations. The Latin American experience
has shown the need to give up the idea that the fundamental stimulus to development arises from uncoordinated
activity in the international economic system. On the
contrary, the adoption of new production and consumption
patterns, as well as the attainment of a minimum degree
of autonomy, requires a shift toward policies of selective participation in the system. This has made it
necessary to move toward a closer coordination of the
foreign policies of the region's countries with the
object of increasing their bargaining capacity. Some
practical expressions of selectivity have been seen in
three specific areas of concern: control and exploitation of natural resources, foreign trade, and problems
related to the transfer of capital and technology and
to the behavior of multinational corporations.

During recent years, an increasing number of Latin
American governments have strengthened their will to
recover or stress their control over existing natural
resources in their territories, resulting in a wave of
expropriations and nationalizations throughout the

region. The premonitory event took place at the end of
1968, when the Peruvian military junta expropriated the
La Brea and the Pariñas oil fields and refineries,
owned by the International Petroleum Company (IPC),
the largest oil corporation in Peru. At the same time,
the military government started rural reform that affected the foreign agricultural interests, particularly
the sugar mills on the coast owned by the Americans and
the vast agriculture and cattle operations of the Cerro
de Pasco Corporation in the highlands. This way, the
IPC take-over not only became the origin and symbol of
the Peruvian Revolution, but anticipated a wave of economic nationalism in other countries. These trends had
already been apparent during the process of "Chileani-
zation" of copper managed by Anaconda and Kennecott,
under Frei's government, that was followed by the expropriation of their fields, unanimously approved by
the Chilean Congress of 1971. One must also remember
the conflict between the government of Guyana and the
Alcan Aluminium Ltd., which ended with the nationalization of the Demerara Bauxite Company (Demba). The laws
on hydrocarbons adopted by Ecuador and, more recently,
the reversion of the old Venezuelan petroleum concessions and the petroleum and iron nationalization by the
government of Acción Democrática in that country are
other examples of this trend. It is not by chance that
a few months before the IPC events the Latin American
governments, gathered within the frame of ECLA, included
in the Consensus of Viña del Mar the recognition "of
the superior right of each country to freely dispose
of its natural resources." As regards maritime law,
as is well known, the Latin American countries pioneered
the 200-mile limit, which confers upon riparian states
a preeminent right to the exploitation of the natural
resources included within those boundaries. This position is complemented by the Latin American countries'
interest in the full maintenance of the international
status of the sea bed, the resources existing in them,
and the establishment of multinational mechanisms for
the administration of these areas. The support given
by all Latin American countries to Panama with regard
to the canal--both on occasion of the meeting of the
Security Council of the United Nations in that country
and in the framework of the OAS and other international
forums--is another manifestation of this trend.

A second area of convergence of the foreign policies of Latin American countries is their trade relations with the rest of the world, particularly as regards primary products. The role that Latin American
countries have played in UNCTAD through the Group of
the 77 is well known, particularly at the meeting of
Alta Gracia in 1964. The countries of the region have
taken active part in actions designed to strengthen

existing agreements on primary products (petroleum,
copper, and tin) or to establish new agreements (bauxite
and bananas). They have also shown interest in the integrated program promoted by UNCTAD, aiming to bind the
different agreements, with the object of progressing
toward the establishment of a huge system of interdependence among different products. The agreements
concluded between Venezuela and Central America about
coffee, for example, represent a new experience, the
establishment of a regulating stock.

A third zone of convergence is related to the
treatment of or control over the flow of external resources. The influence of foreign investment in the
development process of Latin American countries is
greater than one would suppose on the basis of their
share in global investment, which barely surpassed
5 percent during the last decade. This is due to the
tendency of foreign investment to concentrate on the
more dynamic sectors of the economies and, within them,
only in established productive branches and in the most
important companies. This explains the fact that the
sectorial distribution of foreign investment in Latin
America has developed from the traditional activities
(tropical agriculture, mining and petroleum, and public
services) toward new sectors (manufacturing and commer-
cial-financing services). This concentration results
from the tendency of foreign investors to place capital
in industries strongly protected against new producers.
In the mid-1960s, more than half the sales of the fifty
most important companies in Argentina were made by subsidiaries of foreign firms, while more recent studies
in other countries yield similar results. In spite of
this fact, until the end of the past decade, little was
known about the development and the effects of foreign
capital in Latin America. At the very end of the decade,
a number of studies were undertaken--first in Colombia
and later throughout the Andean group--on the basis of
which it was possible to formulate new policies related
to the flow of foreign capital and technology, not only
in the countries of the Cartagena Agreement, but in
others as well. These policies, first incorporated in
Decision 24 and adopted by the countries of the Andean
group in 1970, were reflected in the law on establishment of the National Institute of Industrial Property
of Brazil later that year, in the law on transference
of technology promulgated by the Argentine Republic in
1971, and in the Mexican law on foreign investments of
1972. The common denominator of these policies seems
to be the search for greater control over capital and
technology imports to coordinate contribution of these
factors with national development. Bearing in mind the
existence of important differences between the various

countries, in general we may say that these policies
are designed for the following purposes:

1. To strengthen the bargaining position of
national capital vis-à-vis the foreign investors;

2. To influence the sectorial orientation of
foreign investment by adopting more selective criteria;

3. To prevent foreign investment from being restricted to a financial impact, ensuring that these
investments make a substantial contribution to technological development, managerial capacity, or expansion of foreign markets;

4. To allow the disaggregation of the "package"
that is usually involved in foreign investment, in
which financial, technological, commercial, and managerial elements are bound together;

5. To control the impact of foreign investment
on the balance of payment of the country by regulating
the repatriation of capital and profits and the payments
resulting from royalties, patents, and technical assistance; and

6. To control the influence of foreign investment
on the national economy by regulating reinvestment of
profits and purchase of local entreprises.

It is interesting to note how the legislation of
a country with apparently limited government intervention in business, like Brazil, establishes that its
objective is "to adopt, so as to attain the economic
development of the country, measures capable of accelerating and controlling the transfer of technology and
establishing better bargaining conditions and utilization of patents" and foresees programs designed to
"strengthen national bargaining power and to select
technology imports." The Institute of Industrial
Property of Brazil is one of the most efficient agencies
in this field.

The aforementioned trends--toward increasing growth,
growing cooperation, and greater coordination of their
foreign policies--impelled the countries of the region
to establish the Latin American Economic System (SELA)
in Panama on October 17, 1975. The SELA is a regional
consultative organization for permanent economic and
social coordination and cooperation. The fundamental
aims of SELA are (1) to promote intraregional cooperation, in order to hasten the economic and social development of its members; and (2) to promote a permanent system of consultation and coordination for the adoption of

common positions and strategies on economic and social matters, in international organizations and forums as well as in relation to third countries and groups of countries.

SELA is based on several principles: the acknowledgment that cooperation among developing countries is a strong driving force; the acceptance of ideological pluralism among the countries of the region; the application of essentially pragmatic and flexible procedures to ensure that each initiative is promoted with the direct support of the governments involved; the acknowledgment that the relatively more developed countries must also assume greater responsibilities; and the belief that such a system of regional cooperation should not become an element of confrontation with other regions of the world.

In that respect, the inter-American system will continue the framework through which the multilateral relations of the United States with Latin American countries are channeled. The OAS and other inter-American agencies, like IDB, present an impressive record in the evolution of international cooperation for Latin American development. Latin American countries have recently shown their intention of still using this system to examine their mutual interests, such as trade and assistance, or the controversial aspects that occasionally appear in their relations with the United States (for example, the recent U.S. Trade Reform Act). It would be a serious mistake to think that the new mechanism is called to act as a competitive agency or as a body apart from the organizations making up the inter-American system. On the contrary, the establishment of this regional forum will contribute to clarifying the dialogue between the Latin American countries and the United States in the hemispheric framework, allowing the former to define their positions with greater independence. What is more important, however, is that SELA represents an act of self-assertion by Latin American countries as well as a major step toward coexistence among different regimes, since in SELA are seated together such countries as Brazil, Cuba, Chile, and Mexico.

THE WEAKENING OF THE "SPECIAL RELATIONSHIP"

A clear indication of these recent trends is the relative weakening of the special relationship between Latin America and the United States. I have already pointed out how Latin America remained within the security sphere of the United States at the end of World War II. This phenomenon was accompanied by

a marked loss of interest in Latin American affairs on
the part of the European countries. On the one hand,
the threat of a short-term nuclear confrontation tended
to override the geopolitical considerations that in the
past had dictated a Latin American position as demographic reservoir, source of supplies and raw materials,
and point of support for the communication lines of the
great powers. On the other hand, the leading role with
which the United States emerged from the war drove its
allies to delegate to it the task of keeping the Latin
American countries' security and allignment during the
cold war. The fact that the Cuban Missile Crisis in
1962 had been unilaterally resolved by the United States
without consultation with its Atlantic allies and the
failure of some European countries in their efforts of
rapprochement with Latin America in the mid-1960s
(President De Gaulle's visit to Latin America and the
triangular policy of President Saragat and Prime Minister
Fanfani) clearly show the deliberate withdrawal of the
European countries during the whole period.

However, it was unavoidable that the development
of détente during the 1960s would eventually lead them
to reconsider these attitudes. Thus, toward the end of
the decade, the European countries began to appreciate
the short-term economic advantages that could afford
them a stronger influence on Latin America, instead of
reducing them to the long-term security objectives set
up at the beginning of the cold war. As far as the
United States was concerned, it necessarily tended to
give less importance to a fall in its relative position
in Latin America than to a determination of which countries would step into the sphere of influence left open
by its withdrawal. These new perceptions, arising from
détente, originated a favorable atmosphere for a relative loosening of the hemispheric relationship.

President Nixon's Latin American policy of "low
profile" or "benign neglect" was drawn up within this
frame of reference. An official version of that policy
is found in an article signed by Charles Meyer, former
Undersecretary for Inter-American Affairs, who employed
the term coined by the U.S. President himself: a "mature
association." According to the Secretary of State, the
United States was looking for a new balance in its relationship with Latin America, by loosening up the old
paternal hold over the other nations of the hemisphere.
Nixon's policy involved the acknowledgment that differences in priorities and interests are to be expected,
even through these may be overcome with a spirit of
compromise--and not of confrontation.[12]

Fear has been expressed that a policy of "limited
concern" on part of the U.S. government may leave Latin

American relations in the hands of private U.S. interests, backed up by nationalist feelings often expressed by the Congress.[13] Since the U.S. government
must necessarily watch over the interests of its citizens abroad, through a kind of vicious circle, this
policy would lead to new and more disagreeable forms of
U.S. intervention, as was the case with expropriations
of U.S. investments in the area. Other indications,
however, seem to lead to the opposite conclusion. In
fact, it is not clear that this is the most probable
perspective and, in any case, it does not seem to be
the aim of Latin American policy espoused by the Ford
administration. In an official statement made in 1972,
President Nixon said that "should an American company be
expropriated without adopting the appropriate measures
to grant a quick, suitable and effective compensation
it is assumed that the expropriating country will not
receive new bilateral economic benefits, unless important factors affecting out interests require a different
type of action on our part."[14] In fact, the United
States is in the process of settling the conflicts resulting from expropriation of the IPC in Peru, and it
tried, at least, to adopt an ambiguous position in the
case of copper in Chile.[15] On the other hand, it is
evident that intervention in defense of any particular
firm in the area might endanger other companies' investments, interfere with the business relationship between
the two countries, or block the access to certain raw
materials. These considerations allow me to propose
that in all likelihood the United States is looking for
the reduction of its participation in Latin America.

    Furthermore, this policy is in keeping with certain
trends observed in the evolution of the economic relationship between the United States and the Latin American countries.

    Between 1950 and 1970 the share of Latin American
exports in the U.S. market decreased from 24 percent to
11 percent, while the participation of the Latin American market in U.S. exports decreased to a lesser extent,
going from 17.4 percent to 13.3 percent in the same
period. On the other hand, the importance of the U.S.
market for Latin American exports decreased approximately from 60 percent to 40 percent. The slower growth of
Latin American exports to the United States, as compared
to exports to other regions of the world, is becoming
worse because its structure has undergone little change
lately: the share of primary products in Latin American
exports to the United States decreased only from 95.6
percent to 92.7 percent between the first and the second
halves of the 1960s.

Three additional facts contributed to weaken the
economic ties between the United States and Latin America. First was the delay in the approval of the General
Preferences Scheme by the United States Congress and
the restrictive or discriminatory clauses incorporated
in it, once it was approved.

Second, U.S. investments tended to grow less in
Latin America than in the rest of the world. As is
known, there is a close relationship between investment
and trade. A study made of British investments in
Nigeria concludes that every £100 invested in this
country yield additional trade of about £40. Undoubtedly, if the trend to a lesser relative share of U.S.
investments continues in Latin America, it will affect
the trade flow between the countries concerned.

In the third place, it is also agreed that the
"ties" on funds channeled through foreign aid programs
have an influence on trade. Tied aid provided through
AID increased from 41 percent to 98 percent between
1960 and 1968. For some years now, strong pressure
has been exerted to reverse this trend. The process
began with the announcement made during President
Nixon's speech to the Inter-American Press Society
in October 1969 that the funds furnished by the United
States could be freely used within the region.

Finally, I should point out that the Latin American
share in U.S. direct foreign investment decreased from
38 percent to 16 percent between 1950 and 1968.

It is natural that this lesser influence of the
United States in the area should be accompanied by some
diversification in Latin American relations with the
European Economic Community, Japan, the socialist bloc,
and the Third World. On the eve of World War II, three
countries absorbed two-thirds of Latin American foreign
trade: the United States, Germany,. and the United Kingdom. In 1970, that proportion was shared by seven countries. Trade relation between Latin America and the
EEC, notwithstanding the greater restrictions imposed
by the latter in recent years, increased at an average
annual rate of 6.2 percent during the past decade, as
compared to a rate of 3.5 percent in the case of trade
between Latin America and the United States. One should
recall that at present the Europe of the Nine represents
a market that may be compared to the U.S. market for
Latin American exports, with shares of 27 percent and
29 percent, respectively. Should the aforementioned
growth rates persist, the EEC will replace the United
States in a few years as the principal market for the
exports of the region. The Latin American countries
have been trying, since the end of the past decade, to

diminish the unfavorable effects of EEC regulations on
their exports and to obtain the adoption of cooperative
measures in the trade and economic fields between the
two regions. These efforts permitted the establishment
of standing mechanisms for cooperation and consultation
between both parties, particularly since the Sixth CECLA
Extraordinary Meeting at ministerial level in July 1970.

Although in absolute amounts the trade between
Latin America and Japan is still small, its growth rate
is extraordinarily dynamic. During the past decade
Latin American exports to Japan increased at an annual
rate of 13 percent; Japan's share in its exports have
thus increased from 4 percent in the first five-year
period to 6 percent in the second. This trend was felt
to represent one of the most promising areas for the
development of Latin American international economic
relations. Such prospects are strengthened by the rapid
increase of Japan's share in the world market, as well
as by the levels and type of technological development
attained by that country. In 1971 the countries of the
Cartagena Agreement established an Andean-Japanese Joint
Commission at Governmental Level, which was preceded by
a statement urging the examination of matters of common
interest and the formulation of an agreement. Later on,
during the Fourteenth CECLA Meeting at Experts Level
held in September 1972, a Statement on Relations between
Latin America and Japan was made, one that could provide
the background for establishing a permanent mechanism
of consultation.

Latin American trade with socialist countries during the 1960s was principally absorbed by Argentina and
Brazil and showed certain improvement, although suffering sharp fluctuations. Argentine trade with the Soviet
Union went from $61 million (U.S.) in 1960 to $76 million in 1970, while that of Brazil increased from $71
million in 1960 to $135 million in 1970. It is also
remarkable that the country holding the third place in
the trade with the Soviet Union in 1970 was Colombia
with $37 million, even though their relations had been
practically nil during the first half of the decade.
These figures might lead to the hypothesis that there
would be no correlation between the degree of ideological pluralism and the degree of the diversification of
international relations. Instead, there does seem to
be a connection between (1) the degree of diversification of the economy, (2) the presence of nontraditional
goods in their exports, and (3) the degree of diversification in their foreign relations. It also seems clear
that just as Western Europe and Japan played an important role in the 1960s by furnishing Latin America with
new alternatives (in addition to their relationship with
the United States), the Soviet Union and China will play

a similar role in the 1970s due to their role as great
powers and to their increasing interest in obtaining
greater benefits from the international division of
labor. On the other hand, considering the importance
of their markets, one may forecast that even a minimum
Latin American participation would mean deep changes in
the traditional pattern of their economic and trade relations.[16]

Finally, the need to negotiate with centrally
planned economies or public corporations has led to
opposite opinions. On one hand, it has been pointed
out that although the Latin American countries export
commodities, whose international standardization is
simple and widely known, they import manufactures,
capital goods, and intermediate goods with complex
technical specifications. In products coming from
socialist countries, such specifications usually differ
from those required by the industrial structure of the
Latin American nations. In addition, even if these
differences were not so marked, the fact that both the
specifications and the institutions taking part in the
trade relations are unknown constitutes an additional
trade barrier between the regions.[17] From another point
of view, it has been claimed that the countries in which
the public sector generally has an important economic
role, as in the developing countries, can perhaps more
easily negotiate with centralized economies or with
state-controlled foreign trade within the Western world,
especially with public corporations. Thus, for example,
at the end of the past decade the state-owned Renault
corporation won a bid to establish an automotive assembly plant in Colombia. The unsuccessful bidders--Ford,
General Motors, and Chrysler--considered it foolish
that the successful bidder would undertake to purchase
and market Colombian products--so diverse as coffee and
tobacco, meat and rice--for a value equivalent to that
of the automotive parts imported from France or abroad.
Nevertheless, a state-owned corporation like Renault
had no apparent difficulties in doing so.[18]

THE FUTURE OF U.S.-LATIN AMERICAN RELATIONS

If we were to look at the future, we would not be
optimistic at all about the prospects of this alleged
special relationship--let alone any kind of partnership--
between the United States and Latin America, although we
would still recognize their common interests.

Even if the share of the U.S. market for Latin
American exports of manufactured goods has been growing
in recent years, the Latin American market attracts a
declining proportion of total U.S. exports, with Brazil

and Mexico absorbing 50 percent of the Latin American share. Faced by inflation, recession, unemployment, and the rising power of externally oriented multi-national corporations, U.S. labor is retiring into old protectionist positions. U.S. industry--bearing the burden of an expensive "service economy"--is gradually losing its competitive edge on products manufactured abroad, and the agricultural sector changes yearly with each crop. The generalized preference system enacted by the Trade Reform Act includes so many provisions against foreign products that might "flood the market" that its impact on Latin American exports has been estimated at less than $300 million.

Countervailing duties imposed on Latin American products subject to subsidy schemes, inadequate defini-tions of the value added in countries involved in in-tegration schemes, other restrictive or discriminatory measures--including the import ban against members of OPEC--have been an irritating factor in U.S.-Latin American relations during the mid-1970s and make the future look gloomy.

Financial aid does not brighten the picture. Overall official development assistance provided by the United States in relation to the GNP fell from 0.5 percent at the beginning of the 1960s to 0.3 percent in 1970. In absolute figures, public funds to Latin America rose only from $950 million in 1961-65 to $1.3 billion in 1971-73--36 percent. The U.S. Congress has been reluctant to replenish the weak funds of both the World Bank (IDA) and the Inter-American Development Bank (Fund for Special Operations), and the AID keeps operat-ing at a low level of only $300 million a year. The United States has not shown a constructive position with regard to the International Monetary Fund proposals or to the World Bank supplementary finance scheme to finance LDCs' oil-related deficits, as well as to the issue of the link between Special Drawing Rights and development finance.

Economic considerations at home and a preference for countries that represents a threat to security and for the Third World abroad make it very unlikely that any significant improvement could take place in the flows of public aid from the United States to Latin America.

The same prospects may be true of U.S. direct in-vestment in Latin American countries. The Latin Ameri-can place in U.S. foreign investment has been dropping during the last ten or fifteen years. Furthermore, the climate for U.S. investments is bad and deteriorating in most Latin American countries, as a consequence of the

huge magnitude of U.S. assets in the region, of growing
nationalism among both the people and the technocrats
in Latin America, and of increasing competition from
European and Japanese investors.

But, unexpectedly, here the prospects began to
change. One of the main objectives of U.S. investment
in Latin America is to keep open the access to raw materials that are now in short supply. And reactions
against any economic pressure related to U.S. investment is likely to become stronger in Latin American
countries--and even to spread throughout other development regions--as the Third World consciousness grows.
This is where the new "fluidity" in international relations and the political "scarcity" play a very important role in Latin American affairs. Here, Latin American countries can find a lever to induce positive
changes in the U.S. approach to their basic problem.
I realistically can envisage some improvements in three
areas, especially as Latin America acts increasingly in
coordination with the rest of the Third World.

First of all, as the world is running into major
shortages, the United States will find Latin American
exports of some strategic minerals to be more important
--oil, iron ore, copper, bauxite and alumina, lead, tin,
manganese, and zinc. Since the United States is the
world's major consumer of raw materials, and since Latin
America constitutes a land rich in natural resources,
the U.S. reliance on Latin American exports--reinforced
by traditional links--will undoubtedly grow fast. This
may lead the United States to change its former position
vis-à-vis international commodity arrangements and to
enter into long-term agreements with suppliers to secure
steady access to supplies at reasonable prices. The reverse may even happen: exporting countries may become
reluctant to enter into this kind of agreement as they
perceive greater future shortages and prefer to operate
within the structure of existing or new producers'
associations stimulated by OPEC's success, while pushing
to get access to the markets of the developed countries
for their manufactures in exchange for their supplies.

In the second place, that would open some opportunities for the expansion of nontraditional exports
from Latin American countries. One requirement would
be new policies on the part of the U.S. government,
oriented to helping the sectors affected by the competition and including adjustment assistance to the
industries and reallocation and training of manpower.
However, this change seems consistent with the general
interest of the public, since lower trade barriers
brings more goods at cheaper prices, thus helping to
fight inflation. Moreover, it should be noted that,

in spite of the low growth rates of Latin American exports of manufactured goods to the United States, this market still absorbs 45 percent of the total.

Third, interest in securing access to resources that will be in short supply can be a strong incentive to maintain U.S. investment within the region, in spite of current trends in most Latin American countries to nationalistic policies and a more selective approach toward the process of transfer of capital and technology. Although investment in Latin America as a percentage of total U.S. investment abroad has been declining, it still accounts for one-third of all such investment in the Third World, as well as approximately one-third of total foreign investment in Latin America. The fact that U.S. foreign investment is shifting from the primary to the industrial sector does not exclude such investment from exerting important influence on the governments and the economies of these countries in order to keep them open as suppliers of increasingly scarce raw materials. In fact, Latin America has shown remarkable ability to attract direct investment from the United States in recent years. During 1969-71, such investment constituted 60 percent of overall financial flows from that nation.

In conclusion, as a consequence of worldwide trends toward greater self-reliance among countries of the Third World, changes in power relations between Northern and Southern hemispheres, and regional moves to intensify economic cooperation among Latin American countries, the "special relationship" assumed between the United States and Latin America will not be viable any longer-- unless it is relegated to a rhetorical level at which this unfulfilled assumption could cause serious harm to U.S.-Latin American relations. For the same reasons, economic issues are likely to dominate the agenda during the coming years, political controversies like Cuba and the Panama Canal being raised by other countries to fuel the discussion on economic affairs. It is my feeling that relations may be improved if the United States stops trying to promote new brands of special ties with the Latin American countries and begins to deal with them through the same kind of flexible and carefully designed policies that the United States must follow elsewhere in an increasingly interdependent world.

NOTES

1. Among the literature on the evolution of inter-American relations, see Gordon Connell Smith, The Inter-American System (1966); Federico G. Gil, Latin American-United States Relations (1971); Jerome Levinson and Juan de Onis, The Alliance Which Lost Its Way ·(1971).

2. Arthur Whitaker, "Rio and Bogota: Panamerican Perspectives," Inter-American Economic Affairs, vol. 1, no. 3 (1947), p. 27.

3. Levinson and de Onis, The Alliance, p. 45.

4. When proposing the establishment of a new Far East development agency with the participation of this country, the U.S. President had accepted the possibility of establishing regional financing institutions. With respect to the background of the establishment of the IDB, see Felipe Herrera, General Opinions on the Inter American Bank: A Struggle Decade for Latin America (1970).

5. At a certain moment both developments seemed to converge; e.g., the proposal enunciated by Fidel Castro in the second session of the Committee of 21 to the effect that the United States should supply $30 billion over a period of ten years for financing Latin American development. However, these two lines of evolution were thereafter divided. After Buenos Aires, Fidel Castro was no longer present at any inter-American forum.

6. Richard Cooper, "Trade Policy Is Foreign Policy," Foreign Policy, no. 9 (Winter 1972-73).

7. See C. Fred Bergsten, Robert O. Keohane, and Joseph S. Nye, "International Economies and International Politics: A Framework for Analyses," International Organization, Winter 1975. See also C. Fred Bergsten, The Future of the International Economic Order: An Agenda for Research (1973).

8. For a more detailed approach to this question, see Luciano Tomassini, "Tendencias favorables y adversas a la formación de un Subsistema Regional Latinoamericano," Foro Internacional, vol. 15, no. 4 (1975).

9. Stephen D. Kasner, "Oil Is the Exception," Foreign Policy, no. 14 (Spring 1974).

10. See Luciano Tomassini, "Hacia nuevas formas de cooperación Latinoamericana," Comercio Exterior, April 1975.

11. Mahbub ul Hag, "Employment in the 1970's: A New Perspective" (Paper delivered at the 12th World Conference, May 1971).

12. Charles Meyer, "U.S. Policy toward Latin America: Where We Stand Today," Department of State Bulletin, November 15, 1971.

13. See Luigi Einaudi, "Latin America's Development and the United States," in Einaudi, ed., Beyond Cuba: Latin America Takes Charge of its Future (1974), p. 222.

14. U.S. Foreign Policy for the 1970s: The Emerging Structure of Peace, A Report to the Congress by Richard Nixon, February 9, 1972, p. 76.

15. Paul Sigmund, "The Invisible Blockade and the Overthrow of Allende," Foreign Affairs, vol. 52, 2 (January 1974).

16. U.S. Tariff Commission, Probable Effect of Tariff Preference for Developing Countries (1972); CEPAL, América Latina y la Estrategia Internacional de Desarrollo: Primera Evaluación Regional (1973), pt. 2, p. 13.

17. Herbert Goldhammer, "The Nonhemispheric Powers in Latin America," in Einaudi, Beyond Cuba, pp. 180-81.

18. CEPAL, América Latina, p. 66.

Transfer of Technology:
A Fortuitous Time Machine

César Peña Vigas
Translated by Lillian Morganti

Technology is bought and sold on the market like any other commodity; yet, the processes of its selection and optimum usage are determined in the same manner that children choose their playthings. In other words, technology as such is an apparently harmless economic commodity; but grafting it onto a milieu different from that of its origin is not nearly as harmless.

If by way of illustration one compares the transfer of technology from the developed to underdeveloped countries with the workings of a time machine, the phenomenon is more easily understood. When a new technology is implanted in a society more backward than that which generated it, a brusque leap toward the future apparently takes place, viewed from the historical perspective of the present.

One may then think that the society receiving the new technology is progressing in time. However, that new technology is actually being inserted into a relatively backwards milieu; consequently, it will not get the infrastructural support necessary to maintain it. Further, technology is essentially dynamic and is continually being renovated. When it does not receive the stimulus of innovation in its new medium, minor inconveniences will gradually occasion the diminution of its usage and it will fade out, under the aegis of obsolescence, even though it may still have some marginal utility.

In sum, it may be affirmed that the transfer of technology makes it possible for a backward country to progress toward the future in as many areas of human activity as its financial resources allow; but simultaneously, while the rest of the country unaffected by

the transfer process evolves toward its own future (in
most cases an evolution not centered about the acquired
technology), that fraction which has been invaded by
the new technology is delayed in time with regard to
the world centers where the technology originated.

This phenomenon creates a situation of chronological disorder within the country with different cultural
nuclei coexisting within its boundaries. These may be
visualized as distinct entities, some of which progress
with the passing of time, while others within the same
aggregate regress--if one takes the progress of the
country that generated their origin as a chronological
reference.

AGRARIAN REFORM IN THE TIME MACHINE

Agrarian reform in our own country, Venezuela,
illustrates the foregoing concepts. I shall isolate
three important factors in order to explain my theme:
production of fertilizers, agricultural machinery, and
the supply of water for irrigation.

Production of fertilizers by the domestic petro-
chemical industry began twenty years ago. At the end
of May 1975, the Minister of Mines admitted that the
Nitroven plant, designed to cover domestic demand as
well as to export ammonia and urea, was immersed in
a crisis of such proportions that it would have to be
placed in the hands of foreign management in order to
enable it, in the words of the minister himself, "to
start up properly." We have purchased advanced technologies for the production of fertilizers, but we have
been incapable of permanently supplying our country's
requirements at competitive prices. In addition, it is
evident that we have not even been able to handle maintenance requirements and improvement of the plants in
question.

And, in another aspect, our farmers have not been
educated and trained in the proper use of synthetic
fertilizers through an effective and sustained information program. In addition, local technology involving
the use of organic fertilizers--which originated in the
colonial era--has stagnated and is tending to die out.

As regards agricultural machinery, it has been
almost totally imported. Similarly, the maintenance
of this machinery can be classified as very deficient.
The best evidence of the poor quality of maintenance
are the machinery and tool junkyards scattered throughout our agricultural regions; it is also easy to verify
the lack of specialized mechanical workshops in the

areas where they are most needed. Further, there are
no valid indications that the maintenance of imported
machinery is about to improve appreciably, just as
there are no plans in sight for the design and local
construction of the machinery and implements required
by Venezuela to produce the foodstuffs it consumes.
Until now the only projects have been for the assembly
of tractors and implements. In short, we still do not
possess a farm machinery culture.

The supply of water for irrigation is perhaps the
most critical of the three factors. It is of enormous
importance due to the impracticability of importing
the water needed by our crops. Large irrigation works,
such as the Guarico and Majaguas dams and the Apure
dikes, have been built in our country. [Editor's note:
The Apure dikes, or módulos de Apure, are basically
a network of low dams designed to catch and contain the
large amounts of precipitation that fall during the
rainy season.] These two dams have been partially successful at a very high cost. The dike system promised
better results, since the investment and cost per irri-
gated hectare are relatively much lower. However, the
partial successes noted cannot hide the catastrophe inherent in the destruction of our natural water sources.
Numerous rivers have dried up, and we are on the way to
producing a great wasteland where once greenness and
fertility prevailed. It has not been possible to stop
the desert makers, the peasants who have cut down and
burned the vegetation over a good part of our territory.
The educational campaign efforts of the rural schools to
stem this destruction have been ineffective, and there
is no sign that the situation will change for the better.

THE LACK OF HARMONIOUS PROGRESS

A simultaneous analysis of the three factors
examined reveals that they are not progressing together
in harmony, nor is any single one of these factors advancing independently. As long as there are financial
resources, the purchase of agricultural machinery can
continue; but acquiring the machinery does not mean
that it is automatically accompanied by the water for
our crops or the people who will use the machinery
rationally. We have used the power of the machine to
destroy sources of water, without compensating for this
destruction with an increase in the production potential
of every hectare of land. Along with employment of the
machine and fertilizer technology, it was necessary to
create a network of local organizations that would encourage the efficient use of both and ensure economical
maintenance and domestically manufactured replacements
for the machinery. These local bodies would also see

to it that local, nonimportable factors favorable to agricultural production were kept up and improved.

The fortuitous nature of the time machine to which I have compared the transfer of technology becomes obvious when--in the particular case of technology associated with agricultural production--we realize that even though we have progressed in time through the acquisition of machinery and advanced processes, we have regressed with respect to the potential of our sources of water for irrigation and do not know with any degree of certainty just what our food supply situation will be during the next twenty-five years. Until now, we have proved only that we depend on oil revenues to acquire food abroad, whether directly or indirectly. Nevertheless, we know as little about the future of the fertilizer and machinery industries worldwide, as we do about the facilities for purchasing foodstuffs on world markets in the years ahead or about the future prices of those foodstuffs, which will probably continue to rise.

ORGANIZATIONAL TECHNOLOGY AND NATIONAL CHARACTER

There are other technological entities and artifacts not so clearly suited to commercial interchange. They are characterized essentially by their organizational nature and are consequently quite dependent on the human factor for their proper functioning and for attainment of their objectives. As an example, one can cite an agricultural information service. Such an organization is a technical artifact, but one without the characteristics of, say, a mail truck. The truck may be bought and sold from country to country without its usefulness being appreciably affected. The same norm cannot be applied to an agricultural information service, since its operation depends substantially on the country's national character.

As a notable example of this premise, we can select the information service that connects our farming communities, our technological development centers, and the Ministry of Agriculture and Cattle Raising, pointing out the difficulties it has had throughout its history in improving its services. Though precise historical data is unavailable, the users of this service do not have the slightest doubt about its notorious inefficiency. In the same vein, one can also note that there is no observable tendency toward improvement.

In order for such a service to improve progressively, it is probably not necessary to invest large sums of money, nor to bring in foreign technicians for consultation; rather, the fundamental requirement is to modify

the attitude of those responsible for the service with
respect to such important elements as (1) the value of
information as a means of communication within a technological culture, one that should not be subject to
the discretion of the functionaries manipulating it;
and (2) the value of time, an irrecoverable natural
resource, and the importance of punctuality as a prime
organizational factor in attaining effectiveness and
efficiency in enterprises of any kind.

The inefficient use of information and time that
have typified the agricultural information service will
not be able to change radically by the year 2000. This
is due in part to the need for parallel change in postal,
telephone, and similar services upon which it depends,
in part to other factors that I shall now examine.

EDUCATION, THE KEY TO REQUIRED HUMAN RESOURCES

At this point it is necessary to discuss a determining link: education. This factor will have the
greatest bearing on the image of the nation's technological future during the next twenty-five years.
The reasons pointing to this assertion are contained
in the preceding paragraphs. In brief, (1) the transfer of technology is not an effective remedy for developing a technological capacity sufficient and adequate to supply our particular needs; and (2) organizational technical artifacts are important to technological growth and should be generated within the country
itself, not imported.

Venezuelan investments center on the acquisition
of technological goods that will dot our landscape with
islands representing the technological future of more
advanced countries. We are committed to a race whose
ever advancing aim is to purchase "the latest in technological progress." A shift to thought along more
rational lines is not foreseeable. Gunnar Myrdal
confirms this in the following remarks on development:

> When it comes, however, to the technology
> implied in the industrial processes and em-
> bodied in the machines, which is what is
> usually meant by the transfer of technology,
> there is little choice but to take it all
> without much change. For one thing, a dif-
> ferent technology in this more fundamental
> sense would be likely to call for more tech-
> nological creativity than underdeveloped
> countries demand. The only capital equipment
> available, in any case, is what the developed
> countries are currently employing. That, along

with the problem of finding spare parts, explains why underdeveloped countries have not
equipped themselves with second-hand machinery
from earlier years of technological advance,
as some well-wishers have suggested they should.
What is more, entrepreneurs are reluctant to
accept "second best" equipment (Scientific
American, September 1974, p. 175).

A radical change in this tendency within the next
twenty-five years is clearly linked to governmental
phenomena and/or measures substantially affecting the
nation's economy. But also required are the human resources capable of implementing the necessary transfor-
mations; and these resources we do not have today, nor
do we possess the educational infrastructure that would
allow us to consider the possibility of developing these
resources in less than twenty-five years.

THE EDUCATIONAL SYSTEM AND THE PRODUCTIVE APPARATUS

When education meshes dynamically with the productive apparatus, it does so mainly as an innovative organizing force. The educational system becomes a ship
exploring the future and places the latter within the
reach of national progress. In addition, educational
progress harmoniously integrated into the plans of a
country dedicated to seeking a better future acts as an
agent of selection, for it places every individual in
the production sector where he will be most useful and
where his acquired and potential capacities will be of
the greatest value. An extraordinary example of this
harmony is reflected in "Agriculture in China," an
article by Sterling Wortjan in the June 1975 issue of
Scientific American.

Practically any diagnosis of the Venezuelan educational system underscores tendencies and characteristics
radically opposed to what is desirable. Among these
negative aspects of the system are the following:
1. It is not materially linked to the productive
   apparatus.
2. Lacking the means to promote innovation, it behaves
   like an organization engaged in teaching technological backwardness.
3. It is not an instrument for the selection and placement of the most competent in the work most suited
   to their demonstrated potential. The selection
   process is carried out with a marked tendency to
   channel students into higher education in fields
   of little importance to technological development.
4. There is an informal educational system, constituted
   mainly by the communications media, that has demon-

strated its effectiveness in orienting the population's consumer habits. This orientation plays a
determining role in the educational process of
young children.
5. The educational system has failed to teach values
    regarding the true importance of learning as a means
    to survival. The generalized habit of cheating is
    a notable indication of this phenomenon, which is
    also observable in the popularity of the pseudo-
    science successfully published in Venezuela.
6. Our educational organization has not built up an
    informative infrastructure for the spread of learn-
    ing. There are practically no libraries in the uni-
    versities, high schools, and elementary schools.
    Further, the country lacks important scientific
    publications.
7. The educational process, both formal and informal,
    fails to orient youth toward the formation of values
    such as that of time and its importance within the
    productive process. The Venezuelan's proverbial
    disregard for punctuality, regardless of his social
    status, is an important example. The time lost by
    our educational institutions, without any social
    penalty involved, also bears mentioning.

THE BASIC AIMS: CAN THEY BE ATTAINED?

     If to this gloomy picture we add the fact that no
plan to alter it exists, we may conclude that the nation
will not have the necessary human resources by the end
of the century to work toward attainment of the following aims:
1. To produce the food needed to sustain a rapidly
    growing population with its own resources;
2. To invest its fiscal resources rationally in order
    not to squander them in acquiring the "technological
    islands of the future" I have discussed;
3. To transform education into an institution that will
    inspire the technological innovation the country
    really requires; and
4. To turn basic institutions--such as the agricultural
    information service and the postal service--into
    functional entities.

     Regardless of the governmental administrations
under which we will live, it does not appear that the
features of our technology will be substantially modified during the next twenty-five to thirty years. The
national will looms up as a crucial factor if there is
to be a change in the destructive tendencies I have
analyzed so that the country might steer another course
in its production dynamics by the beginning of the next
century.

If we persist in our present tendency to acquire advanced technology, the operation of which is possible only on the basis of large subsidies, the future of Venezuela will be one of chaos and disequilibrium, a situation that could explode with any drop in income. Our productive apparatus could come to a stop in a very short time without the support of subsidies, and the country would see itself threatened on more flanks than it could effectively protect.

Argentina's Four Types of Inflation

Marcelo Diamand

In a series of papers published in Argentina, and in the book Doctrinas Económicas, Desarrollo e Independencia (Economic Doctrines, Development and Independence) I attributed the numerous failures of economic policies in Argentina and other primary exporting countries in advanced stages of industrialization to the divorce between the ideas that influence societies and the new economic reality of these countries.[1] The main characteristics of this new reality are the simultaneous existence of a primary sector that operates at international prices and an industrial sector operating far above international prices, a pattern that I have named an unbalanced productive structure. In the absence of industrial exports, this productive structure leads, as a natural tendency, to a chronic limitation of growth due to an insufficient supply of foreign exchange. Besides, the phenomenon gives rise to very peculiar secondary deformations within the economic system and to causal interrelationships very different from those existing in industrial countries (at least up to a few years ago), thus originating a new economic model, unknown to traditional theory. The purpose of this study is to analyze one of the most important derivations of this new model, namely the unusual nature of its inflationary processes.

Today the subject acquires importance for the industrialized countries. Because of spectacular new developments within the world economy, the traditional economic theory has lost its relevance when applied to their reality. In the first place, during the rapid growth of 1970-73 there appeared multiple bottlenecks in strategic supplies of primary goods and industrial raw materials. In the second place, the oil balance of payments deficits, which appeared in 1973, are provoking a widespread foreign exchange limitation. Both kinds of bottlenecks--external and internal--bring about effects

previously very little known to the industrialized
countries.

The structural inflation arising from the bottlenecks and coexisting with unemployment, the drop of real
wages, the spectacular increase of budget deficits--
phenomena up to this moment reserved to the underdeveloped world--lead today to worldwide controversy between
the defenders of recessive stabilization and defenders
of inflationary growth, very familiar to everybody that
lived through one of the International Monetary Fund
(IMF) stabilization plans. Therefore, a much better
understanding of the issues that are debated can be
gained from the analysis of developing economies.

THE DIFFERENT INFLATIONARY PROCESSES AND THE
DISTRIBUTION OF INCOME

Two kinds of inflation are commonly recognized in
economic literature. The first arises through increases
in the prices of goods or services resulting from excessive overall demand in relation to the supply capacity
of the productive system. The phenomenon is called
demand inflation.

The second type of inflation occurs as a result of
price increases arising from decisions or agreements regarding goods whose prices are set independently of the
market mechanism. The most important case is provided
by wage increases negotiated between unions and employers' representatives. Since price increases of this
kind are usually stimulated by costs, the phenomenon is
called cost-push inflation.

Besides these two types of inflations that today
present an economic problem in the industrialized world
and are accordingly amply discussed in the specialized
literature, there are two more that typify unbalanced
productive structures. Both originate--directly or
indirectly--in the tendency toward external disequilibria that characterize these structures. Both belong to
the family of structural inflations. The first is
brought about by bottlenecks in domestic supply. Very
often, and much before overall demand has reached the
point at which it outstrips overall supply capacity,
bottlenecks or constraints are created in the supply of
specific items, and excess demand raises the price of
the articles in short supply. The increase is propagated by way of production costs or by way of the cost
of living, giving rise to a compensatory wave of price
or wage increases that affect the rest of the economy.
An inflation of this nature, like demand inflation, has
its origin in an excess of demand over supply, but this

excess is restricted to a single product in short supply
or to a group of such products.

Inflationary phenomena of this nature up to a few
years ago were unknown in industrialized countries.
This fact was due not so much to the absence of bottlenecks in supply, which are found in all kinds of economies, as to the capacity of such countries to replace
the goods in short supply through imports, at least
until 1970-73. In this period the sustained growth
took place simultaneously in all industrialized countries, leaving no sources of available alternate supply
of scarce goods. The bottleneck-solving imports became
unavailable and worldwide structural inflation resulted.
In unbalanced productive structures, on the other hand,
the chronic shortage of foreign exchange makes it impossible to count on the surplus import capacity needed
to be able to use this method. Thereby, even inflations
arising from bottlenecks in domestic supply are an indirect consequence of constraints on the external sector
that prevent them from being solved by importing the
goods in short supply.

In practice, economists, politicians, and the
specialized media tend to confuse the different inflationary phenomena, merging them into a single one under
the common name of "inflation." This is tantamount to
lumping together several types of contagious diseases,
having different origin and calling for different
therapy, under the common name of "the fever." The
hypothetical properties of this fever are discussed,
as are its effects and the proper way to cure it, without noticing that the initial lumping of several phenomena into a single one renders the whole discussion
senseless.

This habit is often justified by saying that, in
fact, the only difference between the several inflationary phenomena is their origin and that once the spiral
is unleashed they become identical, regardless of their
original cause. This is totally false, since the different inflations are distinguished not only by their
origin, but also by the therapy they call for and by
the varying effect they have on income distribution and
the level of employment.

As regards therapy, the ultimate object of economic
analysis is to provide a guide for action. Hence arises
the importance of the diagnosis, since different diagnoses lead to different stabilizing policies. For this
reason it becomes absolutely necessary to differentiate
structural inflations--particularly exchange inflation--
from demand inflation. In the latter, the constraining
factor might be labor or capital, and it is entirely

genuine: it sets a limit to production that cannot be
overcome in the short run. The excess demand over this
limit is a real excess, and the only remedy that can
offset inflation is a reduction in demand.

In a structural inflation, constraint is exerted
on only one item and can always be overcome, or at least
alleviated, by economic policies. Even when it is not
possible immediately to expand production of the scarce
item, the degree of strangulation will depend on the way
this scarce item is used. But any effort to overcome
the scarcity must necessarily be preceded by awareness
of that scarcity's existence, and this awareness is
achieved only through knowing what started the inflation.

This is why the definition is so important. The
streams of ink that have flowed in the controversy between monetarists and structuralists owe their origin
to the philosophical discrepancy implicit in this problem of defining inflation.[2] For the monetarists, the
scarcity that a bottleneck involves is a fact of life,
and activity must adjust to it. Structuralists maintain
that the bottleneck is a variable that obeys economic
policies.

When monetarists use a definition that confuses
both kinds of inflations, they obstruct perception of
a supply bottleneck and, instead of applying specific
policies to correct it, proceed as with demand inflation:
reducing demand in an attempt to eliminate inflation.
In practice this is tantamount to reducing economic
activity to the level allowed by the supply of the
scarcest item, without anyone even bothering to find
out if the scarcity can be remedied.

The most common variety of structural inflation
arises directly from bottlenecks in the supply of
foreign exchange. The excess of specific demand for
foreign exchange relative to its supply renders necessary a devaluation. This generates a general wave of
cost and price increases that spreads to the rest of
the productive system. Since phenomena of this kind
have their origin in a bottleneck in one of the supply
items, inflations of this type--which I shall refer to
as foreign exchange inflations--also constitute a special case of structural inflation. Nevertheless, the
frequency with which they occur in countries of unbalanced productive structure, their complexity, and
the impossibility of understanding them within the conceptual framework provided by traditional economic
theory call for an especially profound analysis of the
subject and justify in this case a separate classification.

Each of the four types of inflation mentioned is characterized by a different income distribution pattern. In demand inflation, the first to increase are domestic prices, and this implies greater entrepreneurial profits, as long as costs remain constant. In the case of cost-push inflation, if the principal impulse is provided by wage increases (the usual cause), it is the wage-earning sector that comes out on top of the others in respect of the distribution of income. In a structural inflation arising from a bottleneck in domestic supply, the advantage goes to the producers of whatever goods are in short supply. Last, in a foreign exchange inflation, the greatest share of income goes to the exporting sector, which in Argentina means the farm sector.

In each of these cases the sector that obtains the increase appropriates a larger share of the national income at the expense of the others. Should the government managing the instruments of economic policy and the acquiescence of other sectors permit it, the system reaches a new state of equilibrium marked by a permanent redistribution of income favoring the sector that took the lead.

On the other hand, if, as usually happens, the other sectors refuse to accept a smaller share of the income and take steps--directly or through pressure on the governments--to recover their position, they set in motion a series of linked price increases that progressively involve the remaining price determinants until an entire inflationary spiral is completed. In this case the increases in nonagricultural prices, in wages, and in the exchange rate follow each other cyclically. But if the original cause persists, then as the inflationary spiral closes, the sector that had first benefited once more takes the lead, thereby dynamically retaining its initial relative advantage.

The difference between the several types of inflation is not limited to their effect on the distribution of incomes, but is also evidenced by their impact on the level of employment. Demand inflation always brings about an increase in economic activity. The inflationary mechanism that operates in cost-push inflation is independent of demand, and the phenomenon is compatible with both full employment or a recession, according to the monetary and fiscal policy that accompanies it. Last, the structural inflations--originating either in bottlenecks in domestic supply or in the supply of foreign exchange--are essentially recessionary, even if they are accompanied by expansive monetary and fiscal policies.

We see, accordingly, that the effect of inflation
is asymmetric. In inflations that do not affect full
employment, the situation of the penalized sectors is
compensated for by the boom in the economy. On the
other hand, in those that bring about a decline in
activity, the fate of those penalized is doubly adverse
since they lose their percentage share of the income
while there is also a fall in the total income generated.
In other words, they are not only served a smaller share
of the cake, but the cake itself is not as big as it
used to be.

A policy that seeks to attain stability without
affecting the level of internal activity should differ
according to whether the price increases are due to
excess demand, to wage pressure, to price increases
in specific items of domestic production, or to a
monetary devaluation rendered necessary by external
disequilibrium.

DEMAND INFLATION

As its name suggests, this type of inflation is
brought about when overall demand for goods and services exceeds what can be supplied by productive capacity fully employed. The reasons for excess demand may
lie in a change of the population's habits that gives
rise to a fall in the customary level of savings, a
strong investment boom, an improvement in international
prices for the country's exports, or, most frequently,
a monetary expansion. The characteristics of demand
inflation are overabundance of purchasing power relative
to overall supply, the total mobilization of the available producing capacity, an increase in the level of
production, sales, and transactions--that is to say,
the well-known inflationary boom.

Although it may seem quite obvious, the existing
state of confusion makes it necessary to insist that
for demand inflation to occur, a true situation of
excessive demand must indeed exist, observable in
reality and characterized by a sellers' market.

Demand inflation never originates in fiscal deficits or monetary issue as such. It occurs only when
the increased demand arising as a consequence is of
such magnitude that it exceeds the supply capacity of
the productive system. If this supply capacity is not
fully occupied and there are idle resources available,
the new demand gives rise to an automatic increase in
production and in the corresponding supply, without
causing inflation. Thus it is that in a recession,
when resources are insufficiently employed, the fiscal

deficit and monetary expansion increase demand, but
without outstripping supply capacity. Accordingly,
instead of bringing about inflation, they represent
the correct mechanism for reactivating the economy.

The expansion of production through monetary in-
jection and fiscal deficit is possible only when there
are idle resources. If an attempt is made to force expansion once productive capacity has been fully mobilized, the new increments of demand that are created do
not encounter corresponding increments of supply and begin to compete for the goods and services that are already booked. The result is an excess of overall demand
in relation to supply, which gives rise to higher prices,
in other words, to demand inflation.

Once demand inflation has set in (assuming that
wages and the exchange rate do not vary at the outset),
the increase in prices generates increased profits in
those sectors that produce for the home market. In this
way demand inflation in Argentina provokes a transfer of
income in favor of nonagricultural entrepreneurs at the
expense of wage-earners--although their disadvantage is
to a great extent neutralized by the boom in the economy[3]--and also of the exporting sector, whose prices
are established by the rate of exchange.

When these two sectors lose their relative share
of the total income, they try to recover it, the former
by means of a nominal increase in wages and the latter
by means of a devaluation tending to reestablish the
former parity. Once wages have been raised and the
exchange rate readjusted, the first turn of the inflationary spiral closes. If prices increase once more
during the time that the original excess demand continues to operate--through the fiscal deficit or credit
expansion--then the entrepreneurial profits of sectors
working for the home market once more increase, and
a new cycle of inflation commences.

It is highly desirable to dispel an idea that is
very widely held in Argentina, according to which it
is possible to create money without inflationary consequences, provided that this money is devoted to
capitalizing the country.

According to this outlook, there would appear to be
a "good" kind of monetary expansion devoted to investment and a "bad" kind devoted to consumption. This sub-
division is fictitious. Demand inflation occurs or
fails to occur independently of the productive or un-
productive character of the expenditure that gives rise
to it. Even when the excess demand arises from investment goods, those goods need time in which to mature

before they contribute to augment productive capacity.
In the meantime, the additional demand generated by
their production exercises an immediate pressure on
supply.

Even though the inflation caused by the growth in
investment may be justified in terms of the growth in
long-term productive capacity that it renders possible,
its short-term effects will be exactly the same as if
the inflation had been provoked by excessive consumption.

COST-PUSH INFLATION

Cost-push inflation may be regarded as the converse
of demand inflation, since it originates in cost increases arrived at by decisions made independently of
the market mechanism. To this category belong the inflations that are afflicting industrial countries to an
ever increasing extent. The most common case, typical
of most countries with powerful trade unions, is that
provided by inflations triggered by wage increases. In
an industrial society wages are ruled not by market mechanisms, but by joint bargaining between the workers'
unions and the employers or their associations or,
occasionally, by government decision. Although the
bargaining positions of the parties involved may be
influenced by market conditions, this influence is
rather indirect.

When the wage increases exceed what the employers
can absorb or consider to be reasonable, they are passed
on, thereby creating a rise in the general level of
prices and setting off an inflationary process. In this
case the motive for inflation is not increased demand,
but increased costs brought about by the wage increment.
The increase in prices takes place as a consequence.
Sooner or later, as occurs with demand inflation, the
exchange rate must also go up in order to restore parity
and to avoid disequilibrium in the balance of payments.

The difference between a demand inflation and a
cost-push inflation is that the former is set off by
excess demand and entrepreneurial profits precede wages,
while in the second case the motive force is the wage
increase and higher earnings for the workers precede
profits.

As in demand inflation, we can here find three
kinds of increases: of wages, of nonagricultural profits, and of the exchange rate. Nevertheless, the
sequence differs, since wages take precedence at the
expense of the other sectors.

When the phenomenon is of recent origin, the type
of inflation may be identified by ascertaining which of
these three price determinants is advancing in relation
to the others. But when the inflation began long ago,
it becomes hard to decide how the process was generated,
since the phenomenon, once unleashed, manifests itself
as an ascending spiral in which each of the several
sectors struggles in turn to obtain the upper hand.
The increment for each sector is justified by the increment accorded to the previous sector and, in its
turn, is the justification of the subsequent increment.

In practice it is easy to distinguish between the
two phenomena by watching the level of employment. In
demand inflation the market is entirely a sellers' one
and the productive system is working at full stretch,
so full employment exists in its most extreme form,
a situation synonymous with the familiar inflationary
boom. On the other hand, with cost-push inflation,
demand does not succeed in drawing ahead of supply
capacity; cases may even occur in which prices rise
in the midst of a recession.

In Argentina the cost-push inflation of the wage-
increase variety is typical of the periods subsequent
to devaluations that have been rendered necessary by
external disequilibria. These devaluations, which will
be examined in greater detail later on, are always
characterized by the fact that the exchange rate gets
ahead of costs and gives rise to a transfer of income
from the wage-earning and the nonagricultural entrepreneurial sectors to the rural landowning and the
financial sectors, accompanied by a recession. Later,
as the economy reactivates, the workers begin the recovery of their share of total income by means of successive nominal wage increases. The process is characterized by a gradual decline in the ratio of the exchange rate to domestic costs. Farm prices rise less
than wages, and, because of this, there is a tendency
to return to the income distribution pattern ruling
prior to the devaluation. That means that as a result
of cost-push inflation, a progressive redistribution
takes place that cancels out the regressive redistribution caused by the devaluation.

Another type of inflationary mechanism that can
drive up costs is provided by the monopolistic increases
applied by certain enterprises--fundamentally, those
producing raw materials or semifinished goods for which
demand is very inelastic, being established by the
volume of output of the stages that they supply.

The problem of monopolistic increases is especially
grave in unbalanced productive structures. Due to the

cushion of protection--difficult to lower if it is desired to avoid an excessive outflow of exchange, which
would be even more dangerous--price control exercised
through imports is less effective than is usually the
case in industrialized countries.

STRUCTURAL INFLATION ARISING FROM BOTTLENECKS IN
DOMESTIC SUPPLY

A clear division between underemployment and full
employment of resources is a simplification; some fields
of activity always become saturated before others. Before full employment is attained, bottlenecks begin to
appear in the productive capacity. If lack of foreign
exchange makes it impossible to overcome this insufficient supply through importation, these bottlenecks
generate price increases in the scarce goods.

When there is productive capacity for these goods
that can be promptly mobilized or when demand falls off
rapidly with higher prices, a small price increase suf-
fices to balance the market. If, on the other hand,
slow-maturing investments are needed to augment supply
and if the inelasticity of supply happens to coincide
with a demand that is also inelastic, a considerable
growth of prices may be required in order to reestablish
market equilibrium. The consequence is an inflationary
pressure throughout the whole productive structure and
a redistribution of income favoring the sector that produces the scarce goods.[4]

In order to analyze this phenomenon, I will take
the concrete and very typical example of beef in Argentina. Supply depends, to a large extent, on the cattle
stock and not only does not increase promptly when
prices rise, but may even decline.[5] Farmers react to
higher prices by building up their herds. They accordingly retain more breeding cows and so reduce the supply for immediate consumption.[6]

In order to bring the market into equilibrium,
then, a reduction of demand is unavoidable. If problems
in the foreign sector rule out the possibility of sacri-
ficing exports--which would be equivalent to making up
for the shortage of other products by way of imports--
the entire burden of the adjustment must be borne by
domestic consumption. The prices begin to rise and
continue to do so as long as the population holds out
against a reduction of its habitual consumption. But
however rigid consumer habits may be, a price is finally
reached that is high enough for them to yield and cut
back their demand to the level of supply.

The price increase required to attain this balancing effect brings about a marked transfer of income in
favor of the livestock-breeding sector, fundamentally
at the expense of the wage-earners' purchasing power.
Mass consumption of goods and services declines, with
recessionary effects for the industrial, commercial,
and service sectors.

At this point there are two options. One is to
attempt to compensate the transfer of income by means
of wage increases. But the frustrating aspect of structural inflationary phenomena is that the regressive
transfers of income that they provoke are not so easily
compensated for. When the cause of the inflationary
process is the physical insufficiency of a certain
product, the regressive distribution of income is a
mechanism by which the market reduces demand so as to
adjust it to this shortage.

Unless direct measures are also taken simultaneously against the bottleneck, the rise in wages increases
the demand for beef and once more throws the market off
balance. This brings about a new growth in the price
of beef, which continues to go up until demand once
again falls off. Thereby, through the agency of a complete inflationary spiral, the regressionary redistribution of income needed to maintain market equilibrium is
restored. Another alternative is to freeze the new distribution of incomes by applying direct government measures or monetary restrictions in such a way as to prevent wages from returning to the level they had lost.
Even supposing that such a procedure were politically
practicable and setting aside social considerations,
we would find its recessionary consequences to be
unacceptable from a purely economic standpoint.

Accordingly, in structural inflations the only
solution that permits a return to the prior distribution
of income requires direct action upon the bottleneck.
In the long term, this means measures capable of stimulating supply and, for emergencies, measures of direct
restriction of demand to replace the reduction of demand
brought about, in the case of an inflationary spiral, by
market forces through the agency of prices.

INFLATION ARISING FROM EXTERNAL BOTTLENECKS OR
FOREIGN EXCHANGE INFLATION

Among the numerous bottlenecks that may develop in
supply, the most important is the one that occurs in the
foreign exchange sector. On the one hand, insufficiency
of foreign exchange may paralyze domestic production of
far greater value. On the other hand, a constraint of

this type may prevent the solution of all other bottlenecks in domestic supply.

External bottlenecks may appear following a process
of domestic inflation--demand, cost-push, or structural--
if the rate of exchange does not keep pace with costs,
as often occurs. This lag encourages imports (although
in unbalanced productive structures its effect is atten-
uated by the protection schemes) and, ultimately, dis-
courages export production.

International experience (before the oil balance of
payments problems) gives rise to an automatic identification of external disequilibria with domestic inflation.
Hence, one of the central premises of the theoretical
models that commonly guide economic policy in unbalanced
productive structures is that their external disequilibria are always a consequence of prior domestic inflations.

This premise is erroneous on two counts: even when
the phenomenon described does in fact occur, it is not
domestic inflation, as such, that is responsible for external disequilibrium, but the government's tendency to
hold the exchange rate behind the growth of domestic
costs. If governments had sufficient foresight to avoid
this delay and to raise the exchange rate in accordance
with domestic inflation, the impact on the foreign sector would be to a great extent counteracted and the
negative incidence of demand inflation upon the balance
of payments would be neutralized.[7]

But the principal error of the traditional model
is that it does not take account of the fact that in
unbalanced productive structures a type of external
bottleneck occurs that is independent of the existence
of prior domestic inflation or of an eventual lag of
the exchange rate behind rising costs. The appearance
of this second type of external imbalance implies such
extensive changes in theoretical premises as to render
necessary the modification of the whole model to be
applied.[8]

In unbalanced productive structures, the sector
that is growing most rapidly--the industrial sector--
practically does not export at all. The export capacity
is fundamentally dependent upon the primary sector,
which, due to limitations of world demand or domestic
supply, never grows at the same rate as the industrial
sector. Accordingly, economic development brings about
a growth of domestic production calling for an ever
increasing need of foreign exchange, without providing
the means to generate it. The capacity to produce
foreign exchange lags chronically behind the growth

of the domestic productive structure, giving rise to a permanent tendency toward disequilibria in the balance of payment.

This kind of chronic imbalance, up to the birth of the oil problem, was unknown in industrial countries, because their domestic production is almost all potentially exportable, and thus its growth brings about a parallel growth in the capacity to generate foreign exchange.

When external disequilibrium brought about by the divergence between imports and exports makes a devaluation inevitable, this gives rise to a wave of increases in costs and prices that leads to foreign exchange inflation. Thereby the traditional relationship between cause and effect is reversed: the external disequilibrium, instead of being a consequence of inflation, now appears as its cause.[9]

The intensity usually attained by foreign exchange inflations is due to the aforementioned rigidity in the supply and demand of foreign exchange. Primary exports respond sluggishly to increases in the exchange rate, due to limitations in world demand or constraints on production. On the other hand, owing to their high prices, most industrial products are not exportable at any reasonable exchange rate. Finally, the import products either are essential for the operation of the economy or, if not, benefit from tariff exemptions or defects in the protection schemes. This means that discouraging imports by means of devaluation is very difficult indeed.

Once a disequilibrium has been produced in the exchange market and once the regulatory capacity of the central bank has been exhausted, the price of foreign exchange begins to rise in search of the equilibrium between supply and demand. But since exports do not increase and--if we limit our analysis to the direct price effect of the devaluation--imports do not decrease either, no effect appears that is capable of bringing the market into equilibrium. The exchange rate continues to rise. Finally, the exchange rate becomes high enough to provoke a recession, thereby indirectly bringing about external balance through a general decline in the level of activity and a consequent reduction in the need for imports.

The recession is caused by the increase in domestic prices that accompanies devaluation. The elevation of the exchange rate leads to an increase in the cost of all imported goods that is transmitted to the prices of industrial goods and services. At the same time, the

increase in export prices, when expressed in local
currency, induces an increase in these same prices on
the domestic market, which in Argentina's case is reflected in a rise in the prices of foodstuffs. In this
way the devaluation brings about a transfer of income
in favor of the farm sector. The victims are the nonagricultural entrepreneurial sector, whose costs go up,
and wage-earners, who see their real income diminish.
In the first instance incentives for investment are
affected; in the second, the demand for mass-consumption
industrial goods and services declines.[10]

When prices increase, with the same nominal amount
of money in circulation, there is a reduction in the
real quantity of money available for transactions. As
a consequence the volume of bank credits is, in real
terms, also sharply reduced. Firms find themselves
without the money needed to operate and the demand for
money grows, bringing about an increase in the rate of
interest ruling on the extrabanking market. This effect,
in its turn, gives rise to a transfer of income in favor
of the financial sector. Monetary illiquidity follows,
and investments decrease even more.

The fall in investment and consumption brings about
a reduction in overall demand. Idle productive capacity
appears together with unemployment, so that--with new
reductions in investment and consumption--the recessionary phenomenon is aggravated. The level of internal
activity declines, there is a reduction in the volume
of imports that the country requires, and external
equilibrium is recovered.[11] Thus, the recession is
converted into a balancing mechanism through which the
market reacts to a bottleneck in the supply of foreign
exchange. The devaluation and corresponding increase
in prices advance just far enough to bring about a decline in activity sufficient to restore the equilibrium
in the external sector of the economy.

Devaluations of this kind should not be confused
with those which take place subsequent to domestic inflations and whose object it is to restore the usual
share of income and incentives to the exporting sector.
In the case now under consideration, the devaluation is
independent of the relationship between exchange rate
and domestic costs. The price of foreign exchange is
driven upwards because the central bank loses control
of the quotation. Instead of remaining fixed at a level
corresponding to the prices and costs of the farm sector,
the exchange rate continues to increase until it reaches
a higher level, one that is sufficient to bring about
a recession and thereby to lower demand for exchange
down to the level of its supply. This balancing mechanism of the foreign sector is associated with an abrupt

increase in the incomes of the farm sector, which rise
beyond their usual values.

Attempts to correct this type of recession by means
of the habitual expansive measures are self-defeating.
If means of payment are expanded or a deliberate budgetary deficit is incurred without eliminating the restriction in the foreign sector, then consumption and investment are increased and the level of internal activity
once more begins to grow. As unemployment declines,
the pressure against wage increases weakens. Wages begin to regain their former level, so that there is once
again a more progressive redistribution of income. Demand increases even further, together with the need for
imports. The balance between supply and demand for
foreign exchange reached as a result of the recession
disappears again, thereby calling for a new devaluation.
Thus the cycle of foreign exchange inflation is completed. Once more costs and prices go up, a new decline
in real wages occurs, monetary illiquidity reappears at
a new level of prices, and another recessionary effect
is induced, thereby neutralizing the expansion that
took place.

Having already analyzed the difference between demand inflation and cost inflation, let us now see how
these two differ from foreign exchange inflation. I
shall begin with demand inflation. Its similarity to
foreign exchange inflation lies in the fact that in both
cases the phenomenon is a reaction to the excess of demand over supply. The difference is that in demand inflation this excess is produced in relation to the
available productive capacity setting the maximum limit
that may be attained in the short run by the country's
production. Accordingly, in this case, there is a
genuine disequilibrium of demand with respect to the
possibilities of overall supply.

In the case of foreign exchange inflation, as in
all structural inflations, the excess of demand is produced in relation to the supply of a specific item--
foreign exchange--the availability of which does not
attain the level required by a fully mobilized productive
capacity.

The first case is comparable to that of a long
highway capable of carrying a certain volume of traffic.
If we try to accommodate traffic beyond this limit, disturbances and jams will occur along the highway. In
contrast, the second case resembles a wide highway with
sufficient capacity to accommodate the traffic, but with
a narrow bridge where vehicles get held up. Here the
disturbance is produced at a single point and is sub-

sequently pushed back along the highway; the volume that the bottleneck lets through limits the traffic behind.

In a foreign exchange inflation, the causal sequence is inverted with respect to demand inflation. First of all, the external imbalance is produced and the exchange rate goes up, generally in advance of domestic prices. Thereby a transfer of income is produced in favor of the farm sector and at the expense of nonfarm entrepreneurial profits and wages. Subsequently, prices go up, so that the incomes of nonfarm entrepreneurs partially regain their former position. The last link in the chain is an increase in the wages that seek to regain the level they had lost. But since the initial external disequilibrium is not eliminated, the exchange rate once more goes up, and the farm sector retains its advantage.

Here, once more, a diagnosis of the type of inflation based on which sectors gained an advantage and which lost in the income distribution would be very subjective, depending upon the moment chosen as a point of reference. A much more objective index would be the level of activity.

Demand inflation can be visualized as a mechanism wherein the monetary roof "pulls" a productive structure upwards and the floor is provided by prices and costs. As long as the structure responds elastically, expanding in response to the stimulation, prices do not move. Once elasticity is lost as a result of full employment being reached, the movement of the roof is transferred to the prices, at which moment demand inflation commences.

In foreign exchange inflation everything takes place as though the productive system were pushed from below by the increased price of foreign exchange and came up against a monetary roof that resisted this pressure. The increase in prices is halted, but at the cost of "compressing" the productive structure until a recession is brought about. The compression is not alleviated by purely expansive measures. The floor is pushed upwards by the reaction of the exchange market to an insufficiency of supply. If, in order to lighten the compression, the roof is displaced upwards, the floor will immediately rise, maintaining the same degree of this compression.

If we now proceed to compare foreign exchange inflation and cost-push inflation, we will find that the resemblance lies in the fact that the latter can also be accompanied by a recession. The difference is that in an exchange inflation, whether through exhaustion of

exchange reserves or through the imminent danger of
a run on the exchange market, the central bank abandons
its regulatory action and the recession is a consequence
of the external problem. In cost inflation, on the
other hand, the central bank retains its power to regulate the rate of exchange in accordance with the development needs of the exporting sector. Even supposing
that a recession takes place, it is due to purely
monetary causes and may be corrected by internal ex-
pansionary measures.[12]

Returning to our metaphor, here we once again face
the movement of the floor that compresses the productive
structure against a monetary roof. But in this case the
movement of the floor can be stopped or delayed at will.
And even when this is not possible, the reaction is much
slower: in the case of wage agreements it can be delayed for a year. Accordingly, when the roof is lifted,
the floor does not necessarily follow--at least not
immediately--and the compression is eliminated.

Exchange inflation, owing to its direct and indirect effects, probably constitutes the most important
source of inflationary phenomena in unbalanced productive structures. Its periodical explosions, in their
turn, release compensatory periods of cost-push inflation, during which wages seek to regain the position
they had lost during the devaluation. This, together
with less intense but more permanent phenomena of
price increases derived from internal bottlenecks,
makes inflation seem habitual. Inflationary expectations aggravate the process and on some occasions themselves provoke it.

STABILIZATION POLICIES IN THE FACE OF DEMAND AND
COST-PUSH INFLATION

Traditional stabilization measures consist in
monetary restriction and especially in action designed
to eliminate budget deficits. This procedure is appropriate when the inflation is indeed one of demand.
But when excess demand does not exist, the measures
designed to reduce it amount to a usually fruitless
attempt to suppress inflationary focuses of another
kind through the agency of a recession.

First let us look at the case of a cost-push inflation, impelled by wage increases. To operate against
these increases by way of a reduction in demand implies
the use of unemployment to check the growth of wages.
Even supposing the procedure to be effective, the cure
would be worse than the disease. Since it is not even

effective, it implies imposing a useless and ridiculous sacrifice upon the country.

Experience shows that the trade unions secure wage increases with a certain independence of the climate of demand, and even in the midst of severe recessions. The employers' attitude toward union demands, although it partially depends on the level of employment, is also determined by other factors--fundamentally, the alternative cost of a possible strike, fear of the violence that this could entail, and, at times, a private conviction that the workers' demands are justified. Furthermore, a moderate depression does not affect all employers to the same extent. Different activities are constricted in different ways. Even within the same activity, producers of articles in short supply are much more concerned about avoiding an interruption of output by strike than about avoiding an increase in wages, and if their influence is strong enough, they will carry with them the remainder of the sector that they represent. Similar considerations may apply in respect to increases affecting monopolistic enterprises that meet an inelastic demand for their products and whose decisions are little affected by the decline in overall demand.

In order to apply a real brake on increases-- whether of wages or prices--through the agency of a recession, the latter would have to be great enough to provoke a regular catastrophe, which would not only be socially and politically unacceptable, but would not even provide a solution from a purely economic standpoint.

We have already seen that any increase in costs always affects the real amount of money in circulation. In order to maintain monetary liquidity without affecting demand, it is necessary to expand the means of payment in step with the increased prices. The usual mechanism for expansion is the budget deficit, brought about by the inflationary phenomenon itself. Whereas fiscal expenditure is effected at current prices, revenue is collected largely on the basis of the prices ruling during the previous period. As a result, cost-push inflation almost always leads to an unbalanced budget. In this case the deficit is not the cause of the inflation, but its effect.

The monetary issue needed to cover this deficit represents one of the possible ways of restoring the liquidity and demand that would otherwise be reduced as a result of cost-push inflation. This issue represents a compensatory tax covering the difference between what the private sector would have had to pay in taxation,

had stability been maintained, and the taxation that
was in fact paid and, although nominally unchanged, was
in fact lower in real terms as a consequence of the loss
of value of the currency.

When a government decides to check cost-push inflation by means of restrictive monetary policies, it is
enough for it to refuse to "recognize" the inflation
and not alter the volume of money in circulation, thus
permitting illiquidity to occur.   In order to do this,
it must refrain from financing the budget deficit by
means of monetary issue.   Nevertheless, the reduction
in economic activity that takes place brings about a
marked decline in revenue collection, even further
aggravating the original budget deficit and trapping
the treasury in a vicious circle.   Since the productive
activity is in recession, it cannot support heavier
taxation; the only remaining way out is monetary issue.
Thus it is that, in practice, the decision to maintain
monetary restriction always comes to grief against the
realities of a budget deficit that is provoked or aggravated by those same restrictive policies.

Since the failure of stabilization attempted by
the application of restrictive measures to cost-push
inflation by Nixon at the end of the 1960s, it became
increasingly clear to academic circles that at present
many prices are set not by the market, but by decision
mechanisms that can be counteracted only by other decision mechanisms.[13]

STABILIZATION POLICIES IN THE FACE OF STRUCTURAL
INFLATION

Once again, the traditional reaction to inflations
of structural origin is to confuse them with demand inflations and to apply restrictive monetary measures.
The real significance of this policy is twofold.   On the
one hand, as a result of the direct recessionary effect,
they give rise to a slump in the level of employment and
overall demand and thus lighten the specific pressure
of demand upon the bottleneck in supply.   On the other
hand, the same recessionary effect helps to maintain
the regressive redistribution of income that is the
other instrument for reducing demand.

These effects are avoided by means of a concentrated action against the bottlenecks in supply.   The long-
term policy must keep incentives stable in such a way
as to provide a timely encouragement of investments in
the potentially dangerous items and suppress these bottlenecks before they actually appear.   The need to prevent these increased incentives from implying a transfer

of income that would be unacceptable for the country
may call for more imaginative policies than a mere
price increase. It may be shown, for example, that
a combination of price increases, subsidies, taxes,
and exchange policies allows incentives for increased
farm production without giving rise to massive transfers
of income in favor of that sector.

The short-term treatment of bottlenecks depends
upon the situation of the foreign sector, because, if
there should be a surplus of foreign exchange, any constraint in supply can be immediately eliminated. If
this surplus is not available, there is no other resource in case of emergency than to ration demand
directly--in the case of beef by temporary bans on
consumption, or by rationing in the case of other
critical items--which constitutes the only procedure
capable of replacing the reduction in demand effected
by the market through price increases and regressive income distribution. But even in this case we must not
lose sight of long-term objectives. The existence of
a bottleneck demonstrates that the incentives for production hitherto in force are insufficient and should
be increased. Accordingly, the missing incentives must
be provided by other means or the direct restriction of
demand must be graduated so as to permit a certain increase in price that will leave enough margin to encourage investment.

The approach that calls for structural inflation
to be fought by means of unemployment is of special importance, because the ideology underlying it is shared--
explicitly or implicitly--by the greater part of the
Argentine governing class, by informed opinion at home
and abroad, and by the academic world in general.

The most important example of a restrictive policy
applied for the purpose of checking an inflation arising
from bottlenecks is that provided by the famous stabilization plans of the IMF, which are customarily applied
when a country has lost its currency reserves and appeals
to that body for help. The plans in question generally
commence with the abolition of controls over the transfer of foreign exchange, with a certain liberalization
of imports, and with devaluation. At the same time,
intense monetary restriction is imposed, reducing the
volume of banking credit and strictly limiting the budget deficit. Issue of new money, save for a very small
margin, is permitted only when supported by holdings of
gold or foreign exchange, so that the growth of the means
of payment becomes strictly linked to the volume of the
central bank reserves. The purpose of the restrictive
monetary measures is to maintain overall demand below
full employment, at a level compatible with the bottle-

neck in the provision of foreign exchange. In the words
of Constanzo, a former high official of the fund: "Any
effect on the balance of payments must be absorbed by
the use of international reserves. In their absence,
an anti-inflationary policy would be called for, that
is to say, credit and money in circulation would have
to be reduced in order to curtail the demand for imports
to the level of the income derived from exports."[14]

The obsessive insistence of stabilization plans on
balanced budgets and restricted banking credit does not
arise from a fear of the direct inflationary effect upon
domestic prices. If the country is in recession, with
idle resources, the monetary issue and credit expansion
will not be inflationary and will even be desirable as
a means of reactivation.

The limitation of issue and credit expansion are
due precisely to the desire to avoid reactivation. Any
of the expansive procedures would annul the mechanism
of monetary restriction that maintains activity at a
level below full employment. As a consequence, activity
will increase to a level at which, though perfectly acceptable from the standpoint of productive capacity, it
would be above the level that can be met by the bottleneck in the external sector. Accordingly, neither the
budget deficit nor the credit expansion would be inflationary through increasing demand to a level that,
though inferior to productive capacity, would exceed
what is permissible from the point of view of the availability of foreign exchange. That is to say, they would
be the cause of a foreign exchange inflation.

Even at the risk of seeming tedious let me once more
summarize the concepts. When a bottleneck in the supply
of foreign exchange occurs, only one of the two things
can happen: either the bottleneck is eliminated, or all
internal activity must necessarily slump and adjust itself to what the bottleneck allows.

In industrialized countries both exports and import
substitution react to an increase in the exchange rate.
This means that the market mechanism (the devaluation
arising from an imbalance between supply and demand) is
capable of overcoming the bottleneck in the external
factor. But in countries with unbalanced productive
structures, the incentives provided by devaluation
operate in a very weak manner. If the weight of the
adjustment of the external sector is allowed to rest
on the forces of the market, which are incapable of
eliminating the bottleneck, these operate in the only
direction that remains open to them by reducing the
level of activity.

According to the monetary policy adopted, the balancing recession of the foreign sector can be brought about only in one of two ways. If monetary circulation is not restricted, the progress of devaluation and of the foreign exchange inflation is automatically left untouched. Costs and prices draw dynamically ahead of the volume of money, and illiquidity persists despite the injections of new money (the movement of the floor always precedes the movement of the roof). Furthermore, also dynamically, the exchange rate maintains its lead over wages and regressive distribution of income. These phenomena keep the economy in a state of recession.

An alternative recessionary mechanism is monetary restriction. When the external disequilibrium is not very intense, this may entirely replace devaluation, as occurred in Argentina in 1969, when economic expansion was curtailed. Its effect is most insidious, since it tends to disguise the insufficient supply of foreign exchange or, in other words, the real nature of the problem.

Normally a combination of the two measures is employed--devaluation followed by restrictive monetary policy, as was the case in 1962. The more severe the monetary restriction, the less devaluation will be necessary in order to attain the same reduction in activities and in the demand for foreign exchange arising therefrom.[15]

The usual criticism of IMF-style stabilization is aimed at the recessionary effects of the policy. This attack--such as it is usually called--would be applicable to the restrictive treatment of cost-push inflation, where a more direct option exists between recession and reactivation. But it cannot be considered the most appropriate formulation in the case of foreign exchange inflation. Here the recession rises from a bottleneck in the foreign sector, and if there were really no way to overcome it, it would be inevitable with or without monetary restriction.

The fundamental error of traditional stabilization plans does not consist in a false option between monetary expansion and nonexpansion, but in the false presentation of the option as such, which distracts public attention from the real problem.

THE CONFUSION OF CONCEPTS INTRODUCED BY THE IMF TYPE OF INFLATION

The absence of industrial exports and--in the special case of Argentina--the inelasticity in the supply

of farm products, which have the effect of limiting
growth through the creation of external bottlenecks,
are not due to economic characteristics inherent in
unbalanced productive structures as such. On the contrary, they derive from the fact that the instruments
of economic policy employed are not adjusted to these
characteristics. The unbalanced productive structure
represents a new phenomenon. The countries in which
circumstances have brought it into existence are still
unaware of the intellectual implications of the new
model they have created. In its presence they continue
to operate with ideas and economic instrumentation
copied from industrialized countries. It is this maladjustment of ideas and instruments to the new reality
and not the new reality as such that must be blamed for
the limitation in growth arising from the bottleneck in
the external sector, for the new inflationary phenomena,
and for economic stagnation.

It has been shown that the redesigning of the exchange, tax, and tariff schemes, based upon the properties of the unbalanced productive structure, makes it
possible to avoid the limitation of industrial and farm
exports and to eliminate the chronic tendency toward
external disequilibria.16

A clear diagnosis of the situation will also provide short-term solutions. The habitual pressures for
the importation of raw materials, intermediate goods,
and capital goods are very powerful. When all government levels do not clearly realize which are the orders
of priority in foreign exchange matters, there is not
enough incentive to withstand these pressures. As a result of gradual concessions to import interests, exceptions and exemptions appear. Exemption from payment of
custom dues is employed as a means of regional industrial promotion; customs evasion and contraband are
tolerated--in short, the country ends up diverting a
considerable percentage of foreign exchange to superflu-
ous purposes, some of which are even contrary to the
economic interests of the country.

In order to reduce the expenditure of foreign exchange and to gain room in which to maneuver, it is
necessary only to eliminate these concessions. This,
in turn, gives time to set long-term policies in motion.
In case of real need, recourse may even be had to exchange control, which even further restricts foreign
exchange expenditure, although direct control measures
always amount to a confession that former policies have
failed and were unable to avoid the need for said controls. Accordingly, in view of the difficulties they
cause, they should be reserved only for emergencies.17

The real damage caused by the traditional stabilization philosophy lies in the fact that the confusion
of concepts that it inevitably introduces prevents the
adoption of long- and short-term measures such as those
I have mentioned.

IDEOLOGICAL FACTORS IN THE ARGENTINE INFLATION

Apart from the harm caused by any inflationary
phenomena as such and from the recessionary effects
provoked by bottlenecks, further injury to the economy
arises from the failure to adjust economic instruments
to the inflation. We have already seen the consequences
of the delay in adjusting exchange rates to costs. Similar considerations may apply to interest rates.

One of the most frequent accusations leveled
against inflation is that it has a discouraging effect
upon the accumulation of savings. This effect is indeed
produced when the interest rate is not high enough to
compensate for the loss of value of the money during the
inflation, that is, when the real interest rate--arrived
at by subtracting the rate of inflation from the nominal rate of interest--is insufficient. But here, once
more, the cause is not inflation, but the lack of adjustment of the interest rate to the inflation. It is
sufficient to correct the latter in order to overcome
the problem.[18] The same can be said with regard to the
taxation system. The notorious decapitalization of companies during inflationary periods occurs when income
tax is applied to nominal profits, so that a company
that is no more than maintaining its real capital during
the inflation shows fictitious profits subject to taxation, which in this case are confiscated. The remedy
that could prevent this from taking place is to include
automatic capital revaluation in the taxation system.[19]

As a consequence, once the conclusion is reached
that inflation is inevitable, the damage can be reduced
by putting it on an institutional basis, that is to say,
by taking it into account for establishing the exchange
rate and rates of interest, taxation, pensions, and the
like.

In the course of the prolonged Argentine inflationary process, there has always been a reluctance to place
it upon an institutional basis because this was regarded
as a demonstration of weakness in face of a phenomenon
that was considered to be basically easy to solve, provided that enough political firmness could be shown to
resist popular pressure. As we have seen, nothing could
be further from the truth. In the countries with unbalanced productive structures, the task of stabilization

is an exceedingly complex one. To the difficulties in
managing credit and fiscal instruments and the need to
meet sectorial pressures in favor of a greater share in
income--such as are common to all countries--must be
added the effort required to avoid domestic bottlenecks
in supply and to counteract the permanent tendency toward disequilibrium in the foreign sector.

The first obstacle encountered in the execution of
this task is the absence of economic theories adjusted
to the realities that must be faced. The second obstacle, which is even more serious, is the permanent influence of imported theories which are based on realities
existing in industrialized countries and which, starting
from false causal relationships, exercise a systematic
drive toward action contrary to the objective pursued.
The situation becomes even further aggravated as a consequence of political interferences deriving from the
relationship between inflation and the distribution of
income. Although theoretically in favor of stabilization, each of the several sectors tends to have its own
idea of what it implies, and each exercises pressure:
1. To secure an increase and consequent transference
    of income in its favor, either by provoking it, as
    in the case of wage increases, or by preventing a
    corrective action that could avoid it, as occurs in
    an exchange inflation when obstacles are set in the
    way of direct action against external disequilibrium;
2. To obtain stabilization from that moment on in order
    to prevent the other sectors from regaining their
    share of income and thus annulling the advantage
    obtained;
3. To rationalize its own position through a one-sided
    diagnosis of the inflationary phenomenon whose pur-
    pose is to accuse the other sectors of being re-
    sponsible for the inflation, thus providing a
    "scientific" basis for the type of stabilization
    that it happens to desire.

In Argentina there exists an explosive combination
of circumstances. The theoretical model, which encourages a distribution of income in favor of the farm
sector, coincides with the analytical model that the
international financial and "scientific" establishments
propound in ignorance of what an unbalanced productive
structure implies. The great influence that the former
exercises on local communication media and on the status
mechanism operating in the society and the international
prestige of the latter give great strength to the traditional model emanating from this circumstantial ideological alliance. Decades of analyses and interpreta-
tions, based on the model in question and propagated
through all the channels of mass communication, have
left the Argentine governing sector at the mercy of

the myths and conventional models that today determine its attitude toward economic problems.

The budget deficit is the source of all Argentina's evils; monetary issue is inflation and inflation arises from an excessive desire for consumption; Argentina's stagnation is due to the lack of sufficient capacity for sacrifice on the part of the population; industry is expensive owing to the absence of foreign competition; any subsidy implies inefficiency; the state ought not to interfere with the free operation of the market, and so on--all these are corollaries of the model in question, accepted as unquestioned truths by a large part of the Argentine governing class.

The powerful intellectual influence of these stereotypes justifies the tendency of large sectors--basically the industrial sector--to adopt systematically institutional attitudes that are contrary to their own interests. It furthermore presents a very grave problem. The economic policy required to face up to the inflationary process and to ensure the development of the country must be exercised in a competent manner, in accordance with a very coherent model, and without descending to demagoguery. This calls for access to the technical and managerial training, to skill in the handling of instruments, to the cognizance of day-by-day economic life, and to the executive experience of the governing class. But this policy also frequently includes deliberate budgetary deficits, monetary issue, and stimulation of consumption. It calls for the ability to distinguish between different inflationary processes. It implies a comprehensive attitude toward cost-push inflations that could lead to its institutionalization when income policy proves to be insufficient. It presupposes continuous action against bottlenecks by means of a conscious management of the market through the global instruments of economic policy: the protection system, a flexible employment of the exchange rates, the use of subsidies as a habitual instrument of economic policy, the employment of taxation to correct the distribution of income, and so forth.[20] In brief, the economic policy that the country requires contains elements that are completely incompatible with the conventional model under whose influence the governing class lives.

This is the main cause of the internal contradiction that paralyzes Argentine society and of the swings of the power pendulem from economic liberalism, technically skilled but inhibited from operating in the direction called for by the reality, to populism, less inhibited and accordingly better oriented in the overall

sense, but devoid of a training adequate to the task
it is called upon to fulfill.

The inflationary problem is only one of the aspects
of the Argentine economic problem, and it has only one
solution: the governing class must become mature enough
to abandon the myths that now inhibit its actions and to
adopt an attitude of critical analysis toward reality.
As a result, there would appear an intellectual blue-
print adapted to that reality, capable of channeling
activities in the right direction.

NOTES

1. Marcelo Diamand, Doctrinas Económicas, Desarrollo e
Independencia: Economía de las Estructuras Desequilib-
radas, Caso Argentino (Buenos Aires: Paidos, 1973).

2. This controversy can be seen in Dwight S. Brothers,
"Nexos entre la estabilidad monetaria y el desarrollo
económico en América Latina; un escrito doctrinal y de
política," Trimestre Económico, no. 116 (October-
December 1962), or in Joseph Grunwald, "Estabilización
de precios y desarrollo económico: el caso chileno,"
Trimestre Económico, no. 111 (July-September 1961).

3. The wage-earner's income depends not only on his
nominal wage, but also on hours worked, including over-
time, and even on other tasks he may engage in outside
his normal working hours. In the case of a family, it
depends on the number of hours worked not only by the
head of the family, but also by his wife and children--
incomes that are very sensitive to the level of employment.

4. Julio H. G. Olivera, in "Aspectos Dinámicos de la
Inflación Estructural," Trimestre Económico, no. 136
(October-December 1967), develops a mathematical model
of inflation originated in a bottleneck.

5. Carlos Díaz Alejandro says that, regarding elasticity problems, no pessimist ever dreamed, even in his
most depressive mood, of a supply curve of exportable
goods that responds negatively to prices, such as occurs
in Argentina. See his Exchange Rate Devaluation in a
Semi-Industrialized Country: The Experience of Argentina, (Cambridge, Mass.: M.I.T. Press, 1965), p. 80.

6. Raúl Yvez worked out an interesting theoretical
model concerning this subject. See "The Investment
Behavior and the Supply Response of the Cattle Industry
in Argentina" (Paper presented at a workshop, Purdue
University, 1971).

7. See, for example, Richard Mallon, Exchange Rate Adjustment in a Semi-Industrialized Primary Exporting Economy (Cambridge, Mass.: Development Advisory Service, Harvard University, 1966).

8. This model is developed in my book Doctrinas Económicas, Desarrollo e Independencia. A much shorter version can be found in Marcelo Diamand, "Seis Falsos Dilemas en el Debate Económico Nacional," Cuaderno del Centro de Estudios Industriales, no. 5 (1969).

9. There are very few and mostly incomplete references to this kind of exchange inflation. Dudley Seers presents explicitly a model of inflation originated in the export-import gap, but does not develop it in detail. On the contrary, Prebisch develops the subject, analyzing in detail the foreign exchange inflationary process and especially the orthodox stabilization policies, but--strangely enough--he never classifies explicitly this phenomenon as a different kind of inflation. Finally, Díaz Alejandro describes foreign exchange inflation, but also without giving it a specific name, merely saying that it is a "price inflation combined with deflation of real income." See Dudley Seers, "Theory of Inflation and Growth in Under-Developed Economies Based on the Experience of Latin America," published in W. Baer and I. Kerstenesky, Inflation and Growth in Latin America (New Haven: Yale University Press, 1964), pp. 89-103; Raúl Prebisch, "Hacia una Dinámica del Desarrollo Latinoamericano," Fondo de Cultura Económica (1963), p. 87; Díaz Alejandro, Exchange Rate Devaluation.

10. For a detailed and well-documented description of this effect, see Díaz Alejandro, Exchange Rate Devaluation.

11. See Prebisch, "Hacia una Dinámica del Desarrollo Latinoamericano."

12. It is convenient to point out an exception. At times governments, faced by pressure from the trade unions, guarantee the level of real wages and, more importantly, guarantee instantaneous adjustment of nominal wages. It may also occur that the guaranteed real wages are higher than what would emerge from the market forces operating within the exchange, tax, and credit context established by the very same government. In other words, there appears an inconsistency between the explicitly guaranteed real wages and the economic measures that establish the context in which the market operates, setting them implicitly. The discrepancy between the promised real wages and the concrete measures impedes their attainment. However, the commitment obliges the government to correct the discrepancies

instantaneously. We thus arrive at a self-propelling cost inflation, of a nature similar to exchange inflation.

13. The analysis of cost-push inflations in developing countries can be seen in Carlos Moyano Llerena, Panorama de la Economía Argentina, 4, 25 (1965); v, 30+31 (1966); and vi, 40 (1969), (Buenos Aires); Nicholas Kaldor, "Economic Problems of Chile," reprinted in Essays on Economic Policy, vol. 2 (New York: W. W. Norton, 1964); Juan Carlos de Pablo, Política Antiinflacionaria en la Argentina 1967-1970 (Buenos Aires: Amorrortu Editores, 1972).

14. G. A. Constanzo, Programas de estabilización económica en América Latina (Mexico: CEMLA, 1961).

15. A more profound analysis reveals that the two procedures are not exactly equivalent. Devaluation is rather less recessionary. Furthermore, they represent different redistributions of income: devaluation is more favorable to the exporting sector, while monetary restriction favors the financial sector.

16. For a detailed description of these policies, see Marcelo Diamand, "Bases para una Política Industrial Argentina," Cuadernos del Centro de Estudios Industriales, no. 2 (1969); Marcelo Diamand, "La Estructura Productiva Desequilibrada y el Tipo de Cambio," Desarrollo Económico 12, 45 (Abr-Jun 1972); Diamand, Doctrinas Económicas, Desarrollo e Independencia.

17. In the short run, recourse may also be had to foreign aid. Nevertheless, much prudence must be exercised in this case owing to the conflicts that appear with other measures in the foreign sector and to the dangers that the procedure represents for the future. See Marcelo Diamand, "Desarrollo Industrial, Política Autárquica y Capital Extranjero," Cuaderno de IDES, no. 16 and Doctrinas Económicas, Desarrollo e Independencia.

18. This point was examined by Ricardo Zinn in a series of articles that appeared in Cronista Comercial (Buenos Aires) September-October 1971.

19. This subject was dealt with by Armando Ribas, "Institucionalización de la estabilidad," Revista Política y Economía, June 1971.

20. See Miguel H. Alfano, "Falsa antinomia agroindustria," Cuadernos del Centro de Estudios Industriales, no. 4 (1970); Diamand, Doctrinas Económicas, Desarrollo e Independencia.

The Emergence of U.S. Control of the Peruvian Economy: 1850-1930

Heraclio Bonilla

No one can be unaware of the decisive weight that the United States has on the internal structure and the destiny of Latin America. The nature of this contact and its consequences have not been identical at all times: they have depended on the internal changes produced both in the United States and in Latin America and on the respective position of each continent within the system of international relations. But in spite of the importance that this country has had for Latin America since the beginning of this century, it has been only in the last decade that social scientists have begun to examine rigorously the most relevant questions. This new awareness is without doubt a symptom of the crisis through which these relations are passing. Such studies, however, tend to concentrate on the most controversial aspects of contemporary U.S.-Latin American relations and are not concerned with putting these relations into a historical perspective.

This essay has a double function. On the one hand, based on the experience of Peruvian-U.S. relations, it attempts to establish a coherent chronological order for the nature of these relations. At the same time, it attempts to show how mechanisms of U.S. control over the Peruvian economy emerged. Rather than being a definitive essay, this study is no more than an attempt to define, in a historical perspective, some of the problems inherent in these relations and the relevance of studying them. A limitation of this study is the fact that its analysis is based entirely on U.S. diplomatic documents and on some of the existing studies on Peruvian-U.S. relations.

THE CONTEXT OF THE NINETEENTH CENTURY

     To speak of the nineteenth century in Peru is to
speak of guano and of Great Britain. Between 1840 and
1880, the four decisive decades in Peru's nineteenth-
century economic history, the Peruvian economy depended
in effect on the exploitation of guano, the fertilizer
found on the coastal islands. The great industrial
power of Great Britain, at the same time, exercised
indisputable, though not absolute, control over the
economy through the mechanisms of trade and finance.

     But in spite of overall dominance by Great Britain,
there was also room for other European powers--France,
Germany, and later Italy--which had some measure of control in the Peruvian economy, particularly in attracting
and making use of profits from local enterprises. A similar role on this side of the Atlantic was played by
the United States. Let us examine its characteristics.

     Between 1840 and 1858 Peru exported 3,277,302 tons
of guano, of which nearly one-fifth went to the North
American market (via Baltimore), while the remaining
four-fifths went to the European markets, principally
that of Great Britain.[1] During this period the year
1854 has particular significance, for the Barreda
brothers, afraid that they might lose their export
rights, shipped 159,654 tons to the United States.[2]
It is necessary to emphasize that even though the North
American market did not consume as much fertilizer as
the British market, North American ships played a dominant role in the transport of the guano to the world
markets.

     From the end of the 1850s, the amount of guano ex-
ported to the United States began to decline considerably. The accumulation of substantial stocks of guano
in that country, the pricing policy of the Peruvian
government, and the competition brought about by other
fertilizers were the major factors in this decline.
The U.S. Civil War (1860-65) consolidated this crisis
and closed the North American market to further importation of Peruvian fertilizer.[3] Moreover, at the end of
the Crimean War, English and French merchant vessels
were freed to compete with North American ships in the
transport of guano. After the end of the American Civil
War the Peruvian fertilizer was never able to regain its
former levels of exportation to the United States because of the now acute competition from other types of
fertilizers. Table 1 shows the fluctuations of guano
exports from Peru to the United States.

Table 1. Peruvian Exports of Guano to the U.S.,
1844-1870

Year	Tons	Year	Tons	Year	Tons
1844	445	1852	25,500	1860	54,134
1845	---	1853	32,152	1861	27,424
1846	1,170	1854	159,654	1862-65	----
1847	1,112	1855	31,316	1866	13,000
1848	890	1856	15,728	1867	30,175
1849	2,700	1857	15,822	1868	1,700
1850	6,800	1858	8,473	1869	7,425
1851	25,000	1859	39,194	1870	41,243

Source: Louis Clinton Nolan, "The Diplomatic and Commercial Relations of the United States and Peru, 1826-
1875" (Thesis, Duke University, 1935), p. 188.

Alongside guano, which was the dominant product,
Peruvian exports to the United States also included--
though in very small amounts--silver, various kinds of
wool, leather, sugar, Peruvian bark dyes, wine, and
liquors. Reciprocally, until the 1870s, North American
exports to Peru consisted of coarse cottons, ready-made
woolens, clothing, boots and shoes, provisions, some
silks, furniture, coal, hardware, naval stores, wine
and spirits, drugs and medicines, lumber, and ice.
Two commercial treaties, signed in 1851 and 1870, regulated U.S.-Peruvian commerce during the nineteenth
century.

Louis Nolan, in a pioneering work on U.S.-Peruvian
commercial relations, has attempted to measure the economic significance of this interchange. Nolan mentions
that between 1825 and 1850 this commerce was insignificant, with an unfavorable balance for the United States.
Beginning in 1850, however, this tendency began to change
noticeably. Between 1841 and 1851 the total value of
commerce was $3,775,611 (U.S.), which represented an
unfavorable balance of $2,163,449 for the United States.
Yet, between 1851 and 1861, the total value of trade was
$11,287,601, this time giving the United States a favor-
able balance of $2,636,635.[4] The increase in trade and
in the favorable U.S. balance becomes even clearer in
the decade 1861-1871, in spite of the negative, yet

relatively short, effects of the Civil War. During this decade the commerce represented a value of $23,042,522, more than double that of the previous decade, and between 1871 and 1875 a value of $32,422,366. During the latter period the trade represented a favorable balance for the United States of $11,992,232.[5]

Another aspect of the U.S.-Peruvian commercial traffic of this period centered on whaling. Until 1850, northern Peruvian seaports, notably Tumbes, were continually visited by North American ships in search of whale oil and bone. Article 12 of the 1851 commercial treaty aimed at strengthening this sea traffic, in that North American vessels were absolved from customs duties and were also permitted to buy and sell merchandise freely up to the value of $1,000 (U.S.).[6] But again the U.S. Civil War, combined with the movement of the whales to the Arctic, put an end to this activity. U.S. Consul Card noted in this respect that eighty-three North American ships anchored in Tumbes in 1861, forty-two in 1862, twenty-five in 1863, and perhaps ten in 1864.[7]

The 1870s in Peru were years of great railway expansion. This expansion represented in effect a victory by the most modern sector of the ruling class, which tried to mitigate the waste of the considerable resources generated by the guano trade that had been indulged in by previous governments. In the same way as immigration the railway expansion within the country represented a response to the demands of an ideology that saw them as the most suitable methods for overcoming the obstacles to economic growth. Again Great Britain, and to a lesser degree the rest of Europe, provided the source of the capital needed for the railway constr c-tion in the form of various loans to the Peruvian governments But the materials necessary for the rail construction came principally from the United States. Between 1850 and 1870 the agricultural economy of the coast also revived, based on the production of cotton and sugar, in response to the demands of the external market. This development required the introduction of agricultural machines on the haciendas, again with the United States playing an important role.[8] Between 1871 and 1880 the value of U.S.-Peruvian commerce reached $36,590,058, over 40 percent above that of the previous decade.

Table 2, compiled by Nolan, shows the annual value of U.S.-Peruvian trade between 1865 and 1880.

Table 2.   U.S.-Peruvian Trade, 1865-1880

Year	Peruvian exports to the U.S. (in U.S. $)	Peruvian imports from the U.S. (in U.S. $)	Balance (in U.S. $)
1865	250,815	781,386	-530,571
1866	807,238	1,215,835	-408,597
1867	1,701,987	1,730,914	-28,927
1868	1,765,397	1,666,355	+98,042
1869	1,381,310	1,673,445	-287,135
1870	2,557,833	1,974,167	+583,666
1871	4,731,430	2,381,005	+2,530,425
1872	1,668,983	4,595,403	-2,926,420
1873	1,186,161	2,864,945	-1,678,784
1874	1,256,286	1,914,871	-658,585
1875	1,291,235	2,480,941	-1,189,706
1876	1,426,043	1,032,898	+393,145
1877	1,479,511	1,300,552	+178,959
1878	1,531,591	1,005,538	+525,953
1879	1,857,859	1,305,362	+552,497
1880	361,308	918,136	-556,828

Source: Nolan, "Relations of the United States and Peru," p. 224.

The value of the imports coming from the United States since the 1870s is even greater if one includes the value of precious metals shipped to Peru. According to Nolan, the value of the precious metals was the following:

Year	U.S. $
1870	1,819,018
1871	1,200,000
1872	4,500,000
1873	1,549,099
1874	707,035

While the commercial traffic was increasing in the 1870s, fundamental changes in the nature of this commerce were taking place. Guano was progressively losing its dominant position with the rising demand for nitrate. But the most important changes were those in the nature of the imports from the United States, in the sense that imports of durable and capital goods began to exceed imports of consumer goods. Table 3 shows the nature of these imports between 1871 and 1875.

Table 3. Peruvian Imports from the U.S., 1871-1875

	1871	1872	1873	1874	1875
Iron, steel, and by-products	561,699	1,374,407	623,028	417,789	1,105,357
Wool and wool products	506,726	1,003,203	491,783	337,550	411,962
Food products	144,007	371,676	381,076	241,923	169,260
Oil, minerals, and refined products	104,923	90,736	67,952	60,506	103,993
Drugs, inks, and chemical products	91,203	46,897	57,113	56,409	27,851

Source: Nolan, "Relations of the United States and Peru," pp. 226-27

The expansion of the railways of Peru, financed through British capital and by mortgaging guano sales, brought about an important commercial exchange between Peru and the United States. Yet, in spite of this trade, the principal control over Peru's economy was still exercised by Great Britain. This indisputable fact resulted from Peru's financial dependence on Great Britain, from the high cost of commercial shipping on the Atlantic, and from Great Britain's control of the shipping routes through its steamship lines.[9] Moreover, there existed an internal system of marketing entirely in the hands of the English, the French, the Germans, and the Italians; the Peruvians' association with European merchants and industrialists naturally tended to reinforce trade with Great Britain and Europe.[10] In spite of this, the early presence of the United States facilitated the opening of the necessary channels for the subsequent establishment of its hegemony.

The so-called War of the Pacific between Peru and Chile (1879-84) dramatically ended the guano cycle in the economic life of Peru. Moreover, the war caused the almost complete destruction of the country's productive potential. Postwar reconstruction was made possible through a sensitive change in the nature of foreign investment--instead of being in the form of loans to the Peruvian government, it came through direct investment in the production of the more important raw materials--through the creation of internal monopolies o through the creation of internal monopolies of productive resources, particularly in land and minerals.

Such were the events leading up to the rise in U.S. hegemony and control of the Peruvian economy, through the progressive replacement of Great Britain and the other European powers within the Peruvian economy. This drastic change in the position of Peru within the world market also resulted from a change in the balance of power between England and the United States, essentially the decline of British power due to the obsolescence of its technological structure.

In 1880, at the height of the war with Chile, Peruvian exports to the United States amounted to only $758,000, with imports from the United States amounting to $94,000.[11] This sudden decline in the level of trade between the United States and Peru, compared with the preceding fifteen years, lasted until 1898. In that year, Peruvian exports to the United States rose to $1,112,400, while the corresponding imports rose to $876,000.[12] The recovery of the commercial traffic between the United States and Peru, which was to improve even more at the beginning of the present century, resulted from two related factors: the strengthening of

the internal structure of Peru and the establishment in
1894 of two steamship lines (replacing the antiquated
sailboats used previously) that provided a monthly connection between New York and the west coast of South
America.[13]

THE BEGINNING OF U.S. DOMINATION

The year 1900 marks the beginning of the spectacular development of commercial exchange between the
United States and Peru: Peruvian exports rose to
$4,640,796, while imports from the United States
amounted to $1,447,472. Moreover, this rise generated
important changes within the Peruvian economic structure. Until the war with Chile, Peruvian exports to
Europe represented close to 80 percent of Peruvian exports, while the U.S. market absorbed only 2 percent.[14]
Imports from the United States in 1877 represented
7 percent of all Peruvian imports.[15] By contrast,
between 1892 and 1913 the percentage of Peruvian imports
that came from the United States increased from 7.1 percent to 29.8 percent,[16] while the percentage of Peruvian exports going to the United States rose from 2.7 percent in 1877 to nearly 33 percent of the total in
1913.[17]

If one observes the annual values of importation
and exportation between the United States and Peru,
particularly between 1903 and 1905, it is apparent that
imports from the United States exceeded Peruvian exports.
This is a significant fact, as it represents the consolidation of U.S. hegemony through the establishment
of the first large imperialist enclaves dedicated to
the exploitation of copper, petroleum, and sugar. From
partial control of the Peruvian market, the United
States, through its growing capital investments and the
formation of the giant corporations, initiated its domination of the whole Peruvian economy in the first
decade of the twentieth century. The installation of
these U.S. enterprises explains not only the growing
consumption of capital goods coming from that nation,
but also the effective relationship between the production of raw materials and the U.S. market. In effect,
the special nature of U.S. trade with Peru was shaped
in response to the demands of empire. For example,
between 1895 and 1899 the U.S. sale of trains, cars,
and railroad track represented an annual value of
$16,300; this amount increased to $192,800 annually
between 1901 and 1905.[18]

The export to Peru of U.S. capital goods also
formed the fundamental base for the U.S. defeat of the
British and the Germans in competition for the control

of the Peruvian economy. Table 4 shows the relative growth of U.S., British, and German exports of these goods to Peru.

Table 4. Annual Average of Capital Goods Exports to Peru, 1895-1904

	1895-1899 (U.S. $)	1900-1904 (U.S. $)	Growth rate %
United States	269,000	810,000	201.1
England	636,000	1,092,000	71.7
Germany[a]	155,000	317,000	104.5

a- From 1897 to 1899.
Source: "Peru's Commercial Progress," Daily Consular and Trade Reports, no. 546 (April 24, 1906), p. 6.

The lack of a U.S. banking system that could finance these industrial and commercial activities prevented the U.S.-Peru commercial exchange from reaching higher levels. If, for example, a manufacturer or exporter asked a New York bank to extend credit to a South American client, the bank could grant or refuse the request only in light of the solvency of the manufacturer or trader, because the financial status of the South American client was not known. In order to avoid these difficulties the U.S. merchants acopted the system of "cash against documents."

Such a policy protected the interests of the U.S. industrialists, who were ignorant of the conditions of South America, but did not completely exclude the use of credit in the exportation of their goods. The merchant houses and the consignee traders in New York were responsible for paying the industrialists in cash, while at the same time they recovered their outlay by discounting the credit notes drawn on clients in South America. The European banks that were operating in Latin America, like the U.S. banks (after the Federal Reserve Act was passed), constituted an efficient market for these discount operations. Hence, the acceptance of a credit document did not depend so much on the solvency of the client as on the reputation of the intermediary bank.[19] The opening of a branch of the National City Bank of New York in Lima in 1920, which facilitated a more direct financing operation, consolidated the U.S. supremacy over Peru's international trade.

THE EFFECTS OF WORLD WAR I

The dominant position in the Peruvian economy established by the United States in the first decade of the twentieth century was consolidated in the course of World War I. This consolidation ran parallel with the strengthening of the Peruvian economy, due to the great demand for raw materials on the part of the nations at war. An indication of this situation can be observed in the spectacular development of Peru's international trade between 1915 and 1917 (see table 5).

Table 5. Peruvian International Trade, 1912-1917

Year	Peruvian import (Peruvian pounds)	Peruvian export (Peruvian pounds)	Balance
1912	5,140,338	9,439,581	4,298,243
1913	6,088,776	9,137,780	3,049,004
1914	4,827,930	8,767,790	3,939,860
1915	3,095,544	11,521,807	8,426,263
1916	8,683,150	16,541,063	7,857,913
1917	13,502,851	18,643,414	5,140,563

Source: "Peruvian Exchange during the War," Commerce Reports, no. 14 (January 17, 1920), p. 334.

Note: The rate of exchange of the Peruvian pound was equal to the British pound sterling or to 4.8665 U.S. dollars.

But the impact of the war was neither automatic nor immediate. In the first months of the conflict there was total disorganization of the international trade of the countries on the west coast of South America, associated with a financial crisis and a drop in the monetary exchange rates. It was in 1915 that these countries began to gain economic strength due to the increased demand for copper, nitrate, tin, and cotton. Once this demand had reestablished the former price levels, the exportation of these products grew in quantity and value. In the case of Peru, the situation was even more favorable because the market for one of its most important export products, sugar, had not been weakened by the initial disturbances of the war.

The great demand for Peru's raw materials also generated a very favorable commercial balance, strengthening the monetary exchange rate. On August 1, 1919, the Peruvian libra was quoted in New York at $5.30; by the end of 1920 this rate had declined to only $4.74.[20] The level of Peruvian imports did not, however, increase

in volume, due to the economic crises of the countries
at war. Given that government income depended to a
large extent on import tariffs, the revenue of the Peruvian government was lower than that of the private commercial corporations within the country.[21]

As mentioned earlier, the war consolidated U.S.
hegemony over the Peruvian economy. In fact, in 1913
the imports from the United States represented 28.8
percent of Peru's total imports, while at the same time
the U.S. market was absorbing 33.2 percent of Peru's
total exports. The percentage of the imports increased
to 54.3 percent in 1918 and 61.9 percent in 1919, while
Peruvian exports to the United States increased to 46.5
percent during the same years. Table 6 indicates the
corresponding dollar values of these exports.

Table 6. Peruvian-U.S. Trade, 1913-1918

Year	Peruvian exports to the U.S. (U.S. $)	Peruvian imports from the U.S. (U.S. $)
1913	14,761,355	8,541,934
1914	14,827,700	7,643,928
1915	25,054,360	7,187,102
1916	50,024,370	24,699,126
1917	54,609,063	43,864,096
1918	48,944,071	27,772,373

Source: "Trade of the West Coast of South America,"
Commerce Reports, no. 140 (June 16, 1919).

During these years exports from the United States
to Peru consisted of iron and steel manufactures, cotton
goods, wood, chemical products, electrical goods, automobiles, meat, coal, and agricultural implements, while
copper was the principal product that Peru exported to
the United States, followed by cotton, wool, rubber,
oil and minerals, and sugar.[22]

It has been indicated that the exportation of this
type of raw materials was the factor that strengthened
the Peruvian economy during World War I. At the same
time, however, this kind of strengthening, which was
dependent on favorable external factors, was bound to
be highly precarious. In the same way as in the nineteenth century, the stimulus for growth was entirely
external to the Peruvian economy, and hence this new
growth also lacked the favorable factors that might
have made possible a more integrated development.

If one examines Peru's three most important export
products between 1914 and 1918--copper, sugar, and cot-
ton--it is in fact possible to find a close correlation
between the price levels on the international market and
the fluctuations in the production and exportation of
these same products. Table 7 shows the price fluctuations of "standard" copper quoted in Lima between 1912
and 1919.

Table 7.   Price Per Ton of Copper in Lima, Peru,
1912-1919

Year	Month	Price in pounds sterling			
1912		£62	2s.	6d.--£79 10s.	
1913		63	15	-- 75 2	6
1914	February	66	5		
	November	51	12	6	
	December	57			
1915	January	56	1	3	
	June	84	10		
	August	65	2	6	
	December	84	5		
1916	January	86	3	9	
	May	142	18	6	
	July	89	5		
	December	139			
1917	January	133	15		
	February	139	13		
	December	110	5		
1918	January	110	5		
	August	122			
	December	112			
1919	January	111	10		
	February	74			
	July	106			

Source: "Foreign Trade of Peru," Commerce Reports,
no. 9 (January 12, 1921).

The fluctuations in the demand of copper determined
the export cycle of copper, which between 1912 and 1917
was exported in the following quantities:[23]

Year	Metric tons
1912	34,830
1913	41,316
1914	29,440
1915	41,015
1916	52,338
1917	49,999

Sugar was exported principally to the United States and to England and on a smaller scale to Chile, Uruguay, and Argentina. The volumes traded also closely followed the fluctuations of the price of sugar on the international market. The prices for each quintal of sugar quoted on the London stock exchange are shown in table 8.

Table 8.   Price Per Quintal of Sugar in London, 1912-1919

Year	Month	Price in pounds sterling
1912		£9s. 11d.--15s. 2d.
1913		9 2 10 3
1914		17
1915		18
1916	January	11 6
	May	17
	December	13
1917		11 9 18 1
1918		15 19
1919		18 8 20 4

Source: "Peruvian Exchange During the War," Commerce Reports, no. 14 (January 17, 1920).

Between 1912 and 1917, the following quantities of sugar in metric tons were exported:

Year	Metric tons
1912	147,410
1913	142,901
1914	176,671
1915	220,257
1916	239,009
1917	212,041

If one considers the total production of Peruvian sugar in 1916-19, then only 15 percent of the total was produced for internal consumption:[24]

Year	Metric tons
1916-17	216,000
1917-18	265,000
1918-19	250,000

Before the war virtually all of Peru's cotton exports were shipped to Liverpool, and from there they were in part reexported to the United States. But the war forced the North American companies to buy the cotton directly in Peru in order to meet the military requirements more quickly. The outbreak of war actually had negative effects on the demand for Peruvian cotton due to the accumulation of great cotton stocks that were not sold in the United States. There were difficulties, too, of transport for a product such as cotton, which required substantial hold space on board ship. The subsequent fall in prices meant that cotton was not planted on several coastal haciendas in 1914. But the development of the war changed this situation toward the end of 1915 and at the same time encouraged the production of long fiber cotton rather than short fiber.

The Liverpool Cotton Exchange classified Peruvian cotton in four classes: rough, semirough, soft or Egyptian, and the Mitafifi and Peruvian Sea Island. The fluctuations of its prices depended on the quotations in Liverpool: the average prices of cotton in these four classes between 1913 and 1919 are indicated in table 9.

The incipient development of the Peruvian textile industry required the consumption of approximately 5 million tons of cotton per year, with the balance for export. The quantities exported between 1912 and 1917 are shown in table 10.

The consolidation of U.S. hegemony, moreover, implied substantive changes in the position of the Peruvian economy within the international market, that is, its movement away from influence and control by the European powers. Between 1910 and 1912, Great Britain was foremost in the countries that supplied the Peruvian market, followed by the United States, Germany, and France. In 1913, one year before the war, almost one-third of the imports from Britain consisted of various types of textiles, while at the same time Great Britain supplied close to one-half of all of the coal imported by Peru. The balance of the imports from Britain consisted of a great variety of manufactured goods, including corrugated iron, hydraulic pumps, agricultural implements, cables, and chemical products. The war resulted in the eclipse of British-Peruvian trade by

Table 9. Price Per Pound of Cotton on Liverpool Stock Exchange, 1913-1919 (In pence)

Year	Rough	Semirough	Soft	Peruvian Sea Island
1913	10.25-- 9	8.85-- 8.50	8.20-- 7.84	11 --10.50
1914	9 -- 8.75	8.50-- 8.40	7.64-- 5.30	10.50-- 8.75
1915	8.75--11.50	8.40--10.40	5.59-- 8.64	8.50--10.50
1916	11.50--18	10.40--17.50	8.88--12.20	10.50--24
1917	18 --32	17.50--30.50	12.06--25.13	24 --34
1918	33 --37	31.50--35.50	27.07--27.05	34 --33
1919	36 --29.75	34.50--25.50	25.80--27.04	33 --27.50

Source: "Peruvian Exchange during the War," p. 338.

Table 10. Metric Tons of Peruvian Cotton Exported, 1912-1917

Year	Rough	Semirough	Soft	Peruvian Sea Island
1912	---	7,498	10,995	555
1913	---	7,240	14,924	1,597
1914	---	4,429	16,267	2,070
1915	703	5,348	12,539	2,426
1916	5,436	1,625	13,375	3,654
1917	1,994	1,225	7,328	6,688

Source: "Peruvian Exchange during the War," p. 339.

closing British supply lines, along with the increase
in transport costs and Peruvian diversification into
new channels of commerce. Table 11 shows the position
of Great Britain and of the other European countries
in Peru's import trade between 1910 and 1913. From
1913 on, during the war years, the United States replaced England as the principal supplier of Peruvian
imports. In fact, between 1914 and 1917 the value of
Peru's imports from the United States was three times
that of imports from Britain. Germany and Belgium, who
before the war had held fairly strong positions in
Peru's international commerce, disappeared from the
picture and were replaced by Spain, the British Indies,
Japan, and Italy. Fifty percent of Spanish exports to
Peru consisted of textiles, and the balance was food
products. Virtually all imports from India consisted
of jute sacks for minerals and sugar, while Japan principally supplied textiles and--in smaller quantities--
rice, paper, and china goods. The source of these
imports between 1914 and 1917 is evident from table 12.

Finally, examining the effects that World War I had
on the consolidation of U.S. hegemony in Peru, one must
add those that resulted from the opening of the Panama
Canal in August 1914. For the commercial exchange between the United States and the Pacific coastal ports,
the Panama Canal signified fundamental reductions in
distances and costs of transport. Both facts brought
about increased exchange of goods and a noticeable reduction in prices. Through the Panama Canal, the trip
from New York to Callao was reduced to only twelve days,
while the distances saved are reflected in table 13.

COMMERCIAL RELATIONS FROM THE POSTWAR YEARS TO THE
CRISIS OF 1929

The end of the war also put an end to the exceptional circumstances that had made possible the development of the Peruvian export economy and the strengthening of U.S.-Peruvian commerce. Between 1920 and 1921,
the value of Peruvian exports to the United States fell
from $74,659,809 to $14,733,000, while the value of
Peruvian imports from the United States dropped from
$46,675,710 to $24,028,000. The contraction of the
external market had negative effects not only among the
local groups that were involved in international trade,
but also on the government finances of Peru, with the
drastic reduction in income from taxes on imports.[25]

From August 1922 to 1929, however, Peru's exports
regained their former status as a result of the growing
role of U.S. capital in the sectors related to foreign
trade and the high sugar prices.[26] But this recovery

Table 11. Value of Peruvian Imports, 1910-1913 (In Peruvian pounds)

Country of Origin	1910	1911	1912	1913	Total
United States	922,678	1,248,942	1,194,890	1,755,252	5,121,762
Great Britain	1,678,701	1,719,832	1,367,977	1,598,606	6,365,116
Germany	790,711	946,207	930,397	1,055,975	3,723,290
Belgium	250,595	333,982	245,226	384,139	1,213,942
France	485,904	289,530	318,431	280,492	1,374,357
Italy	167,790	199,450	254,707	254,473	876,420
Chile	152,189	76,768	195,707	213,077	637,741
Hong Kong	131,686	154,348	154,855	158,221	599,110
Australia	182,153	229,306	239,558	129,895	780,912
Other	218,290	239,881	238,591	258,647	955,409
Total	4,980,897	5,438,246	5,140,339	6,088,777	21,648,059

Source: "Trade of the West Coast of South America," Commerce Reports, no. 140 (June 16,1919), p. 1393.

Table 12. Value of Peruvian Imports, 1914-1917 (In Peruvian pounds)

Country of Origin	1914	1915	1916	1917	Total
United States	1,570,724	1,488,264	5,116,582	8,792,710	16,968,280
Great Britain	1,338,552	662,546	1,496,305	1,934,666	5,432,069
Hong Kong	129,274	181,947	301,914	453,762	1,066,897
Spain	62,547	45,233	170,119	357,621	635,520
Chile	89,618	94,390	298,768	357,256	840,032
British Indies	55,755	87,409	233,174	350,024	726,362
Italy	201,632	157,831	237,248	248,707	845,418
Australia	187,088	12,373	235,417	231,942	666,820
France	155,974	89,067	196,265	225,280	666,586
Japan	12,462	18,383	85,499	129,496	245,840
Other	1,024,304	258,102	311,859	431,387	2,015,652
Total	4,827,930	3,095,545	8,683,150	13,502,851	30,109,476

Source: "Trade of the West Coast of South America," p. 1395.

Table 13. Distance in Miles Between Callao, Peru, and Four Ports

To Callao	From New York	From New Orleans	From Liverpool	From Suez
By the Straits of Magellan	9,613	10,029	9,980	11,057
By the Panama Canal	3,363	2,784	5,937	7,730
Distance saved	6,250	7,245	4,043	3,327

did not reach the levels obtained during World War I.
The average annual value of U.S.-Peruvian commerce between 1922 and 1929 ranged around $40 million. It was,
moreover, a growth interrupted by small recessions, such
as those of 1923, 1925, and 1926, caused by low cotton
prices and by maladjustments in the internal monetary
market.[27]

During those years cotton, copper, sugar, and,
increasingly, oil constituted the principal Peruvian
exports. The exact proportion of each of these products
within its commerce can be seen in table 14.

Table 14. Percentage of Peruvian Exports Provided by
Various Products, 1922-1930

Year	Sugar	Cotton	Rubber	Wool	Oil	Copper
1922	24	25	1	3	22	18
1923	27	22	1	3	18	17
1924	21	22	1	4	23	14
1925	11	32	1	4	24	18
1926	17	22	1	3	28	16
1927	16	23	1	3	27	18
1928	13	21	-	4	28	20
1929	12	18	-	4	30	23
1930	11	18	-	3	30	19

Source: I.G. Bertram, "Development Problems in an
Export Economy: A Study of Domestic Capitalists,
Foreign Firms and Government in Peru, 1919-1930"
(Ph.D. thesis, Oxford University, 1974), p. 31.

Given that the North American market was then the
most important one for Peruvian raw materials, the cotton, sugar, copper, and oil all figured within the
principal Peruvian exports to the United States. Capital goods, food products, and drinks, on the other hand,
constituted the principal Peruvian imports from the
United States.

In summary, the important point to note here is
that during the war and during the years of postwar
recovery the U.S. corporations that had been established
in Peru since the early twentieth century consolidated
their positions. Consequently, it was these companies
that primarily benefited from the expansion of Peru's
exports. The Cerro de Pasco Copper Corporation, for
example, was the second most important exporting company (after the International Petroleum Company) during
the 1920s. Between 1920 and 1930 its exports reached
close to $212 million, or just under 20 percent of the

total export value. Exports by the Northern Peru Mining
and Smelting Company, moreover, during this period were
worth 9 million Peruvian pounds, around 3 percent of
Peru's total exports.[28] These figures in themselves
are sufficient to demonstrate the control of the U.S.
companies over Peru's economy.

THE ORIGIN AND NATURE OF U.S. INVESTMENTS

     During the whole nineteenth century, Britain's
control over Peru's economy was fundamentally commercial
and financial. That is, while the Peruvian market was
influenced directly by the pattern of English production, the whole economy was also considered--after
independence--to be a suitable area for the investment
of British capital. Until the beginning of the War of
the Pacific, the export of capital from England took
the form of loans to a Peruvian state that was permanently in need of money. The fragile nature of Peru's
productive structure, along with a permanent state of
bankruptcy, generated both a colossal accumulation of
external debt and an extremely low rate of return on
capital investment. The end of the war initiated a new
cycle in the nature of British investment, which was
caused by profound changes in both Peru's and Great
Britain's economies. The so-called Grace contract paid
off the external Peruvian debt with British creditors
through the relinquishment of the guano trade, the railways, certain lands in the Perené, and the control of
the guano trade, the railways, certain lands in the
investment took the form of direct investment in commerce, services, and some productive sectors.

     At the beginning of the twentieth century, the
total value of direct British investment reached $27
million, most of which was directed, as indicated,
toward the railways, services, and half a dozen companies oriented to the internal market. From 1900
until 1930, Lobitos Oilfields (petroleum), Duncan Fox
Co. (cotton), and, to a lesser degree, the Sayapullo
Syndicate and the Lampa Mining Company (minerals) were
the only British companies whose production was aimed
at the external market. Companies such as London and
Pacific Petroleum, the British Sugar Company, and other
sugar plantations with substantial British capital were
purchased in this period by new American companies.
This explains why, until about 1900, only 5 percent of
all Peruvian exports were produced by foreign firms;
from 1900 to 1930, on the other hand, the growing
position of U.S. companies in the areas of raw materials
production meant that 50 percent of all exports were
being produced by these firms.[29]

British hegemony over the Peruvian economy throughout the nineteenth century prevented major development
in U.S. investment during this period. With the exception of small investments in agriculture and mining by
the American residents in Peru, Cartavio--acquired by
Grace Bros. in 1882--was the only important U.S. company.[30] But after 1901, and above all during World
War I, when the export of European capital came to
a halt, the influx of U.S. investment became greater
and greater.[31] The rhythm of this growth was closely
associated with the establishment and consolidation of
the first U.S. companies.

Some significant dates are: 1901, the birth of
the Cerro de Pasco Corporation; 1903, the expansion of
W. R. Grace and Co. into the textile industry; 1907, the
appearance of the Vanadium Corporation of America; 1913,
the purchase of the London and Pacific Petroleum Co. by
a subsidiary of Standard Oil; 1916, the establishment
in Lima of the American Mercantile Bank by Guaranty
Trust, Brown Brothers, and J. & W. Seligman of New York;
1920, the opening of a branch of National City Bank of
New York; 1921, the creation of Northern Peru Mining
and Smelting Co. by American Smelting and Refining
Company.[32] Table 15 shows the growth rate of direct
U.S. investment in comparison with that of Great Britain.

Table 15.   Direct Foreign Investment in Peru, 1900-1929
            (In millions of U.S. dollars)

Year	U.S.	Great Britain	Total
1900	3	27	30
1905	15	51	66
1910	30	54	84
1914	38	58	96
1919	111	50	161
1924	145	52	197
1929	162	66	228

Source: Bertram, "Development Problems in an Export
Economy," p. 29.

For the most part, U.S. investment went into the
development of the mining industry, through the operations of companies such as Cerro de Pasco Copper Corporation, International Petroleum Company, Vanadium
Corp. of America, Inca Mining Company, and Northern
Peru Mining and Smelting Company and the awarding of
rights to the Cerro Verde deposits to Anaconda. On
a lesser scale, other sectors of the Peruvian economy
were also penetrated by these initial investments.

These included W. R. Grace and Co. in textile production
and small industry; Wessel, Duval and Co., Pan American-
Grace Airways, All America Cables, and Frederick Snare
Corporation in commerce and in communications; Fred T.
Ley and Co. and the Foundation Company in construction;
J. & W. Seligman and Co., Guaranty Trust Co. of New York,
and the National City Co. in the financial sector.[33]

The control of the internal Peruvian market was
intensified during 1900-30 as the old system of sale by
consignment for U.S. products was replaced by the main
U.S. firms by a method of sales through agencies. Toward the end of the nineteenth century only Singer Sew-
ing Machines had adopted the new system; but in the first
two decades of the present century, U.S. Steel Corporation, Gourock Ropework Export Company Ltd., National
Paper and Type Co., and Ingersoll-Rand expanded their
sales with the opening in Peru of agencies directly
dependent on the parent company.[34]

Finally the public sector became yet another suitable area for U.S. investment, particularly through
various loans during the Augusto B. Leguía administration (1919-30). In this respect it is worth recalling
that the birth of the Peruvian Corporation in 1890 had
canceled the huge debt accumulated by the Peruvian
government during the nineteenth century. A loan written in Germany in 1906 for 600,000 pounds sterling in
exchange for a mortgage on the income of the Estanco
de la Sal (salt monopoly) reinitiated in the twentieth
century a new cycle in Peru's external debt.[35] But the
"eleven years' rule" of Leguía was a period of particularly high increase of Peru's financial dependence.
Thus, while public expenditure amounted to 6.6 million
Peruvian pounds in 1919, it had increased to 25.7 million Peruvian pounds by 1928, an increase financed by
U.S. loans. In 1919, 5 percent of public spending was
covered by this type of financing. This figure increased to 43 percent in 1926, while 56 percent of
public expenditure was financed by external credits
in 1927-28.[36] This prodigality with foreign credit
allowed Leguía to develop an impressive policy of public
works construction, accompanied by an equally impressive
policy of public corruption, in an attempt to consolidate his political clientele. Table 16 shows the main
loans signed by Leguía and by the banks associated in
his financial activities.

The result of all of these operations was the total
indebtedness of the Peruvian state, a process that once
again resulted in the financial and economic collapse of
Peru when the external sources of credit were cut off as
a result of the great crisis in 1929. Table 17 indicates
the changes of Peru's external debt between 1919 and 1930.

Table 16.   Foreign Loans to the Peruvian Government,
            1921-1928 (In millions of U.S. dollars)

Name of Loan	Date of contract	Rate of interest	Banks in charge of issue	Amount
Loan confirming Cumberland's contract	1921	-	Guaranty Trust Co. of New York	0.2
Petroleum loan of 1922	1922	8	Guaranty Trust Co. of New York	2.5
Sanitation loan of 1924	1924	8	Guaranty Trust Co. of New York and others	7.0
Petroleum loan of 1925	1925	7.5	Guaranty Trust Co. of New York and others	7.5
Sanitation loan of 1926	1926	8	Guaranty Trust Co. of New York and others	2.0
Gold Bond loan of 1926	1926	7.5	Guaranty Trust Co. of New York and others	16.0
Province of Callao	1927	7.5	Alvin H. Frank & Co., J. & W. Seligman & Co., and others	1.5
Tobacco loan	1927	7	J. & W. Seligman & Co., National City Co., and others	15.0
Peruvian National Loan (first series)	1927	6	J. & W. Seligman & Co., National City Co., and others	50.0
Peruvian National Loan (second series)	1928	6	J. & W. Seligman & Co., National City Co., and others	25.0[a]
City of Lima	1928	6.5	R. H. Rollins and Sons	3.0

a- plus £2 million
Source: James C. Carey, Peru and the United States,
1900-1962 (South Bend, Ind., 1964), pp. 64-65.

Table 17. Peruvian External Debt, 1919-1930

Year	Total in Millions		Net change	
	Debt in U.S. $	Debt in £ sterling	Debt in U.S. $	Debt in £ sterling
1919	--	1.0b	--	--
1920	--	1.0b	--	--
1921	--	0.9b	--	-0.1
1922	2.4	2.7	2.4	1.8
1923	2.1	3.4	-0.3	0.7
1924	8.8	3.3	6.7	-0.1
1925	13.5	3.2	4.7	-0.1
1926	30.5	3.1	17.0	-0.1
1927	66.4a	3.0	35.9	-0.1
1928	90.7	4.9	24.3	1.9
1929	89.7	3.6	-1.0	-1.3
1930	88.5	3.5	-1.2	-0.1

a- Excludes $29 million of bonds in the process of
   of being retired.
b- Up to June 30.
Source: Bertram, "Development Problems in an Export
Economy," p. 43.

     In short, the process that led gradually to hegem-
ony by the United States over Peru's economy began in
the latter half of the nineteenth century. Initially
it was basically a commercial control, achieved by
U.S. products penetrating into the gaps left by massive
British exports. This was a process that noticeably
increased with the construction of the railways and the
growing demand for rolling stock imported from the
United States. The War of the Pacific, the establishment of steam navigation, and the financial activities
of W. R. Grace allowed the opening of the first channels
to investment of U.S. capital. But it was the establishment of the first agro-mining enclaves, under the direct
control of major U.S. companies, that led the Peruvian
economy to a role of clear subordination to the needs
of U.S. industrial expansion. World War I consolidated
this process, while at the same time it ended the control that the European powers, especially England, had
exercised over Peru's economy since the early 1800s.
The continual demand for credits by a state under the
control of a corrupt administration and the changes in
U.S. commercial operations put Peru's financial sector
under U.S. control and made U.S. domination over the
internal market more complete and efficient.

But the establishment of this hegemony was not only the result of these mechanisms of control. The opening of new markets, the establishment of U.S. firms in the productive sectors of the economy, and the search for favorable terms for these concessions were made possible by the firm intervention of the U.S. State Department through its principal diplomatic agents. The Electric Boat Co., the National City Bank of New York, and All-America Cables are examples of some of the U.S. firms that used the support of their government to initiate and then strengthen their operations in Peru.

NOTES

1. Louis Clinton Nolan, "The Diplomatic and Commercial Relations of the United States and Peru, 1826-1875" (Thesis, Duke University, 1935), p. 187.

2. Ibid.

3. "Letter of the Secretary of State Transmitting a Report on the Commercial Relations of the United States with Foreign Countries for the Year Ended September 30th, 1862," in Annual Report on Foreign Commerce (Washington, D. C., 1863), pp. 692-93.

4. Nolan, "Relations of the United States and Peru," p. 216.

5. Ibid., p. 217.

6. Ibid.

7. Denison Card to Secretary of State, Tumbes, September 1, 1864 (Microfilm publications, T-353, roll 1).

8. "Letter of the Secretary of State Transmitting a Report on the Commercial Relations of the U.S. with Foreign Nations for the Year ended September 30, 1866," in Annual Report on Foreign Commerce (Washington, D. C., 1867), p. 543.

9. "Report of Consul Brent on the Commerce of Peru in 1884," in Commercial Relations of the United States, pt. 2, 1884-1885 (Washington, D. C., 1886), p. 798.

10. "Peru Report of Consul Brent," in Commercial Relations of the United States with Foreign Countries during the Year 1886 and 1887 (Washington, D. C., 1888), p. 689.

11. Report Upon the Commercial Relations of the United
States with Foreign Countries for the Year 1880 and 1881
(Washington, D. C., 1883), p. 118.

12. Commercial Relations of the United States with
Foreign Countries during the Year 1899, vol. 1 (Washington, D. C., 1900), p. 127.

13. "General Survey of Foreign Trade," in Advance
Sheets of Consular Reports (February 13, 1901), pp.
26-27, "Peruvian American Trade," in ibid., no. 3076
(January 17, 1908), p. 5.

14. William Bollinger, "The Rise of United States
Influence in the Peruvian Economy, 1869-1921" (Thesis,
University of California, Los Angeles, 1972), p. 20.

15. Ibid., p. 53.

16. Ibid., p. 16.

17. Ibid., p. 20.

18. "Peru Commercial Progress," Daily Consular and
Trade Reports, no. 2546 (April 24, 1906), p. 7.

19. E. Hurley, Banking and Credit in Argentina, Brazil,
Chile and Peru (Washington, D. C., 1914), pp. 66-69.

20. "Foreign Trade of Peru," Commerce Reports, no. 9
(January 12, 1921), p. 215.

21. "Trade of the West Coast of South America," ibid.,
no. 140 (June 16, 1919), p. 1393.

22. "Foreign Trade of Peru," ibid., no. 9 (January 12,
1921), p. 215.

23. "Peruvian Exchange during the War," ibid., no. 14
(January 17, 1920), 335-36.

24. Ibid., pp. 336-37.

25. "Peruvian Government Seeking to Improve Economic
Conditions," ibid., no. 14 (December 5, 1921), p. 812.

26. "Peru: Exchange Situation," ibid., no. 184
(August 7, 1922), p. 359.

27. "Business Depression in Peru," ibid., no. 1 (January 7, 1924), p. 7; "Trade Continues Dull in Peru,"
ibid., no. 18 (May 3, 1926), p. 265; "Causes of the
Exchange Slump in Peru," ibid., no. 44 (November 1,
1926), pp. 304-5.

28. I. G. Bertram, "Development Problems in an Export Economy: A Study of Domestic Capitalists, Foreign Firms and Government in Peru, 1919-1930" (Ph.D. diss., Oxford University, 1974), p. 96.

29. Ibid., pp. 27-30.

30. Bollinger, "United States Influence in the Peruvian Economy," p. 10.

31. Frederic M. Halsey, Investments in Latin America and the British West Indies (Washington, D. C., 1918), pp. 19, 321-44.

32. Bollinger, "United States Influence in the Peruvian Economy," pp. 10-11.

33. James C. Carey, Peru and the United States, 1900-1962 (South Bend, Ind., 1964), pp. 54-55.

34. Bollinger, "United States Influence in the Peruvian Economy," pp. 48-52.

35. Heraclio Bonilla, Gran Bretaña y el Perú, los mecanismos de un control económico (Lima: IEP, 1975).

36. Bertram, "Development Problems in an Export Economy," p. 46.

IV. PAN AMERICAN VIEWS
OF ETHNICITY

The Afro-American Experience in the South of North America

Gloria Blackwell

My focus on one significant black community in Atlanta, Georgia, and on one major institution in that community offers an approach to the Afro-American experience in the U.S. South. This approach, in turn, suggests more questions than conclusions. The conclusion suggests that Afro-Atlantans need cultural and ethnic infusions to relieve the myopic ambivalence resulting from centuries of southern love-hate rituals in black and white.

ATLANTA

Since its founding in 1837, Atlanta has been essentially and intentionally a black and white city. By 1860 the black population was 21 percent of the 9,500 total. Darker citizens have constituted a major, alert, and aggressive portion of the population and have never dropped below 30 percent since 1870. By 1970, Afro-Atlantans numbered 255,000 of the 497,421 total. Historically, therefore, issues of race and ethnicity in Atlanta have been issues in black and white, of affinities and antipathies. Progress has been both offensive and defensive in nature in this "city too busy to hate."

"SWEET AUBURN"

This black community is in the heart of Atlanta, adjacent to the central business district. It is noted for its rich cultural heritage, internationally famous residents, and outstanding entrepreneurial activity. Wheat Street, racially mixed but predominantly white (renamed Auburn Avenue in 1894), was opened in young

Atlanta in 1853. A century later, Afro-Atlantans owned
more than 95 percent of the Auburn Avenue businesses,
and "Sweet Auburn's" fame spread, especially throughout
the black world.   In a 1956 study entitled "The Negro's
New Economic Life," John Emmet Hughes declared Auburn
Avenue "the richest Negro street in the world." Two
years later, August Meier and John Lewis found that the
Auburn business and residential community had spawned
and nurtured a distinctive black upper class. Afro-
Atlantan John Wesley Dobbs (1882-1961) dubbed the avenue
"Sweet Auburn," influenced by Oliver Goldsmith's poem
and by the money (called "sugar") invested in Auburn
Avenue.

BLACK-CONTROLLED MEDIA IN ATLANTA

        The first black-owned radio station in the United
States, WERD (1949-69), was launched on Auburn Avenue.
The oldest black-controlled daily newspaper in this
country, the Atlanta Daily World (1928-) was launched
and continues to publish on "Sweet Auburn." Afro-
Atlanta's most successful businessmen and civic leaders
frequently became the editors and owners of the black
media operations that grew in number after the Civil
War: Bishop Henry McNeal Turner, Auburn Avenue bookstore proprietor H. A. Hagler, Grand United Order of
Odd Fellows' Benjamin J. Davis, Atlanta University
Professor and Vice-President of Citizens Trust Bank
Jesse B. Blayton, and President of the Atlanta Life
Insurance Company Jesse Hill are examples. In spite
of--if not because of--this impressive history of control
of a medium by independent individuals, Afro-Atlantans
lack a communications network that supports and is
supported by the black community. And, in recent years,
social and physical aspects of the once vibrant "Sweet
Auburn" community have deteriorated. Business activity
has declined. Historic and other structures stand empty
and in need of repair. Thus, local concerns, proximity
of the races, and space negated, diminished, or significantly influenced the focus and needs of Afro-Atlanta.

SELECTED WORKS AND SOURCES EMPHASIZING THE BLACK SIDES
OF ATLANTA

Books

General Works

Allen, Ivan, Jr. Mayor: Notes on the Sixties. New
        York, 1971.

Bacote, Clarence A. The Story of Atlanta University.
    Atlanta, 1969.

Baker, Ray Stannard. Following the Color Line. New
    York, 1908.

Carter, E. R. The Black Side of Atlanta. Atlanta,
    1894.

_____. Our Pulpit, Illustrated. Atlanta, n.d.

Garrett, Franklin M. Atlanta and Environs. New York,
    1954.

Ginsburg, Eli. The Middle-Class Negro in the White
    Man's World. New York, 1967.

Ginsburg, Paul M. The New South Creed: A Study in
    Southern Mythmaking. New York, 1970.

Hunter, Floyd. Community Power Structure. Chapel Hill,
    N.C., 1953.

Jennings, M. Kent. Community Influentials: The Elite
    of Atlanta. New York, 1964.

Lynch, Hollis. The Black Urban Condition. New York,
    1973.

McMahon, C. A. Life Tables for the Population of
    Georgia, 1950-1951. Atlanta, 1955.

_____. The People of Atlanta. Athens, Ga., 1950.

Martin, Thomas H. Atlanta and Its Builders: A Compre-
    hensive History of the Gate City of the South.
    Atlanta, 1902.

Pierce, Joseph A. The Atlanta Negro: A Collection of
    Data on the Negro Population of Atlanta, Georgia.
    Atlanta, 1940.

Woodward, C. Vann. Origins of the New South, 1877-1913.
    Baton Rouge, 1951.

Biography and Autobiography

Davis, Benjamin, Jr. Communist Councilman from Harlem.
    New York, 1969.

DuBois, W. E. B. The Autobiography of W. E. B. DuBois.
    New York, 1968.

_____. Dusk of Dawn. New York, 1940.

English, James W. Handyman of the Lord: The Life and
     Ministry of William Holmes Borders. New York,
     1967.

Johnson, James Weldon. Along This Way. New York, 1933.

Mays, Benjamin E. Born to Rebel. New York, 1971.

Palmer, Charles F. Adventures of a Slum Fighter.
     Atlanta, 1955.

Proctor, Henry Hugh. Between Black and White: Auto-
     biographical Sketches. Boston, 1925.

Thomas, Jesse O. My Story in Black and White. New
     York, 1967.

Torrence, Ridgely. The Story of John Hope. New York,
     1948.

Washington, Booker T. An Autobiography: The Story of
     My Life and Work. Toronto, 1901.

Waters, Ethel. His Eye is on the Sparrow: An Auto-
     biography. New York, 1951.

White, Walter. A Man Called White. New York, 1948.

Theses and Dissertations

Adair, Augustus. "A Political History of the Negro in
     Atlanta." Atlanta University, 1955.

Blackwell, Gloria. "Black Controlled Media in Atlanta,
     1960-1970: The Burden of the Message and the
     Struggle for Survival." Emory University, 1973.

Calhoun, John H. "Significant Aspects of Some Negro
     Leaders' Contribution to the Progress of Atlanta,
     Georgia." Atlanta University.

Conyers, Jean Louise. "The Negro Businesswoman in
     Atlanta, Georgia." Atlanta University.

Daniels, Rufus. "The Historical Development of Mutual
     Federal Savings and Loan Association, Atlanta,
     Georgia, 1925-1961, A Case Study." Atlanta
     University, 1962.

Dinkins, Joel W. "Some Aspects of Economic Life of
     Black Atlantans, 1880-1900." Atlanta University,
     1972.

Haynes, Leroy. "The Ecological Distribution of the Negro Population in Atlanta in 1939." Atlanta University, 1940.

Henton, Leroy Comradge. "Heman E. Perry: Documentary Materials for the Life History of a Business Man." Atlanta University, 1948.

Hopkins, Richard. "Patterns of Persistence and Occupational Mobility in a Southern City: Atlanta, 1870-1920." Emory University, 1972.

Lamar, Bobby J. "Citizens Trust Company and Its Role in the Development of the Atlanta Black Community with Emphasis on the Loan Function." Atlanta University, 1969.

Lyon, Elizabeth A. "Business Buildings in Atlanta: A Study of Urban Growth and Form." Emory University, 1971.

Middleton, Merlissie Ross. "Residential Distribution of Members of an Urban Church." Atlanta University, 1953.

Porter, Michael Leroy. "Black Atlanta: An Interdisciplinary Study of Blacks in the East Side of Atlanta, 1890-1930." Emory University, 1974.

Preston, Howard L. "A New Kind of Horizontal City: Automobility in Atlanta, 1900-1930." Emory University, 1974.

Scott, Olivirea. "A Classified Sociological Source Bibliography of Periodical and Manuscript Materials on the Negro in Atlanta." Atlanta University, 1948.

Slade, Dorothy. "The Evolution of Negro Areas in the City of Atlanta." Atlanta University, 1946.

Taylor, Arthur Reed. "From the Ashes: Atlanta During Reconstruction." Emory University, 1973.

Thompson, Gloriastene. "The Expansion of the Negro Community in Atlanta, Georgia, from 1940-1958." Atlanta University, 1959.

Articles and Periodicals

Alexander, Robert. "Negro Business in Atlanta." Southern Economic Journal 17 (April 1951): 451-64.

Atlanta Daily World (black newspaper). 1928-present.

Atlanta Inquirer (black newspaper). 1960-present.

Atlanta Magazine. 125th Anniversary Commemorative
     Issue, March 1972.

Atlanta University Publications. 1896-1916.

Bacote, Clarence A. "The Negro in Atlanta Politics."
     Phylon 16 (1955): 333-50.

_____. "Negro Proscriptions, Protests, and Proposed
     Solutions in Georgia, 1880-1908." Journal of
     Southern History 25 (November 1959), 471-98.

_____. "Some Aspects of Negro Life in Georgia, 1880-
     1908." Journal of Negro History 43 (1958):
     186-213.

Calhoun, John H. "Black Business in Atlanta." Atlanta
     Inquirer, 1971.

Crowe, Charles. "Racial Massacre in Atlanta, September
     22, 1906." Journal of Negro History (1969): 150-
     168.

Hopkins, Richard. "Status, Mobility and the Dimensions
     of Change in a Southern City: Atlanta, 1870-1910."
     K. T. Jackson and S. K. Schultz, eds., Cities in
     American History. New York: Knopf, 1972.

Hughes, Emmet John. "The Negro's New Economic Life."
     Fortune 54 (September 1956).

Lasker, Bruno. "Atlanta Zoning Plan." Survey 48
     (April 22, 1922): 114-15.

Meier, August, and Lewis, David. "History of the Negro
     Upper Class in Atlanta, Georgia, 1890-1958."
     Journal of Negro Education 18 (Winter 1959):
     129-39.

Phylon.

Shivery, Louie D. "The Neighborhood Union: A Survey
     of the Beginnings of Social Welfare Movements
     Among Negroes in Atlanta." Phylon 13 (1942):
     149-62.

Spellman Messenger.

Voice of the Negro (black newspaper). 1904-7.

Haiti and Black Americans: Relations and Encounters

Richard A. Long

For contemporary black Americans, the fact that
Haiti liberated itself from European tyranny represents
a basic event in their own experience. The moral and
philosophical history of Afro-Americans is filled with
many allusions, references, relations, and contacts with
the first black republic of the world.

As prologue to this history, we can recall an incident, both bizarre and little noticed in the history
of the American Revolution. Still a monarchy, but a
steadfast enemy of England, France greatly assisted the
American colonists in their struggle for independence.
Without this French intervention, a totally different
result of the revolt could have been expected. One of
the unsuccessful acts on the part of the French was
their participation in the Battle of Savannah (a port
city of the Georgia colony), where French troops under
the command of Count d'Estaing took part on the side of
the American colonists during the autumn of 1779. Among
these troops there were more than 500 blacks and men of
color from Santo Domingo, including the young Henri
Christophe, then a bootblack.

The American Revolution was not a revolution; it
was a secession. The social system continued as it was.
Slaves of the colonists remained slaves. It is paradoxical that the American Revolution had a profound

---

Source: This paper was originally written in French
and delivered by the author in March 1975, in Port-au-
Prince under the auspices of the American Embassy there.
The translation was produced by Logical Technical Services of New York and Washington and is used by permission of Mr. Eldridge Greenlee, President of LTS.

influence on the French Revolution, for the latter was
the source of the events in Santo Domingo that resulted
in the abolition of slavery on that island and in the
independence of Haiti.

For black Americans--both those who were emanci-
pated and the somewhat well informed slaves--the epic
of Haitian independence and its heroes was a motivating
force in the search for liberty and human rights. It
was the name Toussaint L'Ouverture that was chiefly on
the lips and in the hearts of black people kept in servitude and oppression by the slave power of the United
States. His spirit influenced slave revolts such as
those of Gabriel Prosser and Denmark Vesey. For the
masters, the name of Toussaint was a source of fear
and terror.

One of the most illustrious personalities of Afro-
American history was the great actor Ira Aldridge. Born
in New York, he began his career on the stage in the
black companies of hard-working amateurs, but his taste
for perfection led him to leave the United States and
to try his luck in England and Europe. Received with
enthusiasm in most European capitals, he played mostly
heroic roles, such as Othello and King Lear. The first
honorary distinction that he received was bestowed by
the Haitian government. It must be recalled that Ira
Aldridge played the role of Henri Christophe in a play
that had a certain degree of success in Germany. On
December 2, 1827, the Haitian government named him as
officer of the regimental guard of the President of the
Republic. There is a possibility that Ira Aldridge
traveled to Haiti to receive this honor, but this is
not certain.

After the War of 1848 with Mexico, the American
government, in all of its departments, fell more and
more under the domination of the South and its pro-
slavery beliefs. A black Episcopal priest, James
Theodore Holly, had the idea of encouraging emigration
to Haiti by freedmen. An invitation was extended by
the Haitian government to black Americans, and in 1858
many black families emigrated. During this era we hear
of an American colony at Saint-Marc (composed of people
from Louisiana) and another at Archaie. After the fall
of Soulouqu the Haitian government redoubled its efforts.
James Redpath, an antislavery white man who had also
interested himself in the emigration of black Americans
to Haiti, received a commission from the Haitian government in 1861 to establish an office in Boston. In the
same year Redpath published A Guide to Haiti, containing
information on the country and advice to future immigrants.

At that moment, one of the greatest of black Americans, one of the great men of modern times, appeared. Frederick Douglass was born a slave on the Eastern Shore of the state of Maryland in 1817. He suffered personally all the humiliations of the life of a slave. Fortunately, he learned how to read and write. He escaped at the age of twenty-one and established himself in New England. After spending three years as a manual laborer, he became a lecturer for one of the antislavery societies. He distinguished himself as a politician and philosopher, meeting with great success at public gatherings abroad, particularly in England. Throughout his long career as an antislavery leader, Douglass was a relentless opponent of projects for the emigration of blacks to Africa. He insisted on the right of American blacks to be free in their own land, the United States.

After the 1850s, Frederick Douglass became so depressed by the reverses suffered by the antislavery movement everywhere that he accepted the invitation of the Department of Immigration of the Haitian government to pay a visit to Haiti. He wrote in his diary, "We are greatly excited at the prospect of standing on the soil of Saint Domingue, the site of events both stirring and heroic, the labor of a people of our flesh." This trip, set for April 25, 1861, was canceled by a most important event in the history of the United States, the attack on Fort Sumter, the naval fortification at Charleston, South Carolina, by the secessionists on April 12. This event led directly to the Civil War, considered by Douglass as a direct link to the freedom of slaves.

In July 1889, President Benjamin Harrison named Frederick Douglass as Minister and Consul General to the Republic of Haiti. Having held the attention of the world for more than forty years, Douglass was considered to be the most eminent black man in the United States. Certain men of his time felt that the act of President Harrison was not so much an honor for Douglass as a trick to get him out of the way. Douglass did not view things in this light, and he accepted the appointment. He arrived in Haiti during the installation of President Legitime. During the presentation of Douglass's letters of accreditation, President Legitime said, "Your reputation is known in both hemispheres. You are the embodiment of the idea which Haiti follows, the moral and intellectual development of the African race by individual effort and training of the mind."

Douglass occupied the role of a diplomat during the difficult business concerning St. Nicholas Harbor, desired by the American navy as a naval base. The Haitian government had rejected the offer in spite of the pressure exerted by the United States. In the American

press, Frederick Douglass was sharply attacked because
he was seen as "permitting his identity with the black
people of Haiti to weaken him in his duty as the American Minister." It was in this climate of bad publicity
in the United States that Douglass resigned. The Haitian people deeply regretted his departure in 1891.
A great honor was bestowed on Douglass by the Haitian
government in 1893 when he was made member of a commission as Honorary Delegate of Haiti to the Chicago
World's Fair.

In Chicago on January 2, Douglass presented a discourse on Haiti that is a masterpiece of American rhetoric. This speech was both a summary of Haitian history
and a defense of its national life. Two years later,
the great Douglass passed away.

In his dissertation Douglass said:

I consider Haiti as the original liberator of
the 19th century. It was her example, both
unique and courageous, which for the first
time shocked the Christian world with an understanding of the manliness of blacks. . . .
Until the moment that Haiti struck its blow
for liberty, the conscience of the Christian
world remained dormant in the presence of
human slavery.

In a certain sense, the mantle of Frederick Douglass was passed not to the black leader most in the
public eye after his death, Booker T. Washington, but
to W. E. B. Du Bois. Professor, writer, scholar, editor,
and activist, Du Bois was, like Douglass, one of the
greatest of black Americans. He spent most of his
career as a professor at Atlanta University and in the
NAACP. For this organization he established a periodical, The Crisis, in 1910 and edited it for twenty-three
years. Later he founded the quarterly Phylon, still
published by Atlanta University.

The ties that bind Du Bois to Haiti are first those
of birth. His grandfather, having been born in the
Bahamas and having spent his youth in New York, went to
Haiti about 1820. He married there and had a son, Alfred, who would become the father of W. E. B. Du Bois.
Alfred was taken from Haiti to the United States by his
father at the age of five. Du Bois did not know either
his father or his grandfather well, but the knowledge
of these Haitian relationships was very important for
him.

During all of his long life, Du Bois had opportunities to renew his knowledge of Haiti and its history for

himself and for the black world. I would like to enu-
merate only a few of these occasions, for the relations
of Du Bois with Haiti would require a detailed study.
In his first book, which appeared in 1896 and covered
the history of the suppression of the slave trade, he
entitled a chapter "Toussaint L'Ouverture and Anti-
Slavery Effort." As ideologist and mover of the Pan
African movement, Du Bois very often had contact with
Haiti and its political figures. In 1919 he worked at
the side of Georges Sylvain and of Dantes Bellegarde
in Paris. Du Bois naturally protested against the
American occupation of Haiti during its entire course
from 1915 to 1933. In September 1944, he made a brief
visit to Haiti, and in his journalistic writings of the
period he talks about that country, its history, and
its problems. He mentions in particular his meeting
with Price-Mars. He published two articles in Cahiers
d'Haiti in September and October of the same year.

Here we might mention some black scholars who had
associations with Dr. Du Bois and also with Atlanta University: Mercer Cook spent much time in Haiti as director of a program on instruction in English. Head of the
French Department at Atlanta and later at Howard, diplomat, translator, he did much to advance the knowledge of
Haiti among black Americans. He wrote many articles and
pamphlets on the subject of Haiti, and he invited Dantes
Bellegarde as a lecturer to both Atlanta and Howard.
A pupil and associate of Mercer Cook, Naomi Garrett,
worked in Haiti as a professor of English. Her doctoral
thesis on the subject of Haitian poetry was published as
The Renaissance of Haitian Poetry by Présence Africaine.
Historian Rayford Logan, who had been associated with
Du Bois since 1919, is the author of a monumental work
on the history of diplomatic relations between the
United States and Haiti that appeared in 1941. He has
also written articles on Haiti. Professor Logan, like
Mercer Cook, worked at both Atlanta and Howard.

The period following World War I was a very animated one for black Americans, especially in the areas
of literature and politics. A distinguished personality
of the Harlem period was James Weldon Johnson. He had
already won a reputation as diplomat, poet, novelist,
translator, and man of politics. As Secretary of the
NAACP, he took a lively interest in the American occupation of Haiti and in 1920 was a member of American liberal groups who visited Haiti to investigate it. Afterwards, he published four articles in a weekly, The
Nation, on the subject of the occupation. Collected
together under the title Self-Determining Haiti, these
were circulated as a pamphlet.

In intellectual circles in the United States,
Johnson carried out such a publicity campaign for Haiti
that one may speak of a "Haitian theme" in American letters. In his autobiography, the well-known Along This
Way, he makes note of his love for Haiti and its people.
He speaks in his narrative especially about Georges
Sylvain. Johnson stayed three months in the country,
and he remained a friend of the country until his death
in an automobile accident in 1938. Johnson was a graduate of Atlanta University and author of the moving
lyrics of the hymn "Lift Every Voice and Sing," called
by some the "Negro National Anthem."

Two very distinguished Americans made a trip to
Port-au-Prince in 1927. They were the best-known composer and violinist among blacks of that period,
Clarence Cameron White, and his colleague, professor
and writer John F. Matheus. Matheus, more than eighty
years old at the time of this writing, recently described the visit. They both came in search of inspiration for an opera on a Haitian theme. They found
it: the opera Quanga, which relates episodes of the life
of Dessaline. Unfortunately little known, the opera had
a few performances twenty-five years ago. Matheus wrote
other stories and a play on Haitian subjects, and during
the 1940s he returned to Haiti to replace Mercer Cook as
director of the English language program.

I would like to note that several black composers
have taken an interest in Haiti. Of these, John Work,
a professor of music at Fisk University, spent a year
in Haiti during the 1940s. His research and his com-
positions, unfortunately, remain unpublished.

A great poet, the best known of the Harlem renaissance, demonstrated a great interest in Haiti. Langston
Hughes, an enthusiast of the black world, made an extended visit to Haiti in 1931 and became acquainted with
the young Haitian writers of the period, like Jacques
Roumain and Philippe Thoby-Marcelin. Later he did several translations of Haitian poets and presented them to
the American public in an anthology, Poetry of the Negro.
His collaborator in the editing of the anthology was the
distinguished Arna Bontemps. Bontemps and Hughes also
coauthored a children's book with Haiti as its theme,
entitled Popo and Fifine. Langston Hughes also collabo-
rated with Mercer Cook in the translation of a novel by
Jacques Roumain, Masters of the Dew.

Countee Cullen, a poet of the black renaissance who
had a deep love of French culture, does not enter the
scene officially as a visitor to Haiti, but, in fact, he
knew Haitians both in Paris and New York and had close
ties with some of them. Moreover, before his death, he

had planned to visit Haiti, perhaps in search of materials for his writings. A writer and anthropologist who
deserves mention is the very witty woman Zora Neale
Hurston, the author of Tell My Horse. In that book her
taste for things exotic and paradoxical overcame her
scholarly moderation, and the result is not to be recommended. But her love for Haitians, particularly the
peasants--whom she sees as sharing basic ties with the
people of other islands, such as Jamaica, as well as
with the blacks of the United States--is undeniable.

When one speaks of Afro-American culture, a key
personality is Alain Leroy Locke, professor, critic,
and philosopher. It was he who in 1925 was the editor
of the anthology The New Negro, which remains a monument
of the Harlem renaissance. In the American tradition,
there are very few books that made such an impression,
not only in the United States, but abroad, in every
corner of the black world. President Senghor has said
that The New Negro was his bedside reading when he was
a student in Paris. Alain Locke was the adviser of
young artists of the period and the sponsor of a movement agitating for a reevaluation of the black man in
the United States. Locke extolled the importance of
black folk and the richness of their ancestral African
culture.

During his life Alain Locke had a great feeling
for Haiti, and in 1943 he traveled to Haiti to give
a series of lectures under the title "The Role of the
Negro in the Americas." These lectures were presented
under the auspices of the Inter-American Committee on
Intellectual and Artistic Relations. Also published in
Haiti, these lectures remain a very important document
in the Haitian-Afro-American dialogue. In his discussions, Dr. Locke made a plea for solidarity on the part
of the blacks in the Americas and analyzed the differences in the relations of the elites and the masses in
different countries. In the first lecture, he spoke of
the novel Canapé Vert, a major work written by the
brothers Marcelin. He said, "We have here a concrete
illustration of what I would discuss, to know how that
which rises to the rank of an art and of universal expression, and that which appears to be only local and
national, can acquire an international meaning and a
positive influence, and remain, in substance, representative of a race." In the second lecture he spoke in
this way: "After the Guyanas, Haiti remains the most
important center of living African expression in America. As such, she constitutes a precious laboratory for
the study of those traces which disappear so rapidly."

Alain Locke remained in contact with several Haitians during his life, and he read all the books and

articles dealing with Haiti over a period of forty
years, publishing reviews of many of them.

The secrets of the African dance are well preserved
in Haiti, and it was in search of their secrets that
Katherine Dunham first came to Haiti. An ethnologist
and a choreographer, she found in Haiti a complete
vocabulary of movement that formed the basis of her
teaching. This teaching revolutionized the dance theater. I also believe that it was the subtle impact of
this theatrical style that contributed so much to the
Africanization of social dancing nearly everywhere in
the world. Katherine Dunham is well known both in Haiti
and outside the country as a friend and proponent of an
art form that originated in Haiti.

Also in the area of the dance, the work and the
contribution of Lavinia Williams, a former collaborator
of Katherine Dunham, are extraordinarily influential.
Lavinia Williams attracted to Haiti many people who
came in search of the vitality of the Haitian rhythm.
She adds to her own talent a great knowledge of Haiti,
and with that she is preparing to develop elsewhere in
the Caribbean the panorama of black art.

The beautiful countryside of Haiti has attracted
many artists and painters--among these, black Americans.
The first to come was William Edouard Scott of Indianap-
olis. He had studied in Chicago and in Paris. As hold-
er of a Rosenwald fellowship, he worked in Haiti in 1931
and held a show in Port-au-Prince. The Haitian government bought twelve of his paintings. Scott's example
inspired Petion Savain. An artist often inspired by
African sources, Aaron Douglass, who was also once
a student in Paris, made a visit to Haiti in 1938.
Even before visiting Haiti, another artist, Jacob
Lawrence, created a series of works (forty-one in all)
on the life of Toussaint L'Ouverture. Now recognized
as a masterpiece of American art in its genre, one may
hope that the series will be exhibited in Haiti. These
works date from 1938, when Lawrence was only nineteen
years old. There are other black painters to remember
here: James Porter, Ellis Wilson, and Paul Keene. But
I end this catalogue with the name of Lois Mailou James
Pierre-Noel, a professor for many years at Howard University and the wife of a distinguished Haitian,
Vergniaud Pierre-Noel. A true devotee of French art
and culture as well as Haitian, Lois Pierre-Noel has
created dozens of beautiful paintings on Haitian subjects. She has exhibited them in Haiti, Washington,
and Paris and recently in an extensive exhibition in
her native Boston.

I have made a brief review of the truly great bonds that exist between the blacks of the United States and those of the Haitian nation. I have not covered the subject entirely: here at the end we are only beginning.

Capital or Labor? The Decision to Introduce the Industrial Stabilization Act (Trinidad and Tobago, March 1965)

Carl D. Parris

> If foreign investment were a key to happiness,
> this would have been a happy place (Eric Wil-
> liams, Nation, February 1, 1963).

> The Act is on the Statute Book and will remain
> on the Statute Book (Eric Williams, Nation,
> October 1, 1965).

In March 1965, the government of Trinidad and
Tobago was faced with increasing demands from organized
labor for strong governmental action with regard to
ownership and control of national resources as well as
demands for drastic change in the area of income distribution. The government therefore was faced with the
choice of either confronting those companies and groups
that were in the main responsible for these social and
economic ills or of confronting labor, in the hope that
by this action it could morally persuade the companies
and groups to assist it in curing the country of its
ills.

The government took the latter option. It introduced and passed in both Houses of Parliament, in one
day, a piece of legislation known as the Industrial
Stabilization Act.[1] This act may be summarized as
follows.

Note: A number of individuals have contributed in
various ways to the shaping of this product. Among
them are Lloyd Best, Kari Levitt, and Eric St. Cyr.
They are not, of course, totally responsible for the
final form.

1. It provides for the compulsory recognition by employers of trade unions and organizations representative of a majority of workers.[2]

2. It establishes an industrial court composed of

a president who shall be a judge of the Supreme Court of Judicature, designated by the Chief Justice after consultation with the Prime Minister, and four other members appointed by the Governor General . . . to hear and determine trade disputes, to register industrial agreements and to hear and determine matters relating to the registration of such agreements. [Further, it shall] hear and determine complaints relating to the price of goods and commodities, and to hear and determine any complaint brought in accordance with this Act.[3]

3. It declares that

a worker shall not take part in a strike in connection with any trade dispute unless (a) the dispute has been reported to the Minister . . ., (b) the Minister has not referred the dispute to the court for settlement within twenty-eight days of the date on which the report of the dispute was first made to him, and (c) the Minister has, within forty-eight hours of the decision to go on strike, been given fourteen days notice in writing by the trade union or other organization of its intention to call a strike or declare a lock-out as the case may be.[4]

The decision of the government in March of 1965 is an important one not only because it marks a sharp break in its official attitude toward organized labor, but also because it demonstrates the narrowing of the options open to a government committed to an economic policy of industrialization by invitation. The fundamental question that I therefore seek to answer is, what factors influenced this specific decision?

THE PNM, THE GOVERNMENT, AND LABOR PRIOR TO 1961

When the People's National Movement (PNM) won the 1956 general election, it did so without any official trade union base.[5] The party leader, Dr. Eric Williams, tells us that in 1955, "three top trade union leaders, all of whom have since opposed the PNM offered to join our party on condition that they came in as what they

called a "faction" with certain offices in our party,
certain seats on our executive and certain constitu-
encies in the elections reserved for them." The People's National Movement refused this offer, he said,
because, "with the experience of the British Labour
Party before us, we were careful not to allow our movement to be dominated by the trade union bloc vote."6

This position taken by the party leaders with respect to the official representation of labor undoubtedly gave them an opportunity to win the supoort of a
wider cross section of the voting public by presenting
themselves to the population and the international community (the British, in particular) as standing above
factions and interest groups, as "a democratic party of
men and women of honesty and incorruptibility, of all
races, colours, classes and creeds."7 Perhaps more importantly for the party leaders, the position taken
freed them from any specific ideological commitment
that might have rendered them "unfit to rule" not only
in the eyes of their colonial masters, but also in the
eyes of powerful local interest groups that benefited
from colonial rule.8 In keeping with this, the party
leader as early as September of 1955 was able to enun-
ciate a position that offended neither local nor foreign
business interests nor organized labor.

Thus in March 1957 the government found itself in
a situation in which trade unionists sought to organize
workers in an American firm that assembled office equipment. The management of the firm opposed the intentions
of the trade unionists, arguing that the welfare of the
workers was already taken care of. The government
sought to support the union and through the Minister of
Labour pointed out to the management that their attitude
would lead to industrial unrest. The Chief Minister,
Dr. Williams, mindful of his earlier position on the
right of unions to organize announced that "any industry
coming in here and behaving decently will be given de-
cent treatment. If they do not like our action, let
them pull out."9

The position adopted by government in this dispute
was important, for moving from a relatively quiescent
labor scene in the early 1950s, Trinidad found itself
in the early 1960s bedeviled by eager trade unionists
anxious to demonstrate to management that they were no
longer willing to "hew wood and draw water." The workers had supported the Williams government in the 1956
general elections and had marched under its banner on
April 22, 1960, demanding the return of Chaguaramas
from the Americans. It could thus be argued that the
nationalist demands of the PNM in the period, especially
over the Chaguaramas issue, had spilled over to the

organized working classes in the early 1960s and that
the upsurge of labor militancy in the 1960-65 period
was a continuation of the 1960 march on Chaguaramas.
This assertion can be established best in terms of the
events of the largest strike that took place between
1960 and 1965.

TEXACO OIL STRIKE, 1960

On June 27, 1960, the Oilfield Workers' Trade Union
(OWTU), the largest union in the country, gave notice of
an impending strike to the management of Texaco. The
strike, which began on June 30 and initially involved
7,000 workers, soon spread to Apex Trinidad when the
latter was informed by Texaco that it would no longer
take Apex crude oil. At this point Apex served notice
on some 600 workers. Apex workers then decided that
"one for all, all for one, we go on strike from tomor-
row."[10] The Trinidad Guardian, which during the Chaguaramas affair was openly hostile to government, quickly
quoted and supported by way of an editorial some local
economists who feared that the strike might have an ill
effect on the territory's industrial and investment
climate.[11] This influential foreign-owned newspaper
further argued that the situation could affect Texaco's
plans for future investment and divert other potential
investors to more favorable areas. The economists also
buttressed their antilabor position by pointing out the
adverse impact that high wages in oil might have on
other sectors of the economy and suggested the possibility that wage increases in the oil industry might result
in higher prices throughout the country.[12]

Despite the pressure from members of the local
professional and business class and from the influential
foreign-owned newspaper, the government's initial position was simply one of "concern about the strike."[13]
When, by July 8, the strike had spread from Texaco to
Apex and then to Shell, the situation in the country
was becoming serious. The strike had affected transportation facilities in the country; the Coconut Growers
Association processing plant had closed down due to a
shortage of cooking oil; the price of coal had increased
considerably; workers at the Trinidad brick factory had
been laid off; and scavenging was going on, creating
a serious health hazard.[14]

Additional pressure was brought to bear on the
government when East Indian opposition leader Bhadase
Maraj threatened to introduce a motion in the Legislative Council calling on the government to declare the
strike a national emergency.[15] The Trinidad Guardian

once more editorialized, accusing the government of not
taking a firmer stand due to political reasons.[16]

Despite this mounting pressure and the fact that
the oil industry was virtually paralyzed, the government's only concession to the business interests was
to call a meeting between the negotiating parties, at
which it was agreed that "all essential services would
be maintained."[17] When the strike ended several days
later, Dr. Williams took the opportunity of giving the
government's view of the situation while addressing
a large crowd in San Fernando. After indicating the
number of workdays and the amount of government revenue
lost during the strike, he said,

> You will have noticed I have refrained from
> discussing the inconveniences to the public,
> the temporary price increases, the shortage
> of food-stuffs. . . . Industrial democracy
> is based on the right of workers to withhold
> their labour by way of strike, even though
> the community is thrown in turmoil.

> Strikes inevitably involve public in-
> conveniences. It is the effective and often
> the only way of bringing the workers' case
> to the attention of the public and winning
> public support and sympathy. I have been
> through so many strikes abroad, many leading
> directly or indirectly to a transport crisis,
> that I for one was determined once basic es-
> sential services were maintained and until
> a total shut down was really threatened that
> I would sanction no step whatsoever which
> savoured of strike breaking.[18]

This speech, with its "right to withhold labour" theme
and its "industrial democracy" view, invites an explanation of the reasons why the Trinidad and Tobago government in March of 1965 introduced the Industrial Stabilization Act (ISA), which essentially contradicts the
position enunciated in 1960. Several interesting factors suggest that the government would not have made
such a statement at this time. First of all, the essentially nationalist and working-class rhetoric of the
leader of the government in 1960, Dr. Williams, was
situated in a context in which (1) the dispute between
the regime and the United States over Chaguaramas was
still officially unsettled and (2) contemporary events
in Cuba had an important impact on the working class of
Trinidad and Tobago and its leaders, whose support the
government would need for the upcoming general elections
of 1961.[19]

That the government was aware of the negatives in the situation is clear, for in the San Fernando speech Dr. Williams ominously added,

> I have restricted my analysis . . . to the question of Government Finance, which is what the union and the company chose to argue about. In that sense the strike was aimed at the government and was fundamentally political in its origin and nature. Extremists on both sides clamoured for governmental intervention; a company representative threatened one Minister that his company would not invest one penny in Trinidad, another company representative accused the government of double crossing the company; irresponsible elements on the workers' side injected race into the strike, talked about emulating Castro, advocated nationalizing the oil industry, threatened a national crisis. . . . These elements sought to lay the ground work for the establishment of a socialist party for the coming General Elections.[20]

Second, the Williams government was looking forward to financial inputs from the United States as a result of the impending settlement of the Chaguaramas affair. Third, having come to power on the crest of an oil boom, the government clearly felt it was in a position to absorb the initial losses of revenue from the strike.

In addition to the government's perception of its economic strength and legitimacy, the upcoming general elections were an important factor in explaining the government's stand on July 24, 1960. Three facts seemed important to their outcome: (1) in the 1956 elections, Williams and his party had had no solid official trade union support; (2) members of the local commercial and agricultural elites joined Williams's party even though many remained in opposition to his Chaguaramas campaign; (3) although the issue of Chaguaramas was not yet officially settled, Williams and his government had abandoned their original position, thus eliminating the possibility of U.S. intervention.

The response of the local population to the government in the 1961 elections was overwhelming, for despite the importance of the race question,[21] the People's National Movement was swept back into electoral power with a two-to-one victory over its opponents. In fact, the trade union vote was crucial. Recognizing the importance of their votes, Dr. Williams wooed this group in a speech that is important to our later discussion of the Industrial Stabilization Act, if only because it exposes the contextual difference between the periods of July 1960 and March 1965:

> If there is any group in the community which
> is going to defend democracy and self-govern-
> ment, that group is the workers. . . . if any
> group is the repository of patriotism, that
> would be the workers of the country. No gov-
> ernment will survive without the point of view
> of the labour movement behind it. . . . You
> workers are the force of the future. . . .
> After the elections I recognize my friends.[22]

If the last sentence was meant in good faith, then it is extremely difficult to understand how the party, containing elements of the already hostile business community and committed to a development strategy that demanded, above all, quiescence among workers, could have recognized its trade unionist friends. Such recognition could have served only to legitimize further the workers' demands for higher wages and better living conditions and thus to push the government into a policy of confrontation with the multinational corporations in oil and sugar. There can be no doubt that all this was well understood by the government, because in the area of political representation, in which it could easily have "recognized" its friends, it significantly failed to do so, while strengthening the hand of business. Examination of the composition of the Cabinet and of both houses of Parliament is revealing. In the 1961 Cabinet there were five members closely aligned to business and no labor representation. In the lower House of Parliament, business had seven representatives, while labor had none; and in the Senate, membership in which was based on appointment, business again had seven representatives, while labor had only two.[23]

Second, the preponderance of such names as Merry, DeFreitas, and Gatcliffe in government appointments to important statutory boards suggests that the government felt no need to change its original omnibus orientation keeping both capital and labor happy. But the domestic situation was about to change in the first half of the 1960s. The government had, in fact, to make a choice between capital and labor. This time it chose an alliance with capital. However, I feel that the decision to introduce the ISA in March of 1965 should not necessarily be seen as indicative of an antilabor attitude; rather, it was a function of the government's deeper entanglement in the international capitalist system.

THE GOVERNMENT AND THE ECONOMY: 1962-65

In the 1962 Throne Speech, the government expressed
its "profound regret that its high expectations and
those of the people of Trinidad and Tobago, of the
Chaguaramas agreement negotiated with the United States
of America in Tobago a year ago, have not been translated into the practical co-operation which was then
confidently anticipated."[24] This disappointment must
be understood in light of the financial state of the
country by the end of 1961. In his Budget Speech of
1962 the Minister of Finance stated that "the point has
now consequently been reached where, at current levels
of taxation, it is no longer possible to finance development from current revenues."[25]

The economic downturn coincided with one of the
government's major tasks--to "present an accurate picture of our political stability and economic climate
to the outside world, particularly to investors."[26]
The government wasted no time in assuring foreign investors of its hospitable attitude. It reiterated that

> in 1956, one of the first acts of the govern-
> ment that was elected in September of that
> year concerned a proposal that the United
> Kingdom and the United States should sign
> a treaty involving . . . a guarantee of
> American investments in various parts of the
> world in the event of expropriation. The
> government of Trinidad and Togabo as one of
> its first official acts told the United
> Kingdom--

>> 'go ahead, sign the treaty, and we
>> will have no objection to its being
>> extended to Trinidad and Tobago.'[27]

The change of government's fortunes in this period
is also reflected in the country's increasing unemployment.[28] And in addition to revenue depletion, unemployment, strikes in oil and in other sectors of the economy,[29] the government at this time faced the possibility
of a strike by its own civil servants. Commenting on
the threatened strike, Dr. P. Solomon, Deputy Prime
Minister, exposed the government's fears that continued
labor unrest could undermine the prospects of the chosen
economic development option: "If there had been a
strike. . . . it would have seemed to the world that we
are an immature, irresponsible, impossible kind of people with whom to deal; and that, pursuant with unrest
in the labour movement, would have put 'paid' to any
chance of investment for possibly the next twenty
years."[30] Thus, the government faced a much tighter

economic situation in 1962 than it had met on assuming
office in 1956. What is more, the public debt had
risen from $72.9 million at the end of 1957 to $137
million at the end of 1962, and the recurrent government
financial balances had dwindled from $32.6 million in
1958 to $2.1 million in 1961.[31]

The impending entry of Britain into the European
Common Market had serious implications for the sugar,
cocoa, and citrus industries, which were crucial in
terms of keeping the lid on the unemployment situation.[32]
The government's confidence in its ability to deal with
this problem and with the weakening of prices for petroleum was influenced by a perception of its small size.
This led to the feeling that the government of such a
small country was helpless in the context of the larger
international economy. But these asymmetrical relations
of dependency, however precarious, were quite acceptable
to the local business elite.

Consequently, when the government sought to raise
internal revenue by (1) the introduction of a "purchase
tax," whose stated intention was to influence the pattern of consumption,[33] and (2) an increase in the rate
of tax on companies, which were formerly allowed to
write off for tax purposes 40 percent of the value of
their capital investment in the year of expenditure
against their profits in that year, the reaction of the
local elite was both swift and hostile. The Chamber of
Commerce in a letter to the Finance Minister wrote that
"if the proposals contained in the 1963 Budget are im-
plemented, they would 'cripple the economy of the country'";[34] and the Trinidad Guardian sought to influence
public opinion by carrying a caption that said "resig-
nation of the Minister of Finance is reported by a reliable source to have been requested by certain groups
in an appeal to the Prime Minister."[35] Commenting on
the criticism of the budget, Finance Minister A. N. R.
Robinson easily recognized that "most of the criticism
was concerned only with sectional interest."[36]

What becomes very interesting at this point is the
awareness by at least some elements in the government of
the role of the larger corporations in the economy.
Finance Minister Robinson pointed out that

> the Commercial Banks run their business in
> a way that is not in the interest of the popu-
> lation . . . and it is commonly accepted . . .
> that their policies have always been dictated
> by their head offices abroad, and consequently
> in the interest of foreign and metropolitan
> powers rather than in the interest of the
> society in which their particular branch bank
> operates.[37]

The government, however, rather than utilizing the
electoral legitimacy it had gained as a result of the
1961 elections, chose to appeal to the "good sense" of
the business sector. In so doing it illustrated its
own awareness of the contradictions of its development
strategy and its perception of its own weakness in the
face of the multinational corporations.

The failure of the business community to respond
to moral pressure induced the government to back down
on its original proposals concerning insurance tax,
income tax, and allowances for children's education
expenses at institutions abroad. The change was implied
by the Finance Minister, who announced that "we propose
to embark upon a prudent measure of borrowing both on
the domestic market and on foreign markets."[38] Furthermore, the draft estimates of expenditure for 1963 indicated that the government was seeking to borrow an
additional $35 million on the world market[39] and that
Texaco had donated $3 million out of a total of $15
million promised to the government's Independence Development Fund.[40]

In addition, the government decided to appoint a
commission of inquiry into the oil industry whose tasks
were
1.   To examine the organization, structure, and finance
     of the oil industry of Trinidad in the context of
     the economics of the world oil industry;
2.   To assess the equity of the shares of the national
     product that accrue to the government and to the
     workers of the country as well as to the share-
     holders;
3.   To appraise the labor policy of the industry with
     special emphasis on job security, retrenchment,
     and redundancy in the context of the Independence
     Development Fund;
4.   To make recommendations designed to assure greater
     stability in the industry.[41]

Fearing that its oil reserves might be dwindling,
government also requested the United Nations Technical
Assistance Board to provide immediately the resources
of an expert petroleum engineer with experience in the
assessment of reserves and the effect of various procedures on the level of such reserves.[42]

At the same time the Prime Minister announced that
the Cabinet had decided that a commission of inquiry be
appointed
1.   To investigate the existence and the extent of sub-
     versive activity within the country, with special
     emphasis on the trade union movement;

2. To appraise the international ramifications of such
    activity;
3. To make recommendations for the protection of the
    nation's democratic patterns.[43]

What is of interest here is that despite the Finance
Minister's complaint of the exploitation of the economy
by large corporations, the government chose to investigate the trade union movement rather than the foreign
corporations.

Thus, by June 1963 the government was forced into
a more unequal economic relationship with local and
foreign capitalist interests; and in exchange for their
financial support, the government began to discredit
those same trade unionists whose demands it had cham-
pioned in 1960.[44] The formalization of dependency became more apparent in the government's Second Five Year
Development Plan, issued in 1964.[45]

The basic assumptions of the plan were that the
rate of growth of production of crude petroleum would
decline and that the population would continue to increase at about 3 percent per year. To finance the plan
it was envisaged that $41.6 million would be raised from
public sector savings, $66.1 million from foreign loans
(including borrowing from "local" foreign banks), $6
million from other capital receipts from local sources,
$50.5 million from the Chaguaramas agreement, and $90.8
million from foreign aid, grants, and soft loans.[46]

Faced with falling prices in oil, sugar, and other
commodities and with a reduction in the rate of expansion of the economy as a whole--as well as the already
"rising" expectations of the working sections of the
population--the government, rather than opting to re-
define radically its economic policy, chose the economic
strategy of "national corporatism." This, in the words
of the Prime Minister, is

> a middle way between outright nationalization
> and the old fashioned capitalist organization
> backed by the marines and the dollars of the
> United States of America. That middle way is
> an active participation between government
> and major foreign investors in both the formu-
> lation and the achievement of the government's
> development targets and the government's
> social objectives.[47]

In keeping with the "new strategy," which called
for the "active collaboration of the private sector,"
the government then instituted discussions with big
business in the oil and sugar industries and sought to
trade its capitulation for their support in its attempt

to diversify the economy, thus alleviating the unemployment situation in the country.[48]

The response of the foreign companies corroborated
the Finance Minister's earlier observation that "the
more concessions that the government granted, the more
the business community wanted." In turn, government
reaction betrayed its inability to resort to measures
other than moral suasion to pressure the multinational
corporations. It was clear that the government was
more than reluctant to use its popular support to continue the psychological decolonization it had begun over
the Chaguaramas issue.

The implications for labor of government's deepening involvement in the international capitalist system
became clearer by the time the 1964 budget was presented
in Parliament. As the Finance Minister pointed out,
"the budget is the instrument by which the development
plan is carried into effect. . . . the budget must also
seek to provide the stimulus to the private sector to
achieve the targets set under the plan."[49] Following
this signal to the business community of the government's intentions to make further concessions, the
Finance Minister, who in 1963 had pointed to the ex-
ploitative role of foreign conglomerates in the economy,
now argued that the government's developmental goals
could be achieved only if labor would play its part.
Thus, the Minister continued:

> There can be no doubt whatsoever, that if we
> are to achieve the rate of progress which is
> necessary and desirable in this country, not
> only is further institutional development
> necessary but an ever more urgent need is
> a better atmosphere for industrial develop-
> ment. A healthy industrial relations pattern
> cannot be achieved on the basis of the turbu-
> lence on the one side or intransigence on the
> other. The process has already gone too far
> and any continuation of this state of affairs
> into 1964 will permanently injure our indus-
> trialization effort and damage our interna-
> tional reputation.[50]

In short, for those segments of organized labor
who opposed the government's economic policy, the writing was on the wall. Labor was now supposed to "behave"
and to subordinate its interest to "community interest,"
the latter being clearly synonymous with business
interests. Furthermore, nowhere in the budget did the
Minister deal with two very pressing domestic problems,
unemployment and the rising cost of living. Rather, the
1964 budget emphasized the need for financial resources

and highlighted still further the financial dependence
of the government over the past year.[51]

Given, therefore, the almost total reliance of the
Second Five Year Development Plan on loan capital, it
is of no surprise that the Budget Speech did not suggest
any intention by the government to deal with big business. Neither did the speech indicate any governmental
intention to change the trade structure of the country.
Not only did the development plan rely on aid, but the
Prime Minister even put forward a case for retention of
the Commonwealth preferential treatment for Trinidad's
agricultural exports.[52]

By early 1964, therefore, it had become very clear
that the Trinidad and Tobago government was under severe
pressure from local and foreign business elites[53] whose
strength within the political system had increased
through occupancy of key positions on statutory boards,
through the government's newly articulated policy of
national corporatism, and through the government's acceptance of financial support for its "Better Village
Programme" from multinationals that were operating
locally (for example, Tate & Lyle and Texaco).[54] Although the economic policy of national corporatism
forced the government to use any financial surpluses it
had gained to service its growing loans, the Prime Minister, rather than rethinking the development strategy,
sought to argue its inevitability by reference to the
country's "geographical location in the hemisphere," its
"inherited economic structures," and, of course, its
small size.

Nevertheless, the government was reluctant to get
tough with labor. During the May-July 1964 bus strike
at the Princes Town Special Bus Company,[55] the government, finding itself accused by opposition members in
the House of Assembly of not using the police to break
the strike, tried to maintain an image of impartiality.[56]
The acting Labour Minister, A. C. Alexis, declared:
"this government have always stood for justice, as has
been evidenced in the past strikes when the workers
themselves remarked that never were the workers of the
country so fairly treated."[57] However, in November of
1964 the Governor General in his Throne Speech indicated
to labor that the die was cast unless labor was willing
to assume the role that the government's economic strategy required. Given Trinidad's small domestic market,
the government had to encourage products for export.
This required that Trinidad's products be competitive
with those in overseas markets.[58] However, neither the
Governor General nor the Finance Minister spelled out
the economic sacrifices expected from labor in the

pursuit of such an economic strategy. Clearly, labor
would have to content itself with low wages.

It is my view that the government had to threaten
and discredit the militant elements of the labor movement in order to obtain legitimacy for its probusiness
policies and to ensure the continued financial participation of business in its economic endeavors. But while
it can be argued that government's financial entanglement with big business would lead to a coincidence of
interests, it must also be realized that this financial
entanglement would bring about areas of conflict.[59]

This last point becomes very clear in the 1965
Budget Speech, in which the Minister pointed out

> that the problem of industrialization in
> Trinidad and Tobago is becoming more and
> more complex.
>
> In the industrial field . . . because
> of the limited size of our domestic market
> and the nature of modern technology and scale
> of production, much will not be achieved by
> import substitution alone. There is a com-
> pelling need for a national aggressive and
> sustained approach to this question of mar-
> kets. But private enterprise must play its
> part.[60]

What is significant about this speech is its admission
of the failure of the government's development strategy,
especially in terms of its reliance on big business to
create the conditions for the further economic development of the country.[61]

If we recall the government's retreat on its 1963
revenue-raising provisions, the standoffish attitude of
the oil and sugar companies toward the government's appeal for cooperation in its industrial diversification
efforts, and the government's frequent reiteration of
the need for a stable industrial climate, then the Minister's "but private enterprise must play its part"
would be seen more as an expression of hope than a
threat to big business.[62] What was still left to be
decided were the terms under which this hope would be
realized. I propose that the price of cooperation by
the business sector in the government's development
plans was governmental guarantees and action regarding
"the atmosphere for industrial development."[63] In short,
the rules of participation would be set ultimately by
big business. The government's concurrence in this was
made clear in the Budget Speech of 1965. The Minister

informed the nation that "it makes no sense at all to
generate hostility against profits."[64]

In response to this situation, the militant segment
of organized labor called on the government to control
and stabilize both wages and profits and to curb inflation.[65] Further, commenting on the economic situation,
it said,

> We in Trinidad were caught in a worldwide net
> of capitalist exploitation, a situation which
> could not be remedied with bargaining, im-
> proved fringe benefits or pension plans. What
> is needed is political action so that we, in
> this country, can control our affairs and find
> a way to reap the benefits of the country's
> wealth without the "help" of foreigners.[66]

This statement coincided with wage strikes at Lock
Joint[67] and at an important American-owned manufacturing concern, Federation Chemicals Limited.[68] Two events
followed these strikes and provided, perhaps, the pro-
verbial straw that broke the camel's back. First, the
Civil Service Association (CSA), through its General
Secretary, James Manswell, threatened to institute
a slowdown;[69] and, second, a strike was called in the
sugar belt, involving large segments of the East Indian
working-class population. In short, the entire bottom
was falling out of the barrel.

By early March 1965, in the context of a struggle
between capital and segments of organized labor, the
government of Trinidad and Tobago had two options.[70]
It faced the choice of tough action against the foreign
and local business elite or of tough action against
organized labor, which, from the government's viewpoint,
was disrupting the smooth running of the economy. On
March 9, 1965, the government announced that it had
chosen the latter option, and a state of emergency was
declared in the sugar belt. On March 15, with the full
consent of all Cabinet Ministers, it introduced the
Industrial Stabilization Act and obtained its passage
in both Houses of Parliament.

ALTERNATIVES: COULD THE GOVERNMENT HAVE DONE OTHERWISE?

It is my thesis that as the pattern of development
chosen by the Trinidad and Tobago government unfolded,
the options narrowed.

By March 1965, option one--to become tough with
foreign enterprise--was no longer feasible, because
the economy had taken a drastic downward turn and the

government's confidence in its capacity to handle the
situation had dwindled. Further, in the context of the
strategy of development undertaken by the government,
foreign capital was needed, more desperately now than
ever. Strikes were seen as detrimental not only to the
successful pursuit of the strategy, but also to the
workers themselves.

The government's strategy demanded a particular
role of its people: cheap labor. The question thus
became, How to ensure this and when? The different
tactics used by the government were primarily the
elimination of the economic nationalists and the passage of certain legislation.[71] Finally, the government
of Trinidad and Tobago was firmly in the Western camp.
In this situation, it was ideologically hamstrung,
because the rules of the game allowed militant action
by governments in the Western hemisphere only at their
own peril. In this light, the fate of Cheddi Jagan in
Guyana, Colonel Arbenz in Guatemala, and the more recent
events in Cuba were not lost on the government. Because
the mechanism for changing what the government realized
were unfavorable economic relations could be conceived
only in legislative and moral terms, we find the government using moral suasion with foreign and local economic
interests and finally attempting legislative action in
the form of the Finance Bill of 1966.[72] Any move other
than that chosen by the government would have upset the
balance for which the government had opted in its development strategy.

What is finally important to our consideration of
the choice made is the timing of the decision. I wish
now to contend that the specific decision to introduce
the Industrial Stabilization Act could not have been
made earlier. The reason was political. First, even
though the government was in a position to absorb the
economic losses caused by the oil industry in 1960, it
could not have introduced this piece of legislation at
that time: it had come to the end of its first term
of office and had to court working-class electoral support in the upcoming elections.

Second, although most segments of organized labor
had gone on strike and its capacity to absorb economic
losses had dwindled, the government could not have done
so soon after the elections because organized labor had
not yet been split. To introduce such an act before
1965 would have narrowed its electoral support since
opposition electoral forces had organized around the
Democratic Labour party, under the leadership of Dr.
Rudnanath Capildeo.

Third, although the government's economic fortunes had shifted in the 1962-64 period, introduction of the ISA at this time would have appeared in the eyes of all segments of organized labor as an about-face on the earlier prolabor position. The government, therefore, had to create the conditions under which its intervention would still be legitimate. In short, the 1962-64 period provided the motivation, but not the opportunity. This opportunity came through the issue of poaching: when sugar workers broke with their established leaders and called upon the leader of the Oilfield Workers' Trade Union to take over their union, the government was provided with the opportunity it needed. Thus, under the guise of a communist take-over, it could capitalize on the ideological split between the leaders of the organized workers and at the same time could maintain its hold on the larger segment of organized labor.

Fourth, since the issues that faced the government in this period were essentially political ones of social justice and of ownership and control of national resources, and since its economic strategy did not allow for this, the government had to make sure of the continued participation of both the local and foreign economic elites before it delivered its part of the bargain.

It is therefore important to recognize that neither the party nor the government of Trinidad and Tobago in the period 1960-65 was concerned with social revolution. They were concerned with management.

NOTES

1. Government of Trinidad and Tobago, Act No. 8 of 1965.

2. Ibid., p. 1.

3. Ibid., p. 6.

4. Ibid., p. 19.

5. This at the time was a unique achievement in Caribbean politics, for up to then most Caribbean political parties had official trade union affiliations. See C. P. Bradley, "Mass Parties in Jamaica," Social and Economic Studies 9 (December 1960).

6. Eric Williams, Inward Hunger (Andre Deutsch, 1969), p. 146.

7. Eric Williams, The Case for Party Politics, Public
Affairs pamphlet (1955), p. 19.

8. This last point is crucial because, coming in 1955,
Eric Williams and his party would obviously benefit
from the experience of Cheddi Jagan in Guyana in 1953,
as well as that of Kwame Nkrumah in Ghana in that same
period. For the latter, see J. Mohan, "Nkrumah and
Nkrumahism," Socialist Register, 1967, pp. 198-99.

9. Trinidad Guardian, March 23, 1957 (emphasis added).
See also Selwyn Ryan, Race and Nationalism in Trinidad
and Tobago (University of Toronto Press, 1972), pp.
177-78.

10. Trinidad Guardian, July 1, 1962, p. 1.

11. Ibid., July 1, 1962, p. 6.

12. For a recent article on this question, see Eric
St. Cyr, "Trends in Wages, Prices, Employment and Unemployment," mimeographed (University of the West
Indies, 1972). For an article that contradicts the
findings, see Havelock Brewster, "The Growth of Employment Under Export-biased Underdevelopment in Trinidad,"
Social and Economic Studies 21 (June 1972).

13. Trinidad Guardian, July 1, 1960.

14. For an abbreviated check list of domestic casualties, see ibid., July 8, 1960.

15. Ibid., July 5, 1960, p. 7.

16. Ibid., July 8, 1960.

17. Ibid., July 6, 1960.

18. Sunday Guardian, July 24, 1960 (emphasis added).

19. See speeches of both W. W. Sutton of the Amalgamated Engineering and Workers Union and Carl Tull of the
Communication Workers Union: Trinidad Guardian, July 5,
1960, p. 2.

20. Trinidad Guardian, July 24, 1960. If one examines
analyses of government-labor relations either in the
Vanguard or in Tapia, no. 27 (May 1972), this latter
piece of Dr. Williams's speech is ignored. This seems
to me to be the cause of later misanalysis of the introduction of the ISA.

21. For interesting documentation of this, see Krishna
Bahadoorsingh, "Trinidad Electoral Politics: The

Persistence of the Race Factor" (Ph.D. thesis, Indiana University, 1966), and Ryan, Race and Nationalism in Trinidad and Tobago.

22. Trinidad Guardian, November 28, 1961 (emphasis added).

23. See R. D. Thomas, "The Muted Voice of the Labour Movement," mimeographed (University of the West Indies, 1972).

24. Official Report, Parliamentary Debates, Hansard (House of Representatives, Trinidad and Tobago), vol. 1, 1961-62, p. 13.

25. 1962 Budget Speech, ibid., p. 633.

26. Throne Speech, ibid., p. 13 (emphasis added).

27. Ibid., p. 79.

28. See Parliamentary Debates, ibid., November 23, 1962, pp. 451-527.

29. According to a government spokesman, "In 28 cases, there was no grievance procedure existing at the under-takings where the strikes occurred, and in the majority of these cases the strikes involved claims for recog-nition by trade unions." See Dr. P. Solomon's speech, ibid., pp. 516-19.

30. Ibid., p. 521.

31. Debate on the Second Five Year Development Plan, Parliamentary Debates, ibid., vol. 3, 1963-64.

32. See Speech by the Opposition Leader, Dr. R. Capil-deo, ibid., vol. 1, 1962-63, pp. 928-34; also 1963 Budget Speech, ibid., p. 2.

33. 1963 Budget Speech, ibid., p. 916. Also, Trinidad Guardian, January 4, 1963, p. 1.

34. Trinidad Guardian, January 11, 1963, p. 1.

35. Ibid., January 12, 1963. This was confirmed by Mr. B. Ramdeen, opposition member, who in the debate on the Income Tax Amendment Bill, May 1963, said: "At the time of the Budget the business community of this coun-try offered us 20,000 signatures to ask government to remove the Minister of Finance" (Parliamentary Debates, vol. 2, 1962-63, May 13, 1963, p. 584).

36. Trinidad Guardian, January 9-10, 1963, p. 1. See
also Speech by the Prime Minister, ibid., Hansard,
vol. 2, pp. 1026-82, where specific references were
made to the positions taken by critics of the budget
in the pages of the Trinidad Guardian, and Speech by
the Finance Minister, A. N. R. Robinson, ibid.,
pp. 1118 ff.

37. Parliamentary Debates, vol. 2, pp. 1128-29.

38. External Loans Debate, Parliamentary Debates,
vol. 2, 1962-63, July 12, 1963, p. 1111.

39. Trinidad Guardian, January 11, 1963, p. 1.

40. Trinidad Guardian, January 16, 1963, p. 1. In
keeping with this decision, by June 1963 the government
sought membership in such capitalist institutions as
the International Monetary Fund, the International Bank
for Reconstruction and Development, the International
Finance Corporation, and the International Development
Association. See International Finance Organizations
Bill, Parliamentary Debates, vol. 2, 1962-63, June 28,
1963, p. 879.

41. Oil Industry Commission of Inquiry, Parliamentary
Debates, vol. 2, 1962-63, April 5, 1963, p. 292.

42. Ibid.

43. Ibid., p. 293 (emphasis added).

44. It is necessary to note that by this time the
labor movement was split between those who accepted
the economic analysis of the business community and
those who rejected it. The Amalgamated Workers Union
led by W. W. Sutton is an obvious example of the first
and the Oilfield Workers' Trade Union is an example of
the latter.

45. See Second Five Year Development Plan, 1964-68
(Government of Trinidad and Tobago, 1964).

46. A comparison of the financing of the Second Five
Year Development Plan with the First shows clearly the
state of the economy and the drift toward reliance on
the international capitalist system.

47. Eric Williams, "Trinidad and Tobago, International
Perspectives," Freedomways, Summer 1964, p. 333. Also
see the Prime Minister's contribution to the Debate on
the Second Five Year Development Plan, Parliamentary
Debates, vol. 3, 1962-63, p. 257.

48. <u>Tripartite</u> <u>Conference</u> on <u>Employment</u> <u>and</u> <u>Unemploy-</u>
<u>ment</u> <u>in</u> <u>Sugar</u> <u>and</u> <u>Oil</u> (Ministry of Planning and Develop-
ment, Trinidad and Tobago, 1964.

49. 1964 Budget Speech, Parliamentary Debates, vol.3,
1963-64, December 16, 1963, p. 2 (emphasis added).

50. Ibid., p. 11. Commenting on this new position on
labor, opposition member B. Ramdeen wittily said, "As
regards government's headaches over the attitude of
Trade Unions, I can only say at this stage that their
chicken has come home to roost" (Budget Debate, ibid.,
p. 849).

51. The 1964 Budget Speech pointed out that government
had raised $11 million from the Independence Development
Loan to which Texaco had contributed. There had been
a loan from the International Bank for Reconstruction
and Development for electricity of $17.3 million and
a loan from the Export-Import Bank for the sewerage
project of $8.81 million. The Minister pointed out
that he had hoped to raise another $15.9 million on the
U.S. market. However, due to an unfavorable balance of
payments position this had to be deferred. Government
did, however, borrow $10 million from Chase Manhattan
Bank at 6 percent interest for three years.

52. Recall that Trinidad at the 1962 Commonwealth Conference had supported British entry into the Common
Market because, as the Prime Minister later said, "we
saw in the British application and the associate status
for Trinidad and Tobago under Part IV of the treaty of
Rome consequent upon that application, the surest means
of preserving the limited preference we had in the
British Market, and extending the toehold we had secured
in the European Market" (<u>Nation</u>, August 13, 1965).

53. This becomes totally evident when one sees the
government's position in the debate on external loans.
See Development Loans Bill Debate, Parliamentary Debates,
vol. 3, 1963-64, pp. 1696-1786.

54. As a result of Tate & Lyle's support of the Better
Village Programme, and while awaiting government's response to the suggestion by Tate & Lyle that mechanical
harvesters be introduced, the organ of the National
Union of Sugar Workers said, "the government has not
expressed any view on the implications of the introduction of mechanization and according to official sources
is not likely to do so in the near future. . . . we <u>are</u>
<u>left</u> <u>to</u> <u>conclude</u> <u>that</u> <u>our</u> <u>government</u> <u>sold</u> <u>the</u> <u>right</u> <u>to</u>
<u>speak</u> <u>for</u> <u>one</u> <u>million</u> <u>dollars</u>. . . . If one is to
associate the million dollars with the mechanization
then he finds the workers have been sold at less than

sixty dollars per head. The colonial massa day done, but God help us under the new Independence massa" (Nuswor News, June 15, 1964, pp. 13-14 [emphasis added]).

55. See Report of Commission of Inquiry Into the Operations of the Princes Town Special Bus Company Ltd. (Port of Spain, Government Printing Office, 1964).

56. See Debate on the Bus Strike, Parliamentary Debates, vol. 3, 1963-64, July 3, 1964, pp. 1671-72.

57. Ibid., p. 1679.

58. This argument is made quite cogently by Finance Minister Robinson on a number of occasions. See the Debate on the IDC, ibid., April 24, 1964, pp. 1354-1422.

59. This point seems valid if one assumes that government is primarily interested in citizen welfare and business in maximizing profit.

60. Budget Speech, 1965 (Port of Spain, Government Printing Office, 1965), p. 17. This budget again confirms the government's intention of wooing financial investors, for unlike the 1963 budget, it allowed for reduction of company taxes. It further suggests the fact that the probusiness elements in the government had won the day over the proreform elements.

61. See also Edwin Carrington, "Industrialization by Invitation in Trinidad and Tobago, Since 1950," New World Quarterly, Autumn 1968.

62. I am of this opinion precisely because of the fundamental differences in the budgets of 1963 and 1965.

63. This interpretation, I believe, is accurate, especially when one sees the Prime Minister's own position in his Reflections on the ISA (Port of Spain, PNM Publishing Company, 1965).

64. See Budget Speech, 1965, p. 23. What was needed was to slow down the rise of average money incomes.

65. Trinidad Guardian, February 2, 1965, p. 1.

66. Ibid. (emphasis added).

67. Workers at Lock Joint employed on a $32-million sewerage scheme went on strike rather than accept the wage increase offered by management. They declared: "It is slavery under a disguise. We can take no more.

They want us to do all kinds of work under the worst
conditions and still don't want to pay us" (<u>Trinidad
Guardian</u>, February 9, 1965). Also consider a statement
by Transport and Industrial Workers Union on the nationalization of the transport system. The union
stressed that the workers must not be lulled into a
false sense of security, nor should they believe their
struggles have ended with nationalization: "The struggle will only be ended when the working class ceases to
be hewers of wood and drawers of water" (ibid., February 17, 1965, p. 6).

68. Ibid., February 3, 1965, p. 1. The workers went
on strike in protest, aainst what they termed the delay-
ing tactics of Federation Chemicals' management over
wage negotiations. They were not acting on union instructions.

69. On March 7, he made a threat of a slowdown by the
CSA if government did not implement the $10-million
wage hike recommended by the report of the working
party in the Civil Service. A resolution was passed
by the CSA Executive, giving the government twenty-one
days (<u>Trinidad Guardian</u>, March 8, 1965).

70. This point is important to bear in mind, for among
those segments of organized labor who were threatening
industrial action there were elements--such as the CSA--
that were not opposed to the government. What I am
suggesting is that those who were opposed to the government were numerically outnumbered by those who supported
it.

71. For this first tactic, see my "Chaguaramas Revisit-
ed" (Paper presented to the Annual Meeting of the International Studies Association, Washington, D. C., February 1975).

72. For an analysis of the Finance Bill decision, see
Carl D. Parris: "Size or Class, Factors Affecting
Trinidad and Tobago's Foreign Economic Policy" (Paper
presented to the Conference on the Independence of
Very Small States [with special reference to the Carib-
bean], University of the West Indies, March 1974).

Race, Class, and Culture
As Explanations of the Black Experience in the Americas

Anthony P. Maingot

The session entitled "The Black Experience in the Americas" benefited from three significant contributions in writing and/or in oral comments: from Emory University, Professor Gloria Blackwell on "The Afro-American Experience in the South of North America"; from the University of the West Indies, Trinidad, Professor Carl C. Parris's "Capital or Labor? The Decision to Introduce the Industrial Stabilization Act (Trinidad and Tobago, March 1965)"; and from Ecuador, Professor Justino Cornejo, who made a formal oral presentation in Spanish. The theme of the session is an important one; the papers, oral presentations, and discussion raised crucial issues and, like most good intellectual discussions, raised many questions not answered right then and there. This is an extension and elaboration of some of those issues.

Although we are most accustomed to hearing about race relations in the United States, it is clear that issues involving questions of race are not rare in either half of the hemisphere. Whatever country of Latin America one selects, the issues of race and/or ethnicity form part of the "social problems" perceived by the nation's citizens. As such, there is ample need for sessions such as this one on "The Black Experience in the Americas." Even in such a "homogeneous" society as Costa Rica, where "race questions" are limited to contact on the narrow banana plantation fringes of the Atlantic and Pacific coasts, the issue has relevance. The increasing migration of Costa Rican blacks from the eastern area of Puerto Limon to the United States is only partly due to language; after nearly half a century of residence in Spanish-speaking Costa Rica, these immigrants from the West Indies still use English as their means of communication. A more important reason is the

ongoing discrimination suffered by the blacks in the
Meseta Central, where the bulk of Costa Rica's white
and mestizo population reside.[1] The removal of blatant-
ly discriminatory racial legislation by the first government of the liberal José Figueres in the Constitution
of 1949 has not fundamentally changed behavioral patterns. Yet one searches in vain for a serious systematic study of race or ethnic relations in that country.

But clearly the lack of any systematic and serious
concern with race in the social science literature on
Costa Rica has parallels in most other Latin American
countries and stands in stark contrast to the overriding
concern with race relations in the West Indies--British,
French, and Dutch--and to the long Brazilian tradition
of a social history in which questions of race and
ethnicity play central roles.

But the widespread concern with race, though varying in focus and degree of intensity, is readily visible
in the belles lettres of the Western hemisphere. So
universal is the concern that there is no lack of data
for a comparative study of race relations that opts to
use fiction in its many forms as its primary source.
Indeed, in many ways attempts at comparative studies of
the racial theme through literature have been more successful than the efforts emanating from the social sciences. Outstanding examples are José Juan Arrom,
Estudios de Literatura Hispanoamericana (1950); Gabriel
Coulthard, Race and Colour in Caribbean Literature
(1962); and Kenneth Ramchand, The West Indian Novel and
its Background (1970). Somewhat short on analysis, but
clearly suggestive and helpful, are the works of Hortensia Ruiz del Vizo, especially Poesía Negra del Caribe
y Otras Áreas (1972). The value of these treatises is
their search for common themes in the prose and poetry
of the whole Caribbean; they constitute a truly comparative literature and stand apart from social science
works such as Magnus Morner's compilation, Race and
Class in Latin America (1970), and Philip Mason's
Patterns of Dominance (1970), which are contrasting--
rather than comparing--studies. Comparison implies
analysis on one central conceptual axis and not merely
the juxtaposition of self-contained case studies. Thus,
Pierre van den Berghe's Race and Ethnicity (1970), although dealing with many of the same societies as does
Philip Mason's work, is of considerably more utility
because of the explicit statement and explanation of
the ideal type that served as framework for his various
case studies. Similarly, H. Hoetink, The Two Variants
in Caribbean Race Relations (1967), remains an example
of a useful study in comparative race relations in the
hemisphere. Though Hoetink's work is debilitated by an
overly psychological set of propositions, its utility

becomes all the more remarkable when particular case
studies, especially his later case study on the Dominican Republic,[2] are analyzed in the context of his
broader conceptualization of Caribbean social relations.
Note the word utility, rather than truth. It is considerably less important whether we agree or not that
Van den Berghe or Hoetink provides us with the truth
about Caribbean or Latin American race relations
(a doubtful proposition in the social sciences, in any
case) than whether we agree that their concepts and
paradigms have utility for the comparative study of
race relations.[3]

    The need for a minimum of conceptual clarity, if
not conceptual agreement, in the study of hemispheric
race relations generally and the black experience
specifically was very much in evidence at the session
on "The Black Experience in the Hemisphere." Three
quite distinct approaches to race relations were apparent, approaches in which one of three concepts was
given central importance: race, class, or culture.
It appeared not that the authors totally ignored the
other concepts, but rather they used one or the other
as the core explanation of the situation.

    The North American concern with race was clearly
reflected in Blackwell's article, "The Afro-American
Experience." Her central question is an important one:
What happens to the racial loyalties and primordial attachments when blacks move out of their neighborhood
and into the wider society, including the power structure? The black neighborhood (in this case "Sweet
Auburn" in Atlanta, Georgia)--can it serve as the
"anchor" of racial attachments? The answer was obviously felt to be yes, and consequently a partial solution
to the black man's problem is to be found in a revival
and regeneration of the racial neighborhood. There is
very little concern here with the class dimensions of
the problem. It was assumed that the neighborhood comprised many classes, that those who had climbed the
social and political ladder (like the Mayor of Atlanta)
were as integrally a part of the problem (and/or the
solution) as were those who remained behind to subsist
in the decaying and poverty-stricken areas of Sweet
Auburn. Culture is clearly perceived as an essential
ingredient, but, again, as "black" cultural "identity,"
as a means of racial defense and survival.

    Note, for instance, Blackwell's statement: "His-
torically . . . issues of race and ethnicity in Atlanta
have been issues in black and white, of affinities and
antipathies." Or, "the conclusion suggests that Afro-
Atlantans need cultural and ethnic infusions to relieve
the myopic ambivalence resulting from centuries of
southern love-hate rituals in black and white."

That cultural and ethnic infusion, in Blackwell's
opinion, could best be had by retaining the racial
strength of Sweet Auburn. It is a strengthened and
regenerated racial neighborhood that will best be able
to help black Atlantans in their dealings with the rest
of society. From there follows Blackwell's overall conclusion that "local concerns, proximity of the races,
and space negated, diminished, or significantly influenced the focus and needs of Afro-Atlanta."

The central concern, then, is with race; the cultural, social, political, psychological, and even spatial dimensions are treated peripherally. The search
is for identity and well-being of all blacks.

There is less concern, thus, to inquire into the
overall significance and theoretical relevance of the
following facts cited by Blackwell:

> Wheat Street, racially mixed but predominant-
> ly white (renamed Auburn Avenue in 1894), was
> opened in young Atlanta in 1853. A century
> later, Afro-Atlantans owned more than 95 per-
> cent of the Auburn Avenue businesses, and
> "Sweet Auburn's" fame spread, especially
> throughout the black world. . . . August
> Meier and John Lewis found that the Auburn
> business and residential community had spawned
> and nurtured a distinctive black upper class.

The apparent correlation between black political-
economic success in the wider Atlanta community and the
decline of the racial neighborhood Sweet Auburn ought
to point to the variable "class" and to the social
mobility resulting from class shifts. The continued
adherence to the exclusive concern with race has origins
best explored through the sociology of knowledge rather
than through a purely methodological debate, a point to
be elaborated on later. Nevertheless, there is ample
evidence that the North American studies of race relations have been moving to redress the imbalance in emphasis between race and class through a new emphasis on
class and social conflict in the study of race relations.[4]

The contribution by Carl D. Parris, "Capital or
Labor? The Decision to Introduce the Industrial Stabilization Act (Trinidad and Tobago, March 1965)," is
an example of the West Indian intellectual's increasing
concern with class and class conflict as principal ex-
planatory variables. Nowhere in the paper is there
a concern with--indeed, even a prominent mention of--
race. In part encouraged by the introductory remarks
of the chairperson, who described the West Indies as

"predominantly black" societies,[5] Parris made the oral
addition that he was talking about "white Capital" and
"black Labor." But when we are confronted with the
historical fact that it was very much the black government's fear of an alliance between rural agricultural
<u>Indians</u> and urban industrial blacks that hastened the
enactment of the ISA in 1965, the racial attribution
seems much less plausible as an explanation of government action in 1965 than does the straightforward class
analysis presented in the written paper. "The issues
that faced the government in this period," Parris
asserts, "were essentially political ones of social
justice and of ownership and control of national resources."

Given that definition of the problem, the task
then was an analysis of government strategy in dealing
with labor and capital. In 1965 this strategy had to
be played out in the midst of an economic downturn.
In that context, moderation to the extent of conservatism seemed the only formula for survival for the party
and government in power, which happened to be black.
Economic constraints made it imperative that the needs
and demands of the local and foreign economic elites be
satisfied. What Parris concludes about government
strategy in Trinidad and Tobago in 1965 could be repeated about so many weak nations, large and small,
regardless of racial composision: "neither the party
nor the government of Trinidad and Tobago in the period
1960-65 was concerned with revolution. They were concerned with management."

Be that as it may, the fact remains that race certainly does play a role in the economic stratification
and distribution of wealth on the island, as the studies
of Camejo and others have demonstrated empirically.[6]
As such, the government's actions of 1965, as described
by Parris, could easily be perceived and interpreted as
kowtowing to the whites, as an abdication of the black
loyalties proclaimed in the early 1960s--when the economic situation was much more favorable. And indeed,
as the events of 1970 demonstrated, this is exactly how
it was interpreted. While Parris's emphasis on economics
and class conflict is to the point, his failure to ex-
plore the racial dimensions, at least in terms of their
impact and influence <u>a posteriori</u>, reduces the value of
the analysis.

This concern with class has certainly been both
cause and effect of the maturing of the most important
body of theory in Caribbean race relations: "cultural
pluralism." A concept first utilized by Furnivall in
British Asia, its most prominent West Indian advocate
has been a Jamaican, M. G. Smith. The theory has now

moved to a plane of theoretical refinement sufficient
for meaningful comparative analysis. Significantly,
the emphasis is on the role of conflict in plural
societies.[7] I shall return to this later.

Neither the North American emphasis on race nor
the West Indian emphasis on class seems to have reached
major areas of Latin American thought on race relations.
The position taken by Professor Justino Cornejo of
Ecuador was very much in the tradition emphasizing
culture, culture contact, and acculturation as agents
of change in race relations.[8] The fundamental motor
of this process of change is miscegenation, the blending
into the dominant group that then becomes something
else--a new "race." This is best achieved through an
ennoblement (in the eyes of the white dominant group)
of the culture of these minorities--the black's contribution to music, cooking, language, folklore in
general. The assumption is that race mixture and culture mixture go hand in hand and are equally "strengthening" and envigorating to the "national" culture or
raza (used in the Latin context, which implies culture).
As might be expected, this position elicited protests
of "genocide" from North American and West Indian blacks
alike, a protest that Professor Cornejo could not understand. His concern was with the cultural revival and
eventually cultural integration of the Latin American
black, just as generations of Latin American social
scientists and social activists have been concerned
with the acculturation of the Indian.

This approach, of course, is not new. It was the
Brazilian Gilberto Freyre who pioneered the cultural
anthropological study of race relations in Brazil, creating (or at least elevating to a "science") a national
myth of miscegenation and cultural/national rebirth.
"What I wanted to save from conventionally narrow points
of view," Freyre asserted, "was a number of such Luso-
Brazilian achievements as miscegenation and the fusion
of cultural values."[9] Freyre eventually went so far as
to speak of a "Luso-tropicology," "a policy of cultures,
in the widest sense of the expression, to be followed by
both Portugal and by Brazil":[10] the study of culture
diffusion, through miscegenation, thus as ideology,
rather than purely as description of social reality.
That miscegenation has not always led to culture diffusion or creation of a "new" culture has been noted by
many. Again, the study of comparative poetry and literature reveals much about the differential consequences
of miscegenation. Hortensia Ruiz Del Vizo notes that
the black is an important element of the Cuban, as well
as coastal Colombian, presence. In Cuba, however, race
mixing led to culture fusion, producing a process of
cultural "mulatización," while in Colombia "the reverse

has occurred: mixture of blood but not of cultures."
The Afro-Cuban "schools" of poetry have no counterpart
in Colombia.[11]

In Brazil, Freyre's theoretical scaffolding of
miscegenation and acculturation began to be dismantled
little by little as more sociologically oriented studies
began to focus on questions of social structure and
social mobility as indicators of race relations.   The
UNESCO-sponsored studies[12] and the subsequent independent analyses by Florestan Fernandes,[13] Fernando
Henrique Cardoso, Octavio Ianni, and others have
opened up new avenues to the study of Brazilian race
relations.[14]

There has been very little diffusion to the rest
of Latin America of this extraordinary blossoming of
Brazilian studies on race relations.   The concern and
emphasis still tends to be on acculturation.   Rarely
has Indo-Latin America been studied with the same framework as has Afro-Latin America by Latin Americans themselves.[15]

Even a cursory acquaintance with sociology of
knowledge approaches helps us understand that the three
focuses described here--race, class, and culture--
reflect in a fundamental way the dynamics of the wider
societies in which the authors reside and write.   Race
is a fundamental factor of American political, social,
and economic life, and no black American scholar can
ignore that existential fact for long.   Scholars in the
black-governed societies of the West Indies tend to
focus on the class stratification.   And certainly, the
lack of any significant social mobility alongside considerable miscegenation tends to focus the Latin American on integration into the national culture.   But
surely social scientists have to transcend their immediate social situation.   Ideas should be more than
ideology (that is, expressions of what is needed and
desirable); they should be heuristic devices assisting
objective analysis.

All three variables (race, class, and culture) are
present in different degrees in different societies.
As concepts, however--as general propositions for the
study of race relations in the hemisphere--total emphasis on one or the other is clearly unsatisfactory,
as this session so vividly demonstrated.

There is a need for truly comparative studies of
hemispheric race relations.   The first step in this
direction is some agreement on a useful conceptual
approach to that study in the hemisphere and on the
ideas and materials there to be used.   The new approaches

to social conflict evident in North American theories
of race relations, the refinements in the West Indian
approach to cultural pluralism, and the post-Freyre
Brazilian concern with social structure and mobility
should point to some common ground. It is not the
purpose here to propose any such paradigm. But surely
the argument above indicates some central themes that
deserve restatement.

It might be helpful to return to some basic conclusions of the UNESCO project. First, the study of
race and ethnic relations has to be made in the context
of a wider awareness of the social structure and stratification system in which they unfold--in other words, in
terms of the wider distribution of power and privilege
in the society. Any focus on the national allocation
and distribution of power and privilege will entail an
understanding of the process of social conflict; that
conflict can be both latent and/or manifest, can have
both a disintegrating and/or integrating impact on the
group.

In order to understand the origin and continuity
of this conflict, one must study a number of factors
falling into two distinct categories. The UNESCO study
labeled these categories as the structural components
of majority-minority relations, and the historical-
cultural components.[16]

By structural components are meant those legal,
political, economic, and social mechanisms and barriers
that the majority builds and maintains in order to consolidate and, if possible, improve its position. They
are logically the ones the minority faces in its attempts to change its position.

The historical-cultural components refer to ideology and historical experiences that provide the basic
setting and the specific motives for intergroup conflict.
The intimate relationship between both categories and
their link to the ongoing process of conflict is apparent from the way Wagley and Harris describe the
historical-cultural components:

it consists of the possibilities offered by
the dominant group's ideology and total sociocultural system for deriving advantages from
the presence of the minority; and it consists
of the degree of culturally-induced prepared-
ness of the minority for protecting and advancing itself against the exploitation and
hostility to which it may become subject.[17]

The lesson, then, is that "The Black Experience
in the Americas" is one dimension of the experience of
majority-minority relations in the hemisphere, of the
ongoing process of social conflict stemming from the
ongoing competition for power and privilege. Granted,
in many ways, the "black" experience deserves special
study; it does have very unique dimensions and idio-
syncratic configurations. But to the extent that this
study ignores the wider social-structural and historical-
cultural issues, they remain--no matter how interesting
in themselves--irrelevant to the wider questions of man
in this hemisphere. Race, class, and culture are all
parts of that question; the UNESCO approach and the
more recent elaborations to that approach in the United
States, Brazil, and the West Indies provide us with an
adequate paradigm in which to handle in a useful, comparative way the variables of race, class, and culture
in the ongoing and future discussions of the black, or
Indian, or white experience in the hemisphere.

NOTES

1. See Carlos Melendez and Quince Duncan, El Negro en
Costa Rica (San José: Editorial Costa Rica, 1972).

2. H. Hoetink, El pueblo dominicano, 1850-1900:
apuntes para su sociología histórica (Santo Domingo,
1971).

3. On comparative literature, G. R. Coulthard notes,
"we are not concerned with whether writers are right
or wrong, but with analyzing how the theme is presented,
with what its possible cultural origins are, and with
trying to define its temporal limits" (Race and Colour
in Caribbean Literature [London: Oxford University
Press, 1962], pp. 40-41).

4. Note, for instance, the attempts to balance "consensus" and social conflict theories in such works as
R. A. Schermerhorn, Comparative Ethnic Relations (New
York: Random House, 1970); Gary T. Marx, ed., Racial
Conflict (Boston: Little, Brown, 1971); and Norman R.
Yetman and C. Hoy Steele, Majority and Minority (2nd
ed. Boston: Allyn and Bacon, 1975). It is not unusual,
thus, for works on race relations to begin with theoretical statements from Lewis Coser and Ralf Dahrendorf,
students not of race relations per se, but of class and
class conflict.

5. The black American emphasis on race was in evidence
again. Trinidad (38 percent Indian) and Guyana (54 percent Indian) are best termed "multiethnic" societies,
especially since the American black-white dichotomy does

not take into account such distinct "ethnic" groups as the colored--in Trinidad fully 17 percent of the population.

6. Acton Camejo, "Racial Discrimination in Employment in the Private Sector in Trinidad and Tobago: A Study of the Business Elite and the Social Structure," Social and Economic Studies, September 1971, pp. 294-318. See also Interim Report of the Commission of Enquiry into Racial and Colour Discrimination in the Private Sector (Trinidad and Tobago Government Printery, 1970).

7. For a good sampling of the "new" approaches in cultural pluralism theory, see M. G. Smith and Leo Kuper, eds., Pluralism in Africa (Los Angeles: University of California Press, 1969).

8. These comments are based on notes taken on Professor Cornejo's presentation in Spanish and a subsequent reading of his work Los que Tenemos de Mandinga (Colón: Editorial Gregorio, 1974).

9. See The Masters and the Slaves (New York: Alfred A. Knopf, 1956), p. xix.

10. Gilberto Freyre, The Portuguese and the Tropics (Lisbon: Executive Committee for the Commemoration of the V Centenary of the Death of Prince Henry the Navigator, 1961), pp. 7-8.

11. Poesía Negra del Caribe y Otras Áreas (1972), p. 120.

12. A good summary of the Brazilian part is contained in Charles Wagley and Marvin Harris, Minorities in the New World (New York: Columbia University Press, 1958).

13. Not surprisingly, Fernandes's study is entitled A integracão do negro na sociedade de classes, 2 vols. (São Paulo, Dominus Editora, 1965).

14. For a good review of these developments, see Octavio Ianni, "Research on Race Relations in Brazil," in Magnus Morner, ed., Race and Class in Latin America (New York: Columbia University Press, 1970), pp. 256-78.

15. Non-Latin Americans have done well in this regard. See especially H. Hoetink, Slavery and Race Relations in the Americas (New York, 1973), and Magnus Morner, Race Mixture in the History of Latin America (Boston: Little, Brown, 1967).

16. Note the similarity with the new North American
stress on theories of conflict cited above and with
M. G. Smith's refinement of his initial "cultural
pluralism" approach. He now recommends that the study
of pluralism take into account the relationship between
three levels of pluralism: structural, social, and
cultural ("Analytic Framework of Pluralism," in Leo
Kuper and M. G. Smith, eds., Pluralism in Africa
[Berkeley, University of California Press, 1969]
pp. 415-58).

17. Wagley and Harris, Minorities in the New World,
p. 256.

"Now or Never Is the Time": Anthropology, Government Policy, and the Concept of the Vanishing Indian

Brian W. Dippie

John Collier, the future United States Commissioner of Indian Affairs, tartly observed in 1923 that the Smithsonian Institution, the Bureau of American Ethnology, the American Anthropological Association and the American Association for the Advancement of Science "might as well not exist in so far as their existence is measured in terms of influence on Indian policy." His complaint, elaborated elsewhere, was that anthropologists had so exclusively focussed on primitive or pure aboriginal cultures, so completely ignored contemporary Indian cultures, that their work had proven of limited usefulness to reformers and administrators while lending credence to the Bureau of Indian Affairs' official line that the native cultures were decaying and soon to disappear forever as the Indians assimilated, amalgamated and assumed their rightful place as ordinary American citizens, indistinguishable from their white compatriots.[1]

Collier was speaking as an Indian reformer. But his perspective on American anthropology and his assumption that it should be an applied science were not original. Back in 1803, Thomas Jefferson had instructed Meriwether Lewis "to acquire what knowledge you can of the state of morality, religion, & information" among the Western tribes "as it may better enable those who may endeavor to civilize & instruct them, to adapt their measures to the existing notions & practices of those on whom they are to operate." In 1847 Henry R. Schoolcraft persuaded Congress to handsomely subsidize the compilation of reams of material on the Indians on the grounds that the resulting volumes, six in all, would greatly facilitate informed policy-making. In 1878 John Wesley Powell recommended that Congress create a Bureau of Ethnology on similar grounds:

> The rapid spread of civilization since 1849
> has placed the white man and the Indian in
> direct conflict . . . and the "Indian problem"
> is thus forced upon us, and it must be solved,
> wisely or unwisely. Many of the difficulties
> are inherent and cannot be avoided, but an
> equal number are unnecessary and are caused
> by the lack of our knowledge relating to the
> Indians themselves. . . . I think it will be
> apparent from what I have said that a thorough
> investigation of North American ethnology
> would be of great value in our Indian Office.

Anthropology, in short, merited federal support because
it promised to shed light on the Indian cultures and
thus put the management of Indian affairs on a scientific footing for the first time.[2]

There was another, perhaps even more pressing reason that Powell advanced to justify government patronage
for ethnological research:

> The field of research is speedily narrowing
> because of the rapid change in the Indian
> population now in progress; all habits, cus-
> toms, and opinions are fading away; even lan-
> guages are disappearing; and in a very few
> years it will be impossible to study our North
> American Indians in their primitive condition
> except from recorded history. For this reason
> ethnologic studies in America should be pushed
> with the utmost vigor.

All told, it was a strong case, and it found a sympathetic hearing, for within a year the Bureau of Ethnology had been created and Powell appointed as its
first director. Yet almost half a century later Collier could assert--and assert accurately--that anthropology's influence on Indian policy had been negligible.
The question we are left with is why.[3]

For Powell and his generation the answer seems
close at hand. Lewis Henry Morgan, a Rochester, New
York lawyer by profession, was the doyen of American
anthropology in the 1870s. His Ancient Society, a mam-
moth treatise describing the course of human social evolution from savagery through barbarism to civilization,
had captivated an age that loved sweeping generalizations and universal laws, master explanations that
brought order where before there was only the chaos of
countless facts. Morgan argued that human cultures
evolved through successive ethnic periods, seven in all,
each of which was characterized by a particular technological development that dictated progress in every

other area of human endeavor at that level of attainment. Social evolution occurred in states, then, and
since these stages were absolutes, cultures evolved
strictly parallel to one another. Social progress
could not be speeded up by artificial stimuli. Indeed,
since barbarians possessed barbaric skulls and barbaric
brains, it was obvious that they could advance to the
next level only after hundreds of years of gradual improvement. "We wonder that our Indians cannot civilize;
but how could they, any more than our own remote bar-
barous ancestors, jump ethnical periods?" Morgan asked.
Since they were barbarians, the Indians "must grow towards civilization as all mankind have done who attained
to it by a progressive experience."4

     The evolutionary parallelist viewpoint represented
scientific orthodoxy till almost the end of the nineteenth century. Certainly Powell and the Bureau under
his direction subscribed to its principal tenets. Consequently, when Powell was approached for his opinions
on the viability of allotting Indian lands in severalty
and turning the tribesmen into individual landowners as
a means of hastening their progress towards civilized
self-sufficiency, he could only advise great caution in
implementing a policy that so clearly flew in the face
of ethnological truths. Powell's ability to influence
policy-making was severely constricted by his evolutionary precepts, since they forced him to demand the
one thing that reformers could not concede: time, in
copious quantities, for the Indian to make the slow
transition from tribesman and hunter to individualistic
farmer and grazer. In proposing the creation of the
Bureau of Ethnology, Powell had bluntly stated his
position:

     The attempt to transform a savage into a civ-
     ilized man by a law, a policy, an administra-
     tion, through a great conversion, "as in the
     twinkling of an eye," or in months, or in a
     few years, is an impossibility clearly appre-
     ciated by scientific ethnologists who under-
     stand the institutions and social condition
     of the Indians. This great fact has not in
     general been properly recognized in the ad-
     ministration of Indian affairs.

Specifically on the question of an allotment policy,
Powell contended that first the Indian would have to
abandon his traditional social forms and adopt the
civilized family's structure, learn the value of individual property, embrace the concept of lineal in-
heritance and give up the pursuits of savagery for
those of civilization. These changes would have to
take place "slowly and contemporaneously." Then, and

only then, the Indian would be ready to benefit from an
allotment policy.[5]

It goes without saying that Congress in the end
listened to the reformers and their political allies,
not the anthropologists. The Dawes Act or the Allotment
in Severalty Act passed in 1887 made only one small concession to the need for a transition period. The Indian
allottee was to become a citizen at once, but would have
to wait twenty-five years, during which time he was expected to demonstrate his ability to manage his land for
himself, before receiving clear title to his quarter-
section plot. Once again Powell's "great fact" of
social change--time, measured out in evolutionary
dollops--had been ignored, and despite the accumulated
wisdom of the Bureau of Ethnology, anthropology's impact on policy-making remained as slight as ever.

The dominant influence of Morgan's ideas helps
account for the failure of ethnology to make a real
impression on policy: reform could not wait for evolution to take its gradual course. But anthropology itself underwent a theoretical revolution years before
John Collier made his disparaging observation on its
practical inutility in 1923. Indeed, all the social
sciences had been transformed by a university-based
professionalization that saw their emergence as academic
disciplines. Rigorously inductive methodology now militated against the facile generalizations that were a
stock-in-trade of nineteenth-century social science,
and lock-step evolution was cast into disrepute as a
valid organizing principle. Free-wheeling amateurism
was succeeded by academic sobriety. Franz Boas, for
example, was cut from a very different cloth than Powell.
His caution became as legendary as Powell's fondness for
grand schemata and pseudoscientific jargon. Under the
guidance of Boas and others professional anthropology
dedicated itself to exacting fieldwork and the collection of those facts upon which an ethnological science
could alone be based. The universal laws of cultural
development would have to wait. For now, ethnographic
research was everything. At long last it would seem
that anthropology was in a position to offer sound information on matters affecting the Indian and thus Indian policy. Yet Collier found the work of the first
generation of trained professionals--towering figures
like Clark Wissler, Robert Lowie and Alfred Kroeber--
barren of social significance. Academic anthropologists
apparently had no more to contribute to Indian policy
than their amateur predecessors.[6]

The problem, simply put, was that anthropology had
made its commitment to the preparation of thorough ethnographic studies of relatively intact primitive cultures,

not to the study of those in transition. Morgan for
one had warned that Indian culture was "perishing
daily," and information presently obtainable would soon
become "impossible of discovery." Thus it was up to
Americans "to enter this great field and gather its
abundant harvest." Powell echoed these sentiments.
So, as it turned out, did Franz Boas and his contempo-
raries. A sense of urgency dominated early ethnological
research, producing an aura of fatalism that served to
strengthen the notion that the end was rapidly drawing
near for the American Indian cultures. In no time at
all the Indian as Indian would be gone from the land.
No trace would remain of him save for an ever-diminish-
ing biological strain that, because it could not be re-
plenished, would inevitably be absorbed. Eventually
the red race would be swallowed up in whiteness. The
process was already well under way; it could not be
checked or reversed, and, for that matter, it should
not be. The anthropologist's task was scientific, not
political or administrative. His concern was not with
policy or its goals, but with the preservation of as
full and accurate a record as possible of the aboriginal
culture that remained. Thus professional anthropology
in the United States from the beginning was dedicated
to an "immense salvage operation" that in its zeal to
procure ethnographic records of the old-time Indian
cultures neglected the living entities and helped
popularize the vulgar myth of the Vanishing American
moving inexorably to racial and cultural extinction.[7]

Sent to British Columbia by the British Association
for the Advancement of Science to conduct research among
the coastal tribes, Franz Boas submitted a preliminary
report in 1888 accompanied by "a few remarks on future
researches on the ethnology of British Columbia." Only
in limited areas could one still study native customs
"uninfluenced by the whites," and it was just a matter
of time before all would be corrupted. With the coming
of the white man, the Indians' physical features had
been blurred through racial intermixing, and even their
languages were "decaying." "For all these reasons,"
Boas summed up, "an early study of the ethnology of the
provinces must be considered a necessity. . . . A few
years hence it will be impossible to obtain a great part
of the information that may now be gathered at a com-
paratively slight expense."[8]

Boas never tired of repeating this theme. In 1906
at Quebec City he addressed the International Congress
of Americanists on "Ethnological Problems in Canada."
"Day by day the Indians and their cultures are disappearing more and more before the encroachments of modern
civilization, and fifty years hence nothing will remain
to be learned in regard to this interesting and important

subject," he warned. Three years later, "prompted by
its urgency," he returned to the same topic at a meeting of the British Association for the Advancement of
Science, prefacing his remarks with another stirring
appeal: "With the energetic economic progress of Canada, primitive life is disappearing with ever-increasing
rapidity; and, unless work is taken up at once and
thoroughly, information on the earliest history of this
country, which has at the same time a most important
bearing upon the general problems of anthropology, will
never be obtained." These pleas, reiterated by others,
determined the course of anthropological research in
North America for a generation.[9] The devoted accumulation of data--Boasian historical particularism or phe-
nomenalism--has seemed to some to border on anthropological antiquarianism. But the data for Boas were the
means--the correct means--to a larger end, the solution
of theoretical questions scientifically. "Forcing phenomena into the strait-jacket of a theory is opposed to
the inductive process by which the actual relations of
definite phenomena may be derived," he argued in 1896.
He still believed at that time that "certain laws exist
which govern the growth of human culture, and it is our
endeavor to discover these laws." But the important
problem was to recognize that "the solid work is still
all before us."[10]

It was because they enjoyed such peculiar natural
advantages that American anthropologists felt compelled
to exploit them quickly. Their European counterparts
had to be satisfied with secondary evidence, archeo-
logical and linguistic, while Americans had the opportunity to study primitive cultures at home first hand.
In their pure state Indian societies in all likelihood
approximated those of ancient man in the Old World, and
thus they offered invaluable clues to a scientific understanding of human social development in prehistoric
times. It was an exciting opportunity given Americans,
and the French ethnologist Claude Lévi-Strauss expressed
it well when he remarked rather wistfully on what the
death of Alfred Kroeber meant to anthropology and to
him personally: "He is the last of the North American
ethnologists to have known the Indians. Not untamed
Red Skins--certainly they are no longer--rather those
who had been so in their youth. . . . With Kroeber it
is truly the America before Christopher Columbus which
has died completely." Here is a clue to that intense,
almost religious fervor with which the early professional anthropologists pursued their mission of preserving ethnographic records of the native cultures.
"Now or never is the time in which to collect from the
natives what is still available for study," one of Boas'
protegés insisted in 1911. "What is lost now will never
be recovered again."[11]

So American anthropology became vigorously committed to its salvage operation which, under the auspices
of the Museum of Natural History, concentrated on the
Northern plains. The Southwest, opinion agreed, would
hold out longer. The various Pueblos and the Navajo
could be studied later, after no trace remained of the
old plains Indian cultures. Consequently it was on the
plains for the most part that the first anthropologists
trained in American universities gained their field experience. Boas until 1905 and Clark Wissler thereafter
directed the salvage operation as young scholars headed
West to study a succession of tribes in a race against
time. Wissler himself went to the Blackfeet, the Dakota
Sioux and others--a total of ten reservations between
"the dawn of the present century," as he put it, and
1905--Alfred Kroeber to the Arapaho, the Gros Ventre,
and, briefly, the Ute, the Shoshone and the Bannock,
Paul Radin to the Winnebago, and Robert Lowie to the
Northern Shoshone, the Blackfeet, the Chippewa, the
Assiniboine, the Hidatsa and the Crow.[12] In his memoirs,
Lowie vividly recalled the sense of urgency, even desperation, that had him hopping from tribe to tribe between 1906 and 1908, unable to gain mastery over the
cultural data of any one or enjoy the luxury of "intensive linguistic study." The need to record as much
information as possible before the "native cultures
. . . vanish[ed] under the influence of white civilization" took precedence over all else. Erosion of the
old ways on the reservations was everywhere evident,
and the hopelessness that had settled over the Western
tribes by the end of the nineteenth century communicated
itself to the early fieldworkers, corroborating the impression of a vanishing race. The future apparently
held nothing for these Indians, and anthropology could
not shake the conviction that they were doomed to disappear. Thus their present seemed of marginal interest
at best, and their past alone worthy of serious study.[13]

It was this viewpoint, entrenched in American anthropology by 1920, that Collier deplored. As late as
1907 a trained anthropologist would write of the contemporary Indian, "as a hewer of wood and drawer of
water, he may incite sympathy and attract the philanthropic or economic side of our nature, but he does not
gain our admiration. To the ethnologist he becomes a
thing of but little value." Such was the kind of cavalier disdain for the Indian as nothing more than a quaint
ethnological specimen that so aroused Collier's ire.
"By the latter part of the nineteenth and the first
decades of the twentieth century," he wrote years later,
"anthropologists (there were some exceptions) became
apologists, not for the Indian Bureau, but for the
Bureau's view of Indians and Indian cultures as inferior
and dying--as fast-fading curiosities in the modern

world." That cultural pluralism that after World War I transformed American attitudes towards the Indians naturally left an impression on the social sciences generally and anthropology in particular. Accultura- tion studies came into their own in the 1920s and by the 1930s had become one of American anthropology's preoccupations. Cultures changed in intricate and fascinating ways. Even in a highly coercive situation they made adjustments, borrowing some things and spurn- ing others, preserving some traditional elements and discarding others.[14]

As anthropologists shifted their attention to this acceptance and rejection process, the dynamic area in culture change, they viewed afresh the existing Indian cultures and found in them something more than simple decay. The contemporary Indian's situation for the first time became a subject of intensive scientific scrutiny. This new concern inevitably brought many anthropologists face to face with the problems of applied science.[15] Some traditionalists regretted a departure that they could only regard as a perversion of pure science, but even Boas, at best a reluctant re- former unconcerned with "the application of anthropology to practical questions," took a small interest in Indian policy in the 1930s.[16] The practical and the theoreti- cal were at last in partnership.

Speaking before the American Association for the Advancement of Science in 1929, Fay-Cooper Cole told his colleagues that there was something "radically wrong" with anthropologists if, "after forty years of intensive research and the publication of numerous books, we have made so little impression on Congress, on the Indian service, on missionary boards and other Indian workers." He challenged his co-workers to be- come involved and to contribute their specialized knowledge to policy-makers and administrative personnel alike. After John Collier became Commissioner of Indian Affairs in 1933 he attempted to create a formal liaison between government and the social sciences, and in 1934 he won a pledge from a meeting of anthropologists at Pittsburgh to assist "in the work of rehabilitating Indian communities and developing an Indian program directly related to the life and needs of Indian people."[17]

The actual role of anthropology in the Indian New Deal--a mixture of high hopes, dismal disappointments and some solid accomplishments--is outside the scope of the present discussion. What is germane is the fact that anthropological fatalism had been effectively dispelled at last. Clark Wissler, still ensconced at the Museum of Natural History from which the cultural

salvage operation had been launched more than thirty
years before, in 1934 proclaimed the "rebirth of the
'Vanishing American.'" The science of man had finally
discovered the living fact of the American Indian.[18]

NOTES

1. John Collier, "America's Treatment of Her Indians,"
Current History, XVIII (Aug., 1923), 781.

2. Thomas Jefferson to Meriwether Lewis, June 20, 1803,
in Donald Jackson, ed., Letters of the Lewis and Clark
Expedition, with Related Documents, 1783-1854 (Urbana,
Ill., 1962), 62-3; and J. W. Powell to Carl Schurz,
Nov. 1, 1878, in "Surveys of the Territories," House
Misc. Doc. No. 5, 45 Cong., 3 sess., 26.

3. Powell to Schurz, "Surveys of the Territories," 26.

4. L. H. Morgan, "The Indian Question," Nation, XXVII
(Nov. 28, 1878), 332-33. This is not to suggest that
Morgan did not take an interest in Indian policy or
have ideas of his own on the subject. See his "The
Hue-and-Cry against the Indians," Nation, XXIII (July 20,
1876), 40-1; "Factory System for Indian Reservations,"
ibid. (July 27, 1876), 58-9; and Morgan to President
Rutherford B. Hayes, Aug. 6, 1877, in Bernhard J. Stern,
Lewis Henry Morgan: Social Evolutionist (Chicago, 1931),
56-9.

5. Powell to Schurz, Nov. 1, 1878, in "Surveys of the
Territories," 26-7; and Powell to John T. Morgan, Jan.,
1881, which was read by Morgan to the Senate on Jan. 25,
1881, and printed in the Cong. Record, 46 Cong., 3 sess.,
911. Powell struggled against the limitations that his
own evolutionary precepts entailed, but like others of
the same cast of mind he was a prisoner of the laws he
had helped formulate. See William Culp Darrah, Powell
of the Colorado (Princeton, 1951), 382; and Robert H.
Wiebe, The Search for Order, 1877-1920 (New York, 1967),
144-45.

6. See Hamilton Cravens, "The Abandonment of Evolutionary Social Theory in America: The Impact of Academic
Professionalization upon American Sociological Theory,
1890-1920," American Studies, XII (Fall, 1971); esp. 5-9.

7. Lewis Henry Morgan, Ancient Society; or, Researches
in the Lines of Human Progress from Savagery through
Barbarism to Civilization, ed. by Eleanor Burke Leacock
(Cleveland, 1963 [1877]), Preface; and Ruth L. Bunzel,
"Salvaging the Ethnology of the Northern Plains," in
Margaret Mead and Bunzel, eds., The Golden Age of
American Anthropology (New York, 1960), 340.

8. British Association for the Advancement of Science,
Fourth Report of the Committee . . . appointed for the
purpose of investigating and publishing reports on the
physical characters, languages, and industrial and
social condition of the North-western Tribes of the
Dominion of Canada (London, 1888), 2-3.

9. Franz Boas, "Ethnological Problems in Canada,"
Congrès International des Américanistes: XVe Session
tenue à Quebec en 1906 (Quebec City, 1906), 152; and
"Ethnological Problems in Canada," Journal of the Royal
Anthropological Institute, XL (1910): 529. Also see
Douglas Cole, "The Origins of Canadian Anthropology,
1850-1910," Journal of Canadian Studies, VIII (Feb.,
1973): 33-45.

10. Franz Boas, "The Limitations of the Comparative
Method of Anthropology" (1896), in his Race, Language
and Culture (New York, 1940), 276-77, 280. The cri-
tiques of the Boasian tradition in American anthropology
range from Leslie White's dogmatic The Ethnography and
Ethnology of Franz Boas, Bulletin of the Texas Memorial
Museum no. 6 (Apr., 1963), 35, 53-6, 59, to Murray Wax,
"The Limitations of Boas' Anthropology," American Anthropologist, LVIII (Feb., 1956): 63-7, 72, and Marvin
Harris, The Rise of Anthropological Theory: A History
of Theories of Culture (New York, 1968), esp. Chp. 9.

11. "Humanity, What Is It?: An Interview with Claude
Lévi-Strauss" (1960), Kroeber Anthropological Society
Papers No. 35 (1966): 41, 43-4; and E. Sapir, "An
Anthropological Survey of Canada," Science, XXXIV
(Dec. 8, 1911): 793.

12. Clark Wissler, Indian Cavalcade: or, Life on the
Old-Time Indian Reservations (New York, 1938), 5-6;
Theodora Kroeber, Alfred Kroeber: A Personal Configura-
tion (Berkeley, 1970), 48-51; and Robert H. Lowie,
Robert H. Lowie, Ethnologist: A Personal Record
(Berkeley, 1959), 4-40.

13. Lowie, Robert H. Lowie, 12, 90, 106-7. Also see
Wissler, Indian Cavalcade, 5-7, especially the remark:
"So if the Indian personalities you meet seem restrained
and melancholy, remember that twilight enveloped them
and that there was to be no dawn." Boas continued to
convey the urgency of ethnographic research to his
"second generation" of students. See Margaret Mead,
"Apprenticeship under Boas," in Walter Goldschmidt, ed.,
The Anthropology of Franz Boas: Essays on the Centen-
nial of His Birth, American Anthropological Association
Memoir No. 89 (Oct., 1959), 30; and her Blackberry
Winter: My Earlier Years (New York, 1972), 127, 137,
292-94.

14. A. J. Fynn, The American Indian as a Product of
Environment, with Special Reference to the Pueblos
(Boston, 1907), 260; and John Collier, From Every
Zenith: A Memoir and Some Essays on Life and Thought
(Denver, 1963), 216. Marius Barbeau, an associate of
Boas with the National Museum of Canada, in 1933 said
of the Indians: "Their culture, with almost the single
exception of their languages, is now a thing of the
past. . . . the Indian is now a creature of the past,
who can be studied mostly in books and museums."
("The Disappearance of the Red Man's Culture," Scientific American, CXLVIII [Jan., 1933] : 22-3.) Some
preconceptions apparently die hard.

15. See Melville J. Herskovits, "The Significance of
the Study of Acculturation for Anthropology," American
Anthropologist, XXXIX (Apr.-June, 1937): 259, 263-64;
Oliver LaFarge, Raw Material (Boston, 1945), 181; and
Audrey I. Richards, "Culture Change and the Development
of Anthropological Theory" (1947), repr. in Morton H.
Fried, ed., Readings in Anthropology, Vol. II: Cultural
Anthropology (New York, 1959), 375.

16. Melville J. Herskovits, Franz Boas: The Science
of Man in the Making (New York, 1953), 112-14. Collier
found Boas of no help to the cause of Indian policy reform in the 1920s. (From Every Zenith, 216.) By 1932,
however, Boas was corresponding with the Commissioner
of Indian Affairs about courses that might be required
for certain appointments in the Indian Service. (Ruth
Benedict to Margaret Mead, Aug. 17, 1932, in Mead,
An Anthropologist at Work: Writings of Ruth Benedict
[Boston, 1959], 322.) Eventually Boas endorsed the
policy initiatives of the Indian New Deal after Collier
became Commissioner. (See Jay Nash, et al., The New
Day for the Indians: A Survey of the Working of the
Indian Reorganization Act of 1934 [New York, 1938], 4-6.)
Nothing irritated Collier more than the notion that the
Indian New Deal owed its existence "to the cooperation
of many prominent American ethnologists who understand
the Indian spirit, who know the place that cultural
tradition plays in the life of the Indian . . ." (Julius
E. Lipps, "Ethnopolitics and the Indian," Commonweal,
XXI [Mar. 15, 1935]: 563.) In his memoirs he would
vigorously deny that "the purposes of the Indian New
Deal and its various implementations" were "supplied by
anthropologists." Simply, until the 1930s, long after
the basic Indian New Deal had been worked out, anthropologists were in no position to make such a contribution. (From Every Zenith, 217))

17. Fay-Cooper Cole, "The Relation of Anthropology to
Indian and Immigrant Affairs," Science, LXXI (Mar. 7,
1930): 250; and "Anthropologists and the Federal Indian

Program," ibid., LXXXI (Feb. 15, 1935): 170. For an excellent contemporary appraisal of the part it was hoped "dynamic anthropology" would play in the Indian New Deal, see Felix S. Cohen, "Anthropology and the Problems of Indian Administration," Southwestern Social Science Quarterly, XVIII (Sept., 1937): 171-80. David L. Marden, "Anthropologists and Federal Indian Policy Prior to 1940," Indian Historian, V (Winter, 1972): 22-5, makes a few interesting points, but is superficial and factually unreliable. We can expect much more from Joan Chandler of the University of Texas at Arlington and others currently working in this area.

18. Clark Wissler, "The Rebirth of the 'Vanishing American,'" Natural History, XXXIV (Sept., 1934): 415-30.

V. STUDYING THE UNITED STATES

American Culture: An Enigma to Be Taught?

Ezequiel Theodoro da Silva

The United States/North America, Brazil/South America: Powerful satellites link these two countries by sending messages, images, music, language, films, goods, and values from one to the other. The mass media bring the United States and its culture into South American living rooms, Brazil and its culture into North American living rooms. We are heading toward an international homogeneity of culture. We are already living in the global village.

Two significant illustrations:

Pedro Silva lives in Brazil. Married. Four children. To clean the house his wife, Maria, uses Ajax. Pedro owns a 1974 Ford and a 1975 Chevrolet. The children, who wear practical Lee and Levi's trousers, often drink Coca-Cola, Pepsi-Cola and Seven-Up. On television the family watches "Bonanza," "The Virginian," "Columbo," "Kung Fu," "Mission Impossible," Disney cartoons, and "Kojak." Wimpy's, Kentucky Fried Chicken, Red Balloon, Blue Balloon, and Yellow Balloon (names that they actually do not know how to pronounce) are some of their favorite restaurants. They are very much worried about the assassination of U.S. Presidents.

John Smith lives in the United States. Married. Two children. His seventeen-year-old daughter bought a tanga (Brazilian bikini) to go to the beach. His son started taking soccer lessons to become a new Pele. Sometimes the family barbecues à la Brazil. They do the samba and the bossa nova. They are very much worried about the devastation of the Amazon and the extermination of Brazilian Indians.

These two short narratives, full of important details, clearly indicate that the geographical borders
of a country are no longer barriers to the penetration
of cultural information from abroad. Whether this is
good or bad--that is, whether we can really distinguish
between the mass media as instruments of information
and entertainment and as instruments of manipulation
and indoctrination--is a point that this paper does not
intend to analyze. Nevertheless, "cultural permeability"
would be an excellent topic for any American Studies
course. The main objective of the classes I organize
is to make my students discover how U.S. citizens live
in different situations, rather than to put forward my
opinions and ideology.

Having stated my impartiality and the inevitable
presence of the United States in Brazil, I ask, Why
don't we take advantage of this very presence to study
U.S. culture? If in the past one had to learn about
a foreign culture through books (which take a long time
to be published and cannot keep up with the rate of
change of a society), nowadays, because countries are
not spatially confined and because modern media are
instantaneous in effect, the student has a chance to
follow what is happening in the United States or elsewhere by just switching on a television set. This constant contact facilitates the teacher's work because
students already have items in their repertoire of experience on which to anchor the new learning they will
acquire in a course on U.S. culture.

Despite the strong tendency toward the homogeneity
of cultures, every society retains cultural idiosyncra-
cies that cannot be grasped via the mass media. Some
situations are so specific that they have to be experienced by the student in a different way. Although the
media can show overt information about a country (where
and what happened), they are not able to transmit those
tacit or covert cultural aspects that underlie the culture (why it happened).

One of my students told me that she had made a trip
to the United States before taking my course. I asked
her to verbalize her experience, and she said, "Well,
New York and Washington are just as we see them on TV.
Los Angeles is just as we saw it before the 'earthquake.'
The Americans look like Americans, too, but I had a hard
time communicating with them. They are terrible, cold
people." After listening to complaints for five minutes,
I came to the conclusion that this girl had some superficial knowledge about the overt culture of the United
States, but she did not know a thing about the society's
covert culture. Teachers of U.S. culture must be quite
aware of this cultural iceberg in order to include both
facets of the target culture in their programs.

In order to solve the enigma and avoid dilemmas on the part of the students, teachers must show them the overt culture of the country and at the same time create cultural situations that have to be lived by these students. The following program is an attempt to make students see both sides of the coin and, during the process, help them get to the essence of the reality of the United States.

PROGRAM: U.S. CULTURE COURSE

I. Objectives of the Course
    The main objective of the U.S. culture course is to guide students toward an understanding of the U.S. code of behavior. In addition, students will
    A. Use reference libraries;
    B. Critically read information written about the U.S. code of behavior;
    C. Synthesize cultural information, using correct language, and present findings by applying creative strategies;
    D. Examine what is overt and covert in the culture of the U.S.;
    E. Increase their ability to communicate with U.S. citizens inside and outside Brazil;
    F. Increase their understanding of the Brazilian culture.

II. Requirements of the Course
    A. Readings about U.S. culture
        1. Alvin Toffler, Future Shock
        2. Jennifer Rogers, Foreign Places, Foreign Faces
        3. Time and Newsweek magazines
        4. Mimeographed material
    B. Written synthesis and presentation of research findings
    C. Presence, punctuality, and participation in discussions
    D. Tests and final examination

III. Evaluation

    Participation   20 points
    Test 1 (April)   20
    Test 2 (May)   20
    Research and Presentation   20
    Test 3 (June)   20
                                 _____

    Total   100 points

Criteria:

MB--excellent	90-100 points
B--good	80-89
R--fair	70-79
I--insufficient	less than 70

IV. Methodology and Course Content
  A. Unit Blue
      1. Phase A: Absorbing (March/April). This
          consists of lectures, slide projections,
          films, and group discussions. Topics
          include:
          a. Culture: an overview
          b. National Anthem and other patriotic
              songs
          c. U.S. holidays
          d. The U.S. educational system
          e. The U.S. family
          f. Food in the U.S.
          g. Drug addiction in the U.S.
          h. Media in the U.S.
          i. British and U.S. English
      2. Phase B: Selecting and preparing a topic
          (March/April). Students will select a
          specific topic, do research on it, and
          think of creative strategies for its pre-
          sentation. Topics include:
          a. Leisure time in the U.S.: Walt Disney
          b. U.S. politics: John F. Kennedy
          c. The U.S. press: The New York Times
          d. Cinema in the U.S.: nostalgic movies
          e. Sports in the U.S.: football
          f. Women's Liberation: Betty Friedan
          g. Minorities in the U.S.: New York City
          h. Music in the U.S.: George Gershwin
          i. Black discrimination: Martin Luther
              King
          j. The Watergate crisis: The Washington
              Post
  B. Unit Red
      Presenting and debating (May). Five research
      groups will present the topics they chose in
      unit blue, phase B.
  C. Unit Yellow
      Listening, judging, and reacting (June). This
      consists of lectures delivered by U.S. citizens
      and group discussions. Topics include:
      1. Religion in the U.S.
      2. Labor unions in the U.S.
      3. Children and adolescents in the U.S.

American Studies, Pedagogy, and Programs in Canada

Peter Buitenhuis

In the light of subsequent remarks by conference participants from Central and South America I must modify somewhat the optimism I expressed in the following paper about the role of multinational corporations in the Western hemisphere outside the United States. Many of the participants believe that these corporations have not significantly liberalized their policies in their countries, nor have they contributed much to the general raising of cultural and educational standards. It seems that too little of the profits of these corporations are being returned to the home governments in the form of taxes that could then be used for social and educational benefits.

What particularly impressed me about the discussions in the wake of the papers on this subject and others was the feeling that American Studies organized in the United States was not a method readily transferable to the other Western hemispheric countries. The concept of American Studies as widely used in the United States and in some European countries does not seem at this time of often quite passionate nationalism to be of great value in this hemisphere. This impression was confirmed by a subsequent session of the conference in Mexico City, where I discovered that some comparative studies similar to those outlined in my paper were going on at the University of Mexico.

What was striking to me also at these meetings in San Antonio was the similarity of the problems facing American Studies, in the largest sense of that term, in the hemisphere outside the United States. We Canadians tend, I am afraid, not to think very much in hemispheric terms in this as in many other respects, and it seems to me that the New World Conference was a good beginning

for many of us in Canada to start breaking down hemispheric isolationism.

I wonder if there was an unconscious symbolism in
the Canadians' choice of a work to represent themselves
in celebrating the Bicentennial of the American Revolution? This was Louis Riel by Harry Somers and Mavor
Moore, presented recently by the Canadian Opera Company
at the Kennedy Center in Washington, D.C. It is the
story of an unsuccessful rebellion against a superior
government power that ends in a martyrdom.

There has been a lot of martyrdom going on in
Canada recently vis-à-vis the United States. Some
writers regard the plight of Canada as a crucifixion
on the U.S. cross of gold. Others regard it in the
less dramatic metaphor of the dairy industry--mere
homogenization into the vast Milky Way of U.S. life.

Five years ago a social scientist in an article in
the Canadian Review of American Studies (vol. 1, no. 2)
discussed the homogenizing process taking place in Canada that tended to make of North America a single society
on the U.S. model, a process known as "continentalism."
In this article, "Continentalism in Canadian Education,"
author H. T. Wilson wrote in essence that the most
potent agency of this continentalism was the university
itself. He pointed to the social sciences and the prestige and power that they wield in the modern university
as a major source of homogenization through what he
called "the theology of technique." Wilson saw the
modern university, with its emphasis on service-oriented
research, as being completely acquiescent in the goals
of a technological society. "The emergence of the status and power of professionalism in the Canadian university," he wrote, "is a significant manifestation of
that kind of imperialism which I have called continentalism." And he ends his article with a sort of lament
for the unawareness of human values that this approach
embodies.

One of the intellectual underpinnings of this
article is George Grant's book Lament for a Nation:
The Defeat of Canadian Nationalism (1965). This was
an early document in the history of Canadian nationalist
thought and is a conservative's attempt to explain how
Canadian national identity and nationhood itself were
being rapidly destroyed by U.S. ideology, technology,
and economic and cultural imperialism.

Since that time the attack on continentalism has
grown until today I can say that the word is almost an
obscenity in Canadian intellectual circles.

This has profound implications for the nature and
future of American Studies in Canada. On the one hand,
there can be no question that the study of U.S. history,
institutions, economics, and literature still goes on
apace at most Canadian universities and colleges. A few
years ago, I conducted a survey among leading Americanists in Canada about the state of their discipline.
A few reported declines in enrollments owing to a shift
in interest to Canadian subjects as a consequence of
Canadian nationalism . One reported that there had been
a decline, but now enrollments were picking up again
since Canadian nationalism had begun losing its power.
But most respondents to my questionnaire reported that
enrollments were holding up and, in some cases, were
increasing in traditional U.S. history, politics, economics, and literature courses. (The statistical nature
of these enrollments is covered in my own survey of
American Studies in Canada published in American Studies:
An International Newsletter, Autumn 1971). What is,
however, more significant than these enrollment statistics and their local variations is the general pattern
of American Studies in Canada now and a prediction about
its future pattern.

The problem was stated most concisely at a meeting
of the Canadian Association of American Studies that
took place in Waterloo, Ontario, on October 22-25, 1975.
In one of those sessions Fred Matthews, a historian, expressed the view that, I believe, found wide acceptance
among the participants at the meeting. This was that
among students and even among many of our colleagues in
Canada there existed the notion that to be engaged in
American Studies in any systematic way was somehow to
be party to American cultural imperialism. This fact
has, no doubt, militated against the setting up of
interdisciplinary programs in American Studies at
Canadian universities on the model of those in the
United States or in Europe. One of my correspondents
from the History Department of the University of Manitoba, Winnipeg, put it succinctly: "Apparently, the
vocal nationalist feels that knowing that the U.S. is
enemy is enough. Our students seem to be inward-turning,
at least to those who like to think of the university as
a place where intellectuality generates cosmopolitan interest." I believe that I am correct in saying that the
only interdisciplinary program in this field that is
presently operating in Canada is the one which I founded
in North American Studies at McGill in 1968 and which is
still operating. However, this program has never attracted more than about twenty-five students at any one
time and operates only at the undergraduate level.

Whatever our past hopes may have been about cosmo-
politanism and about the obvious practicality of our

studying in Canada a civilization that has such a profound effect upon every aspect of our life, we have to
confront, understand, and cope with the solid fact of
anti-American nationalism. Of course, the problem is
not simply confined to Canada. It is an obvious factor
in the Western hemisphere and remains a factor in the
United States itself. For example, in April 1963 Midge
Decter wrote a piece in Harper's magazine called "Anti-
Americanism in America" that painted a picture of emo-
tions as virulent as any that exist outside the United
States. She also pointed out how fashionable anti-
Americanism simplified issues, exaggerated effects, and
neglected the complexity of all the problems that it
raised. I have the impression (and it is only an impression) that such anti-Americanism has decreased since
the end of the Vietnam War. It would have been logical
to predict that the feeling would have lessened in
Canada, too. But it seems not to have done so. A specific irritant has been removed, but the complaint remains. Indeed the complaint--against American cultural
and economic imperialism--is being expressed just as
strongly now as it was two or three years ago. One of
the most noticeable recent moves to alleviate American
influence can be seen in the attempt by the Canadian
federal government to jam commercial messages that are
part of the programs beamed across the Canadian border
by U.S. television networks. The theory behind the
attempted jam is that the advertising revenues paid by
Canadian companies to American networks would then be
diverted to Canadian networks. But many observers in
Canada would say that this is merely putting a Band-Aid
on a cancerous sore. Let me give you an example of one
who believes that the cancer is terminal.

Recently publisher Mel Hurtig gave a talk at Simon
Fraser University. Hurtig was one of the founders of
the Committee for an Independent Canada, which for
several years has been blasting away at so-called
American cultural and economic imperialism. This talk,
which he presumably gave at many Canadian universities,
was apocalyptic in tone. Echoing George Grant, he
announced that Canadian nationalism was dead and that
the country was on the verge of becoming "the epitome
of a colony, a banana republic." To support this argument he pointed out that foreign ownership in Canada
has more than doubled in the last ten years and has
grown at a record rate every year since 1970: "We have
reached the point now where foreign ownership will
double within the next fifteen years, even if no foreign
capital enters the country. The investment capital will
come from the retained earnings of foreign corporations
earned from Canadian banks." He added that nowhere did
he see signs that people in Canada were angry enough to
stop this trend and to save the country, claiming that

Canadians would soon be "tenants in a country which
could have, which should have, been their own." In support of this view, Hurtig said that last year there was
a $2-billion deficit in the Canadian current account
payments and that in 1975 the deficit would be between
$5 billion and $10 billion. He stated that the government's policy in the face of this problem has been to
sell off more and more natural resources and thus to
bring in still more foreign capital. This simply increases the problem which is already mortal to a separate Canadian nation and identity.

The economic facts may well be beyond dispute.
However, the interpretation of the facts cannot be as
simple as Hurtig claims. For example, in a recent article in the Saturday Evening Post, reprinted in the
United States Information Agency magazine Horizons USA,
called the "Multinational Corporation: Economic Colossus of Modern Times," Lester Brown printed a table rank-
ing nations by gross national product and major multinational corporations by gross annual sales. General
Motors, Standard Oil, Ford Motors, Royal Dutch Shell,
General Electric, and IBM all have larger annual sales
than the gross national product of Chile, whereas the
combined revenues of these companies is greater than
the gross national product of Canada or Mexico or Brazil.
It would be an easy step from this recitation of figures
to the conclusion that the governments of these countries are more or less dominated by these and other
corporations mentioned in this table and that their
economies are being bled white by what Mel Hurtig calls
"a massive hemorrhaging of capital out of the country,"
represented by the dividends of these corporations.
But this would be indulgence in the kind of oversimpli-
fication that Hurtig himself goes in for.

It is clear that there are many more factors in the
equation than the figures represent. While not seeking
to deny the fact that there has been great exploitation
of underdeveloped countries by multinational corporations and considerable influence on government policy,
I find recent evidence, as Lester Brown showed, of a
much greater sense of responsibility in the management
of those corporations and a far wider dispersion of
capital holdings. For example, the shares of most of
the leading multinationals are listed on many international stock exchanges, and management is increasingly
decentralized from New York offices. In addition, many
of these corporations are changing from a resource exploitation endeavor to a manufacturing endeavor. In regard to Canada, I need only cite the 1965 agreement between the United States and Canada that abolished tariffs
on automobiles. This has permitted the free movement of
parts and completed cars across the border. The con-

sequence has been a decentralization of effort and, for
Canada, a vastly increased production of certain models
of cars that are exported direct to the United States.
As Brown pointed out, economic integration that takes
place through the efforts of multinational corporations
lessens the prospect of war and quickly increases gross
national product. He also stated that there are signs
that many of the corporations are becoming more respon-
sive to local and national needs. The only point I wish
to make in this economic chitchat is that the discussion
of multinationals is only one example, although probably
the most blatant, of a general, vast oversimplifying
process that takes place all the time in talking about
relations between the United States and other hemispheric
nations. This serves to obscure or, indeed, make almost
impossible the rational discussion of the problems we
face. As Cornelius F. Murphy, Jr., wrote in an article
called "The Future of North America" appearing in
Queen's Quarterly:

> The current spirit in Canada is one which is
> hostile towards continentalism. Such obsta-
> cles must not prevent us from devising, in
> freedom, political structures to meet our
> needs. What has not been sufficiently appre-
> ciated is that beyond the rhetoric of nation-
> alism, there are inexorable forces which in-
> tertwine our destinies. Canada and the United
> States co-exist on a vast continent under con-
> ditions of profound interdependence. Together
> they must begin to consider how the people of
> North America can be best assured of a full
> life for the future.

Our major problem in American Studies in Canada is precisely this: to get beyond the rhetoric of nationalism
to those inexorable forces and somehow to begin to
appreciate, understand, and interpret them.

I see the process as a long, slow one of the education of attitudes as well as the treatment of subject
matter. Politically it seems out of the question in the
immediate future to contemplate the setting up of interdisciplinary American Studies programs. My correspondents in the survey mentioned earlier were just about
unanimous on this point. We must work through existing
structures in order to educate, and I want to devote
the rest of my time to suggesting some of the ways that
this can be done.

First, it must be our task to encourage the critical attitude in this as in all studies. The assumption
that one studies a nation's culture in order to praise
it or accept it is, I must confess, beyond my comprehen-

sion. And yet it seems one of the most common assumptions that we have to cope with in American Studies.
A case can be made for quite the opposite consequence.
To study the work of, say, Thoreau, Melville, Henry
Adams, Henry James, Dos Passos, Mencken, Arthur Miller,
C. Wright Mills, Margaret Mead, V. L. Parrington, Thor-
stein Veblen, John M. Blum, David Potter, and Studs
Terkel--to name only a few artists and social scien-
tists--is to study a radical critique of American
society. The problem remains of how we get the insights
of these persons and many others into the curriculum and
against the bias of our students. Probably the best way
to do this is through a comparative study appraach.

The historian at Manitoba whose letter I quoted
earlier went on to say that the challenge that the
students have presented to him and his colleagues in
terms of anti-American nationalism has caused them to
change the nature of their teaching:

> One teaches Canadian history in addition to
> American, plus social science methodology;
> another does North American Indian history;
> another does Canadian-American urban history,
> and world history since 1945. The result has
> been not at all unhealthy. Those who have
> diversified have come to appreciate the prob-
> lems inherent in any national history, and
> as a group have become much more interested
> in comparative history. This is reflected
> not simply in their teaching interests, but
> also in their research interests. Most his-
> torians these days would regard this as a
> positive development, as the uniqueness or
> significance of specific events can really
> only be judged by standards outside the
> events themselves. The uniqueness or sig-
> nificance of national phenomena takes on
> meaning insofar as it can be compared to
> developments elsewhere.

Another respondent from Manitoba told me that there is
a Latin American Studies minor, which makes comparisons
with North American cultures, and that the Geography
Department goes in for North American cultural comparisons, as they do at McGill, Toronto, Simon Fraser, and
other Canadian universities.

Another fruitful field for comparison is in litera-
ture. Modern courses in Canada increasingly include
American and Canadian literature, comparing for example,
Hemingway and Morley Callaghan, Mordecai Richler and
Philip Roth, or Leonard Cohen and Norman Mailer. My own
course in North American literature, which I taught for

some years at McGill, carried this approach from the
work of Haliburton, the early nineteenth-century Canadian author, and of Mark Twain through Sarah Jeannette
Duncan and Henry James, up to Austin Clarke, the Canadian black writer, and to James Baldwin. This is only to
suggest the infinite riches that are available to students in fields as diverse as history, literature, economics, sociology, geography, and anthropology in terms
of the comparative method. The comparative approach
also opens to students and researchers in these fields
the immense contribution that American scholarship has
made, particularly in the last twenty-five years. There
can be little question that such scholarship has led the
way in richness, diversity, and boldness in most fields
since World War II. To neglect such resources through
the myopia of cultural nationalism is to do our students
and ourselves a major disservice.

One of the most productive scholars in the comparative field in recent years has, of course, been Professor Marshall McLuhan, of Toronto's Centre of Culture
and Technology.* Emerging from a traditional English
literature background, McLuhan has roamed throughout
the world in his imagination, but especially over the
world of U.S. culture, which his particular stance in
Canadian life has enabled him to view with an analytic
and, often, sardonic eye. McLuhan's influence has been
increasingly felt in Canadian education and has given
rise to the spread of communications studies. A particularly interesting example of this is in the McGill
University communications program, which is an adjunct
to the Department of English. This is run largely by
Hugo McPherson, former Professor of English at the University of Toronto, former Director of the National Film
Board of Canada, and now head of the communications program at McGill. One graduate seminar that he teaches
there is called "Whitman to the Present." It includes
American, British, and Canadian material in fiction,
poetry, film, the press, and advertising, plus one or
two Swedish or Italian films; scenarios are used where
possible. In the communications program, which is interdisciplinary, film and media are used significantly, and
there are contributions from the Departments of English,
Sociology, and Psychology. Similarly, the communication
program at Simon Fraser University, although not attached to the English Department, is concerned with the

---

*A footnote on McLuhanism and homogenization: A recent
vacuum-cleaner commercial, originating in Seattle, but
relayed, of course, to the Vancouver area, featured an
immaculate actor called Marshall MacLean (pronounced as
in the toothpaste ad), demonstrating his all-engulfing
wares.

nature and content of television and film and thus of
necessity with a great deal of American material.

What I am suggesting then is that American Studies
seems to be growing in contexts outside of those which
we have, until quite recently, considered the traditional fields of the subject, which has been centered
largely in the Departments of English and History.
Courses that are team-taught, as at York University in
Toronto, or are taught by two or more individuals from
varying disciplines and using a rich spectrum of materials and methods can embody a wide variety of American
materials. In this way the labeling that is so often
a deterrent to American Studies outside the United
States is avoided. The naive and blocking assumption
that because one is studying a culture one is therefore
praising it or being unduly influenced by it is not confronted, and the materials of study are made to serve
a wide variety of needs.

Nationalism has at least had this good effect: it
has caused us to look once again and more closely at our
approaches to our materials as well as at the materials
themselves. It has caused us to diversify and compare
and to rethink our premises. This is what, I take it,
we academics should always be doing.

About the Contributors

William H. Goetzmann is Stiles Professor in American Studies and Professor of History at the University of Texas at Austin. He was president of the American Studies Association at the time of the New World Conference.

Reyes Antonio Pérez Rojas is Professor of Philosophy and Dean of the Humanities Faculty at the Universidad Nacional de San Carlos de Guatemala.

Hernán Asdrúbal Silva is Associate Professor of American and Argentine History at the Universidad Nacional del Sur, Bahia Blanca, Argentina.

David V. J. Bell is Associate Professor and Director of the Programme, Graduate Programme in Political Science, York University, Canada.

Mario Alberto Carrera Galindo is Director of the "Casa Flavio Herrera," Cultural Center of the Universidad Nacional de San Carlos de Guatemala.

Antônia Fernanda Pacca de Almeida Wright is Assistant Professor of History at the Universidade de São Paulo.

Jesús Velasco Márquez is Assistant Professor of History at El Colegio de Mexico.

Carmen Cecilia de Mayz is Professor of Languages in the Facultad de Letras, Universidad Católica "Andres Bello," Venezuela.

Antonio Pasquali is Director of the Instituto de Investigaciones de la Comunicación, Venezuela.

Roberto Da Matta is Associate Professor and Coordinator of the Graduate Program in Anthropology at the Museu Nacional, Brazil.

Isabel Aretz is Professor of Anthropology in the Facultad de Humanidades y Educación, Escuela de Antropología e Historia, Universidad Central de Venezuela.

Walnice Nogueira Galvão is Professor of Literary Theory and Comparative Literature in the Facultade de Filosofia, Letras, y Ciencias Humanas, Universidade de São Paulo, Brazil.

Evelyn J. Hinz is Assistant Professor of English at the University of Manitoba, Canada.

Michel Brûlé is Professor of Sociology at the Université de Montréal, Canada.

Bruce A. Lohof is Professor of American Studies at the University of Miami.

Basil A. Ince is Senior Lecturer, Institute of International Relations, at the University of the West Indies, St. Augustine, Trinidad.

J. L. Granatstein is Professor of History at York University, Canada.

Luciano Tomassini is Staff Member at the Instituto para la Integración de América Latina, Argentina.

Cesar Peña Vigas is Professor of Sociology at the Universidad de Carabobo, Venezuela.

Marcelo Diamand is Staff Member at the Instituto de Estudios Económicos y Sociales, Argentina.

Heraclio Bonilla is Senior Researcher at the Instituto de Estudios Peruanos, Peru.

Gloria Blackwell is Professor and Chairman of the Department of English at Clark College, Atlanta.

Richard A. Long is Professor of English at Atlanta University.

Carl D. Parris is Professor of Sociology at the University of the West Indies, St. Augustine, Trinidad.

Anthony P. Maingot is Professor of Sociology and History at Florida International University, Miami.

Brian W. Dippie is Associate Professor of History at the University of Victoria, Canada.

Ezequiel Theodoro da Silva is Assistant Professor of English and American Civilization at the Universidade Católica de São Paulo, Brazil.

Peter Buitenhuis is Professor of English and American Studies at Simon Fraser University, Canada.

Index